MW01631249

CATCH THE VISION OF *The Well-Educated Heart*

VOLUME ONE: PHILOSOPHY

MARLENE PETERSON

Libraries of Hope

Catch the Vision of
The Well-Educated Heart

Volume One: Philosophy

Cover Image: Julia Gathering Roses, by Daniel Ridgway Knight, (c. 1900). In public domain, source Wikimedia Commons.

Libraries of Hope, Inc.
Appomattox, Virginia 24522

Website www.librariesofhope.com
Email: librariesofhope@gmail.com

Printed in the United States of America

Table of Contents

Introduction

Welcome!

You are about to embark on a journey of a lifetime in which learning and understanding will unfold layer upon layer and deepen over time. This introductory course is designed to help you start a daily habit of feeding your heart. Your bodies need to eat food every single day, and your heart has the same requirement. Overeating or eating too fast causes indigestion. So allow yourself time to reflect on what you are learning. There's no rush here. And the learning is never going to end. Even five minutes a day will begin to yield good fruit.

For some of you, the ideas presented here will go against everything you've ever thought about learning. For others, the ideas will resonate with beliefs you already carry with you. Either way, I hope you will enter with an open heart and that you will find something that will enrich your life and the lives of your children, if you have children. This course is not just for women with children. It is for all mother-hearts. It is for anyone who wants to live a richer, more abundant life; for anyone who feels like there is something 'missing.'

The course is designed after the same Pattern for Learning you will learn about. This Introductory Course is largely the 'heart' part where you will begin to catch a vision of possibilities and increase your desire to learn more. No one is going to tell you exactly what you should read or what you should get out of it—which is the same process you will be encouraged to use with your children in their heart years. Rather, you'll find yourself taking from it what you are ready to take from it. If you go back through later, you'll find new connections and insights, not because the words or pictures have changed, but because you will have changed.

These volumes are a compilation of podcasts, presentations and other writings. Each entry stands alone, so you may want to skip around and read that which catches your attention. But there is a flow of ideas so you may benefit from starting at the beginning and working your way through. It would be greatly beneficial to keep a journal nearby to write down impressions that come to you as you look for principles or as ideas strike your heart. The most important learning that will take place will happen in the white spaces between the lines. Remember—the more you write, the more you learn. Repetition is key to learning and writing thoughts down is part of that repetition process. In time, you'll want to teach your children the same process.

This is a joyful journey. I'm so happy to have you along!

Love, Marlene

Let Me Start by Introducing Myself

Since we'll be spending quite a bit of time together, you may wonder who is talking to you. So I'd like to start by introducing myself and telling you a little bit of the story behind Libraries of Hope. My name is Marlene Peterson and I am the founder of Libraries of Hope and the finder of the Well-Educated Heart philosophy of learning.

Let me give you a context of how old I am.

I knew I was getting old when I realized one day that I was old enough to have lived in the olden days. We trusted our car to the man who wore the star as he checked our oil and washed our windshield while pumping 17-cents-a-gallon gas.

We had a knob on our television set that we had to stand up and turn when we wanted to change one of the three channels. I watched in high anticipation as I heard all the talk of color TV and couldn't figure out why our peacock still looked black and white. I still remember that magical moment when we unboxed our new color TV set.

My friend, Mary, and I walked several blocks by ourselves uptown to the Saturday matinee every Saturday—and we weren't even ten years old. We always got there an hour early because we wanted to be sure and get the front row seats. Our little Montrose theater always showed a double feature on Saturday and the movies changed every week. If you missed one, you missed it. They didn't come around again and you never knew if or when it would be on TV. The movies weren't rated and my mom never had to consult a parental advisory site to see if the movie would be appropriate for us to watch.

We used slide rules in High School. When my husband and I were college students, a calculator salesman stopped by our house and amazed us as he demonstrated all its capabilities—it added, subtracted, multiplied *and* divided. We just had to have one even though the price tag was a hefty $75.00 and we were making a dollar an hour.

When I look at how far we've come with technology in my lifetime, it is nothing short of miraculous. We surely live in the best of times.

But I'm afraid we are also facing the worst of times.

I was part of the hippie generation of the 60s and 70s. It was the day of mini-skirts, psychedelic colors and peace symbols and we talked about love, not war. My friends and I burned strawberry incense. I had no idea at the time that my generation was the generation that was throwing out all the rules of right and wrong. We were, literally, turning the world upside down.

Maybe it's a carry-over from those hippie days, but in our technologically advanced world, I find myself still thinking about love and world peace while hearts grow colder and the world grows darker.

Somewhere deep inside, I feel an obligation and a desire to right some of the wrongs of my generation before I make my exit. Especially now that there is more at stake. You see, I'm a grandma. And if you think you love your children, just wait until you have grandchildren. Their sweet faces are before me night and day, and oh! How I want a better world for them!

My husband, Brent, and I have raised nine children. (My husband always says all of them are boys except eight of them.) I graduated from Brigham Young University with a degree in Child Development and Family Relations, but my real learning has taken place in the laboratory of my home. I have always been restless where education is concerned. That is why we homeschooled, public schooled, private schooled, charter schooled, online-schooled, unschooled and did combinations of all of the above. By current educational standards, you might say we are a success story. All nine of our children have graduated from universities with several earning advanced degrees.

We are proud of their accomplishments, but I always felt like something was missing.

About fifteen years ago when our youngest daughter was getting ready to leave home, a friend asked if I'd like to help her with a little school she had adopted in the slums of Nairobi, Kenya. This educational restlessness returned as I looked into the faces of these little children in the pictures she showed me. They met in a makeshift classroom with hot tin walls. The chiggers bit their bare feet on the dirt floor. Many of them were orphaned and showed up to school with hungry bellies. But there they were–sitting on crude wooden benches, eager to learn.

But to learn what? Many of these children would likely never grow to adulthood. Few would have a chance to go to college. There weren't a lot of jobs for them. Because there were no books, they had to rely on rote memorization of facts in order to pass standardized tests. And I wondered, what's the point?

And it got me thinking—I really wanted to know—what is the purpose of education? I saw one study where 365 people were asked that very question. They got 365 unique answers. How can we think we can design a uniform system of education when we can't even agree why we're doing it? What I wanted to know was what is God's purpose and reason for education and what are His methods? If I could find the answer to those questions, I knew that the lives of these little children would be blessed no matter what life dealt them.

It set me on an intense course of study for the next year. I turned to the writings of great spiritual leaders and to the scriptures themselves. Along the way, I compared what I was learning with different educational models. I took hundreds of pages of notes. All that learning distilled down to two basic truths for me:

> I have come to believe the purpose of education should be to prepare children to live lives of maximum joy and the method can best be summed up in a phrase I took from the writings of Charlotte Mason: True education is between a child's soul and God.

A simple pattern for learning unfolded and I came to appreciate the powerful influence of fine literature, art, poetry and music and the sweet influences of nature on the hearts of our children and a mother's unique role as the best educator of a child's heart. Let me remind you again: if you are a woman who has never had children of your own or whose children are all grown up, you are still a vital part of this work. Your influence will be felt in ways you may not now imagine. All the things I talk about will bring an added measure of joy into your life.

As I have shared what I have learned with other moms, they have felt it resonate within them, as well. Instead of the frantic anxious worries of falling behind or ruining their kids' chances of getting into college, the word I hear most often from these moms is they feel peace. They are feeling joy in the journey.

I know what I am going to share with you isn't going to appeal to everyone. It will require much of you and may cause you to step out of your comfort zone and look at schooling and education through new eyes. It is very simple, but not always easy.

My thoughts are aimed at other restless souls who are looking for more than fulfilling requirements and passing tests. I'm looking for moms who, deep down, feel they have a purpose and a calling to do something really remarkable—like, maybe, reset the course of history and bring the world back into balance. And yes, even help usher in that era of world peace the ancients and sages have dreamed of for centuries and my young heart longed for.

I am convinced this is the mission given to young mothers of our day.

I watched the 1946 version of Anna and the King of Siam. The king is trying to learn how to civilize his people. As he lies on his death bed, his final words embody the truth he has come to realize: "True progress shall lie in man's heart. Et cetera. Et cetera. Et cetera." It is your divine privilege to act as the guardians of our world's greatest natural resource—our children's hearts.

And because of your potential influence on the hearts of children, the hand that rocks the cradle will indeed rule the nations.

And now I'm going to go out on a limb and share some deeply personal thoughts. But if you're going to take this journey of the heart with me and trust the teachings I am going to share with you, it's important you understand more of the why behind what I am doing.

I think the why can be traced back to a simple prayer that has been a constant in my life: Lord, please make me an instrument in thy Hands. Without Him, I am nothing. I am not the Founder of the Well-Educated Heart philosophy; I'm a finder. I have more questions than answers. But I love sharing with you what I am learning along the way. When some of you tell me you want to meet me, it makes me uncomfortable in some ways–not that I don't want to meet you–I absolutely do! I love you! But like Mr. Rogers used to say–I'm not a fancy person. I stumble over my words in private conversation. I'm awkward and actually very shy. And there's a part of me that worries that you'll be disappointed with me and that somehow I'll be a stumbling block to the message I feel to deliver.

Yet, I cannot deny the clear and distinct impressions that have come to me over the years, starting many years ago when I felt to create a small library of books and to call it Libraries of Hope. It was to be filled with books that would give children hope because they would be filled with truth and light. I had no idea how to go about such a thing. More than one person said,

"You know, children aren't reading very much any more. Especially old books without any pictures. There really isn't a market for what you are doing." And I was asked how I planned on marketing this; what my business plan was; how was I going to get the funds to publish the books. The truth was, I had no business or marketing plans. I didn't exactly know why I was doing what I was doing. I was just doing what I felt I had been asked to do. And the feeling that I had was to not concern myself with that. In my heart, I was told the Lord was preparing a network of mothers and when the time was right, He was going to start writing messages on my heart, that when I delivered them, it would resonate in their hearts and these mothers would be drawn to the message and would want to learn more.

I believe you are the fulfillment of that promise.

For years, the work I was doing was met with apathy and disinterest. And then those messages started coming into my heart. And I have been amazed as I have watched the Lord do His work. I have heard from mothers from around the world–from Australia and New Zealand, from Denmark, Norway, Germany, Italy, Africa, Mexico. From all over the United States from Alaska to the East Coast. And frequently they say this: I don't know how I found you, but when I heard your message, it resonated in my heart and I want to know more.

A few years into the project, I became discouraged. So very few people cared about the books I was gathering. Was I just wasting my time?

In that state of mind, I woke up one morning with one clear thought on my mind: Read the Book of Enoch and my first reaction was, "Is there a Book of Enoch?" I can tell you there is–I found it online in the Apocrypha. The Book of Enoch is said to contain Enoch's vision of our day. I started to read and wasn't really getting anything, but I felt to just keep reading. When I got to the very end, the words lit up and made my heart burn. Enoch saw the books of our day! First he said that "sinners will alter and pervert the words of righteousness in many ways, and will speak wicked words, and lie, and practice great deceits, and write books concerning their words." We see that, don't we?

But here's the good news: "To the righteous and the wise shall be given books of joy, of integrity and of great wisdom. To them shall books be given in which they will rejoice and acquire the knowledge of every upright path."

I am here to say we have been given that great gift! We are living in the day of the harvest when all the greatest books from all the greatest hearts of all the ages have been preserved and gathered and placed in the hands of children in even the humblest home, thanks to our modern-day gift of technology. As John Ruskin wrote: "Will you go and gossip with your housemaid or your stable boy, when you may talk with kings and queens, while this eternal court is open to you, with its society wide as the world...the chosen, the mighty, of every place and time?'

Your job is to awaken the desire to read them which will largely be accomplished through the books you read aloud.

Sometimes when I wonder if the gathering of books is worth the time, I think of a couple of sweet mothers I met at a conference who live in a remote area in Canada. They had internet, but had little access to books. With great emotion, they said they had found my Library of Hope and were so thankful they now had books with which to teach their children.

If I had millions of dollars and could have hired New York's finest marketing team, they could not have designed a marketing strategy that would have had the direct global reach the Lord has quietly been accomplishing as He gathers mothers one by one.

I am constantly reminded by Him that numbers don't matter. For those of you who are frustrated that your efforts to gather others often seem futile, you're not alone. I think it's worth sharing part of an article that addresses this very thing. It was written in 1936 by an Albert Jay Nock, a journalist I believe, and it was entitled "Isaiah's Job."

The writer started by describing a conversation he had had with a man who felt like he had a philosophy and a message that would save mankind and that he was going to spend the rest of his life spreading his message far and wide in an attempt to try and reach the masses.

Nock mustered the courage to tell the man that the masses would not care two pins about his doctrine and he proceeded to paraphrase the job of Isaiah. In a time of great commotion and unrest, the Lord commissioned the prophet Isaiah to go out and warn the people. He said, in essence, "Tell them what is wrong, and why and what is going to happen unless they have a change of heart and straighten up. Don't mince matters. Make it clear that they are positively down to their last chance. Give it to them good and strong and keep on giving it to them. I suppose perhaps I ought to tell you," he added, "that it won't do any good. The official class and their intelligentsia will turn up their noses at you and the masses will not even listen. They will all keep on in their own ways until they carry everything down to destruction, and you will probably be lucky if you get out with your life."

Isaiah had been willing to take on the job, but now a new face was put on it. It raised the obvious question: Why, if all that were so–if the enterprise were to be a failure from the start–was there any sense to starting it?

"Ah," the Lord said, "you do not get the point. There is a Remnant there that you know nothing about. They are obscure, unorganized, inarticulate, each one rubbing along as best as he can. They need to be encouraged and braced up because when everything has gone completely to the dogs, they are the ones who will come back and build up a new society; and meanwhile, your preaching will reassure them and keep them hanging on. Your job is to take care of the Remnant, so be off now and set about it."

Now I make no claims to be an Isaiah or a prophet—far from it! But the same feeling has been placed in my hear—to tend to and strengthen the Remnant, even if that number is very small. The writer goes on to say that in any given society the Remnant is always an unknown quantity. He said when you are called to tend to the Remnant, "Two things you do know and no more: first, that they exist; second, that they will find you." In fact, they will find you without you doing anything about it.

But the Lord knows who they are. Elijah had been given the same job as Isaiah and he finally fled to the desert because he feared for his life. The Lord asked him what he was doing out there and his answer implied that he was afraid if he was killed, the truth would die with him. He thought he was the only one left when the Lord told him, "I don't mind telling you that there are seven thousand of them back there in Israel whom it seems you have not heard of, but you may take My word for it that they are there."

Sometimes you may feel all alone. You may feel obscure, inarticulate, rubbing along as best as you can. But the Lord knows you and you are counted and valued by Him. He takes the weak things of the world and makes them strong. He is an artist and you are His masterpiece in progress. And how do you know if you are of the Remnant? If you love the Lord and seek to do His will, you are of the Remnant.

Throughout the history of the world, in the middle of chaos and destruction, He is always preparing and preserving seed for a new planting. I know from the seasons that winter is necessary for an abundant spring. I've seen the seasons in history. There is no question in my mind that we are living in a day of great harvest, but winter is coming. And the seed must be preserved if there are to be green shoots in the spring.

The Old Testament prophets were masters of imagery and of layered and even hidden meanings. Many interpretations have been given of Malachi's words where he expressed that the hearts of the children shall be turned to their fathers and the hearts of the fathers turned to the children, or the earth shall be wasted.

As I study history, I find my heart turning to the wisdom of our fathers. The beauty of our day is that we don't have to start from scratch. We have so many lessons to draw from that teach us how to govern nations, how to live together in harmony, how to live lives of joy and abundance. Many of those lessons come from seeing what hasn't worked. Yet, as I see solutions that are being proposed in today's world, they are coming from a place of total ignorance of how they played out before. History seems doomed to repeat itself because our hearts will not turn to the wisdom of our fathers who came before us. Nor do we make decisions based on the consequences our choices will have in the lives of our children and those who come after us. We live very much in a day when we think only of ourselves; what's good for me. We've largely lost that spirit of the Pilgrims who understood they were only laying a foundation for those who followed.

Turning 60 a couple of years ago was a turning point in my life for me. I suddenly realized I don't have a whole lifetime ahead. There are things I am not going to be able to do. If I plant a tree in my yard, I may not live long enough to see it grow big enough to give me shade. But the thought struck me, then plant it for those who will come after you, that they can sit under the tree that will give them shade.

I feel that may be one of the messages of Malachi to us—we are the connecting link between the past and the future. We have to look backward, and using the lessons of the past, make wise decisions with an eye to those who will follow us.

That is why you see me placing history at the center of all learning at the WEH (Well-Educated Heart). But it's history in a broad sense—it's a way of learning the lessons of our fathers. And those lessons have been preserved in art, in music, in literature, in poetry as well as the pages of historical fact. For me, History is not just a subject in a curriculum to be checked off a list.

I keep saying it—there has never, in the history of the world, been a generation that has had access to the wisdom the world has left us as this generation has. And there is no other group in the world that has the influence on the generations to follow that a mother has. That's why I constantly encourage you to store up the lessons of history in your own heart; to learn the languages of art and music and poetry and fine literature so that you can understand what our fathers are trying to tell us. And then, as you find those gems of wisdom, to preserve them in Books of Remembrance, not only for you, but for your children, grandchildren and great grandchildren who will follow.

I have a vision of a Remnant of mothers of refined tastes; who are well-educated, cultured and articulate. They are to be a force of great influence in the world—Mothers of Influence. That will never happen without effort and of doing hard things. I totally get that you're busy. Like Martha, you are careful and troubled about many things. But I believe, because I have experienced it for myself, that if you have but the desire in your heart, and will act upon that desire by doing what you can do, the Lord will magnify your efforts, whatever they are.

A caution: Don't get caught in the letter of what you're reading. Don't make it a checklist of things to do. There's something beyond the words themselves you are looking for. Like Mr. Rogers taught, it will be a voice found in the white space between the lines. C.S. Lewis wrote:

"The books or the music in which we thought the beauty was located will betray us if we trust to them; it was not in them, it only came through them, and what came through them was longing… For they are not the thing itself; they are only the scent of a flower we have not found, the echo of a tune we have not heard, news from a country we have never yet visited…"

And as to the white space learning, Lewis continued: "Almost our whole education has been directed to silencing this shy, persistent inner voice."

It is hearing this inner voice that is at the heart of what you will be learning going forward.

I share 18th century educator Pestalozzi's desires as he wrote: "I wish to wrest education from…cheap, artificial teaching tricks, and entrust it to the eternal process of nature herself; to the light which God has kindled and kept alive in the hearts of fathers and mothers; to the interests of parents who desire that their children grow up in favour with God and with men… [Love is] the sole and everlasting foundation in which to work. Without love, neither the physical nor the intellectual power will develop naturally."

Knowing how to nurture the heart of a child is of great worth. Our world desperately needs more mothers who have learned this prized and rare art. Are you willing to pay the price to learn?

God's Ways Are Quiet

When Christmas Comes by Joseph Fort Newton
(Found in *Christ and the Fine Arts* by Cynthia Maus)

Only God could have thought of Christmas. Its beauty is beyond the wit of mortals, so simple in its sublimity, so homey, yet so heavenly. On a tapestry woven of stable straw and starlight it unveils a picture to soften and purify the heart and to bring us back from a wisdom that is not wise, because it is hard, unholy, and unhopeful. Man would have made of this event a pageant, its stage direction as follows:

Array of Great Ones
The Army marches by
Fanfare of trumpets
Enter the King!

Man-made pageants pass and fade, but God works in slower and more secret ways. He blows no trumpet. He rings no bell. He begins within, seeking His ends by quiet growth, and by a strange power men call weakness, a wisdom often mistaken for folly. Man has one answer to every problem—force; but that is not the way of God. He did not send an army to conquer the world. He sent a babe to make a woman cry. The divine method is different: Instead of noise and parade there was—

A Mother and a Babe
No cradle, just a manger
A wandering Star.

Such wisdom bends the knee; such beauty breaks the heart—and mends it. It is a scene to sanctify the world, as if to teach us that God enters the life of man by lowly doors, attended by starry ideals and simple shepherd sentiments—the birth of Jesus, just 'one of the children of the year.' They are wise men who bow at such a shrine, linking a far-off pilgrim star with the cradle of a little child. By such faith, men are truly wise, knowing that no hope is too high, no dream too holy to be fulfilled—even the hope and dream of 'peace on earth among men of good-will'…

Men of spiritual awareness in all lands feel that a time has come in the history of man when he must take a step into a higher range of being, or else lose and slip back…

Over an armed camp, in a hard old Roman world, the song of the angels rang out, proclaiming 'Peace on earth among men of good-will." How far off it must have seemed on that night! How far off it seems today! Yet it will come true. It is not a myth; it is not a mockery…

It is a song out of the heart of God for a hungry world. It means much that we can hear it, despite gray fears and grim facts, forever singing above the din of strife; and, hearing it, take up its strain in the busy world of today. Not in our day, not in many days perhaps, but at last it will be fulfilled. The world will fill up with men of good-will who keep step with its music and live by its law—men who know that man was made for love, because God is love, and that love and joy must blend in the final note of the great world-song."

The Mother's Heart

A Mother's Influence

"Let me say to parents: Make the home-life beautiful, without and within, and they will sow the seeds of gentleness, true kindness, honesty and fidelity, in the hearts of their children, from which the children reap a harvest of happiness and virtue. The memory of the beautiful and happy home of childhood is the richest legacy any man can leave to his children. The heart will never forget its hallowed influences. It will be an evening enjoyment, to which the lapse of years will only add new sweetness. Such a home is a constant inspiration for good, and as a constant restraint from evil.

"We may by our blindness live in a world of darkness and gloom, or in a world full of sunlight and beauty and joy; for the world without only reflects the world within."

--B.G. Northup

"The field is white and all ready to harvest, but we are faced with a generation that has little desire to read. Mothers, this is your moment in history. Within your homes are the chosen harvesters and it is your privilege and upon you rests the responsibility to light fires of desire within their hearts.

"No one can do it better than you!"

--Marlene

"Oh! If the world could only stop long enough for one generation of mothers to be alright, what a Millennium could be begun in thirty years!" –Helen Hunt Jackson

Address Delivered at the World Congress of Families IX

The banquet hall was filled to overflowing. Men and women from all walks of life were waiting with excitement for the arrival of their honored guests. Enthusiastic cheers were heard when the tall, fine-looking young man took his seat near the center of the guest's table. He was their newly-elected mayor, the youngest mayor they had ever had. The townsfolk had watched him grow up and they were so proud of him!

Minutes later, an old white-haired lady entered to more applause and was seated to the left of the mayor. She had been away for many years, but she was the one who had given them their college, their library and their playground.

Dinner was served, the tables cleared and then the mayor rose to speak. After reflecting a bit on growing up and the recent election, he said, "I believe that every man is master of his own fate. I believe in being a self-made man and while I am serving as your mayor, I will do all in my power to ensure every young person in this town is given every opportunity for a good education and a fine career. One can make of himself what he will if he has enough determination and courage. I am here to serve you all." And he returned to his seat amidst thunderous applause.

Not once during the address had the eyes of the little, white-haired lady been taken from the speaker. She seemed to be studying him rather than his address. She was so deep in thought, she almost missed her introduction as the next speaker.

She made her way to the podium and began, "Years ago, in this very town, there lived a teacher of ten bright, happy girls. They played and worked together and loved each other dearly. Sadly, the teacher's husband became very ill and she had to move far away.

"It was hard for the teacher to leave. She had tried to help the girls the best she could, but she wasn't sure if she had done enough. The day came for her to leave and she invited the girls to spend one last evening with her in her home. She asked each girl to write a letter to her and share their dreams of what they hoped to be when they grew up. One by one, ten little heart-to-heart letters were laid on the table.

"Five days later as she was traveling, the teacher opened the letters and read them over and over to herself.

"Jennie wanted to be a great singer; she wanted to go to New York and study opera.

"Katherine wanted to be a kindergarten teacher.

"Mary wanted to be a lawyer—a criminal lawyer.

"Louise wanted to be a nurse. As she read, the teacher felt reassured and smiled at the thought of the influences for good these girls would be." Then, turning to the mayor of the city, the little white-haired lady said, "Sir, I believe the contents of one of those letters will be of interest to you more than the rest. I was the teacher of those girls, so I can give you the exact wording of the last letter I read:

> Dear friend,
>
> You have asked us to give you our dearest wish. I have many wishes for the future but the wish I want most of all is to be a fine and noble woman and some day to be the kind of mother you have told us so much about.

"The girl who wrote that letter, sir, became your mother. Fourteen years before you were born, your character was being formed, your ideals were being molded, your future was being safeguarded. I congratulate you, sir, on being elected to the office of mayor; but I congratulate you more for being the child of my little girl of the long ago who at sixteen could write, 'I want most of all to be a fine woman and some day to be a noble mother.' To her you owe much. Inspire the girls of the town if you plan for great men. A self-made man needs a noble mother to build the foundation of his character. There is no better way."

Then the speaker sat down and there was silence in the banquet hall.

Over a hundred years ago, Helen Hunt Jackson exclaimed: "Oh! If the world could only stop long enough for one generation of mothers to be alright, what a Millennium could be begun in thirty years!"

It is my dearest hope that we will see that generation of mothers, and so I would like to address my remarks to mothers of young children.

Everything man creates in this world is but an outward expression of what is treasured in his heart. As Luke, the physician, wrote, "A good man out of the good treasures of his heart bringeth forth that which is good."

You mothers are the guardians of the world's most important natural resource: the hearts of children. For far too long, you've been made to feel that the work done in your home is beneath you; that there are more productive ways to spend your time. That is a lie.

When a child's heart is the most open and impressionable, you are there. As you hold your newborn baby close to your heart, your skin is soft and warm. Your voice is sweet and melodic. The lullabies you quietly hum bring a sense of calm and order to the chaotic world your baby has suddenly entered. You provide the nourishment that satisfies the gnawing hunger in his belly. Cradled in your arms, your baby feels safe. Long before he understands words, long lasting impressions are being made deep in his heart that reassure him, "I matter. I belong. I am loved." The bond between a mother and a child is strong and powerful.

It is because of your closeness to your child's heart that your influence and impact is so great. Your direct link to his heart is the reason why the hand that rocks the cradle is the hand that rules the nations. If you don't like what you see going on in the world, the truth is, you are the one who can change it, for all true change must take place in individual hearts and, as Frederick Douglass wisely observed, "It is easier to build strong children than to repair broken men." Your heart-work is vital to society and we need to rally around, protect, encourage and support you.

Your baby's heart develops before his brain within the womb, and his emotions develop before his intellect outside the womb. While minds are fed with facts, information and words, hearts are fed with impressions, feelings and images. Nature has reserved the first years of your child's life—particularly the first eight years—for making impressions on the heart. The wise mother will use those years to fill her child's heart with the good, the beautiful and the true.

There has been a shift from heart to mind in childhood education over the last hundred years. This shift from heart to mind has not happened by accident or overnight. It has been by design and with steady effort. Some of the most influential men and women of the last century, especially those who influence education, have dreamed of a world governed by reason. Reason, they say, will give us solutions to all our problems. Reason, they think, can give us a new moral code that's more realistic and practical. And what reasonable person would ever think war is reasonable?

And so we see academics and skills to train minds introduced to our children at younger and younger ages while their hearts are being neglected. The experiment has gone on long enough to see results and the result is, our world has turned upside down. That which used to be good is now viewed as bad, and that which was bad is now held up as good and desirable. It is a grave mistake to train the intellect of a child before we have tended to his heart.

Our world will only be brought back into balance when we place heart and mind in their proper order. This course correction won't require any governor's signature or committee to debate its merits. It will require no government funding. In fact, it doesn't require any funding at all. It's free to implement. And it can be implemented today.

More than 200 years ago, Swiss-educator Pestalozzi wrote, "It is for a long time the business of the heart, before it is the business of reason… The eternal laws of nature lead me back to your hand, mother! Mother! I can keep my innocence, my love, my obedience, the excellences of my nobler nature with the new impressions of the world, all, all at your side only."

The shift from mind back to heart will be found in the music you play in your home, the art you hang on your walls, the poetry you recite by heart because you love it, and above all, the stories you tell. Music, pictures, poetry and story are the languages of the heart. The more you use these languages with your young children, the more they will comprehend.

The story is one of your most useful tools. Telling a story is how you can convert words into moving images that your child's heart will understand and to which it will attach feelings.

Storytelling is an ageless and beautiful art that has been used for hundreds and thousands of years to convey values and traditions from generation to generation and from heart to heart. In those quiet hours when the lights are low and your children are in a calm, reflective mood, the stories you tell them will never be forgotten and they will influence them for the rest of their lives. And in the process, your hearts will be knit together in love.

And now, mothers, I will tell you why I think you are going to be able to do what no generation of mothers has been able to do before you. You live in the season of the harvest and what a bounteous harvest it is! For 6000 years, mankind has been preserving its finest ideas and ideals in art, music and literature. And now, modern technology has delivered the ripened fruit right to your home where it will do the most good. The eyes of all those who sweat and suffered, sacrificed and labored are upon you. They have gifted you with all you need to raise the noblest, most refined, and wisest generation that has yet walked this earth.

Where much is given, much is required and what is required of you is to first, fill your own heart with good treasure from the harvest because what is in your heart will naturally flow into your child's heart. It is your love of all that is good and beautiful combined with your love for your child that will enable you to do what no one else can.

Then, you will need to re-learn the lost arts of heart education that have been brushed aside in our age of Reason. But there is good news. Just over a hundred years ago, there was a revival in the art of storytelling among mothers and teachers of young children. As part of that revival, warm-hearted educators—heart specialists—wrote careful instructions on how to educate children's hearts and then left us a treasure trove of stories to tell; stories that inspire the heart with possibilities and goodness; stories from nature, from history, from great lives, from fine art and music; fairy tales and tales of epic and legendary heroes; and stories of faith. Many of these writings have been buried in dusty corners of university libraries during this reign of the mind. But they've been brought back into the light for all of us to read and study, thanks to the digitizing efforts of such organizations as Internet Archives, Gutenberg and Google.

Vincent Van Gogh said, "It is good to love many things, for therein lies the true strength, and whosoever loves much performs much, and can accomplish much, and what is done in love is done well."

To help a child love much is the divine charge given to mothers and divine gifts are given her to accomplish the task. This is the day of the harvest. It is a day to thrust in your sickle and reap with diligence because you know what follows Fall's harvest. Already you may be seeing signs of approaching winter. The leaves are changing color and starting to drop off the trees. There's a bit of a chill in the air. But you don't have to be afraid. Within the harvest are lessons on how to survive harsh winters. And if you've been wise, you will have stored enough to sustain yourself through cold winter months when nothing grows. Winter can be a time to rest from heavy labors, to wrap up in a warm blanket, sit in front of a fire and reflect on things that really matter. Even on the coldest day of winter is found great beauty. Some of the greatest masterpieces of literature, art and music have come from history's winters. And if the winter's day seems especially long and dark and dreary, you can hold on to the hope and promise of spring, because spring always follows winter. Always. It will be a time of new beginnings; of clearing away rotting leaves and digging new furrows in the earth to plant the seeds saved from the fruits of fall's harvest. And there will be fresh scented breezes.

I realize the number of harvesters may be small, but I've baked enough bread to know a little bit of leaven raises the whole loaf. Mothers, will you be that leaven?

By small and simple means, you can bring great things to pass. Remember this story with which I will close:

A certain man had a friend who was a beekeeper. Upon visiting him one day, he found his friend in great despair. "I'm ruined," he cried. "All my honey is bitter." The man carefully and thoughtfully considered the situation and then suggested they rise early in the morning and try to follow the swarm of bees to see what they were feeding on, which they did. They found them at an old abandoned bottling factory where, out back, there were barrels of rotting, gooey, icky syrups from which the bees were filling their little pollen sacs and flying back to the hives. The man offered, "Change what your bees are feeding on, and you'll change the quality of your honey."

Mothers, as you pay attention to the quality of stories your children are feeding on, you will not only improve the quality of their lives, you will improve the quality of the world. Stories can heal our hearts. Stories can heal our homes. Don't underestimate the power of a story.

A Special Dream

Lana Vawser

"Last night I had a dream and in my dream, I heard the voice of the Lord booming with such authority, expectancy and destiny. He said, 'I am raising up a company of women with fire in their bellies.' Followed straight after that I heard the Lord decreeing Isaiah 60:1: 'Arise, shine, for your light has come, and the glory of the Lord rises upon you.'

"A new day is upon women right now!

"He is raising up women now who know Him; modern-day Esthers, Deborahs, Marys to stand with passion and conviction on their platform of influence.

"This large company of women He is raising up, who know Him and His heart, who carry His fire are about to meet new doors of influence in their lives to release His fire...

"I saw a tidal wave of creativity crashing in on women in this season. Chains that have held many women down from knowing who they are and what they were created to do, and how to express that creativity of heaven, it's being broken. God is awakening creativity in women. Watch and see women who know Him being positioned in greater positions of influence in areas of creativity to begin to lead the world in the creativity of heaven."

It's an exciting time!

Do you feel it? I do.

The Cedars of Lebanon

By Marley Billings

In the snowy mountains of northern Lebanon there is a small grove of trees. The people call it the Cedars of God.

The mountains were once covered by these trees. They are extraordinarily strong and majestically tall. The prized trees were revered and sacred.

Today there is only a remnant.

Cedars of Lebanon have special significance. The righteous shall grow like a Cedar of Lebanon, and flourish, bring forth fruit. (Psalm 92)

The roots of the trees run exceptionally deep. This slow and methodical growth anchors the tree and keeps it connected to an underground spring.

Then begins the great climb upward. Growing for thousands of years, the towering trees stand as devoted sentinels.

As they age, the crown begins to flatten and the side branches form great reaching arms. Ezekiel called it a shadowing shroud—an encircling shelter and refuge.

We are sisters. All part of the same forest, we are pushing our roots deeper striving upward in our learning and ever reaching outward to influence for good.

By small and simple things…are great things brought to pass.

Mothers of Influence

You are a Mother of Influence. Marley Billings, Jen Goostrey, and I have chosen the Cedars of Lebanon to be our symbol. Like our symbol, the Cedars of Lebanon, we want to grow deep roots, strive upward and reach outward. We encourage gathering other Mothers of Influence together for strength and support. We need each other.

The story is told that many years ago, a young boy visited his uncle who worked in the lumber business. They were looking at the trees in the lumber camp when the boy noticed a very tall tree standing alone on the hilltop. Full of excitement, the boy showed his uncle the towering tree. "Look at that big tree!" he exclaimed. "It will make a lot of good lumber, won't it?"

To the boy's surprise, his uncle shook his head. "No," he said, "that tree will not make a lot of good lumber. It might make a lot of lumber but not a lot of good lumber. When a tree grows off by itself, too many branches grow on it. Those branches produce knots when the tree is cut into lumber. The best lumber comes from trees that grow together in groves. The trees also grow taller and straighter when they grow together."

Invite older women whose children are grown, high school daughters, single women who have no children of their own, women of all faiths and political persuasions, neighbors, co-workers and friends. If your group grows too large, branch off and form new groups.

A Mother of Influence tends hearts: her own heart, the hearts of children, the heart of her home, and the heart of her community. By tending her own heart, she creates roots that are deep and sturdy. From the depth of her soul, she begins to nourish the hearts of her children as she strives upward and creates a lifegiving home of becoming and belonging. And then, reaches outward to bless the community in which she lives.

> "If we mean to have heroes, statesmen and philosophers, we should have learned women." --Abigail Adams

A Mother's University has been created to help women re-learn the lost arts of educating hearts of children. Even if a woman has no children of her own, the things she will learn will add a measure of joy and satisfaction to her life and will bless all who are in her sphere of influence. The teachers and mentors at this University are a group of educators who lived a hundred years ago. Their writings have only recently resurfaced.

The study is designed as a twelve-month rotation schedule so that you can learn line upon line, layer upon layer, drawing on what you're ready to take in the first time through and deepening the understanding each time you return as you spiral upward and outward. These writings are supplemented with articles and research of educators today who confirm the wisdom of the past which will give you confidence as you move forward.

Keep notes of what you learn. The Mother's University is free online. When you come to your group meeting, share your experiences as you begin to apply the lessons in educating and warming hearts.

Your home will then become the outward expression of what you treasure in your heart. We love Sally Clarkson who has had a twenty-year ministry of helping mothers create lifegiving homes. She says, "Making a home is a functioning of making time to love." She had her first child at the age of 31. Having never changed a diaper or spent one day babysitting, she had no idea how to be a mother or to make a home. But she learned. Her ideas are simple and practical with suggestions for each month of the year. Check out her ideas in her book, *The Lifegiving Home*.

And now, as the tree reaches maturity, it begins to reach outward to provide shade and refuge in the community. Learning that has no outlet grows stale. While we encourage political and civic activism and raising voices in regards to policy and lawmaking, the scope and vision of Mothers of Influence is as a cultural lift, not as an activist organization and we ask that you not use the name Mothers of Influence in connection with worthy activities that are not part of our purpose and mission.

We encourage Mothers of Influence to always be mindful of ways to add beauty and refinement to the community at large. As a group, and with your families, consider ways to serve such as planting flowers in the community, even if only a planter box, reading inspirational stories to children in a homeless center or donating quality books for the children there, influencing the libraries to increase the number of wholesome and inspirational books on library shelves, placing fine art in public places, joining with other Mothers of Influence and sponsoring talent shows, art galleries, putting on plays, bringing in guest speakers and musicians, writers and poets to inspire young hearts. Sponsor art and music contests for young people. Always keep your eyes open as to where you can plant a little beauty and add a little light to your community.

A lesson drawn from Robert Browning's Paracelsus is this: "There is an answer to the passionate longing of the heart for fulness… And the answer is this: Live in all things outside yourself by love and you will have joy. This is the life of God; it ought to be our life."

It's amazing what a little Light can do.

A daring experiment run in 1982 during the war between Lebanon and Israel was referenced by Gregg Braden in a book called *The Spontaneous Healing of Belief*. Researchers trained a group of people to 'feel' peace within. At appointed times on specific days of the month, these people were positioned throughout the war-torn areas of the Middle East. During the window of time when they were feeling peace, terrorist activities ceased, the rate of crimes against people went down, the number of emergency-room visits declined and the incidence of traffic accidents declined. When the participants' feelings changed, the statistics were reversed. This study confirmed the earlier findings: When a small percentage of the population achieved peace within themselves, it was reflected in the world around them.

The study became known as the International Peace Project in the Middle East and the results were eventually published in the Journal of Conflict Resolution in 1988.

In the preface of an old 1892 book about the 15th century world of Henry V, it reads:

"Old faiths had lost their inspiration. Old forms of government were breaking down. The very fabric of society seemed to be on the point of dissolution. It is however part of the irony of history that a great ideal too often finds its finest expression only when the period of decline has already commenced.

"The remedy for present evils was sought not in the creation of a new order but rather in the restoration of an old ideal. To bring back the Golden Past must be the work of a hero who could revive in his own person its virtues.

"Henry of Monmouth, deriving his inspiration from the past, was the champion of unity against the forces of disintegration."

Being a champion of unity against the forces of disintegration is the work of a Mother of Influence. After the name was chosen, we noticed the initials formed the word 'moi' and it made us think of Lancelot, in Camelot, singing: C'est Moi—'tis I! And so we ask: "Who can make a change in the world? C'est MOI! 'Tis I."

Cedars of Lebanon planted around the world will provide an ever encircling reach of refuge and hope. We believe angels are standing by ready to assist you in this important work. A little leaven, a little salt, even a single candle in a dark room can make a difference.

By small and simple things, great things will come to pass.

Over a hundred years ago, Herbert Spencer imagined someone from the future trying to piece together who we were from our schoolbooks. He wrote: "I see here an elaborate preparation for many things; but I find no reference whatever to the bringing up of children. They could not have been so absurd as to omit all training for this gravest of responsibilities."

Ahhh. But we have been so absurd! We are still not only neglecting the preparation, we are demeaning and devaluing the very worth of a mother. Let us correct the course going forward, for as a wise man asks of us:

"When the real history of mankind is fully disclosed, will it feature the echoes of gunfire or the shaping sound of lullabies? The great armistices made by military men or the peacemaking of women in homes and in neighborhoods? Will what happened in cradles and kitchens prove to be more controlling than what happened in Congresses?"

We answer with a resounding "YES" for we know the hand that rocks the cradle is the hand that rules the nations.

Priceless is the influence of a mother.

The Richest Gift a Mother Can Give Her Child

Adapted Story by Elizabeth Harrison, *In Story-Land*

Long ago, and far, far away, when fairies could be seen by mortals, a sweet baby boy came to live in a humble home. As his mother cradled the newborn in her arms, and wondered what kind of man he would become, she softly whispered, "How I wish that I could give to you, my darling child, the richest gift on earth, so that Kings and Emperors might be proud to call you their companion."

"So you can," said a gentle voice beside her that startled the mother. "I can give him the greatest and most wonderful gift on earth." The mother looked around the room and her eyes fell upon a perfectly beautiful little creature, no bigger than your thumb, with two wings as thin as gauze gleaming with every color of the rainbow. Upon its head was a slender gold crown and its small face was bright with a merry smile.

"What will you do for my child?" cried the mother. "Will you give him comfort and ease and fill his days with endless pleasure?"

"Ah, no," replied the fairy, "I will give him something far better than pleasant food and a soft bed and fine clothes."

"Then will you make him great and powerful so that men may bow down before him and honor him?"

"No! No," again replied the fairy shaking her head. "I will give him something of far more worth than fame and power!"

"Then you will make him rich, so rich that he will never have a financial worry or care; so rich that he never has to work?"

"Nay, good woman," said the fairy seriously. "These are foolish things for which you ask. My gift is greater than all of those put together. Pleasure and influence and wealth a man may earn for himself–and he may be very miserable after he gets them, too," she added with a shrug of her shoulders. "The gift that I would bestow upon your son will make him the happiest of mortals and will give him the power of making many, many others happy."

"Tell me," cried the mother, "how will you make him so happy? No human being is ever sure of happiness."

The fairy replied, "Let me kiss him upon his two eyelids as he lies there asleep and do you the same each returning birthday and all will be well."

A step was heard approaching the door. "Quick! Quick!" exclaimed the fairy, "I must be off before the door opens. Shall I give him the magic kiss or not?"

"Yes," cried the excited mother. "I trust you will do no harm to my precious child." Instantly the fairy fluttered down and, as she kissed each closed eyelid, gently whispered, "He shall be called 'Blessed Eyes.'"

The door opened and the fairy was gone.

Most of the mother's friends and relatives thought Blessed Eyes was a very strange name to give a child, but as the boy grew into a sweet and healthy childhood, loving and kind to everyone, little Blessed Eyes became a favorite.

Long before her child could talk, the mother noticed how closely he observed everything around him. He saw the first red glow of the evening sunset. His eyes were the first to spy out the early spring flower and in the autumn when the wind was sharp and cold, he would bring home some red mountain berries or a withered leaf wrapped around a little caterpillar. No stone nor cloud nor stream nor tree but gave him pleasure.

"Ah," thought the mother, "this is the birthday gift. She has made his eyes to see the beautiful everywhere."

But then she heard these words whispered gently in her ear: "More than that, far more than that! Kings and princes shall yet call him great." She seemed to hear the soft but distant singing of the words,

Love well, love well, love well,
That the heart within may swell.

Years passed by, changing little Blessed Eyes into a tall young man, and each succeeding year added to the wonderful power which his eyes possessed, of seeing the best that was in everything and everybody. He was the friend of rich and poor. All sought his companionship, for he was constantly pointing out to them so many beautiful things in the world about them which they would never have seen but for him. All loved him dearly, for he was just as constantly finding the best that their inner world contained, and encouraging them to live according to their noblest ideals of how true men and women should live.

Long years passed and Blessed Eyes became the King's Chief Counsellor. One day as he was walking through the streets, he heard a deep sigh of someone in great trouble. He turned to see a poor laboring man with his head bent forward upon his hands.

"What is the matter?"

"Ah," replied the poor man, "all the jobs in the shops are taken and I can find no work; my children are starving for want of bread."

"What large, strong arms you have!" said Blessed Eyes. "Why do you not seek the King and offer to quarry the beautiful white marble that lies in yonder mountain range. Those great strong arms of yours could do a grand work in the King's quarry."

The man softened, "I will go."

The King gladly accepted the offer and sent him with crow-bars and drills and soon there came a wagon load of beautiful white marble, and then another and then another. The King was so pleased, he sent another ten men and then twenty and then a hundred and soon a vast pile of the glistening, white marble had been collected and the poor and discouraged man had become the most famous stonemason in the world.

Not long after this, as Blessed Eyes and the King looked at the shining white marble and wondered how it could be used to make beautiful the city, they noticed a man standing beside it, measuring it with his eye.

"It's a fine sight, is it not?" commented Blessed Eyes.

But the poor man looked at him sadly, shook his head and wrote, "I cannot hear a word that you say; I am totally deaf, and therefore I am the loneliest man in all the King's realm."

Blessed Eyes heart was stirred with pity for the lonely man. He took his pencil and wrote, "You evidently have a very correct eye for measurements."

"Yes," replied the man, "I think I could estimate the weight of any one of these great stones within half an ounce."

Blessed Eyes wrote quickly: "With such good eyes for measurement, you would surely be a good builder. This is the King. Why do you not offer to make for him some beautiful buildings out of this white marble?"

The lonely man's face brightened. The King accepted his offer and the new architect set to work at once drawing plans for several buildings which were to surround a charming lake in the King's park.

Soon, scores of men were laying foundations, while others shaped the marble into blocks and pillars, all under the direction of the new architect. When all was done and the buildings stood in their full majestic beauty with their long colonnades shining in the sunlight and their graceful towers rising airily in the upper air and their beautiful gilded domes crowning all, the scene resembled fairyland. People came from the farthest ends of the earth to enjoy its beauty and the sad and lonely deaf man had now become the most famous architect in the whole world.

As beautiful as the buildings were on the outside, inside they were cold and bare and one day as the King and Blessed Eyes consulted how the inner walls might be made as beautiful as the outer ones, they heard a group of boys making fun of a stranger in their midst. With a feeling of indignation, Blessed Eyes pressed forward: "What is your difficulty, sir?"

The stranger blushed and stammered, "I-I-I ca-ca-canno- no-not sp-speak your language wi-without st-st-stammering."

At this the boys roared with laughter. Blessed Eyes turned an angry look at them, and slipping his arm through the stranger's, he said, "Will you walk with me? I noticed you have strong, artistic hands. Surely you must be able to draw and paint."

The stranger's face lit up—he had hoped to get work there as an artist.

He was taken to the King, and soon the three were deep in plans for decorating and making beautiful the inner walls of the white buildings. It was not long before the stammering artist had proved that he was not only an artist, but a master artist. Lesser artists and new pupils flocked to him from all parts of the land. In less than a year, the walls were decorated with wonderful pictures of faraway landscapes; of beautiful sunset clouds, and best of all, true and lifelike portraits of the noblest men and women of the nation and the stammering stranger had become known as the greatest artist of the age.

Now the next question that arose was the best way to use these magnificent buildings, so that all might enjoy them. One day, as Blessed Eyes pondered the matter, he came upon a man, pacing the halls with his hands clasped behind him. He soon noticed the man was completely blind.

"Ah! That is the step of Blessed Eyes! Much as he has done to help others, there is nothing he can do for me!"

"Indeed," replied Blessed Eyes. "If you can tell a man by his step, you must certainly have good hearing. Surely a man whose hearing is so acute must be a good musician."

"Yes, the man cried impatiently, "I am the finest conductor of an orchestra in the whole world, but for what use? Nobody cares for good music now!" And he shrugged his shoulders.

"Come with me to the King. I think he has need of you."

After a long talk with the King, the King offered his generous support that the people might learn to love good music. The blind man became such a marvelous director of musicians that soon, thousands upon thousands came to hear the afternoon concerts which were given in the largest of the beautiful, white buildings.

One bright, spring morning, as Blessed Eyes started out to enjoy the sunshine and flowers, his eyes fell upon the tear-stained face of a woman. "Dear Madam, is there anything I can do for you?"

"Alas, what can you do for a broken-hearted mother whose four little children have been taken by death from her arms. Unless I have children to love, life has no brightness for me."

"Surely," said Blessed Eyes softly and compassionately, "there are yet many children who need your love. Will you not come with me to the palace of the King?"

The woman looked perplexed, but followed. I do not know just how it happened, but soon there were voices of happy children who followed her as she told them stories and taught them songs and led them in charming games, and trained their hands into skillful work. So full of motherly love was the woman's work that other beautiful and noble women came and joined her until at last there was no child in the whole city who had not learned how to love sweet music, enjoy beautiful pictures and how to be kind and thoughtful towards others.

In time many of these children grew into manhood and womanhood and became musicians, artists, authors, physicians, clergyman and wonderfully skilled workmen of all sorts. Many of the women married and became loving and wise mothers because of the training they had received from the pale-faced childless woman who was now filled with joy.

At last the good King died, and the question arose, "Who shall be our King?" The counsellors sent to the stonemasons and the great stone-mason cried, "Let Blessed Eyes be our King! Did he not teach me how to use my strong arms? Has he not furnished bread for us and our families?"

And the architects said, "Let Blessed Eyes be King! Have we not, from him, learned to make beautiful whatever we build?"

And they sent to the mills and the factories and the designers said, "Why not make Blessed Eyes our King? It was he who first introduced Art into our land and showed us how to make as beautiful as pictures our carpets and curtains and walls.

Then they sent to all the colleges and schools of the land and the superintendents said, "We know of no better man than Blessed Eyes. He first taught us that a love of the beautiful should be part of each child's education."

Soon the whole nation seemed to cry out, "Blessed Eyes, Blessed Eyes, Long live King Blessed Eyes!" There is none among us whom he has not helped. When the news was brought to Blessed Eyes, he smiled gently and said, "I had hoped to rest now, but if I can serve my country, I must do it."

So he was made King and the nation became wise and great and powerful under his reign. For the little children grew up learning to love the beautiful and to see it everywhere until at last there was a whole nation of blessed-eyes, and every city in the land became as beautiful as the White City by the Lake.

"*You cannot parent a child whose heart you do not have.*" --Dr. Gordon Neufeld

THERE ARE TIMES WE ALL FEEL INADEQUATE…
YOU ARE A GARDENER OF SOULS.

Educating the Educator

I would like to respond to this mother's request: "I would like a podcast about the education of educators' mothers and how to let go of the idea of perfection. I think we get stuck thinking we have to do it 'right' and we are continually feeling like failures. Please help us to lift the burden of thinking perfection is required and help us to see we are doing just fine."

I frequently hear other moms saying the same thing. I've heard more than one mom, after one of my presentations, say, "Oh! I wish I had known these things when my children were little. But now it's too late. I've failed them." Or they tell me they feel like their own heart is so hard and they don't know how to warm it up.

Comments like that make me sad. First, there is no such thing as too late. And second, there is rarely a heart so hard that it cannot be softened. I remember reading a news story of a hardened serial killer awaiting his execution on death row who was befriended by a man whose heart was filled with love. That Love changed the heart of the killer who left this life with a heart of a child. He had never had a single person in his life who loved him until this man came along.

Learning to soften hard-hearts is our task at hand. We live in a very hard-hearted culture. What we're seeking to do here at the Well-Educated Heart is to soften and warm hearts, which is no easy task. It's extremely challenging to go against the norm. I often refer to you as pioneers blazing new trails because that's what you are. What we are attempting to do has never been done and no generation in the history of the world has had the resources and tools we have been gifted to get the job done.

I don't know why me, but a vision has been planted deep in my heart. I can see something and feel something that is so glorious and beautiful, I can't begin to describe it. I feel like an artist who has been endowed with a great painting in his heart, but that painting can only be re-created in the outer world one brush stroke at a time. I feel so inadequate and unskilled to bring forth such a thing. But the pieces that come out often feel very lofty and I think sometimes that can have the effect of making moms feel inadequate because it's so far above us. All of us. But when I want to bring it closer to earth, the impression comes, "No, we stretch by reaching for that which is above us."

So please know—I don't think anyone has yet reached what I am only beginning to unfold. But there can be and will be great joy in the journey.

I read this quote from a wonderful book I own called *One Thousand Beautiful Things* compiled by Marjorie Barrows, who also compiled the 16-volume Children's Hour Series I've recommended before.

The words were written by Donn Byrne.

"My dear son, God has put wisdom in my head and beauty in yours. Wisdom is needed for the governance of this world, but beauty is needed for its existence. In arid deserts there is no life.

"Birds do not sing in the dark of night. Show me a waste country, and I'll show you a brutal people. No faith can live that is not beautiful…

"The beauty God has put in your heart, child, you must always keep."

I believe you have been prepared and preserved for this time to help plant beauty in the world through keeping alive the beauty that has already been planted in the hearts of your children. How are you going to do it? I felt to re-read *The Secret Garden* by Frances Hodgsen Burnett. If you haven't read it, I encourage you to read it now. And if you've already read it, read it again through the eyes of a well-educated mother's heart. Or listen to it with your children.

This is the story of a little girl whose heart was hardened from neglect, and the Magic that healed it.

We live in a world of instant gratification and quick fixes. If our computer takes more than five seconds to load, we get impatient. If our hamburgers take longer than 5 minutes to get to us, we get annoyed. We're used to problems being solved in a 30-minute TV show and 13 of those minutes are for commercials.

It's no wonder we expect ourselves to change right now. We want our homes to be different right now. But growing a flower garden teaches us all that is worthwhile takes time. The process can't be rushed. There is no flower without planting a seed and watering and nourishing it and clearing the weeds away.

The secret is that you have a garden within you that needs tending and your children have the same. Seeds have to be planted and given time to grow. And those seeds are in the form of thoughts and ideas, images and impressions.

Do you remember this part of *The Secret Garden*? "In each century since the beginning of the world wonderful things have been discovered. In the last century more amazing things were found out than in any century before. In this new century hundreds of things still more astounding will be brought to light. At first people refuse to believe that a strange new thing can be done, then they begin to hope it can be done, then they see it can be done—then it is done and all the world wonders why it was not done centuries ago."

Just a side note—I hope that's what people will say about well-educated hearts. At first, people may refuse to believe it can be done, then they will begin to hope it can be done, then you will show them it can be done, then it will be done and all the world will wonder why it wasn't done centuries ago.

Now to continue from the book:

"One of the new things people began to find out in the last century was that thoughts—just mere thoughts—are as powerful as electric batteries, as good for one as sunlight is, or as bad for one as poison. To let a sad thought or a bad one get into your mind is as dangerous as letting a scarlet-fever germ get into your body. If you let it stay there after it has got in, you may never get over it as long as you live.

"So long as Mistress Mary's mind was full of disagreeable thoughts about her dislikes and sour opinions of people and her determination not to be pleased by or interested in anything, she was a yellow-faced, sickly, bored and wretched child. But when her mind gradually filled itself with robins, and moorland cottages crowded with children, with queer crabbed old gardeners and common little Yorkshire housemaids, with springtime and with secret gardens coming alive day by day, there was no room left for the disagreeable thoughts.

"So long as Colin shut himself up in his room and thought only of his fears and weaknesses and his detestations of people, he was a hysterical half-crazy little hypochondriac who knew nothing of sunshine and the spring. When new beautiful thoughts began to push out the old hideous ones, life began to come back to him."

Two things cannot be in one place.
Where you tend a rose, my lad,
A thistle cannot grow.

We're tending roses here. I believe a beautiful new era is going to break forth upon the world, after a winter season when roots deepen and prepare for a new season, and Satan will be bound because there will be no place in people's hearts for him because their hearts will be filled with that which is good, and true and beautiful.

Those thoughts have to be planted one seed at a time and given time to take root and grow. As the garden came to life in the book, there was joy in the expectation and at every new bud that blossomed. The joy didn't have to wait until the work was finished, because the work would never be finished. If you are waiting for a moment when you are perfect and doing it all right, you'll be waiting forever. It won't happen. So take your delight in every seed you plant and water and nourish. Some will bloom in spring and some will bloom in autumn.

In the front of the 1000 beautiful things book I just told you about is where I found the philosophy of Goethe. He was once asked by a friend what he would suggest as a daily exercise for spiritual betterment. He said:

> I would like to read a noble poem.
> I would like to see a beautiful picture.
> I would like to hear a bit of inspiring music.
> I would like to meet a great soul.
> And for my fellow men I would like to say a few sensible words.

I have taken his recommendation to heart and it has changed my life. When I feel those discouraging or depressing thoughts try to take hold, I'll turn on some music or reach for a poem. I had one of those moments this week. I often feel overwhelmed and inadequate. So I've been taking time to spend with a great soul—Professor Laurence Jones whose, as the book cover says, courage and invincible faith created a miracle of hope and education for the forgotten Negro communities of Mississippi. Here is the complete account of a modern Booker T. Washington, and of the Piney Woods Country Life School, which he created against tremendous odds.

I read a little every day and he is teaching me about faith and not giving up and love.

And I find myself telling my husband stories I am learning from Laurence and my husband is lifted, too.

You are not alone. Trailing clouds of glory do your children come from heaven which is their home, as Wordsworth wrote. As much as you love your children, there is a Heavenly Parent who loves them infinitely more. But ever polite and patient, He waits for the invitation to come into your home and lives. He will make up for the part you cannot do. You can plant seeds, but He provides the Magic.

Your child is actually not an empty bucket. He is as a seed fully endowed with the potential to reach the full measure of his creation. What you provide is the water, the nourishment and the pulling of weeds. No rushing is possible. And you'll be sadly disappointed if you are expecting a peony if your child is meant to be a daisy. He is part of a Heavenly Design in which your child has a unique role to fill. I love pink roses, but thank heavens there is an endless variety of other colors, textures and shapes. It makes the world beautiful and whole.

Try not to be hard on yourself. Chase those bad thoughts away with inspiring ones. Spend time in the Mother's University and keep learning.

We had one of the best Mother's Day talks I've ever heard last year in church. The man who gave it said that his mother only did one thing right in her whole life. She was a selfish alcoholic and a drug addict and had a mess of a life. But when she became pregnant and everyone told her the best thing she could do was to abort that baby, she chose to give him life. With tears running down his face, he said, "Thank you, mom, for giving me life. Because I love life."

Somehow, even though he grew up in that kind of turmoil with the most imperfect of mothers, he emerged as a kind, compassionate, caring man who is doing much good in the world.

There is nothing that is required of you but that you will be able to do. There are many forces at work in your child's life—for good and for bad. It is not for you to shoulder the burden that you are solely responsible for the outcome of your child's life.

When I graduated from college with a degree in child development, there is only one thing I remember from the graduation ceremony. The speaker said something that has stuck with me all these years. He said—actually it may have been a she, I don't even remember—the speaker said, "Every child needs and deserves to have at least one person in his life who is wildly crazy about him."

Love makes up for a multitude of other shortcomings. Let that wildly-crazy-in-love-with-a-child person be you.

Then keep tending the garden, one seed at a time. And watch it bloom.

Here is a little poem to memorize—your simple guide for educating a well-educated mother's heart.

Love the Beautiful
by Moses Mendelssohn

Love the beautiful,
Seek out the true,
Wish for the good,
And the best do.

A Message to Pinterest-Fail Moms

When I was a young mother, I had a couple of friends who were definitely in the Supermom realm. Their homes were always immaculate even though they had little children. Their children were dressed to perfection and everything seemed to run so smoothly in their homes. They had carefully planned Family Home Evening lessons with laminated pictures and darling chore charts, which their children actually followed. They were great cooks and were always involved in the best activities—sports, music lessons—they were picture-perfect families. One of these friends even had a big cage of guinea pigs in her kitchen and her kitchen was still always immaculate. You could have eaten off her kitchen floor. I remember one day I popped in to visit and there were toys all over her living room floor and I silently rejoiced—Ah-hah! She is mortal like me. And then she said, "Oh, please excuse the mess. I'm just disinfecting the toys." Disinfecting the toys? Is that a thing?

Oh man, I am such a failure as a mother.

I loved these friends, but we had 8 children under the age of 11 and my husband was always gone. Our house was chaotic. I was either morning sick or nursing a baby. We were always short on money and while I would have loved to dress my kids the way they did, I was more likely to be holding a pair of shoes together a little longer with duct tape. And I definitely wouldn't have recommended eating off my kitchen floor.

I aspired to be more like them, but I always fell way short.

Today, you young mothers are daily bombarded with images of perfect families in matching outfits, adoring husbands, and Pinterest-perfect homes. While I find no fault with any of these families—bless their hearts—I want to talk to you moms who feel like you are failing as a mother because you don't look like them.

Who you are is way more important than what you do or what your house looks like.

Let me introduce you to another friend of mine. I actually have never met her, but I like hanging around with her because she reminds me good things can come from messy lives.

She was the youngest in her family—the 25th of 25 children. How is that even possible?

She had 19 children of her own. Her third baby died when just a few months old. Then she lost twin boys when they were only a few weeks old. After three more daughters, another set of twins-a girl and a boy—died shortly after birth. Another baby died when her husband took the 3-week-old baby to a nurse to nurse while the mother was recovering. This woman fell asleep on the baby and suffocated him and in a panic, threw the little lifeless body in the mother's arms in the middle of the night.

Only 10 of her 19 children lived to adulthood, 3 sons and 7 daughters and three of those adult children preceded her in death, one dying of a broken heart when she was only 32 years old;

another daughter dying in childbirth.

Well, you might say, she must have had a very supportive husband to help her through things like that. Actually, no.

She met her husband when she was 13 and married him at 19, but they only knew each other through written correspondences. When they started living together, she realized they had little in common with each other—except their stubbornness. He was seven years older than she was. He never provided well for his family—he frequently got fired from his jobs because he was so hard to get along with or he found fault with the job. He fancied himself a writer and accepted invitations to speak but the offers rarely included payment and he was expected to pay his own way. He was impulsive and piled on massive debts for the growing family. He used what money he had to provide the best education he could for his sons, but he kept his wife and daughters in poverty. His daughters blamed their mother's illnesses on his poor financial decisions.

When she was expecting their first baby, things got so bad financially that she had to live in a boarding house and after the baby was born, they had to live with her parents. At one point her husband was thrown into debtor's prison. She sent him her wedding rings to help him pay off his debts and have him released, but he wouldn't accept them. When her husband died, she inherited his debts and was hounded by the debt collectors, one of whom even had her arrested. She was homeless and spent the remaining years of her life staying first in the home of one child and then the home of another and then another.

One of his jobs moved the family out into an obscure part of the country where she felt even more isolated. As they continued to fall deeply into debt, her husband became depressed and disappointed in himself and actually rode off one day, abandoning his family for 12 months. But the reason he left wasn't because of his shortcomings; he was angry because his stubborn wife would not say "Amen" to the prayer for the king. That's because she didn't accept this new king as her king. And she would never go against her own conscience.

The only thing that brought him home was the house caught on fire, nearly killing their small daughter. The fire destroyed most of the house and their belongings.

As he rebuilt the house, this mom took on the education of her children and became a homeschooling mom for the next 20 years. There was no formal teaching until the age of 5, but on their 5th birthday, her children were expected to learn all the letters of the alphabet. Textbooks were scarce and she didn't like what she saw anyway, so she took it upon herself to write her own. Although girls were rarely educated in those days, her own father had encouraged her to learn and she had read the many volumes in her father's personal library as a young girl. She was a deep thinker and had grown up in a home where many interesting and prominent people came to visit, and she learned much from the conversations and debates she heard going on as she grew up.

She lived in a time of great political disagreements—just like today—and things got so bad that those who opposed her husband's views tried to destroy the family. It was in this time of turmoil that her little baby was suffocated. One of her husband's enemies is the one who threw him in debtor's prison and tried to starve the family. It is suspected their house was deliberately set on fire a second time. This time the house burnt to the ground. The fire started in the middle of the night and this poor mother, at first, thought she had lost her entire family in the flames, but, miraculously, they were all found safe.

She gave birth to her 19th baby one month later.

While the house was being rebuilt—and her husband never did get around to fully finishing and furnishing it—it was necessary to send all the children to live in various homes of friends and family for the next year. It grieved this mother to see her children exposed to worldly things she had tried so hard to keep away from her children. When they were together again, she worked hard to re-teach them, but it changed some of them for the rest of their lives.

One daughter fell in love with a man that her father refused to give permission to marry. The girl ran away and returned home later— 5 months pregnant. Still the father would not allow her to marry the father of the baby and forced her to marry a man she didn't love. The baby died shortly after birth as did her next two babies. And the man she was forced to marry became a heavy drinker. Years later she finally divorced him.

You older mothers can relate to the sorrows we feel at what many of our grown children go through.

And yet, in spite of the messiness of her life, this mother changed the world. And she didn't even know it.

This Christmas season, as you sing "Hark, the Herald Angels Sing Glory to the Newborn King"—think of this mother. For it was her son, Charles Wesley, who composed it along with over 6000 other hymns. As Eric Metaxas says in his story of her: Few human beings have influenced the world as Susanna Wesley did. The manner in which she taught her children greatly influenced the work of her son, John, and the Methodist movement he founded led to world-changing revival and to such an array of social reforms as can never be calculated. The abolition of the slave trade and slavery are at the top of a long list that included penal reform, the end of child labor in England, laws against cruelty to animals, and the establishment of countless private societies and organizations dedicated to caring for the poor and suffering. The denomination he founded today claims eighty million members around the world, along with many Methodist hospitals, colleges, and orphanages…

This is the effect of one woman of virtue. When she made the decision to teach her children—her girls as well as her boys—she knew that above all she must teach her children to love God. As Metaxas says, "As far as she was concerned, the state of their souls formed the focus of her education." She wrote: "Though the education of so many children must create abundance of trouble and will perpetually keep the mind employed as well as the body; yet consider 'tis no small honour to be entrusted with the care of so many souls… It will be certainly no little accession to the future glory to stand forth at the last day and say, 'Lord, here are the children which Thou hast given me, of whom I have lost none by my ill example, nor by neglecting to instill in their minds, in their early years, the principles of Thy true religion and virtue.'"

Through all the struggles and disruptions of life, there was one constant in her life—she never failed to keep her daily appointment with God. When the house was busy and crowded—as it always was—when the children saw their mother pull her apron over her head, they knew to quiet down and not interrupt her—this was her place to pray in peace. According to her children who were witnesses to it, just a few hours before she died, she awoke and declared, "My dear Savior! Are you come to help me in my extremity at last?" And per her request, as she passed through the veil, her children sang a psalm of praise to God.

I couldn't help but notice that she began and ended her days with singing. Was it a coincidence that it was through a hymn that John felt his 'heart strangely warmed' that set him on the course of teaching others to feel the warmth of the Spirit and that he and his brothers used hymns to carry their message, not in man-made walls of stone, but out in open fields under God's canopy of heaven.

As I was reading about Susanna, I learned of another woman of influence I'll introduce you to at another time. From her story, I copied these words that I hope you, who feel like Pinterest fails, will take to heart:

"If the work itself be true, much of the effects will be hidden from human sight; all labour which is brought to bear upon the soul of man must be supported by faith and confident trust that the blessing of God does make vital the good seed, and that it is as surely germinating as is the cornseed in the dark earth of the ploughed field, before the green shoots appear. To work only for results, to look constantly for them, to exhibit them to others, and to make them alone the ground of hopefulness, is but a shallow egotism rather than a true devotion."

And now I'll close with Eric Metaxas' summary of her life:

"Anyone believing that the life of a woman dedicated to her family must be less than optimal cannot know the story of Susanna Wesley. Despite poverty, illness, a difficult marriage, and heartbreak in endless forms, she used her intellect, creativity, time, energies and will in such a way that can hardly be reckoned. The world in which we live owes much of the goodness in it to her life."

And so will the world owe much of its goodness to you sweet, dedicated mothers who diligently move forward in faith.

You Are Not Alone

"So, *so* sick of 'the baby is the lesson.' I get it. I do. But if I have to cancel one more field trip minutes before we're leaving because apple cider is dumped all over everyone and into the carpet, or because the couch just got decorated with purple marker or I find 23 apples we picked the day before each with one bite out of them and in a pile by my clueless 18 month old…if I have to turn down one more 'will you read to me please?' or 'can we play a game' request from my hungry-to-learn 4-year-old because I need to wipe poop from a child's back and belly and my kitchen wall… If I have to rush my 4-year-old through one more museum or orchard or nature walk that he's loving because my baby won't stop screaming and my toddler won't stop throwing tantrums on the ground… I. Am. Going. To. Lose. It. I know. This is a no-good vent. I'm sorry. But not really. I find so much positive support and ideas in this group…but today I just need lifted up. That's it. Right now, my brain is shut down to discussions on curriculum and implementation ideas. I just need to be reminded that they *will* get older. My poor preschooler. He is so ready to absorb everything. I'm sick of the baby years and so is…

"… So, I was going to say, 'and so is he.' Well, as I was typing, my 4-month-old started crying and because, well because I just feel like crying myself right now, I ignored it. Something I never do. Like, ever. And I continued to type. My 4-year-old looked up from his bristle blocks and said, 'Mom! You're not responding to Paige! She's trying to communicate something to you. We don't ignore people in this family when they have something they need to say.'

"I picked her up, thanked him for reminding me and for being her advocate, and sat down to nurse her. He got up and asked if I wanted a pillow and the laptop to finish what I was doing and now is sitting next to me stroking Paige's hair with one hand and showing his 18-month-old brother the maps in his Bible with the other.

"Perhaps we are learning after all."

As I unfold the resources I'm going to share with you, I don't want you to think I've forgotten how busy and chaotic your days are sometimes. With my 9 children falling within an 11-year span, I remember well. It's important to keep in mind that in a heart-based education, the lessons aren't all in the books. The heart is being educated by life that's happening all around them. What I will be describing is actually just a small portion of your day in the beginning.

What I'm trying to say is, please don't feel overwhelmed by the resources I'm going to show you or think you need to incorporate them all today. Focus on some simple basics, and it will unfold naturally, even on chaotic days. In fact, my hope is that after your children's hearts are sufficiently warmed and they are older, they will take charge of their own education, with you as a support.

I remember an object lesson in a class years ago. The teacher put an empty jar on the table. Next to it was a pile of rocks and a cup of sand and the object was to make it all fit in the jar. First she filled the jar with sand and tried to add the rocks, but they didn't fit. So next, she put the rocks in first, and the sand fit in all around it.

I would like to suggest four rocks to build your day around. Goethe recommended them. Every day, listen to some fine music, look at a masterpiece of fine art, recite a poem, and read a piece of fine literature, which I would translate into "story." This is solid heart food. But maybe the image I should try and impress on your heart is not that of rocks, but of priceless, sparkling gems. Diamonds and emeralds don't take up much room but are of great worth and value. If you accomplish nothing else in your day, know that you will have left a lasting impression on your child's heart of great worth.

If your child goes to public school and you want to balance out with more heart activities at home, focus on these gems. One little story may seem small and insignificant, but over the course of ten or so years, you will have planted nearly 4000 stories in your child's heart, one day at a time; 4000 stories that wouldn't be there if you didn't take those few minutes to share it. Add to these four gems the lasting impression of being snuggled in your arms and listening to your voice; of knowing you are there; and you've given your child the whole apple of a heart-based education. Most everything else is just sand.

Remember—we are not left alone to figure out how to reach our children's hearts. I know each mother learns this lesson in her own way. For me, the lesson came many years ago when our little six-week-old contracted meningitis. I felt so helpless watching his little body stretched out on the icy sheet as nurses worked to bring the fever down, the little dixie cup taped to his tiny head to protect the IV tube. I knew how serious meningitis was and it frightened me. The doctors weren't even sure what course to take.

I had gone home to shower and change my clothes and as I drove back to the hospital, my tearful pleading intensified. "Please, God, make him well. Don't let him die. I love him so much. I know I've only had him six weeks, but I can't imagine life without him."

It was a gray, dreary, rainy morning and as I pulled up to a red light, the windshield wipers swishing back and forth, I cried even louder, "Please, please, don't take my son away from me."

In the moment of silence that followed, came the life-changing lesson to my soul. It was as though unseen hands had grabbed me firmly by the shoulders to get my attention, and the words formed clearly in my mind, "Marlene, he was My son before he was your son. Don't you think I care?"

In that moment, a vague concept turned into a clear reality as I felt deeply in my heart the shared interest we had in the fate of that little boy. I had loved Michael for six weeks. God had already spent an eternity with him.

From that moment, I have never felt alone in this often crazy yet wonderful world of parenting. Rather, it has been a very real partnership. There continues to be joys and sorrows, but I have found His grace more than compensates for my shortcomings. He wants me to succeed and He wants you to succeed—these are His children, too. And that is the source of hope for all parents—that we are not alone; that someone much wiser, who loves our children even more than we do, stands ready to help, if we let Him. He patiently waits to be invited. It's okay if you don't know everything. He does. And He is anxious to teach you.

"The Spirit itself beareth witness with our spirit, that we are the children of God." Romans 8:16
"...all of you are children of the most High." Psalm 82:6

Building a Temple Within

I frequently get letters from moms that start similarly to this:

> Dear Marlene—
>
> I love the philosophy of the Well-Educated Heart, but our lives are pretty chaotic right now. I hope we can get back to normal so that we can incorporate some of these beautiful ideas.

Let me give you a sampling of the very real problems faced by families in our group: Death of spouse after a long, terrible illness. Sudden death of spouse by suicide. Divorce. Separation. Infidelity. Spouse addicted to pornography, alcohol, drugs, video games or social media. Children addicted to pornography, alcohol, drugs, video games or social media. Loss of job. Financial stresses and massive debt, often occurring in the midst of vital medical procedures. Homelessness and uncertainty. Little children sexually, physically and emotionally abused by trusted adults or strangers. Rape. Flashbacks of profound sexual abuse, an awareness that has only surfaced in adulthood. Paralyzing depression. Post-partum depression. Overwhelmedness. Mothers battling debilitating illnesses, cancer, chronic pain. Loss of children either through death or by their decisions to separate themselves from their families. Infertility. Crises of faith. Bullying. Autism. Dysgraphia, dyslexia and other learning disorders. Social anxiety. Major differences between husband and wife in educational philosophies and goals. Physical handicaps requiring a heavy load of care on the mother.

My heart goes out to all the families who are suffering.

And although no one has directly said it, I get hints that there are moms out there who think I live in an unreal world of rainbows and flowers and sunshine all day long; that when I talk about music and poetry and fine art, it's because I live in a different world than the messy world in which they sometimes find themselves.

But I can tell you that within my own family, we are dealing with a number of the things listed above. It's all part of life. I think about a card my friend sent me. On the cover it said, "Let's get together when things get back to normal." And inside it said, "But what if this is normal?"

And that's my point. Life is messy. By design. We don't grow strong through ease and lack of opposition. We are here to overcome. But not through our strength alone. "In the strength of the Lord, I can do all things."

Which brings me to the point: the principles I am teaching here in the Well-Educated Heart are the very means by which you will be able to navigate whatever challenge you may be facing. The arts are the life jacket when you are drowning in the ocean and the sharks are circling. And the mother who equips her child with the arts will prepare and fortify that child for life's battles ahead. I know you are worried about decoding words and memorizing math facts and constructing sentences. But in the hierarchy of needs in childhood, although necessary, they are not my central focus. Like the Garden of Eden, childhood provides a unique window of opportunity in which to plant deep impressions of beauty and truths that will be anchors to their souls in the lone and dreary wilderness that we all pass through one way or another. We have to be so careful that we don't get caught in the thick of thin things. When your heart is breaking, I guarantee you won't be reaching for your multiplication tables.

This idea of building a temple within my heart that I have talked about elsewhere has been a life-changing concept for me. I cannot heal the damage done to my soul in this fallen world. I cannot fix most of the problems I face. But there is One who can. And if I focus on preparing a place for Him to come, and keep it clean and pure and quiet, He does come and in His love, I feel joy and peace and beauty and safety even though the sharks are still circling.

And isn't this the gift we want to give our children?

But only He can teach you how to do it for your children which is why you must first tend to building the temple within your own heart—preparing a place he can commune with you. Brigham Young taught: "Mothers, let your minds be sanctified before the Lord, for this is the commencement, the true foundation of a proper education in your children..."

He knows, "The mothers are the moving instruments in the hands of Providence to guide the destinies of nations."

I received a couple of letters from moms who have been trying to interest their friends in the Well-Educated Heart. And sometimes they will begin, but they say it's too hard and they leave it behind and choose one of the open-and-go curriculums. They asked me why I thought they did that and I answered that I believe it's largely driven by fear. We live in a tower-climbing world. People are watching where you are on the tower as far as teaching your children and all they can measure is what level of reading or math or writing they are on. There's a lot of pressure to not fall behind. And it's the familiar world. The activities in most curriculums are the kinds of learning activities we all grew up with and we always gravitate towards the familiar. It's safe. And many moms lack the confidence that they can teach their children at all. You can measure progress in these academic programs and many moms live in places where they are required to report such things under stiff penalties of not complying. I get that.

It's a huge challenge for us in this generation.

But everything within me urges me forward in laying a path for a new way—really, restoring an old way, even if the followers are few. I have experienced this way of learning and living for myself and my only regret is that I am so inept at transferring the vision in a way that doesn't overwhelm you. Because it really is simple, as all truth is simple. And although we may not be able to do it to perfection right now, we can begin in small and simple ways to move away from being a tower-climbing people towards being a temple-building people in education where the Lord can be the teacher because, as I have often quoted from Charlotte Mason's writings, "True education is between a child's soul and God." As Heber C. Kimball wrote: "Which would you rather possess in education—the real flower, or the artificial one? Would you not rather have true education, direct from heaven, than the artificial one of the world? The one educates the head and the heart, the other the head alone."

Or as Brigham Young wrote: "When a man is full of the light of eternity, then the eye is not the only medium through which he sees, his ear is not the only medium by which he hears, nor the brain the only means by which he understands." We tend to be so unwilling to allow that kind of learning to happen; to relinquish our control. And in that control, which is primarily seen in our focus on academics in childhood, I truly believe we are hardening the hearts of our children. Hard heartedness is a real condition and will block their ability to feel the influence of the spirit.

The primary function of the arts is to soften and open hearts. So let me briefly review again how the languages of the heart—the arts—help us in building the temple within.

Music changes lives at the deepest level of our being. It travels where words alone cannot reach. Music brings harmony and order to our souls. Or rather I should say, the right kind of music. Some of you may have watched the same YouTube going around that talked about the music of today. I always say it all sounds the same to me and this explained why. After listing a long list of today's top performers, it said that 2 people whose names none of us would recognize are writing the vast majority of their songs. They are using hooks to hook people into the music and people are drawn to its familiarity. They are also compressing the music in a way that turns it into noise. And in another YouTube, it went through the 40 top hits and all 40 used the same 4 basic chords.

My takeaway from this is that our children are being desensitized to music. Strong, repetitive, rhythmic beat in the absence of melody shuts down thought and feeling. Not to mention that so many of the songs never go 'home.' They leave you dangling at the end.

That inspired music that heals our souls and our bodies and even reveals the very glory of God to the deepest parts of our beings is rejected because of a lack of sensitivity to this finer music. I won't spend the time here, but part of the solution is to help make classical music familiar to the ears of your children. You can't force it, but you can play it in your home because you want to hear it.

There is also much that happens when we sing. I've mentioned elsewhere that the voice is the connector between mind and heart. The Greeks understood that and is one of the secrets of their greatness. Those whose hearts are hard or closed often find it very difficult to sing because singing is so emotional. But the lesson in *Sound of Music* isn't lost on me—when the Captain opened his mouth and sang, his heart softened.

Jesus sang a hymn with his disciples at the last supper—a hymn, that evidently, according to Jewish tradition, would have lasted an hour. What might it have done to prepare him for what lie ahead? Singing is a bonding activity and there is great strength in a family who sings together. I sat next to a woman in church this morning who only recently joined our church. She is from Poland and her English is very limited. But there we were, sharing a hymnbook. The songs are unfamiliar to her, but I felt her trying to blend her voice with mine. And it was a sweet unifying moment with her even though our normal language is a barrier. Music is a universal language. Songs can plant deep eternal truths in the hearts of children in a pleasurable way. So singing is a vital and prominent part of education in a Well-Educated Heart home and should be used in abundance.

Our study of fine art is really a study in recognizing beauty in the world all around us. It opens our eyes so we can see and, as Charles Kingsley wrote, Beauty is God's handwriting. The beautiful images are hung on the walls of the temple within where we can be reminded of the truths painted by the hearts of inspired artists.

Our focus on drawing is because drawing produces an exactness of thought. I am far more interested in helping a child learn to draw what he is seeing than to write words. Learning to write words for a child who has spent a lot of time drawing is an easy transfer at the right time. And pictures are far more interesting to a child than letters. As we sketch, we begin to see things we never would have seen if we didn't develop a habit of sketching that which we see. When the camera was invented, John Ruskin spent years trying to convince the people to not stop sketching because he knew we would lose our ability to see. And isn't that happening? We take thousands of pictures, looking, but not really seeing.

I have started applying Jack Laws tools he gave us to apply in nature journaling to the fine art I look at. The three tools are: "I notice," "I wonder," and "That reminds me of." It has brought my appreciation to a whole new level and the images are much clearer in my memory. I will demonstrate it elsewhere.

The mission of poetry is to make glad the heart of man. Poetry is also music. And pictures. It does not teach—it inspires. As one of the heart educators described, "Poetry pierces past the outer husk of things into their inner reality, which it interprets for the soul." Poetry ministers to the inward life. "[T]he true poet has been given, not only a soul awake to all the beauty of the world, but the power to translate his vision into the beauty of human language." Yet, most adults lack the faculty that can appreciate it because it was never nurtured and developed in childhood.

For the child who is raised hearing the music of poetry, to which their hearts are naturally drawn, he will be so blessed in later years. Poetry is meant to be read aloud in order to feel the music. Don't assign poems to be learned and copied—let a child freely look for those poems that connect to him and connects to his own heart. We are all different. The same poem won't mean the same thing to you as it does to me. At the suggestion of the heart educators, I picked up a blank book at A.C. Moore and every time I come across a poem that grabs my heart, I take the time to hand copy it in my book and it has become such a treasure of comfort and inspiration to me.

Finally, we are drawn to stories like a moth to a candle. Can we get enough of them? Blessed is the child whose childhood is immersed in worthy stories. The hearts of these children are filled with treasures that will enrich them their entire lives. And when you tell a story 'by heart,' there is a bond and a connection made between you and your child that is difficult if not impossible to break. There is nothing else in the world like it. No wonder Jesus went about the countryside telling stories.

I have spent the last 15 years immersed in the stories of great men and women and they have truly changed my life. They help me see life in a thousand different ways and hoist me up on their shoulders for a higher view. I am surrounded by them and influenced by them in every moment of my day. Many of these people have been friends of the Savior and they show me what the path of discipleship looks like. They teach me and comfort me and give me courage. I cannot be influenced by a story that has never been planted in my heart and neither can your children.

Stories have opened up the beauties of nature. Just to walk outside, I feel wrapped in the arms of God's love, which is a huge blessing when my heart is weighed down with the troubles we are facing. Stories have given me eyes to see and a heart to understand in ways I never before imagined.

I have loaded the Libraries of Hope website with the kind of stories that will feed the hearts of your children—and you!—in an ennobling and uplifting way if you take advantage of them.

The thing about the arts is that when you are engaged in them, you are living in the moment. You are not living in the regrets of the past or the fears of the future. I think it was Emerson who said, "We are what we think about all day long." When your moments are filled with art that connects you to that which is good and beautiful and true, in a very real sense it goes into the very building materials of your soul. And when your soul is a place of beauty, the Spirit of the Lord will come and dwell with you and inspire you, using the very materials with which you are building your temple to teach you. The arts are some of the finest building materials you can quarry for that temple within.

The foundation stones belong to Him. After all, it is a house built for Him. It is through the arts—the stories, the pictures, the hymns, the poetry—that we best come to know Him because only these languages will reach into our hearts and enable us to see Him through spiritual eyes.

Through the arts, in words borrowed from John Taylor, our "souls are like a well-tuned harp, when [we] are touched by the spirit of inspiration there is a kindred chord in [our] bosoms, they vibrate to the touch, and [we] are filled with sacred melody."

When we tend to the inside, the outside will take care of itself. Beautiful hearts will build a beautiful world.

So the classroom of the heart—which should be the classroom of childhood—is filled with song and music, with story and poetry, with pictures and conversation and drawing and love. Nature provides the perfect classroom because it is filled with all these things.

This advice is given to mothers by Brigham Young: "Instead of being behind the whip, always be in advance, then you can say, 'Come along' and you will have no use for the rod. They will delight to follow you, and will like your words and ways, because you are always comforting them, and giving them pleasure and enjoyment."

I know these words will still fall short for many of you. It may not make sense. It may still be really hazy. It is my biggest challenge to translate a vision into words. I am so weak in that. But when I take my frustration to the Lord, I am always filled with the comfort that He can deliver the message in spite of my awkwardness and weakness of my words. So I keep trying, trusting that He will make up the difference.

This morning the thought struck me that baptism is a symbolic representation of being born again—really, being born into spiritual things—the realm of things which are unseen. Many churches baptize by immersion. And that word immersion is really what I am trying to do—to immerse you in the writings of the heart educators in the hopes that they will give you new eyes and new understanding. That's why I do so many podcasts and am preparing other things—because I know you are busy but there is no way to truly do this way of learning without seeing through new eyes and new understandings. I hope by making audio recordings, you can listen while you are doing other things in your day that need to be done.

Mothers of Influence in connection with the Mother's University has been organized to help you mothers come together and strengthen and encourage each other as you learn the art of cultivating hearts through the arts. You plus one other person is all it takes to start. And if you have no one near you who is interested, please join in the conversation in one of our online groups. You don't have to do this alone.

Let me close with one last thought that I think best sums up the direction I am trying to take you:

"Thrust a man into prison and bind him with chains, and then let him be filled with the comfort and with the glory of eternity, and that prison is a palace to him. Again, let a man be seated upon a throne with power and dominion in this world, ruling his millions and millions and without that peace which flows from the Lord of Hosts—without that contentment and joy that comes from heaven, his palace is a prison. When a person is filled with the peace and power of God, all is right with him."

Please don't give up. Baby steps work. By small and simple means great things will be brought to pass.

"[D]on't ever sell yourself short as a woman or as a mother… Do not let the world define, denigrate, or limit your feelings of lifelong learning and the values of motherhood… Lifelong learning is essential to the vitality of the human mind, body and soul. It enhances self-worth and self-actuation. Lifelong learning is invigorating mentally and is a great defense against aging, depression and self-doubt."
--Robert D. Hales

"The world has enough women who are tough; we need women who are tender. There are enough women who are coarse. We need women who are kind. There are enough women who are rude; we need women who are refined. We have enough women of fame and fortune; we need more women of faith. We have enough greed. We need more goodness. We have enough vanity, we need more virtue. We have enough popularity, we need more purity." --Margaret Nadauld

"My mother was the most beautiful woman I ever saw. All I am I owe to my mother. I attribute all my success in life to the moral, intellectual and physical education I received from her." --George Washington

"*Let France have good mothers and she will have good sons.*" --Napoleon Bonaparte

"*Feed your heart. I can't emphasize this enough. If you want your children to sing while they work, you sing while you work. They need to work beside you so they can see what you're doing. They don't instinctively know how to organize toys. If you want them to love beautiful music, let them see you love beautiful music. If you want them to love reading, let them see you reading. If you want them to keep a nature journal, let them see you keep a nature journal.*

"*Show them, don't tell them!*

"*Their hearts don't understand telling.*" --Marlene Peterson

"*Give me good mothers and I will save the world.*" --Pius IX

The Mother's University

Not one of us can grasp the whole of anything in one sitting. Understanding will layer in over time, line upon line, here a little and there a little as impressions deepen and expand within our own hearts. The Mother's University was created with this understanding in mind. You can study it on your own, or many moms have joined groups of other Mothers of Influence to discuss and practice what they are learning. There is even an online discussion you can join if there is no one in your personal circle of friends or family to invite.

What I will provide you each month is a Study Guide with way more things to read and study than you'll be able to do in one month. Some of you are at a season of life that you may be doing good to watch one 2-minute video. And that's okay. Others of you will have the time to read and ponder much. Take it at your level and your pace.

There are 12 topics—one for each month of the year. No worries for whatever you don't get to— you'll be back around the next year and the next—for as long as it takes. And as you come back each year, you'll bring impressions and experiences that will deepen your understanding until this becomes a way of life. As has been said, only the warm heart can kindle warmth in another. This study group is for warming your heart. And your children will be blessed by that.

The Mother's Learning Library is part of the Mother's University. Each month you will find a volume from this Learning Library that corresponds with the monthly topic. These books are collections of writings from the heart educators of the late 19th and early 20th centuries. The books I am reprinting are my personal favorites. After awhile, they will begin to feel like dear and trusted friends and mentors. These books are a good place to start, even if you don't get the entire book read on the first round.

You will also find articles to read, videos to watch, activities to try out and additional books you may like to read. Choose what appeals to you. This is an explore and discover activity. I don't tell you what you are supposed to get out of it or even where to start and finish.

Let me take you on a brief tour of the 12 topics.

Month One is all about A Mother's Influence—The ancients looked to the mothers as the source of the improvement of society. They held, as an indisputable truth, that mothers were the ruling influence on the characteristics of their children. Today, in one study I read, only 16% of those surveyed felt a mother's value was greater in the home than in the work-place. This devaluation of motherhood has been going on for quite some time.

Don't listen to them. Stand tall. You're a mother of great worth.

In this volume of the Mother's Learning Library, I share several quotes from the writings of Heinrich Pestalozzi, who I would call the modern-day father of heart-based learning.

Month Two, we'll look at Nature Study as a way of opening eyes of wonder and awe. "If the trees and flowers, the clouds and the wind, all tell wonderful stories to the child he has sources of happiness of which no power can deprive him." Our current love affair with science has kids setting up experiments in kindergarten, yet, once outside, they can't tell a birch from an oak tree; a peony from a rose. They know little of the world in which they live much less love it. Nature Study is emotional. Science is intellectual. If we wish to have more scientists, we need to first give our children eyes to see the wonders of nature that surround them every day.

Don't fall into this trap I wrote down from a 1947 text:

"[I]f a poor child picked strawberries, the experience was turned into an arithmetic lesson. If he rolled a snowball, he learned about levers and proceeded from those to wedges. If he took a walk, he had to observe every bird, beast, stone and occupation of man. Day and night these ardent [well-intentioned educators] stalked their children, allowing never a moment for play or fancy…"

Month Three will be devoted to opening hearts to hear the messages found in Music. Yes, music study will increase your child's SAT scores, but that's not the best reason to study music. Martin Luther said: "Music makes people more gentle and meek, more modest and understanding."

Why do we study music? Number one reason is for the happiness it gives us. Music is pure emotion; a universal language. It reaches a place in our hearts that words can't reach and has the power to lift us to great and pure thoughts.

We'll be studying Art in Month 4. As one of my educator friends wrote, "It will take years before you come to a full appreciation of art; but when at last you have it, you will be possessed of one of the purest, loftiest and most ennobling pleasures that the civilized world can offer you."

A child's heart that is trained to receive the impressions of great art will discover more and more of beauty, not only in pictures, but in life. Great masterpieces of art will become a tremendous source of rest, delight and inspiration.

Month 5 is dedicated to Poetry. The stories of history teach us that when a people have lost their heroic spirit; when their hearts have grown cold; it's not the scholar or the scientist who fans the flame again. It's always the poet—a Thomas Moore in Ireland or a Lord Alfred Tennyson in England—who rises up and breathes new life and plants new hearts in nations. As someone said, "The soldier fights for his native land, but the poet touches that land with the charm that makes it worth fighting for. The statesman enlarges and orders liberty in the State, but the poet fosters the love of liberty in the heart of the citizen." Helping our children love poetry may be the very thing that saves us some day in the future.

Next we'll spend a month on Storytelling—putting the book down and telling stories by heart. Storytelling is an ageless and beautiful art. When the lights are low and your child is in a quiet, receptive mood, the stories told him will never be forgotten and their influence will follow him the rest of his life.

Imagination is the topic for Month 7. Albert Einstein said that if you want your child to be intelligent, read him fairy tales and if you want him to be more intelligent, read him more fairy tales. If you want your child to learn from the lessons of history, he first needs to have impressions of right and wrong, justice and injustice, good and evil. These impressions are the gifts of fairy tales. With no imagination, there are no dreams or visions. Without vision, the people perish.

Month 8 is all about the stories of History. Jean Fritz who has brought history to life in many children's books spent her childhood in China in the early 1900's. She looked forward to coming 'home' to America and starting school, but was disappointed when the first history text was handed out. She wrote:

"Opening the book to the first chapter, *From Forest to Farmland*, I skimmed through the pages but I couldn't find any mention of people at all. There was talk about dates and square miles and cultivation and population growth and immigration and the Western movement, but it was as if the forest had lain down and given way to farmland without anyone being brave or scared or tired or sad, without babies being born, without people dying."

History is only boring when it's reduced to facts and information. When it becomes the story of people, the study of history becomes a lifelong and valuable pleasure. Like Rudyard Kipling said, "If history were taught in the form of stories, it would never be forgotten."

And now, in Month 9, we'll get to Language Arts. Some of you may be bothered that it's taking so long to get there. These heart educators taught first impressions, then expressions. It's a later step in learning, not the first. One of the selections in the Learning Library will be a wonderful little book about writing and it teaches, "If thou wouldst write, thou must first live." Like Tock said about words in *The Phantom Tolbooth*, "They're fine if you have something to say." Nothing is more frustrating than being forced to write when your heart has nothing to say. Writing happens when your heart is so full, it just has to find a way to express itself.

When Harriet Beecher Stowe wrote *Uncle Tom's Cabin*, she said she didn't give one thought to style or mechanics. The words just poured out and the influence it had on the nation and the world is astounding. She never once concerned herself if the book would make any money. Wanting to capitalize on its success, however, publishers asked her to write another book. Few people read or have even heard of it. As one critic put it: "She wrote *Uncle Tom's Cabin* because she had a book to write. But she wrote *Dred* because she had to write a book."

It doesn't mean your kids won't be doing any writing along the way. They'll be doing lots of storytelling and copying the words of the greatest writers ever, gaining impressions of their style in the process. The teaching of grammar doesn't have to take years—it can happen very quickly when working with a well-stocked heart.

Month 10 will be devoted to Math. There is a heart-based way for Math, too. Many kids struggle with math because they learn the language, but they don't understand what it's saying. If a child is introduced to numbers by drawing the number 2, and then has to add another number 2 and somehow that makes 4 and "I don't know what that is either, but I have to remember it," math is going to be a real problem down the road. I know the value of the number 2 because I have handled 2 apples. Two isn't very many. And I've cut the apple in two and given half of it to my friend. And sometimes my friend has given me 2 more apples and now I know that 4 apples is more than just 2 apples. We have a daughter who still has a problem with numbers because she somehow missed those sense-impression years. She really wanted a jeep when she was in High School, and one day she came home very excited because she saw a jeep for sale up the street. She said, "It was either $8000 or $80000. Is that a lot?"

I told her we better warn her future husband about her issues with numbers…

Here's something I only learned recently. It may be a 'duh' to you, but I had never before made the connection. The word 'digit' comes from the word 'digitus' meaning fingers. Do you know why our math system is based on tens? It's because we have ten fingers. The language of math developed as it helped to express things seen in the real world. And that's where a love of math starts.

Eighty-five years ago, an educator I think Pestalozzi would have approved of, ran a series of experiments. Louis Benezet delayed the formal instruction of math until after the 6th grade. Instead, the children told stories, played games, discussed ideas, used language. There was a joyous spirit in those classrooms in contrast to the other drill and test classrooms where, he observed, "The effect of early instruction had been to dull and almost chloroform the child's reasoning faculties." The children in the delayed math group mastered the same skills in just a fraction of the time that the other students had spent years on.

Trust the process.

And now, month 11 is for Science. I hope that with all this talk of heart and feelings, I don't mislead you into thinking that I downplay the role of science, although I'm a late-comer to appreciating it. I spent too many years being forced to learn science in a way that didn't relate to anything I could hold on to. But I'm starting to see the wonders of what I missed. For the Learning Library this month, I'm reprinting a science book first written in 1850 that I think will help you see science in new ways, especially if you've been a reluctant scientist like me.

Unfortunately, our modern world thinks Faith and Science cannot co-exist. I love the old science books because there was no separation.

And finally, Month 12 answers the question, what's the point of all of this? And the answer is: Joy. To the current educational establishment, the purpose of education may be to turn out global workers for the global economy. But I—and Pestalozzi—hope for much more for our children.

We want to prepare them to live lives of maximum joy. Happy people create happy lives and a happy world.

So, for the Learning Library this month, I found a really thought-provoking and enjoyable book on this quest for joy where the author draws from the lessons of many of the great thinkers throughout history. You will also find a thought about happiness for every day of the year.

Our upside-down world has also been turned inside-out. Or, rather I should say, outside-in. It teaches us that if you can take care of all the external things, you'll be happy. If you can just get into the right college, land the right job with the highest salary, build the biggest house, earn enough awards, gain enough recognition or be skinny or pretty enough, then you'll be happy. But it's a lie. None of those things have the power to give true and lasting joy and satisfaction. What happens when beauty fades, when riches crumble, or the world stops applauding you? You have nothing.

Joy is forever.

Dawn of Woman's Day 1888

By Frances Willard

(I am including excerpts from this address as it is interesting to see that the roots of the woman's movement was grounded in home and motherhood.)

There is a prayer, uttered or unexpressed, that brings us face to face, and it is this: "Help me to heal the heart-break of humanity."

Mother-love works magic for humanity, but organized mother-love works miracles. Mother-hearted women are called to be the saviors of the race.... We all know that organization is the one great thought of nature. It is the difference between chaos and order; it is the incessant occupation of God. But, next to God, the greatest organizer on this earth is the mother. She who sends forth from the sanctuary of her own being a little child has organized a great spiritual world, and set it moving in the orbit of unchanging law. Hence, women, by her organism, is the greatest organizer ever organized by our beneficent Creator.

But in the nature of the case, the mother, patiently preoccupied in deeds of love for those about her, has been slowest of all to reflect on her own innate powers, and has not until recently so much as dreamed of the resistless force of the world's aggregated motherhood. When I was graduated from college in 1859, there was not on the face of the earth, I venture to say—certainly there was not in my native land...—a national society of women. [Note: The Relief Society, known as one of the oldest and largest women's organization in the world, had been founded in 1842, but had temporarily disbanded in the year referenced. The Relief Society became a charter member of the National Council of Women in 1891. A General Relief Society President, Belle Spafford, served as President of the National Council of Women from 1968 to 1970.]

We worked on in weakness and seclusion, in loneliness and isolation. But we learned at last the gracious secret that has transformed the world for men and made them masters. We learned the mighty difference between the wide, open hand with individual fingers impotent because separate, and the condensed, constructive, organized power of those fingers when combined.

We learned that floating timbers on the sea are not more futile as compared with the same timbers when organized into a ship than are solitary human beings as compared with the same persons when organized and instructed, unified and equipped in societies and guilds...

From this time on the world will have in it no active, organic force so strong for its uplifting as its organized mother-hearts. You will notice the breadth of my generalization. I do not say "all mothers," because all women who are technically mothers are not "mother-hearted," while many a woman is so, from whom the crisscross currents of the world have withheld her holiest crown.

In my own quiet refuge at Evanston, where we talk of all these things, I once said to Susan B.

Anthony, that noblest Roman of us all:

"Bravely as you have trodden it and glorious as has been your via solitaria, have you not always felt a sense of loss?"

She answered in the gentle, thoughtful voice that we all love:

"Could I be really the woman that I am and fail to feel that under happier conditions I might have known a more sacred companionship than has ever come to me, and that the companion could not have been a woman?"

But that she also felt God's call under the unhappy conditions that exist to go her own victorious way alone is proved by her reply to a good man and leading publicist who once said to her:

"Miss Anthony, with your great head and heart, you, of all women I have met, ought to have been a wife and a mother."

Our noble pioneer answered him after this fashion:—

"I thank you, sir, for what I take to be the highest compliment, but sweeter even than to have had the joy of caring for children of my own has it been to me to help bring about a better state of things for mothers generally, so that their unborn little ones could not be willed away from them."...

If there is a spectacle more odious and distasteful than a man who hates a woman it is a woman who hates men...

It has required more than a generation of training within the sheltering circle of the church...for our true position as the equal partners of men in the great world and its work...

It is the unanimous voice of this council that all institutions of learning, and of professional instruction, including schools of theology, law, and medicine, should, in the interest of humanity, be as freely opened to women as to men.... The representatives of organized womanhood in this council will steadily demand that in all avocations in which both men and women engage equal wages shall be paid for equal work; and, finally, that an enlightened society should adopt, as the only adequate expression of the high civilization which it is its office to establish and maintain, an identical standard of personal purity and morality for men and women.

The general declaration of the National Council of the United States as well as of the World's Council was as follows:

> We women, sincerely believing that the best good of our homes and nations will be advanced by our greater unity of thought, sympathy, and purpose, and that an organized movement of women will best conserve the highest good of the family and the state, do hereby band ourselves together in a confederation of workers committed to the overthrow of all forms of ignorance and injustice and to the application of the Golden Rule to society, custom and law...

I have never known a movement among women so enthusiastic and spontaneous. The time for it has fully come; the clock of God has struck the hour, and the best manhood and the manliest nation reaches out a brother's hand of help to us as we move forward bearing woman's white flag of peace, inscribed, "For Home and Humanity."

This is the latest outgrowth of that gospel which raises woman up and with her lifts toward Heaven the world....

Here is a Protestant woman who thinks there is no good in Catholics, never was, and never will be, but she is placed on the Public Library Committee with a communicant of the Cathedral, and finds her "so much like other folks" that she would really have supposed her to be a devout Presbyterian, while the Catholic sister comes into kindly fellowship with her Baptist committeewoman, and will never again believe but that Protestants are really reputable people and quite likely to be saved.

Thus in a thousand ways the blessed education into a tolerant spirit goes swiftly on; the cobwebs of ignorance are brushed away; the rusty chains of prejudice are filed in two, and sectarianism is replaced by sisterly love...

Wherever there is a sister more downtrodden than any other, more helpless and forgotten, there by the law of spiritual gravitation they will delight to invest the weight of their power and the momentum of their united enthusiasm...

The boardinghouse...would disappear to the incalculable advantage of husband, mother, and child...while the bachelor who now leads the sorry life of a "young man about town" would find his pathway to the marriage altar far less hedged about with financial briars and brambles, a "home of his own"—that dearest wish of every true man's heart—having become possible on easy terms...

"And the earth helped woman," is one of the Bible's grandest prophecies, fulfilled for us and yet to be far more perfectly fulfilled in the material inventions whereby woman shall be relieved from the drudgery of daily toil and lifted to the level of her highest and her holiest ministries.

But with these varied cares and perpetual annoyances removed, how will the homemaker ...employ her time? In the care of her children, the companionship of her husband, and in the works of philanthropy, by which the coming epoch shall be hastened forward when there shall be no classes that are not well to do...

Women in council working to improve that sanctuary of their hearts will find grievous inequalities in the laws that relate to property as between husband and wife; they will find that in most of the States a wife cannot bring a civil suit for damages against her husband; that as a rule the crime of despoiling a woman of her honor is not punished so heavily as the stealing of a cow; ...that in all the thirty-eight States but four still make the father the natural guardian of the children, and that as against all but his wife he can will away the guardianship of his child, whether born or unborn, while she cannot will away hers as against all but her husband.

To show how gladly good men help us toward better law let me recite an incident. In the winter of 1856-57 Judge Waite was sitting in his law office in this city when a woman came in and said her husband was about to convey the homestead and have her put out of doors. She asked if this could legally be done. The judge told her he feared it could be, but would examine carefully. She came in the next day, and he was obliged to tell the poor woman that her husband could take away her home. But Judge Waite immediately drafted a bill to prevent such action in this or any case...and it was passed at once...So that we must not only say. "The earth helps the woman," but that the good and true man everywhere is more than glad to help her.

A great world is looking into sight.... The greatest right of which we can conceive, the right of the child to be well-born, is being slowly, surely recognized. Poor old humanity, so tugged by fortune and weary with disaster, turns to the cradle at last and perceives it has been the Pandora's box of every ill and the Fortunatus casket of every joy that life has known.

When the mother learns the divine secrets of her power, when she selects in the partner of her life the father of her child, and for its sacred sake...then shall the blessed prophecy of the world's peace come true.

Society and government are two circles which interplay like rainbows round a fountain, and that fountain is the home...we shall learn a thousand ways of helping that we do not dream of now, while the public sentiment we can arouse and educate will wonderfully hasten the better day.

"Hearts Within, God O'erhead"

[**As a side note, Frances recommended the reading of the book, *The Duties of Women* by Frances Power Cobbe. Here are a few additional notes from the early women's movement.]

[I]t would be idle to veil from myself that the path of progress on which women have now entered, and of which we have done our best to open for them, is a road which leads up a steep hill of difficulty, and from which there are turnings to the right and left, running down all manner of quagmires and precipices. So many, indeed, and so grave are the dangers on either hand, that I cannot blame those who see more to fear than to hope from the movement in question, and raise around us rather a cry of alarm than a cheer of encouragement. But dangers must be faced whenever any time-honored evil is to be swept away or any new good achieved. The woman's movement could not now be stopped, if we desired it; nor do we desire to stop it, if it lay at our option to do so....

I have striven to warn my hearers against that neglect of social bienséances, that adoption of looser and more "Bohemian" manners, and, worst of all, that fatal laxity of judgment regarding grave moral transgressions, which have appeared of late years among us as the inevitable extravagance of reaction from earlier strictness. These faults and mistakes constitute, I conceive, deadly perils to the whole movement for the advancement of women; and with all my strength I would implore every woman who sympathizes with that movement to set her face like a flint against them.

It is our task to make society more pure, more free from vice, either masculine or feminine, than it has ever been before.... If women were to be become...less conscientious, less unselfish, less temperate, less chaste—then I should say: "For Heaven's sake, let us stay where we are! NOTHING we can ever gain would be worth such a loss."

The Delphian Study

For all you mothers who sometimes feel like your brain is getting soggy or who regret never having gone to college, I have something to share with you that has the potential to fill your heart right up. I was at a library sale and picked up 10 volumes of an old 1913 series called The Delphian Reading Course. I had no idea the treasure I had just brought home.

Let me read to you from the Delphian handbook: "Woman has always recognized as her chief business the task of making the world a better place to live in—In civilization as well as in savagery men strive for the means of living, and women make the living worth striving for." I know that's not very politically correct in our world today. We've lost the idea that we need a balance of feminine and masculine working together and are trying to make men and women the same. But we are not the same. Women are softer and have been given divine gifts of nurturing.

As part of the movement of elevating the role of women, the Delphian Society was formed in 1910 with the purpose of educating women. It was difficult for busy moms and wives to go away to college, so they brought college home to them. A Reading Course was designed that gave women the equivalent of a Bachelor's Degree in Classic Studies, even if a woman could only spare 15 minutes a day.

The study included history, literature, philosophy, poetry, fiction, drama, art, ethics and music. The focus was on culture—it was a study for cultivating the heart. "To know the best that has been thought and said in the world" with the aim of personal improvement of each member who, in turn, would lift all of society. As they said, it was all about "the business of life, not just learning of facts and information. It was about making of the mind, a mansion of all lovely thoughts."

As the Delphian handbook says, "If a love for things worthwhile—the lasting and enduring thoughts and sentiments of men—increases, and the desire for wider knowledge is aroused, the hopes and ambitions of the Delphian Society shall have been largely realized."

The name was inspired by the Delphian oracle of ancient Greece—a vaporous, voice of an unseen priestess who inspired wisdom and comfort. Doesn't that describe the role of a woman—quiet whisperings to the heart of a child in the dark, words of encouragement to a discouraged husband. History books may not give her credit, but such quiet voices have influenced and even changed the course of history.

Understanding and appreciation were the objectives of the course. They were taught: "For the many problems that confront us, we need understanding, and for the enjoyment of all the beauty in which the world abounds, we need appreciation."

When the reading course was first released, it was intended for individual study. But it soon became apparent that the study was so much more beneficial when women came together once a month to engage in conversation and share what they were learning, and so Delphian chapters were formed. Within 20 years, there were over 2000 Delphian chapters operating across the nation. In the front of their handbook are the words: "Ten small discussional groups in a community will do more to create a new way of life than a hundred mass meetings with a thousand in attendance at each."

> Who can estimate the value of these circles, which are multiplying throughout the country? Who can fail to see the possibility for the future in thus banding together earnest women of each community? Broader vision, fewer prejudices, greater tolerances must necessarily follow in the wake of centers where enthusiasm for a higher plane of thought is being enkindled. Everywhere are vast resources of the wealth that is most needed today, that of mind and spirit.

If we would improve a community, we must first improve the individuals who make up the community. Libraries, art galleries, and museums would be wasted in a village where none could read or write. To make them of any use, the individuals must be brought to improve themselves. And that is the focus of these study groups.

"When one busy housewife" — I know—I hate that word too, so I'll change it. "When one busy [mom] finds time to call over the telephone in order to discuss with her friend some phase of the Renaissance or a Bach fugue; or when the conversation turns from personalities to modern poetry, or art, we may then truthfully say that the interest in cultural subjects has become an everyday habit instead of an occasional diversion. And this is what invariably happens when two or three Delphians are gathered together."

Women who were part of the Delphian movement turned knowledge into a living force in their everyday lives.

It was after learning all about this movement of women and the work of the Delphians that I called a couple of friends, Marley Billings and Jen Goostrey, and I said, "I think it's time to help organize the moms." They were already feeling it too, and Mothers of Influence was born. They had been meeting with a circle of friends for a couple of years and felt the power of those relationships in their lives. Later, we changed our minds. You don't become a Mother of Influence by forming or joining a group; you already are a Mother of Influence just by having embarked upon this journey. But if you are able to join with others, it will be a blessing in your life.

But getting back to the Delphian Reading Course, I was absolutely thrilled with what I read. If I could have designed a college level course of study for the moms in this group, this is what it would look like. This is a study for the heart—with an emphasis at looking at the languages of art, music, poetry and literature of the ages with just enough history to put it in context. And I especially love that when you study the Ancient Egyptians or Babylonians or Greeks or Medieval times, you get a glimpse into their homes and their family lives; their systems of education and learning, things that are relevant to us in our everyday lives.

Although you may be able to find a set of used books through eBay or Amazon, we have posted all of them in the library. Free digital copies can be found on our Forgotten Classics page. We have also brought them back into print so that you can use a hard copy to underline and take notes. They're available in our store.

I also tracked down the nearly impossible to find study guides that went with them and compiled them into a study guide with questions that can help to direct your thoughts. I usually don't like study guides like that, but I find that this one is very helpful to pick up on concepts or ideas I may have missed in just reading through the text.

Although you can start in Volume I and read straight through, it's really not necessary. And so I broke down all the topics and placed them into the Rotation schedule. You will find Delphian reading in the High School sections as well as in the Mother's University topics. They are in the yellow blocks. I was also excited to find that many of the books they recommended to read for further study are available on Internet Archive and so I linked those books as well.

If you do it with the Rotation schedule, you will be learning the same things as your kids but at a different level. You may even have high schoolers who are interested in going through the Delphian Course.

Margaret Eggleston, my first storytelling friend, tells moms how to develop a rich personality:

"By loving the beautiful, by reading the worthwhile, by filling the mind with those things that are worth passing on, by cultivation of a cheery disposition, by striving toward high ideals."

All these things are accomplished with the Delphian Reading Course. It may not be the study you begin with, but I just wanted to share with you what it is for when you are ready.

Introduction to Johann Henrich Pestalozzi

I'd like to introduce you to a friend of mine, Johann Heinrich Pestalozzi, born in Switzerland in 1747. You will want to get to know him because I would call him the father of the modern-day heart-based education movement. And he loved mothers. Let me give you an impression of the man as described by his German biographers:

In 1780, a man is on his way to Basel, on foot, wearing a worn-out coat. The man has money problems. He is carrying the manuscript of a book that he has written in the pocket of his coat. He wants to show it to a friend in Basel. In front of the city gate there sits a crippled beggar, stretching out his hand.

"Sir, some coins, please!"

The man rummages through the pockets of his coat, searching for coins. He does not find any. Embarrassed he looks down at the ground. He then sees the silver buckles on his shoes. He bends down, takes the buckles off and places them in the beggar's hand. Then he looks for a few strong blades of grass in the field nearby and, as well as he can, ties his shoes with them.

On his tombstone, it was written, "He did everything for others; nothing for himself."

Through poverty and personal sacrifice, through ridicule and misunderstandings, he moved forward with his desire to help people live happy lives. Happy lives should be the aim and purpose of education. He was interested in ennobling the race; of lifting civilization to higher grounds.

He lived in the aftermath of the Renaissance. A love affair of books had taken hold of the people and they were anxious to get the children into them and so started their lessons in Greek and Latin while they were still very young. Yet, the books by themselves were not improving society. Instead, he saw misery and empty, soulless eyes. He wrote, "[E]ver since my youth, has my heart moved on like a mighty stream, alone and lonely, towards my one sole end—to stop the sources of the misery in which I saw the people around me sunk…in the midst of jeering taunts, which I read on all lips, the mighty stream of my heart ceased not, alone and lonely, to struggle towards the purpose of my life…"

Many of his experiments in education took place in his home and with the many orphans he took in and cared for. He died feeling like he had not achieved his purpose, but hoped that, even if it took 300 years, that one day his idea of teaching heart before mind would take root.

Little could he have imagined how far his influence would reach. Within a decade of his death, using his methods, illiteracy was wiped out in Switzerland and he was given due credit. If you have ever been drawn to the philosophies of Charlotte Mason, Maria Montessori, or Rudolf Steiner who started the Waldorf schools, you have come under the influence of Pestalozzi. I recently read that Karl Maeser wove Pestalozzi's ideas into the founding of Brigham Young University where I graduated.

Pestalozzi's education method can be summed up in one word: Anschauung. Translators have had difficulties translating this German word, and I have difficulties pronouncing it, but the English translation that seems to fit the best is 'sense-impression.' The philosophy is: feeling precedes knowledge.

A mind approach to astronomy is to memorize the names of the planets in order. A heart approach—the sense-impression approach—is to take your four year old out, even if it's past his bedtime, to the backyard, snuggle him in a warm blanket, and tell him stories of the stars.

Value of knowing the names of the planets at age four? I'd give it two cents.

Value of spending an evening with your little boy out under the stars telling stories? Priceless.

Pestalozzi knew that mothers are the best teachers for the heart years because love is such a vital part of the education process and no one loves a child more than the child's mother. The challenge he faced—and that we face—is how to prepare and teach the mothers. Friedrich Froebel studied Pestalozzi's ideas and came up with the idea of kindergartens—the German word for 'child-gardens.' The intention of the kindergarten was to teach mothers how to teach their children in their homes. His invitation to all mothers was, "Come! Let us live with our children." There's not a life happening in four walls of a classroom, sitting at a desk for hours a day moving words around on a piece of paper.

I believe Pestalozzi and Froebel would be heartbroken if they saw what we've done to our kindergartens. We've separated the children from their mothers and we're back to working on words instead of love.

Many of Pestalozzi's frustrations came because he understood the principles, but he had so few tools to work with. He would be thrilled with what you have for your use!

He understood the power of singing and music, but there were no children's songbooks. Beethoven was just a child. The great masters of music had yet to compose their music. And even the music that had been composed was certainly not available to a poor home of orphans.

He understood the need for picture books, but Caldecott had not yet been born. Bonheur, Millet, Corot and Landseer didn't paint their much-loved-by-children masterpieces until decades after his death.

He saw the ordering effect of rhythm which poetry offers, but he had no Child's Garden of Verses, no Mother Goose book of rhymes. Longfellow, Wordsworth, Tennyson, Emily Dickinson, Eugene Fields, Christina Rossetti had yet to write their poetry.

And although he loved stories and understood their value, Hans Christian Andersen and the brothers Grimm had not yet put their fairy tales in writing. Neither had any of the storytellers who went out and gathered in the stories of the world. There was not yet a David Copperfield or Tom Sawyer or Jo March or Jane Eyre when Pestalozzi was trying to teach his children. No one had yet written the stories of history in a way a child could understand. In fact, most of the history our children now study hadn't even happened.

If you choose to pursue a heart-based approach to learning, you are likely to run up against the same opposition and resistance as Pestalozzi did. Even though the children were joyful and engaged in their learning, the questions were, even in his day, "Where are your reading scores? And your writing scores?" It meant more to parents to have their child recite an entire passage of scripture from memory, even though he had no sense whatsoever what he was saying, than to see that child as a happy and engaged learner.

When your well-meaning family member or friend is alarmed that your child is out playing in a stream or dressed up as a knight in shining armor or taking fresh baked cookies to the widow up the street instead of doing his suffix worksheets, very sincerely reply, "Thank you so much for your concern for my child, but right now we feel we need to be working on his Anschaaung."

Pestalozzi condemned "words crammed into sleeping powers."

He wrote, "The power and experience both are great at [young ages]; but our schools are essentially only artificial stifling machines for destroying all the result of the power and experience that nature herself brings to life in them."

Ouch.

He continues:

> You know it, my friend. But for a moment picture to yourself the horror of this murder. We leave children up to their fifth year in the full enjoyment of nature; let every impression of nature work upon them; they feel their power; they already know full well the joy of unrestrained liberty and all its charms... And after they have enjoyed this happiness of sensuous life for five whole years, we make all nature round them vanish from before their eyes; tyrannically stop the delightful course of unrestrained freedom; pen them up like sheep, whole flocks huddled together; pitilessly chain them for hours, days, weeks, months, years, to the contemplation of unattractive and monotonous letters (and, contrasted with their former condition), to a maddening course of life.
>
> Friend, tell me, can the sword that severs the neck and sends the criminal from life to death have more effect upon his body than this change from the beautiful guidance of nature...to the mean and miserable school course, has upon the souls of children?

Mothers. Come, let us live with our children while we can. "Let us keep our children for our own, during their earlier years. The world will have them long enough afterward." (Lydia Sigourney) Absolutely for the first eight years of life and to a large extent, to the first 14 or 15 years. These are the ages nature reserves for making impressions on the heart. And no one can do it better than you.

Two thousand years ago, a humble carpenter tried to get the world to understand inside-out learning. Many people rejected his teachings. They wanted him to take care of the externals—if only he would overthrow their tyrannical government, then they would be happy. Instead, he taught them to tend to the inner kingdom of the heart; to lay up treasures there. If they would do this, all else would be added unto them. Those who lay up their treasures within find joy even in captivity or in poverty; no matter what is going on externally in their lives, the joy remains.

These are the diamond souls of history whose hearts never fail when everything is crumbling around them. They stand as a beacon of hope and light in the midst of darkness.

Tending hearts is the mission of motherhood. And as our good friend, Pestalozzi, reminds us:

"It is for a long time the business of the heart, before it is the business of reason. Let not [the child] attempt to [climb the ladder heading to heaven] by the cold calculations of the head or the mere impulses of the heart; but let all these powers combine, and the noble enterprise shall be crowned with success.

"What shall I say more? The eternal laws of nature lead me back to your hand, Mother! Mother! I can keep my innocence, my love, my obedience, the excellences of my nobler nature with the new impressions of the world, all, all at your side only.

"If no one has taught you to know the world, then come, we will learn it together, as you ought, and I must.

"Friend! I must be silent. My heart is moved, and I can see tears in your eyes. Farewell!"

I love that man.

A group of educators from England visited Switzerland to visit his school to observe what he was doing. They saw him asking questions and so they thought, "Ah-hah! The secret of his success is asking questions."

So they went back to England and started questioning children from morning to night. It was a miserable experience for all and the educators finally declared the 'Pestalozzian method' was a failure.

What they failed to see is what only the heart can rightly discern—that the true secret of Pestalozzi's success was love. He worked with orphans and he had a special love for these children and they felt it. The questions he asked poured out of his heart out of love.

Love is the glue that holds all of this together. The scriptures tell us to search diligently; to teach diligently. I love looking up words in the 1828 Webster's dictionary and I learned the word 'diligence' comes from the Latin word 'diligo,' which means 'to love earnestly.' So to teach diligently is to do it with love. And who loves a child more than you which is why you are a child's best teacher.

It was the prayerful, tear-filled voice of Monica that turned a wayward son, Augustine, into a Saint who later wrote, "It is to my mother that I owe everything. If I am Thy Child, O my God, it is because Thou gavest me such a mother. If I prefer the truth to all other things, it is the point of my mother's teachings. If I did not long ago perish in sin and misery, it is because of the long and faithful tears with which she pleaded for me."

"When the real history of mankind is fully disclosed, will it feature the echoes of gunfire or the shaping sound of lullabies? The great armistices made by military men or the peacemaking of women in homes and in neighborhoods? Will what happened in cradles and kitchens prove to be more controlling than what happened in congresses?" --Neal A. Maxwell

A Mother's Heart

By Karen Latham

I am not a teacher! The youngest mom boohooed;
So she wiped a tear and held him tight, and sent him off to school.

I am not a hairdresser! She said to no one there;
So she strapped him in his car seat and drove to cut his hair.

I am certainly no seamstress! She said after a fall;
So she threw away his torn t-shirt and took him to the mall.

I am definitely not a nurse! She said every time he sneezed;
So she took him to the clinic to doctor his every need.

And then one day she looked around when she was needing aid,
And all the world had closed its doors, no services today!

The COVID took her school teacher, her doctor, and her barber;
It took all that she counted on to help her to be a mother.

She cried out on the internet, isn't anybody there?
Someone who can teach my child, nurse him, cut his hair?

That's when something buried deep inside her started stirring;
An idea so much out of place, it was almost disturbing.

When her boy came down with a little cold, she nursed him back to health;
And when his hair grew way too long, she trimmed it up herself.

Then when "distance learning" became too much of a fight,
She thought she would grab a book and teach him herself tonight.

Her confidence grew all the more with every passing day,
Deciding to turn off the screens, she went out with him to play.

Their relationship grew and blossomed then with everything she did
She came to the conclusion that she genuinely liked this kid!

The seed God planted long ago way down within her heart
Had been buried under all the doubt and fear the world imparts.

And when the world shut down and she was forced to look inside
She found that same seed waiting there for her to give it time.

She nourished it with work and play, with conversations sweet;
She tucked her child into bed with patience, lovingly.

In those moments she realized that she had found her place;

Moments sweeter than what the world had taught her to embrace.

One night near that sleeping boy she dusted off a prayer
To thank her God for giving her this child for whom to care.

I may not be trained as a nurse, or a teacher or a barber,
But God, I know I am all that and more, for I have the heart of a mother.

A Change of Heart

Blazing Trails

"For the child...it is not half so important to know as to feel. If facts are the seeds that later produce knowledge and wisdom, then the emotions and the impressions of the senses are the fertile soil in which the seeds must grow. The years of early childhood are the time to prepare the soil. Once the emotions have been aroused—a sense of the beautiful, the excitement of the new and the unknown, a feeling of sympathy, pity, admiration or love—then we wish for knowledge about the object of our emotional response... It is more important to pave the way for a child to want to know than to put him on a diet of facts that he is not ready to assimilate." --Rachel Carson

"The problem facing us is that we have become a very academic-oriented culture where we measure, test, and compare. It takes courage to trust this process of root building that can't be seen—especially when your neighbor or family members have children who are reading and writing and doing math at a level your child is not because you have been placing your focus on internal matters. It's always hard to go against the norm..."

You are a Pioneer blazing new trails.

The Difference Between Mind and Heart

Before we go any further, I want to help you understand what I mean when I differentiate between mind and heart. Let me try and illustrate.

Imagine you're walking down the street and you notice a man walking on the other side of the street. After a few moments, a second man comes up from behind and taps the first man on the shoulder. The first man turns around and after a brief interchange, he reaches into his pocket, pulls out his wallet and hands the second man a hundred-dollar bill. The two men then walk away in different directions.

What is the fact of what you just saw? You saw a hundred dollars transfer ownership from the first man to the second. Is that all you need to know?

Let's try again and this time I'm going to add the story so your heart can understand what your mind just saw. What if I told you the second man was a robber; when the first man turned around, he said, "I've got a gun in my pocket, hand over all your money or else."

Or let's try this. What if I said the two men were old friends. The second man was down on his luck and had previously phoned his friend and asked if he could borrow a hundred dollars and they had agreed to meet there.

Or what if it was the other way around? What if the first man had been the one to borrow the hundred dollars and he had asked his friend to meet him so that he could pay him back?

Let's go back to the first robber scenario. What if I told you the first man was a multimillionaire? No, let's say he had been unemployed for several months…no, let's say several years. He has just been to the bank and withdrawn his last hundred dollars. He has a little girl at home and she's sick. In fact, the doctor told him if he didn't get medicine for her right away, she was going to die. He was on his way to get that medicine and now his money was gone.

Isn't it interesting—that same hundred-dollar bill yielded greed, joy, sorrow, anguish, gratitude, love, despair and annoyance. All things that only the heart can understand. The fact that it was a hundred-dollar bill really was the least important piece of information of all. It gave us a point of reference, but that was about it. And notice—if I were to ask you to tell me in words what greed or joy or anguish feels like, could you?

Our eyes saw the fact. Our hearts grasped the truth.

The heart understands things that cannot always be expressed in words or directly taught. But still, it knows. And as the fox in *The Little Prince* so rightly observed, "It is only with the heart that one can see rightly. What is essential is invisible to the eye."

Or, if you remember Virginia's letter to the Chicago Sun asking if there really was a Santa Claus, in part, the answer was: "The most real things in the world are those that neither children nor men can see."

Which causes more pain? A broken leg or a broken heart? It is this realm of the heart that separates humans from machines and it's all these feelings that make life worth living.

Some 'Heart' Wisdom from the Tin Man and Scarecrow from *The Wizard of Oz*

TM: Why didn't you walk around that hole?

SC: I don't know enough. My head is stuffed with straw, you know, and that is why I am going to Oz to ask him for some brains.

TM: Oh, I see. But after all, brains are not the best things in the world.

SC: Have you any?

TM: No, my head is quite empty, but I once had brains, and a heart also; so having tried them both, I should much rather have a heart.

SC: And why is that?

TM: I will tell you a story, and then you will know.

He then goes on to tell the story and ends with:

"Brains do not make one happy, and happiness is the best thing in the world."

Romancing the Heart and Building the Kingdom Within

One of my little granddaughters, almost from the time she first learned to talk, always included this request in her every prayer: "Please bless us that we will all have good imaginations." My daughter and I had no idea where that came from, but it lasted for several years. Given what I now know about the importance of the Imagination, all I can say is, "Out of the mouth of babes..." What a different world we would have if we all had good imaginations.

I had an old book randomly appear when I was searching for something else one day. It was written in 1885 by a Dr. Curry and it was called *Imagination and Dramatic Instinct: Some Practical Steps for Their Development*. I want to share several sections from this book to pass along some of his insights. It's pretty heavy thinking so stay with me. He opens with a quote from Professor Charles Eliot Norton: "In the curriculums of most of our…institutions of learning…no place is given to that instruction which has for its end the cultivation of the imagination and the sentiments, through the refining of the perceptions and the quickening of the love of beauty." He continued, "Education, say some of our legislators, must give a means of making a living; our public schools must train up practical citizens; boys and girls must be educated in the practical arts of life; the ornamental has no place in the school-room."

But—he says, they utterly fail to grasp the nature of the imagination and its relation to daily life. And I love his definition of imagination: It's the 'thinking of the heart.'

The 'thinking of the heart' is what Mr. Rogers taught: "I want to be more concerned with a sense of wonder than with information. I want to place a higher value on those things that are not seen than those things that are seen." He taught that everything that really matters isn't found in the words on a page—they're found in the white spaces between the words; the white spaces between the lines. They are the ah-ha moments when the light goes on and we get flashes of pure inspiration.

This is the realm of the imagination.

The heart with no imagination is a hard heart.

And then Dr. Curry goes on to list its benefits:

Work without imagination is drudgery, but with its humblest employment is lifted into the realm of beauty and art.

The imagination is the source of all inspiration and interest in life.

Imagination gives charm to the humblest home.

A neglected imagination is one of the leading causes of the degradation of character, while its right use is one of the highest characteristics of the human being.

It is vital for creativity. It gives man taste and refinement.

Without imagination, we cannot comprehend universal principles. We cannot comprehend all that Nature has to teach us.

Imagination not only creates all art, but it appreciates art. Without its presence there can be no genuine love of art; without it, the language of art is unintelligible, its voice unheard, its spirit unfelt.

Imagination makes the individual an heir to all the ages; By its power, we can become a Greek, and see as the Greeks saw, and feel as the Greeks felt.

The faculty which gives birth to ideals is imagination. Without it, there can be little improvement in the ideals of a man or a nation. And no age, no nation, no individual can be elevated except by elevating its ideals.

It is the part of the soul that gives hope because it enables us to see a new and better world in the midst of the old, a new life in the midst of death, a new character in the midst of degradation. Without imagination, there is no hope. Where there is no vision, the people perish.

Imagination enables us to enter into sympathy with our fellow-man. By its power alone can we appreciate the point of view of those different from ourselves. Without imagination, each of us would be alone; each of us would be cold and selfish.

Imagination gives us the power to penetrate to the heart of Nature; it is the faculty which sees beauty and loveliness.

Imagination alone enables man to realize eternity. The ordinary conceptions of the mind cannot embrace infinity, or God. Imagination alone enables men to transcend time and space, to see the eternal through the temporal, the spiritual beneath the physical, the soul underlying all.

This makes me think of the Beatitude: Blessed are the pure in heart for they shall see God, I believe not only in a life to come, but they will see Him everywhere now—in nature, in art and music, literature and poetry, and in lives of men and women and the histories of nations. The hard heart— the heart without imagination—cannot see Him anywhere.

The imagination is the fountain-head of all noble feeling, and upon its discipline depends any true education of the emotions. It is needed to prevent isolation of ideas, and the hardening of truths into mere facts. It is needed to place ideas and facts in sympathetic relationship with one another; to give the spirit and not the letter, truth and not mere fact, the soul and not the mere body.

It sees truth from the heart, and not by the external. It creates, as Nature does, from the centre outward, [from within, out]. Imagination does not perceive fragments; it sees the whole at once.

It is always characterized by simplicity, by unity and truth. It is the soul of all inspiration.

Imagination vitalizes all knowledge...and enables the soul to feel the life of the universe permeating every object.

(Let me just interject here. If you have a difficult time comprehending and capturing the vision of educating the heart, I wouldn't be too hard on yourself. Most of us grew up in a mind-based system that never developed the imagination or the thinking of the heart. But as you engage in the languages of the heart that you will learn more about, you will find new neural pathways opening up and your vision will enlarge and expand as you go along.)

Dr. Curry goes on to explain that the dramatic instinct is closely tied with the imagination; drama in the sense that it is about acting; acting upon the impulses of the imagination. The little child who is imaginative always shows it by dramatic actions in his play. The man who has killed his dramatic instinct has become unsympathetic, and can never appreciate any one's point of view but his own. The dramatic instinct trains us to a deep insight into the motives of man.

Together, they redeem the mind from narrowness and selfishness; they enable the individual to appreciate the point of view, the feelings, motives and characters of his fellow-men; they open his eyes to read the various languages of human art; they enable him to commune on a higher plane and lift him into communion with the art and spirit of every age and nation.

Where the imagination is inactive, all expression is mechanical and cold. A lack of sympathy is a lack of imagination.

Can you begin to see why that simple prayer—Bless us all that we will have good imaginations—would change the world?

And then Dr. Curry goes on to teach how to train and develop the imagination. And the answer is simple as all Truth is. Basically, it's to do the opposite of what we are doing in the education of our children right now. Our focus on academics in childhood—the mechanics of learning—is hardening the hearts and killing the imagination of our children.

The act of decoding a word does not make a child a reader. The act of constructing a sentence does not make a child a writer. Only an active imagination can do that. But where do we place our attention?

Dr. Curry taught the method of studying and training these powers that he recommends is essentially the same as that adopted in the schools of the early Greeks—the Greeks of the Golden age—whose development of the artistic nature is universally considered to have been the highest ever known.

He says the best method of developing the imagination is by the study of Nature and poetic expression. So sending your kids out to play in nature and the rhymes you share is one of the best things you can do in childhood! He continues: "A sympathetic love of the beautiful in Nature is characteristic of noble imagination. The influence of Nature in the education of the human mind cannot be over-estimated. Wordsworth has taught us to realize the power of Nature to stimulate and unfold the energies of the soul. All art proceeds from wonder."

Nature alone, however, is inadequate to secure the full power of imagination. Thousands have grown up in the midst of the greatest beauty of Nature with low and sensuous ideals, and without having their sense of beauty awakened. Art is therefore needed to awaken us to her gifts. That is the role of art—to awaken feeling within us.

What form of art should be studied? Every form as far as possible; for each art is a distinct language, which expresses some aspect of the human soul and reveals some truth which can be apprehended in no other way. Music, poetry, paintings—all are needed.

Every great art is a special language of the human spirit, and he who desires to awaken his artistic nature will learn to read all these languages. Let me repeat that so you won't miss it. Every great art is a special language of the human spirit, and he who desires to awaken his artistic nature will learn to read all these languages. That is the course of study of the Mother's University—to learn to read all these languages.

Dr. Curry wrote, "At the present time, a majority of the studies in all grades of schools concern themselves chiefly with the acquisition of knowledge."

That hasn't changed, has it?

"The too exclusive study of science is slowly leading to the realization of the inadequacy of facts to develop the whole man harmoniously and completely."

There it is again—Mind is only half of what is needed!

Charles Darwin reflected, "Up to the age of thirty, or beyond it, poetry of many kinds—such as the works of Milton, Gray, Byron, Wordsworth, Coleridge, and Shelley—gave me great pleasure; and even as a schoolboy I took intense delight in Shakespeare, especially in the historical plays. I have also said that formerly pictures gave me considerable, and music very great, delight. But now for many years I cannot endure to read a line of poetry; I have tried lately to read Shakespeare, and found it so intolerably dull that it nauseated me. I have also almost lost my taste for pictures or music... My mind seems to have become a machine for grinding out general laws out of large collections of facts. If I had to live my life again, I would have made a rule to read some poetry and listen to some music at least once a week; for perhaps the parts of my brain now atrophied would thus have been kept active through use. The loss of these tastes is a loss of happiness, and may possibly be injurious to the intellect, and more probably to the moral character, by enfeebling the emotional part of our nature."

That which we don't use, atrophies from disuse. By neglecting the Arts in the education of our children, we are hardening their hearts. And what little attention we give the Arts is through mechanical and scientific means—analyzing its parts. Art can only be studied as art and by means of art. Which is a lot of what you will be learning as you go through the writings in the Mother's University.

I know I've spent a lot of time quoting Dr. Curry's words, but I think they are powerful. But now let me turn your attention to the most important part of what he suggests in the education of the imagination.

Here is what he said: "The most adequate method of...developing the imagination and artistic nature is by means of the spoken word—the simplest and most natural form of Art. It was the attention given by the Greeks to the spoken word that caused them to be the most artistic of peoples. By far the most of the work of their schools was the study and recitation of the works of their poets. While they may have slighted the written word, and exaggerated too much the importance of speech, we in our day have gone to the other extreme, and are exaggerating the importance of writing as an agent of education, to the exclusion of the earlier and more simple and natural method of the human voice.

"The voice is the little child's first conscious agent of expression; it is man's chief means of communication; it is the fullest of the life and energy of the human soul; it is the simplest and most natural agent of the faculties of the mind. Some may consider the Greeks to have been the greatest masters of writing in the world, and this is true; but their writing was great because it was founded upon and developed by their speech.

"The voice connects thought and emotion. The action of the mind in writing is not the same as that in reading and speaking. Vocal expression is the direct result of the free, spontaneous impulses of mind and heart."

So let me leave Dr. Curry for a minute and share what I see. From the moment a child can hold a pencil, we are intent on making him write and to read words on a page. But developmentally, is that the best place to start? He can express himself far more naturally in speech. If we allow and encourage the vocal expression of story and poetry and thought and conversation, written language will flow quite naturally in its proper time and place.

The child who hears the music in the voice of the mother reading aloud to him will have much greater comprehension when he begins to read. I think it's interesting that Abraham Lincoln had the habit of reading great literature aloud, even to himself. It was that connection to emotion through the voice.

So let me pull together these lessons for educating hearts.

If we want to build strong imaginations, we must learn the languages of all the Arts—Music, Pictures, Poetry and Story. That is the focus of the next section—to begin to paint a picture of what that looks like. Childhood is the best time to engage in heart languages because their hearts are open and impressionable and not yet cluttered with all the activities of the mind.

And always look to the voice as the greatest teacher of all. Pay attention to the music in your voice as you read to your children and teach them. Allow them ample opportunity to use their voices in expression, in recitation of poetry, in expressing thoughts and ideas in conversation. Encourage them to read aloud. Engage in dramatic experiences like the plays you'll find in the Enrichment section. The more you focus on writing skills in childhood, the more you will shut down this gateway to the heart and to the imagination.

I thought the use of the word 'romance' was strange when I kept coming across titles in the older children's books like Romance of the Civil War or Revolutionary War or Romance of Scotland. Was it all about the love affairs going on? Because that's what I think of when I hear the word romance. The modern definition is all about courting and wooing and the relationship between two people who love each other. But when I checked Webster's 1828 dictionary, I found it had to do with "interesting the sensibilities of the heart, or the passion of wonder and curiosity."

With that definition, isn't that what we are trying to do—either within our own hearts, but especially in the hearts of our children—to interest the feelings of the heart and awaken the passion of wonder and curiosity? Your job as a mother is to romance their hearts. I like that. And I tell you what—if my husband had introduced himself and immediately invited me over to do his laundry and scrub his toilet, the relationship would not have gone very far. It was the flowers and the chocolate and the sweet nothings whispered in my ear that romanced my heart and has kept him my best friend for nearly 44 years now.

The Arts are what make it possible for you to Romance your children's hearts. Sometimes I hear a mom say that she feels like she is neglecting her children's education because all they are doing is reading aloud lots of stories and her kids just want to engage in imaginative play all day or go outside and play in nature. Well, guess what. That's exactly what they should be doing if you want to tend to their imaginations. You have been called to be an artist, not a technician.

Remember the story of Sleeping Beauty? In the story, Beauty had gone to sleep, and when she fell asleep, the entire kingdom became lifeless and colorless. Soon noxious briers and thorns and tangled vines grew around the sleeping kingdom. Prince Philip valiantly drew his sword of truth and protected himself with his shield of righteousness to make his way through the tangled mess and fight the evil Maleficent. But that isn't what brought the kingdom back to life—the thing that brought the kingdom back to life was his love of Beauty. When Beauty received true love's first kiss, Beauty awoke and the kingdom gloriously sprang to life.

We're romancing hearts to awaken beauty.

Louisa May Alcott wrote a little poem that begins: I have a little kingdom where thoughts and feelings dwell.

It is to that little kingdom within the hearts of your children—and your own heart—that you want to tend and cultivate. And here are the decorating tips: Fill the air with worthy music. Line the walls with masterpieces of fine art. Furnish the rooms with poetry. Invite great souls to dine with you and listen to their stories. And beautify the grounds with fields of flowers and canopies of trees.

For as Luke said, "A good man…or a good woman…out of the good treasures of his or her heart bringeth forth that which is good."

Bless us all to have good imaginations.

From Amy Steedman's When They Were Children

"Play is the work of childhood and large chunks of a child's day should be cleared for free, open, magical, imaginative play. Pestalozzi used the term 'sense-impressions' to describe the work for these early years. The more children are allowed to touch and feel and experience, the deeper the learning will be in later years."

The world has many stately palaces and great cathedrals that tower in their loveliness high above the humble dwellings around them, and their beauty and wonder are the delight of our eyes. We look up at their high walls, their gilded roofs, their slender spires pointing to the sky; we admire the great strength and delicate traces of their stonework, and whether in the sunshine or under the stars, they stand out as splendid monuments of what the mind of man has power to plan and his hands have skill to fashion.

But the foundations on which these buildings rest are hidden from our eyes, buried deep down in the darkness. Yet though unseen and seldom thought of, in every case there has been the patient laying of stone upon stone, without which the stately building could never have been reared.

It is much the same with the great lives which tower above the ordinary ones around us. Here and there we note them; we mark the noble deed, the courage, the heroism, the flash of genius, the habit of self-sacrifice, but we are apt to forget that all this did not come into being suddenly, that in each case there was a long time of preparation, a patient laying of foundations in the years of childhood, act by act, as stone is laid upon stone, before it was known what manner of life would be built up.

So whenever it is possible it is well to consider the time of preparation as well as to admire the finished work, and we shall learn to know these great men and women all the better for hearing something of what they thought and did when they were children.

> "Souls are built as temples are—
> Sunken deep, unseen, unknown,
> Lies the sure foundation stone;
> Then the courses framed to bear
> Lift the cloisters, pillared fair;
> Last of all the airy spire,
> Soaring Heavenward, higher and higher,
> Nearest sun and nearest star."

Heart and Art

by Ella Wheeler Wilcox

Though critics may bow to art, and I am its own true lover,
It is not art, but heart, which wins the wide world over.
Though smooth be the heartless prayer, no ear in Heaven will mind it,
And the finest phrase falls dead if there is no feeling behind it.
Though perfect the player's touch, little, if any, he sways us,
Unless we feel his heart throb through the music he plays us.
Though the poet may spend his life in skillfully rounding a measure,
Unless he writes from a full, warm heart he gives us little pleasure.

So it is not the speech which tells, but the impulse which goes with the saying;
And it is not the words of the prayer, but the yearning back of the praying.
It is not the artist's skill which into our soul comes stealing
With a joy that is almost pain, but it is the player's feeling.
And it is not the poet's song, though sweeter than sweet bells chiming,
Which thrills us through and through, but the heart which beats under the rhyming.
And therefore I say again, though I am art's own true lover,
That it is not art, but heart, which wins the wide world over.

Sandcastles, Diamonds and Singing Songs of Joy

I grew up close to the sunny, sandy beaches of Southern California so I got to build lots of sandcastles, which I loved to do. I had to build them close to the water because the water made the sand stick together. But that meant that when the first big wave of the high tide came in, my sandcastle always washed away. Not one of them is still standing.

Sandcastles come to mind when I think about what I remember learning in school. I can only recall a handful of state capitals. The moles I couldn't wrap my mind around in High School Chemistry have returned to being the furry little blind creatures to which I can relate. Although I scored in the 99.9% in a national High School math competition, I can no longer plot *x* or *y* on anything. I wouldn't recognize the quadratic equation in a line-up nor can I tell you what it's used for. I remember missing the meiosis-mitosis question on my Tenth Grade Biology exam. I never could keep them straight. But in the 40+ years since then, the question has not come up again even one time. When I think of the college exams I stayed up all night studying for, if I had to retake them today, I doubt I'd pass any of them.

Some studies estimate the average person loses 90% of the information they learn in school. I've done my own informal 'research' poll among family and friends and found a similar response unless it was a subject they loved or continued to use in their lives or they had one of those rare photographic memories.

Is there anything I remember from school? Actually, yes.

I remember my Eighth Grade Graduation dance because I had a huge crush on Dan Reed. He was late to math one day because he was out shooting a TV commercial. That's how cool he was. I, on the other hand, was a geek. I stood at least a head taller than every other girl in my class. I had glasses and braces and as if that wasn't awkward enough, my mother had hand-sewn me a pale pink graduation dress to wear to the dance. In a day of mini-skirts, she wanted me to be modest. The white lace scallops at the bottom of the dress fell very modestly below my knees.

So there I was at the dance, hugging the walls, watching everyone out on the dance floor. Especially Dan Reed. And then it happened. He was looking my direction. I checked around to see who he might be looking at, but it was just me standing there. Then he started walking towards me. My heart started racing as he held out his hand, looked me in the eyes, and smiling, asked, "Marlene, would you like to dance?" Of course I was too terrified to actually dance with him and I made up some lame excuse, but inside my heart I was dancing on clouds. The whole detailed event plays through my memory as clearly as if it had happened yesterday.

Overall, the things I remember from school so many years ago are the feelings, the disappointments, the embarrassments and the impressions that went into my heart, not what went into my mind. I earned straight A's in school so I must have had all the 'necessary' information in my mind at one time, but so much of it has washed away, just like my sandcastles.

My school days were filled with information. The fact that I cannot tell you the difference between meiosis and mitosis is of no consequence to the world.

Today is different. Today the buzz words are high-order and critical thinking skills. We administer SAT reasoning tests to our students so they can demonstrate their proficiency in rejecting all beliefs that cannot be backed by hard evidence. We train kindergartners to rely on that which can be seen, touched and measured. Emotional thinking is frowned upon.

Scientific reasoning reigns supreme.

Which is why we are living in dangerous times.

Hans Christian Andersen wrote a little story 150 years ago warning us of the very danger we are facing. Disney's *Frozen* is based on this story, but if you've read Hans Christian Andersen's *The Snow Queen*, you know the movie is much different and they left this part of the story out all together. So I think it's worth taking a few minutes to revisit the story as Hans Christian Andersen told it.

Long, long ago there lived a hobgoblin—a demon, really—who one day made a mirror that had a particular power. Everything that was good or beautiful that was reflected in it was made to look small and ugly while everything that was bad or ugly was magnified, and every little fault could be plainly seen.

The scholars in his demon school carried the mirror all over the world until there wasn't a land or a people who had not been looked at in this distorted mirror. They thought it would look even funnier if they could carry it high up into the heavens to look at the angels in it, but the higher they rose, the slipperier the mirror became until it slipped from their fingers and crashed to the earth, shattering into millions of pieces.

Now the mirror caused even more unhappiness, for if a speck no larger than a grain of sand lodged in a person's eye, it had the property of the whole mirror and they viewed everything the wrong way. They could neither see rightly nor justly. And even worse, if a tiny shard entered the heart, the heart grew as cold as ice. The pieces soon covered the whole earth.

The demon laughed so hard at the mischief he had caused that he nearly split his sides.

Now, in a large town lived two poor little children who loved each other dearly. Kay and Gerda often played under the red rose bush that grew near their homes. One day, just as the clock struck twelve, Kay said, "Oh! Something has struck my heart. And it feels like there's something in my eye." When Gerda asked what was wrong and started to cry, Kay mockingly told her to stop crying because she looked so ugly when she cried. There was nothing wrong with him. "But look!" he said. "Look at the worm on that rose and why is that rose crooked? And what an ugly little box they grow in." He kicked the box and ripped off the two roses as he ran off to play with the boys.

By and by he began to make fun of the townspeople and the people laughed and thought he was very clever. He now thought the picture books and stories his grandmother told were very stupid.

One day as he was playing on his sleigh, a large white sleigh carrying a white figure wrapped in white fur circled the field. Kay was intrigued, grabbed hold of the back of the sleigh and off they flew. Faster and faster they went. He tried to let go, but he couldn't. He was afraid and tried to pray, but all he could remember were his multiplication tables. At long last, the sleigh stopped and the driver stood up. She was tall and beautiful—a Snow Queen. She opened her warm fur coat for Kay to snuggle in. "Are you still cold?" she asked as she kissed his forehead. Although his heart was now almost a lump of ice, he somehow no longer felt cold or afraid.

He thought the face of the Snow Queen was the most beautiful he had ever seen. He could imagine nothing more perfect. He proudly told her he could do arithmetic as far as fractions in his head and that he knew the number of square miles and number of inhabitants in the country and the Snow Queen smiled. Off they flew again, over woods and lakes, over sea and land. And Kay felt perfectly safe.

Meanwhile, little Gerda didn't believe what the townspeople said—that Kay must have drowned in the river. She set off to search for him and after a hard and difficult journey, arrived at the magnificent ice palace of the Snow Queen. There were hundreds of empty, vast and cold rooms in the palace, all made of drifted snow. The largest hall stretched for several miles. In the midst of this empty, endless hall of snow was a frozen lake and there, in the center of it, stood the Snow Queen. She called the lake 'The Mirror of Reason' and said it was the best, and indeed the only one, in the world.

When Gerda finally found little Kay, he was quite blue with cold—almost black. But he didn't feel it, for the Snow Queen had kissed away his icy shiverings. There he was, dragging sharp, flat pieces of ice to and fro, trying to get them to fit together in different ways. It was the icy game of reason he was playing and in his eyes, the figures he created were very remarkable and of the highest importance. Yet, try though he may, he could not create the one figure he desperately wanted to make. He was trying to form the word, 'Eternity," for the Snow Queen had told him, "When you find out this, you shall be your own master, and I will give you the whole world and a new pair of skates."

Gerda ran to Kay and threw her arms around his neck. "Kay, dear little Kay! I've found you at last!" But he sat quite still, stiff and cold. Then Gerda wept hot tears that penetrated his heart and began to melt the lump of ice until Kay also burst into tears, washing away the speck that had lodged in his eye. "Gerda, where have you been and where am I?" As he looked all around him, he exclaimed, "How cold it is, and how large and empty it all looks."

The two danced, crying tears of joy, until they fell to the ground, wrapped in each other's arms. And as they lay there, their figure formed—at last—the word "Eternity" and Kay was forever free from the Snow Queen's power.

The two made their way back to their red rose bush where they both sat, grown up, yet children at heart—and it was summer; warm, beautiful summer.

I see evidence of the Snow Queen's influence all around us. That which is good and wholesome is made to look small and insignificant, even ridiculed, while the bad and the ugly is magnified. That which used to be good is now called evil and that which was evil is now called good. The biographies written 100 years ago inspired hearts. Today, we've knocked all our old heroes off their pedestals and their modern biographers focus on their flaws and weaknesses.

The comments in comment sections are mean-spirited and cruel. Intellectuals mock feelings and demand scientific studies and factual evidence as the only grounds for discussion. If an idea cannot be measured or tested, it is rejected. Emotion is scorned.

I often pick up old children's books at book sales and then go online to read what other people have said about the books. I find comments like these:

"This book changed my life."

"I've read it so many times, my copy is falling apart."

"The pages of my book are covered with tears."

"I read the book 60 years ago and I just reread it. I love it even more today than I did then."

These comments are made by an older pre-Snow Queen generation. Then I read comments made about the same book by young readers today:

"This is the most boring book I've ever read."

"I hated this book. No one should ever have to read it."

"It moved so slowly, I wanted to die."

"I hated all those feelings."

This shift from heart to mind hasn't happened by accident or overnight. It's been by design and with steady effort. Many of the most influential men and women of the last century, particularly those who influence education, have dreamed of a world governed by reason. Reason, they say, will give us solutions to all our problems. Reason can give us a new moral code that's more realistic and practical. And what reasonable person would ever think war is reasonable? Their philosophy can be summed up with these words found in *A Humanist Manifesto*: "Reason and intelligence are the most effective instruments that humankind possesses. There is no substitute."

Those sound like Snow Queen words, don't they?

The experiment has gone on long enough to see the results and the result is, the world has turned upside down.

It's a grave mistake to train the intellect of a child before we have tended to his heart. Much of the frustration of young kids in school comes from forcing them to engage in academic activities for which they are not developmentally ready. We ignore the fact that childhood years have been reserved by our Creator for warming their hearts. Children can feel before they can reason.

But we've tasted the fruits of science and technology and they taste really good. We can hardly wait to see science's next big reveal or technology's latest gadget. And there's nothing wrong with that. It's all very exciting. We do want children to develop scientific reasoning and critical thinking skills. We want scientists and engineers. But it needs to happen in its proper order: heart first and then mind.

And the reason for that is clear. .

Science and technology in the hands of evil or foolish hearts can and will destroy us. Only when it is in the hands of good and wise hearts will it bless us.

Science is a wonderful servant but a dangerous master.

By abandoning making long-lasting impressions on the heart in favor of facts and information in childhood years, we've created a massive educational system of sandcastles. But it's not only our learning we're having a hard time holding on to. Everything around us is getting slipperier. We're having a hard time holding on to our jobs, our homes, our money, our relationships, our faith—even our freedom. I blame the Snow Queen's hold on us. Only by paying proper attention to 'heart' can we bring our world back into balance.

For the amount of time, money and worry that go into educating our kids, I'm not satisfied with sandcastles, as fun as they are to build. I want diamonds. Diamonds are one of the few things in our world that don't decay or fall apart over time. If I find a diamond that was buried in a treasure chest 1000 years ago, it will still sparkle today just as brightly as the day it was buried. Diamonds are forever.

I want a 'forever' system of education.

I want learning that will last.

I want to form the word 'Eternity,' like our little friend, Kay.

Which is why I am a big proponent of common core standards. I think that not only all 50 of our states should adopt common core standards, I believe the whole world will benefit from them.

But the common core standards I have in mind are not the ones being implemented in our schools, because I have a different objective in mind. Our schools hope to make our children college and career ready. They want to prepare global workers for the global economy. I think our kids deserve much more than that. We can't go wrong when we align our will to God's, and His will is: "Man is that he might have joy." So my objective is to prepare children to live lives of maximum everlasting joy, in which a job will certainly be part of the journey, but will not be the ultimate destination.

My proposed common core standards won't require any governor's signature or committee to debate them. They need no federal funding. In fact, they don't need any funding at all. They're free to implement. And they can be implemented starting today, in your home and in mine.

These common core standards provide the antidote to the Snow Queen's poison.

I have them from high authority.

The site for the current federal common core standards says they can explain theirs in 3 minutes. I can express mine in just 3 words:.

1: Faith 2: Hope and 3: Charity

Let me show you what they look like.

FAITH

Faith is the first thing to go in a Snow Queen's reign because she demands full trust in only those things that can be seen, tested and measured. Faith, on the other hand, requires us to trust in a higher force or power that usually can't be seen and often asks us to suspend reason. Reason would have had the children of Israel surrender to Pharaoh's army. What possible chance did they have? Only faith would have thought of parting the Red Sea so they could cross safely on dry ground.

The world seeks Truth by Reason. God teaches, "There is a Spirit in man: and the inspiration of the Almighty giveth them understanding." And He reveals that understanding of truth with a feeling…a burning…in our hearts. We feel when something is right. In our day, we see men ever learning but never coming to a knowledge of the Truth.

Truth, Light, Spirit, and Living Water are all words that are used interchangeably in the scriptures to describe what I call spiritual sunshine and we all know what would happen to us if the sun stopped shining. It requires faith to believe in the existence of this spiritual sunshine. It can't be studied under a microscope, but you know when it's present because in its rays is felt love, joy, peace, patience, gentleness, goodness and meekness. It infuses joy into our souls and becomes part of us which is what differentiates it from mere pleasure. Pleasure is usually temporal and temporary. The pleasure of eating a chocolate chip cookie lasts only as long as the cookie. Spiritual light, on the other hand, is satisfying and everlasting.

It is Eternal.

All light can be traced back to its source and I know of only One who has claimed to be the source of this Light I am describing. The good news is He freely shines His light on everyone—the believer and the unbeliever. What varies from person to person is the capacity to capture this light. The greater the capacity, the greater the joy. The value of a diamond is also determined by its capacity to capture light. Some diamonds sparkle more than others.

Spiritual sunshine quickens feelings; it animates us and makes us feel alive. It opens up our understanding. To be 'inspired' literally means to take in breath or to take 'in spirit.' Brahms relied upon inspiration to compose his music. He described the process this way:

"I will now tell you...about my method of communicating with the Infinite, for all truly inspired ideas come from God. Beethoven, who was my ideal, was well aware of this. When I feel the urge, I begin by appealing directly to my Maker... Straightway the ideas flow in upon me, directly from God, and not only do I see distinct themes in my mind's eye, but they are clothed in the right forms, harmonies and orchestrations."

He went on to say it was the same power by which all the great composers like Mozart, Schubert, Bach and Beethoven drew their inspirations.

Is the day of greatness behind us? I like the hopeful words of Orson Whitney who said, "We will yet have Miltons and Shakespeares of our own. God's ammunition is not exhausted. His brightest spirits are held in reserve for the latter times." But I can't see it happening until we undo the damage of the Snow Queen and re-open the channels of inspiration to our children.

Which brings me to my Common Core Standard for Faith: Prepare the child's heart to be inspired.

Goethe was asked how he kept spiritual light flowing inward. His response was that, every day, he gazed upon a masterpiece of fine art, read a piece of fine literature, recited a selection of poetry and listened to beautiful music—exactly the things the Snow Queen is eliminating from our classrooms. She may argue with me that they're there, but what is remaining of the Arts is to be looked upon and analyzed with intellectual eyes, not felt by the heart. She doesn't trust the heart.

By filling the hearts of our children with beautiful images of art, literature and poetry, we are giving the Spirit something to light up. If I go out on a dark summer night with a flashlight and shine the beam straight up in the air, I won't see the light unless it reflects off dust particles in the air or maybe an occasional moth. To really see the light, I need to shine it on the leaves of the trees or the ground ahead of me. We can increase the light within our souls and the souls of our children by giving the Spirit a large surface area to light up. By following the admonition of Paul and treasuring up in our hearts those things which are virtuous and lovely and of good report and praiseworthy, we provide lots of surface area for the Spirit to light up. Light cleaves to light. And in that Light will be felt great joy.

When we block spiritual sunshine, the same thing happens to our world as happens to a flower bed that is covered with a sun-blocking tarp: everything underneath it begins to rot and decay.

If we wish to prepare out children's hearts to be inspired, we need to give the Spirit room to do its work. Several months ago, I was looking for Christmas stories to include in our Christmas volume. When I finished reading one of the selections, I was so overcome with emotion, I buried my face in my hands at my desk and wept. The emotions I felt made me want to be kinder; to be better. They lifted me up. I felt my heart enlarging. The book itself was not a literary masterpiece. It was sentimental and predictable—no action scenes or compelling conflict to resolve. There were even hints of political incorrectness. Despite all these things, I felt my soul being filled.

Had I read the book in school, I'm sure I would have been asked to pinpoint character, plot and setting. I may have been asked to search for and circle use of literary devices such as alliteration or compare and contrast two of the characters. I might have been required to identify and analyze what words the writer used to evoke emotion. I'm sure I would have been given a list of questions to answer about the text. And in the process, it would have killed the Spirit of the story.

The letter killeth, but the spirit giveth life.

When heart work is going on, often silence is the best teaching method. The deeper a message travels into the heart, the fewer words there are to describe the feeling. The ocean at its greatest depth is silent. The Spirit communicates with the 'deeps' of our souls.

Allowing room for the Spirit to work is a big part of applying the Common Core Standard of Faith: Preparing our children's hearts to be inspired. As we make room for the Spirit to work, we'll keep spiritual sunshine flowing in our world.

HOPE

Hope has been the second casualty of the Snow Queen's reign. Hope is an expectation or desire for something better and is what keeps us moving forward. Hope is dependent on vision—"Where there is no vision, the people perish." Nothing has ever been created or accomplished that didn't first exist as an image or as a vision in someone's heart.

In the excitement of filling our children's mind with facts and information, stories have been left behind. Yet, it's the stories that give vision to our hearts. They illustrate life. They set dreams in motion. Our children need to clearly see all the possibilities of life. And for the most joyful life, they need to see what 'good' looks like. The Snow Queen may argue that being 'pure' is old-fashioned and unreasonable, but it's the diamond of greatest purity that is the most prized. The flawless diamond is virtually incorruptible.

The world's vision for our youth is not the Lord's vision. I am not alone in the belief that His long-awaited kingdom is about to be established here upon the earth. This is not the day for building sandcastles. This is a day for diamonds.

Most diamonds are formed under prolonged periods of high heat and intense pressure, a process that can be repeated to make the diamond harder. Diamond souls fit for the Kingdom of God will be formed in the same way.

One night I was saying my usual prayer: "Please watch over my children. Keep them safe from all harm or accident. Bless them with health and strength and with every good desire." But this particular night, my prayer was gently interrupted with these words that formed in my mind, "Marlene, are you asking Me to keep them from the very means that have brought you to know Me?" I knew it was true. It wasn't the times when everything was going right that I felt His power. It was those times when I was backed to the wall with nowhere to go—the times when Reason offered no solution—that I experienced His miracles and felt His healing spirit pour into my soul. Yet, it didn't seem right to pray that horrible things would happen to my children. So I said, "Then I'm not sure what to pray for." Immediately, the sweet feeling came, "Pray for more trust in Me." That's a much harder prayer to pray, but I'm trying.

What we can do to keep hope alive in the hearts of our children through the troubling but necessary diamond forming stretches ahead is to make sure we have filled their reservoir of stories with examples of others who have struggled through challenges and overcome difficulties. We need to give them a vision of the world as it can be to look forward to. And especially, we need to show them what faith in God looks like. They need to know God always keeps His promises and that nothing is impossible to Him. It's the diamond souls with clear vision who will stand strong when everything around them is falling apart. They will inspire hope in those whose hearts are weak.

By giving our children a vision of good things to hope for—the second Common Core standard—we will ensure there will be diamond souls who can withstand the heat and lift those around them to higher ground in the days ahead. Their hearts will not fail them.

CHARITY

Charity is the pure love of Christ and this Love is the superglue of the universe. Take love out of a marriage, and the marriage falls apart. Take love out of a family, and the family breaks up. Take away love of one's country—patriotism—and the nation starts to crumble. Take away love of God, and faith vanishes. Take love out of learning, and the learning doesn't stick.

This pure love is a gift of spiritual sunshine. As the Snow Queen blocks access to that Light, love grows colder. But by following Common Core Standard One, our children's hearts will be inspired, and in the light of that Spirit, the hearts of our children will be filled with pure love. It's not enough to just capture that love, though. The love needs to be put to use and reflected outwards. Likewise, the value of a diamond is not just in its capacity to capture light; it's also in its capacity to reflect that light.

In Robert Browning's *Paracelsus*, Festus and Paracelsus are lifelong friends. Paracelsus longs for the life of the scholar. He can imagine no greater happiness than uninterrupted time with his books, digging out the deep meaning of the truth of the ages. Surely, this will be his great gift to mankind—to share his vast knowledge and understanding.

The two friends meet twenty years later. Paracelsus is a wreck; he's miserable and he's dying. But he has learned a priceless lesson—though too late for himself—as he now understands: "There is an answer to the passionate longings of the heart for fulness, and I knew it. And the answer is this: Live in all things outside yourself by love and you will have joy. This is the life of God; it ought to be our life."

There is a right use and a wrong use for all things. If you tweak the word 'righteousness' just a little, you have 'right-use-ness.' The right use yields joy. The wrong use yields sorrow. This standard of right-use-ness can be applied to business, money, education, art, music, the internet, sex—everything in our world—great blessings in their right-use and great sorrow in their mis-use. Common Core Standard 3 is: Teach the right-use of all things in love. It's a formula for long-lasting joy. In the world's economy, the richest man is the one with the most money. In heaven's economy, the richest man is the one with the greatest capacity for joy. As love increases, joy increases. If we wish our children to be heavenly rich, we will need to give them a clear vision of what love looks like: "Love suffereth long, and is kind. Love envieth not; vaunteth not itself, is not puffed up, does not behave itself unseemly, seeketh not her own, is not easily provoked, thinketh no evil; rejoiceth not in iniquity, but rejoiceth in truth."

Ten years ago, the American Psychiatric Association revealed a study where they estimated the average 18 year old in the United States will have viewed over 16,000 violent deaths and over 200,000 acts of violence. How many acts of love will we have given them to view in those same formative years?

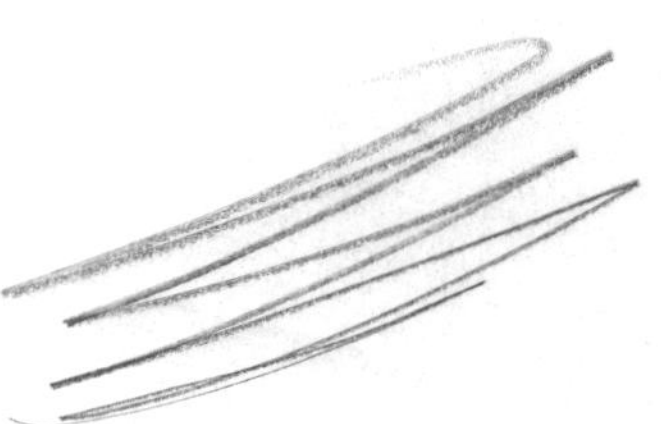

How important is this love? Let me put it this way.

One day I asked my husband to go to the store and buy me some broccoli for a casserole I was making. When he came home, he had several bags of groceries on his arms. There was milk and bread and butter, cookies, chips and cereal. Although everything he brought home was good, the one thing I needed wasn't there: the broccoli.

Love is the broccoli of life.

To paraphrase 1 Corinthians, though a child should score a perfect score on the SAT, graduate with honors from Harvard, write a New York times bestseller, head up a major corporation, find the cure for cancer or be awarded the Nobel Peace Prize, if that child has not love, he is as sounding brass or tinkling cymbals.

On the other hand, though a child speaks not three languages, fails Algebra twice, cannot compare or contrast two characters in two major works of literature, never marries, lives out his life in a small one-room cottage and never does one single notable act in the eyes of the world, if that child's heart reflects love towards all God's creations, he will find his name in God's book of everlasting treasures.

He shall have discovered 'Eternity' and will have become master of his own soul.

God is Love.

Now, I believe common core standards need frequent assessments. In fact, I recommend a daily test be administered to every parent. The same three test questions can be used each day:

> Question One: Today, what did I do to prepare my child's heart to be inspired?
> Question Two: Today, what vision of great things did I give my child to hope for?
> Question Three: Today, what did I teach the right-use of in love?

If we adopt these three common core standards, the outcome that we can expect is to see a new heart and a new world emerge in just a few years—a Golden Age of peace.

For thousands of years, poets, prophets and sages—the dreamers of the world—have longed for a world of peace ruled by love, beauty and justice. Yet, the history of the world has been almost one continuous story of war and bloodshed; of conquering and being conquered. Still, the dream persists.

Julia Ward Howe, who gave us our Battle Hymn of the Republic, shared this vision:

"One night I experienced a sudden awakening. I had a vision of a new era which is to dawn for mankind and in which men and women are battling unitedly for the uplifting of the race.

"There seemed to be a new, a wondrous permeating light, the glory of which I cannot attempt to put in human words—the light of new-born hope blazing. And then I saw victory. All of evil was gone from the earth. Misery was blotted out. Mankind was ready to march forward in a new era of human understanding—the era of perfect love, of peace, passing all understanding."

Upon being awarded the Nobel Peace Prize in 1954, Albert Schweitzer gave these words in a memorable speech:

"The idea that the reign of peace must come one day has been given expression by a number of peoples who have attained a certain level of civilization. In Palestine it appeared for the first time in the words of the prophet Amos in the eighth century B.C. and it continues to live in the Jewish and Christian religions as the belief in the Kingdom of God. It figures in the doctrine taught by the great Chinese thinkers: Confucius and Lao-tse in the sixth century B.C. It reappears in Tolstoy and in other contemporary European thinkers. People have labeled it a utopia. But the situation today is such that it must become reality in one way or another; otherwise mankind will perish...

"Decisive steps must be taken to ensure peace, and decisive results obtained without delay. Only through the spirit can all this be done. Is the spirit capable of achieving what we in our distress must expect of it? Let us not underestimate its power, the evidence of which can be seen throughout the history of mankind...

"Many a truth has lain unnoticed for a long time, ignored simply because no one perceived its potential for becoming reality.?

Faith, Hope and Charity will lift our world.

To borrow the words from another dreamer: "What shall I say...To awaken in your hearts...the desire to realize this glorious anticipation?... I can only call upon God...to make my words as sparks of fire, to fall upon the tinder of your hearts and kindle them into flame. That from this hour your souls may be lit up with the light of your glorious destiny, that you may live for God and His kingdom, not simply for yourselves and the perishable things of the earth."

Or in other words, to live for diamonds, not just sandcastles.

Do you remember the Magic Eye books that were popular a few years back? When you looked at the pages, they just looked like random designs. But if you looked at them long enough and in just the right way, a clear 3D image would suddenly pop out at you.

I had a Magic Eye moment with history recently. That's the best way I can describe it. I had been studying the stories of many of the nations of the world and I was looking at a world map, thinking of these stories. As I looked at each country one at a time, I noticed how many of them had a time in history when they seemed to take center stage, with a spotlight shown on them. And in that light, they left a lesson for the world, and then faded into the background and another nation took its turn. I thought about what I had learned from each one:

Ancient Greece: beauty
Ancient Rome: law and justice
China: respect for elders and honoring ancestors
France: equality and equal justice
Israel (Hebrews): the fatherhood of God and liberty in law
Saracens: love of learning in an atmosphere of freedom
India: power of peaceful measures
Africa: simple and pure faith emerging
Native Americans: reverence for Nature

England: refinement through literature
Holland, Scotland/Ireland: liberty is worth dying for

It was primarily Irish and Scotch blood that flowed in the veins of our early patriot fighters.

Other nations left behind painful lessons. They showed us the misery and suffering under the hands of tyranny and oppression. They taught us about the cruelty of greed and corruption in nations whose highest ideal is gold. And they displayed the savagery and barbarism—the rot and decay—when spiritual darkness sets in.

Some people are offended at the thought of American exceptionalism. I am not. I say to the world, we are exceptional because we are your children. Admittedly, lately we have behaved as spoiled children always do who are lavished with too many unearned gifts. But please give us another chance. Let us turn our hearts once again to you, our fathers, and learn from your stories all the lessons you have taught us. And from those many stories, let us, for the first time in human history, gather them into one great whole—*e pluribus unum*, out of many, one.

But there is one story, one lesson, one Truth that has not yet been brought to center stage for all the world to see. Maybe America has not yet had her chance to shine. Maybe this final story before ushering in an era of peace will be ours to tell. Interestingly, it's a story embedded deeply in the spirit of the German people, and according to the 2000 Census, there are more Americans with German roots than any other single nationality. Wagner, the great German composer, set the story to music. It's the story found in part in The Niebelungenlied and it briefly goes like this:

In the Rhine River lived three beautiful maidens—the Rhine daughters. Carelessly, one day, they lost the gold that had been entrusted to them by their father. They knew whoever molded the gold into a ring would have all power upon the earth, save love. The hideous little creature, Alberich the Niebelung, who seized it, laughed wickedly, "What do I care for love if I have all the gold I want?" Under his cruel power, the people cried out, "That wretched Alberich, with his ring of gold has made us all slaves! With it he drives us down into the earth to get more gold. This curse of gold has filled our world with despair."

The gold ring passed from one owner to another, causing misery to all who possessed it until it came into the hands of the beautiful and noble Brunhilde who courageously returned it to the rightful owners, the Rhine-daughters. At long last, gold no longer held power over the hearts of men. Hurry, worry, falsehood, greed and envy vanished from the earth. Anxiety disappeared from the brows of the tired fathers. A new happiness came into the eyes of the mothers. A greater power than gold had come to rule the world, and that power was Love.

You young mothers and young fathers who are closest to the hearts of the rising generation: The heavens are watching and the earth is waiting for you.

May we adopt a new Common Core standard. If we will prepare the hearts of our children to be inspired; if we will give them a vision of wonderful things to hope for; and if we will teach them the right-use of all things in love, we will yet see the rising of that city shining upon a hill seen in vision by our Pilgrim fathers and our ancient prophets.

"And the Gentiles shall come to thy light, and kings to the brightness of thy rising," saying, "Teach us your ways that we may go home and teach our people," and righteousness will flood the earth, just as Isaiah prophesied.

And our sons and daughters, and their sons and daughters, will be found singing songs of everlasting joy.

"It is the business of the heart for a long time before it is the business of the mind." --Pestalozzi

Pattern for Learning

A Pattern for Learning

HEART	MIND	SPIRIT
Impressions, Feelings, Images	Facts, Information	Light, "Spiritual Sunshine"
ARTS	SCIENCE	FAITH
Desire	Rules	Creation
Random, Spontaneous	Systematic, Sequential	Purposeful
Long-term Memory	Short-term Memory	Infinite, Eternal

And now I'd like to unfold a simple pattern for learning.

As you have read, we are a very academically-minded culture. Our schools are focused on training the *minds* of our children. You know when you are in the realm of the mind because it can be tested and measured. The buzz words are critical thinking skills and scientific reasoning. Minds are fed with facts and information, words, that can conveniently be organized into grade-level curriculum and tested, providing measurable outcomes demanded by those who hand out the money to the schools.

The mind functions in the realm of Science, which is, in essence, all about discovering the laws, rules and principles upon which everything in the world and universe operates. And so we teach our children the rules of math, the rules of grammar, punctuation and spelling. We teach them the laws of physics, the laws of thermodynamics and the laws of economics. The words 'law' and 'order' go together. Complying with rules creates order. If you've ever traveled to a foreign country where there are no traffic laws, you know how chaotic and dangerous it is to drive. On the other hand, scientists who gaze out into the universe are awe struck at the perfect order, harmony and majesty of galaxies and stars and planets all abiding the laws within their respective spheres.

There are also principles and laws by which civilizations prosper and flourish; our liberty is in law; even happiness is governed by law. Law is a good thing. Which is why it puzzles me when I've heard of students asking their teachers why they have to learn all the rules and the teacher responds, "You have to learn the rules so you can break them." Throwing out all the rules seems to be the hallmark of our generation. Just do whatever feels good. We have millions of little girls singing, "No right or wrong, no rules for me, I'm free. Let it go." For a system that prides itself on reason and logic, spending all this time learning rules so we can break them is, in the word of Mr. Spock, "illogical." But I digress.

This type of learning is systematic and sequential. You have to learn the rules of arithmetic before you can master the rules of algebra.

Facts and information are very hard to hold on to and most go into short-term memory. Much of the time in school is spent trying to get information to stick. A child may hold on to facts long enough to take the test, but then they tend to wash away. We use words like cold and hard to describe facts.

And we use a word for the type of learning that goes on in school. We call it academic learning. Have you ever looked up the definition of *academic*? This is what I found in the Merriam-Webster online dictionary: "having no practical importance; not involving or relating to anything real or practical; having no practical or useful significance." And as if that's not bad enough, we don't just want academics. We want rigorous academics. Rigorous and rigor-mortis have the same root word–rigor, which means stiffness and rigidness; even voluntary submission to pain. We use painful words like drilling facts into kids. And we want to extend the academic year and start academics at younger and younger ages?

Do you remember what Aristotle said over 2000 years ago? "Educating the mind without educating the heart is no education at all." Plato also understood: "All learning is based in emotion." The heart is what pumps life into the brain. A person is still alive as long as the heart is pumping, even if brain waves have ceased. But a brain cannot function without the heart. Yet, here we are, cutting the heart out of education.

The heart is fed with feelings, impressions, and images which are delivered by the Arts, which include music, pictures, poetry and story. The heart is the realm of the Imagination. This stage of learning is all about desire; of warming and opening the heart. As Dr. Rich Melheim writes: "The brain is filled with gatekeepers designed to keep information out... [Y]ou have to open the kid before you open the book." These gatekeepers respond to pleasurable experiences, which the Arts provide. When you "get to the emotional centers, the gates of intellect fly open wide."

Learning in this stage can be random and spontaneous because impressions made on the heart go into long-term memory and are held onto long enough to connect and interlace with other impressions. If a fact can be connected to something the heart cares about, it places the fact in long-term storage.

Cutting out the heart is not good. Studies reveal the emotional well-being of college students is at the lowest level in 25 years. Over half of college students in one particular study reported severe feelings of hopelessness and despair. Half! And in the job market, as one employer put it, they're getting lots of resumes from hopeful engineers, but what they're looking for and not finding are engineers with personality.

These are symptoms of heart problems arising from our neglect of the heart.

The final part of this pattern of learning is not allowed in our schools: Spirit. I was reading an old 1900 Chemistry textbook and it talked about the elements the Ancients identified: air, water, earth, fire and the fifth was an element they could sense was there, but couldn't quite put their finger on it. It was a spiritual element and they called it ether. In the spirit of scientific inquiry that tests and measures only that which you can see and handle, the fifth element was dropped, yet we still hold on to the word 'ether' in the word 'ethereal' which describes something heavenly or celestial, something of another dimension. Something higher than us. This Spirit is like a Spiritual Sunshine to us. It is inspiration–to be inspired means to take 'in spirit.' In the Creation story, Light was the first order of the day, and the source of that light wasn't the sun. The sun didn't come along until later in the creation process.

It requires our Faith to believe in its existence because you have to believe in something you cannot handle or measure. It is the same evidential demands of scientific inquiry that keeps talk of the spiritual out of our schools. I can't see the wind, either, or hold it in my hands, but I can see it moving the leaves on the trees and can feel it blowing on my face. If we have not felt it ourselves, we can still see the Spirit's effect in the lives of others. We recognize its presence by its fruits: Joy, Peace, Love, Kindness, Gentleness.

This Spirit or Light is a creative force. It tends to lift, expand and multiply, and everything created under the influence of the spirit yields joy, peace and love. It is the spirit that gives understanding to our learning. The architect who loves the beautiful and learns the skills of building, under the influence of the Spirit will create structures that are not only functional but which inspire the heart with beauty as well. The businessman who loves fairness and people and who learns the rules of success, under the influence of the Spirit will create businesses that will bless and bring joy to many lives. Michelangelo, whose heart loved the beautiful and who mastered the skills of painting and sculpture, wrote, "My unassisted heart is barren clay." He knew the source of his inspiration and genius.

Charles Kingsley wrote, "Jesus Christ, remember, is the Light who lights every man who comes into the world. And no one can think a right thought, or feel a right feeling, or understand the truth of anything, in earth and heaven, unless the good Lord Jesus Christ teaches him by His Spirit which gives men understanding."

But the spirit cannot create something from nothing. Rather it organizes the raw materials we gather through our learning and turns them into a usefulness. The more we give the Spirit to work with, the more it can accomplish through us. This is the right-useness of learning. The purest stream, if there is no outlet, will eventually stagnate and stink. The purest knowledge and desires, with no outlet, with no right-useness of them, will eventually rot. Just like our friend Paracelsus learned in the Sandcastles talk I shared with you.

This stage of learning is very purposeful and customized to the calling and mission of the individual. And the learning is everlasting and eternal. This is the True Education described by Charlotte Mason, between the child's soul and God.

I now find this pattern all over the place. Both the Old and New Testaments are front-end loaded with stories to warm and open hearts. Most of the stories we're familiar with are in the book of Genesis and the Four Gospels. Then come the laws, commandments and doctrines. Finally, the back end has books that require much preparatory learning. The true meaning of books like Isaiah and Revelation can only be revealed spirit to spirit.

John the Baptist's role was to warm and open the hearts of the people so they would be prepared to receive Jesus who taught the law of the gospel in preparation for receiving the Holy Ghost, whose role is to "teach us all things which we should do."

I also notice the first commandment is to love, not to obey. Obedience is second. The desire for the good and the beautiful along with obedience to correct principles will create not only heaven on earth, but heaven in the world to come.

I see the pattern in history–the ancient Greeks were known for their love Beauty and the Arts, the Romans, their love of law and justice, and then came Jesus who taught of a spiritual kingdom.

I see the pattern in nature. The seed that is planted in the ground will not begin to grow until the ground is warmed. And much of that first growth is in developing a strong root system. Without that root system underground–unseen to the eye–the plant will never grow long enough to flower. The stem will wither and die. The flower alone contains all the seeds with which to multiply and replenish the earth.

I see the pattern in music. The heart is the melody, the mind is the rhythm or beat and the spirit brings in all the harmonies.

And I see it in the development of us as human beings. The heart develops before the brain within the womb and emotions develop before the intellect outside the womb. The first 8 years, in particular, are reserved by nature for tending to the heart when a child's heart is open to impressions and feelings because the mind is not yet too cluttered. To me, an ounce of morning is worth a pound of afternoon where inspiration is concerned. Inspiration comes to me in the very early morning hours, often before the sun comes up, when my mind is uncluttered. Childhood is the early morning of life.

So how does this pattern apply to learning? I would suggest, don't attempt to teach any principle, doctrine or academic subject until after you have sufficiently warmed and opened the heart. Leonardo da Vinci wrote: "Study without desire spoils the memory, and it retains nothing it takes in." And Plato agreed: "Knowledge which is acquired under compulsion obtains no hold on the mind." Front-end load the learning experience with story, rhyme, song, images and love. And then, make sure you leave room for the Spirit to do its work. When you ask all the questions and structure all the learning, you interfere with that individualized, customized spiritual learning experience. Like St. Exupery advises: "When you want to build a ship, do not begin by gathering wood, cutting boards, and distributing work, but waken within the heart of man the desire for the vast and endless sea."

Take away the Spirit, take away the heart, and all that's left is purely academic.

"When the multitudes cease to flow into the sanctuary to bathe themselves in God's divine ether, to wash the grime from the soul's garments, to sharpen the dulled instrument of the spirit, that moment the bloom and beauty will begin to pass from our arts, our literature, our music, our laws, and the very springs of civilization will dry up." --President Hopkins of Williams College

My Wish For You

I've been thinking of what I might say to you at this New Year that will give you renewed hope and vision of what we're trying to accomplish here at the Well-Educated Heart. I've written several podcasts already that I've erased. They just didn't seem right. Then yesterday, the thought struck me, "Search the meaning of 'the spoken word of the Lord.'" And I was astonished at what I learned. It confirmed again that the things that I am sharing with you that I have been learning—especially the Pattern for Learning I keep referring to—are not things that I have made up. I believe they are true. I leave it to you to experiment upon the things I say and prove for yourself whether or not they are true by the fruit it bears in your life.

Just a warning—I'm taking this topic to a deeper spiritual level than we usually go. Everyone is at a different place—I respect that and all are welcome to all the resources in The Well-Educated Heart to use as you wish. But I feel that I should share these thoughts with you today.

This is what I learned about the spoken word of the Lord. And you can do your own research! Just Google it. The New Testament was translated from the Greek into the English language. While we read just one expression—the word of the Lord—if you go back to the original Greek, there were two different words that were used. One word was *logos* and it referred to the words that were given generally to all people. But the other word that was used frequently was *rhema,* which has an entirely different meaning. Let me quote some of what I read: "*Rhema* refers to a divinely inspired impression upon your soul; a flash of thought or a creative idea from God. It's divine illumination that is always accompanied by a deep inner assurance. As the scriptures say, 'The spirit of the Lord giveth understanding.'"

As I see it, *rhema* is dependent upon having something stored up within—a stockpile of ideas and words—that can be illuminated or brought to life with the purpose of a lesson or benefit to the individual or his personal mission.

So one person may read the *logos* of the scriptures, or I would expand that to say the written word of anything, and never have those words brought to life. They're just words on a page. But another person will read those same words and be given flashes of inspiration of how they apply to one's own life or learning. It's as though the words are illuminated. The first is *logos* and the second is *rhema.* At least that's how I'm understanding it.

This act of divine illumination is another way of saying what Charlotte Mason taught: True education is between a child's soul and God. Or Isaiah when he taught that the day would come when all our children would be taught of the Lord. Not about the Lord, but by the spoken word of the Lord—*rhema.*

Such instruction is "not helped or hindered by our vocabulary or eloquent speech" because it unfolds deep within our soul. As the article said, you can learn many things at college, but you cannot go to school to learn God. You either learn from Him or you don't know Him at all.

Rhema is that still, small voice.

So that sounds like a discussion for church, right? What does that have to do with The Well-Educated Heart and educating our children? Well, in a nutshell, hard hearts cannot feel *rhema*. Hard hearts look but don't see. They listen but don't hear. They know but don't understand. They think but don't feel.

Those flashes of illumination apply to all our learning whether scriptural or historical or scientific or artistic. So, in order for this kind of learning to happen, we need to keep our children's hearts warm and open and pure. To hear this "spoken word of the Lord" requires living in harmony with divine laws and principles. As we learn from literature, history, art, music and nature, we're constantly searching for those universal true principles by which we teach our children to govern their lives. And they test the truth of those principles by the fruit it bears in their lives. As their hearts grow to love that which is good, true and beautiful and as they are obedient to right laws, this creative power, this divine illumination, will flow into their lives and bear good fruit in the world. It's an individual, personalized course of learning. And its fruits are increased joy, love, and peace.

Hearts are growing hard and cold for a lot of reasons. For one, electronic media is rewiring the brains of our children—they are living in a virtual world and losing touch with the real world about them; with real relationships and real joys. It's a big problem and challenge for us to overcome. This generation seeks for the instant gratification of entertainment and pleasure which can never satisfy. We are living in an age when we are surrounded by all stirring things, unmoved.

And, as I have said before, the world has turned upside down. That which, just a short time ago, was seen as good is now seen as bad and that which is bad is seen as good. Every good is mocked and every fault is magnified. Man's reasoning is creating his own moral code and is creating chaos and confusion in the world.

Goethe's suggestion to every day, listen to some inspired music, look at some fine art, read a few lines of beautiful poetry and spend time with a great soul, which easily happens through story, as well as to spend time with the Creator among His creations is how we can warm and soften and *stir* the hearts of our children and turn things around because hard hearts cannot feel *rhema*.

The arts are for the heart.

A mom in our group wrote that it was necessary to put her kids back in public school recently. One day her 11-year-old came to her and asked if she had noticed that he was a little blah when he came home from school. She said that yes, she had noticed. And he responded, "I don't know what it is, mom. I just feel dead." A little while later she found him pulling out a story from France to read and put on some music which he and his siblings listened to while they drew. He instinctively turned to those things that would warm his heart because his mother had previously given him that experience.

So, yes, we spend a lot of time here learning about how to awaken a love and desire for the arts—Music, Paintings and other Fine Art, Poetry and Story—in the lives of our children. And we encourage them to spend time in nature that is actually naturally filled with music, beautiful imagery and even poetry and story to those who have eyes to see and hearts to feel.

But as only a warm heart can kindle warmth in another, we first tend to our own hearts.

So, to hear that still small voice and feel that divine inspiration, *rhema*, we have to warm our hearts. But it also mentioned that this Spirit needs something to light up. We need to provide the stockpile of ideas to draw from.

The rotation schedule is simply a way to stockpile the heart in a broad way and in this phase of learning, that's really all we have to worry about doing. We don't need to draw the conclusions for our children or fit everything together for them. We just need to facilitate the planting of knowledge and ideas.

I love this perspective of an English poet, John Drinkwater, that I included in the Mother's Learning Library poetry book. Let me quote a section from it:

"Nothing in the world gives people so much real pleasure as making things. And have you ever tried to think exactly what making a thing means? It doesn't mean making something out of nothing in a magical way, but it means taking a thing, or a number of things that are already in existence, and so arranging them, that in addition to the things that have been used, an entirely new thing comes into being."

I would insert here that *rhema* is what helps us in that creative, organizational process.

"For instance, a man may take thousands of bricks, each of which is a separate thing that has already been made, and out of them make an entirely new thing, a house. And in building a house the man is happy for two reasons—because he is making a useful thing, a place where he or someone else can live, and also because he is able to take a lot of bricks that have been lying in heaps, that do not seem to mean anything, and arrange them so that they become a house, which means a great deal. And there is nothing which gives us so much satisfaction as this ability to make disorder into order and give a useful meaning to things that until we have arranged them—just as the man arranges his bricks into a house seemed to have no use or meaning at all.

"It is a curious thing that we are able to get just this same kind of pleasure, which is so good for us, without having any real things to arrange. If you shut your eyes and then think of a horse, for example, it is certain that there is no real horse that you are looking at, and yet in some wonderful way you have been able to make a horse in your mind out of nothing. And the truth is that the idea of a horse which you have been able to call up in your mind, is just as real a thing, and just as important to you, as the horse that you may see in the street.

"And nothing will help you more in your life than the habit of seeing things in your mind very clearly; the habit not only of making things with your hands, but of making them in your mind as well. And just as, if you were building a house of bricks, you would not get the greatest possible pleasure unless you built a good, well-shapen, and complete house, so you will not get the greatest possible pleasure from the things that you make in your mind, unless they too are well-shaped and complete. You will find, for instance, that if you think about a horse with your eyes shut, that is to say, if you make a horse in your mind, you will get far more pleasure if you have learnt how to make it very exactly and clearly, than if you are only able to make it uncertainly, so that the horse in your mind is a confused kind of thing.

"I have said that the pleasure that we get from making things, whether with our hands or in our minds, is good for us. That is so because, ever since the earth began, the greatest purpose of the life on it has been to grow from a confusion that cannot be understood into clear shapes that can be well understood, and when we make anything clearly and exactly we are helping this purpose."

Can you begin to see why our emphasis on the arts—paintings, poetry, and stories that rely upon imagery to help us see and feel clearly—are so important in childhood?

And a little further on, Drinkwater adds: "[B]y far the most important matter is to like a good thing..." It's that first step in the Pattern for Learning—desiring that which is good. These years of childhood and young adulthood are for gathering bricks, which is not the end of learning, but the beginning of a lifetime of creation. That's why when someone asks which month a book should be studied, it doesn't really matter. Often it will fit in several different months. The rotation schedule is just a means to add a little order and rhythm to the gathering stage. We're simply gathering the raw materials with which to arrange and build, the creation stage—which will come later on in the learning process. The more raw materials they have to build with, the more ideas they can see—the more complete and clear they are—the more can be illuminated and used for good purpose.

When you sketch something from nature, when you follow a melody line in a piece of music, when you memorize a few lines from poetry you love, when you copy words that have touched your heart, when you see and feel a story so clearly that you can retell it, when you try and recreate the details of a work of fine art in your memory, you are bringing order to your internal world from the chaos and confusion of the outer world. These activities help you work towards stockpiling ideas with clarity and completeness of vision, which can then be arranged to good use.

Columbus understood this process. He wrote, "It was the Lord who put into my mind (I could feel his hand upon me) the fact that it would be possible to sail from here to the Indies. For the execution of the journey, I did not make use of intelligence, mathematics, or maps..."

As did Michelangelo: "My unassisted heart is barren clay, that of its native self can nothing fell."

These are not rare events. They were common and frequently talked about in older schoolbooks before we cut the spirit out of education. I don't expect we'll produce another Shakespeare or Michelangelo or Beethoven until we once again allow and encourage the flow of inspiration.

I have a feeling that these things that I am saying so imperfectly with my words will only be understood by the same spirit of learning I am trying to describe. I can tell you that I have been practicing the very things I am sharing with you. It truly is a joyful journey. It is the same process I am encouraging you to take the time to do in The Mother's University—stockpile your heart with good things, apply principles and then trust in that *rhema* that will teach you to adapt it to your life and circumstances.

Do your part. Warm and stir the hearts of your children, teach them the joy of obedience to correct principles and then trust the process of what will naturally follow.

"One thing is certain, in the light of human history. With all the advancement of science, with all the material progress of men in matters of mechanical invention and efficiency, with all the cultivation of the human intellect...Man's need of light is persistent, and every honest man recognizes it. ...Nature, science, reason, faith, hope, love, all unite in confirming the convictions that our God, as we know him in nature, will not fail to give to his needy children the adequate light of life to guide us into the way of the fullest realization of our noblest capacities and powers." --Howard Johnson

"For the child...it is not half so important to know as to feel. If facts are the seeds that later produce knowledge and wisdom, then the emotions and the impressions of the senses are the fertile soil in which the seeds must grow. The years of early childhood are the time to prepare the soil. Once the emotions have been aroused—a sense of the beautiful, the excitement of the new and the unknown, a feeling of sympathy, pity, admiration or love—then we wish for knowledge about the object of our emotional response—it is more important to pave the way for a child to want to know than to put him on a diet of facts that he is not ready to assimilate." --Rachel Carson

"There is only one way to improve the taste of a nation. It cannot be done in a hurry and it cannot be done by force. It can only be accomplished by exposing the people patiently to that which is truly "good," to that which is truly "noble"... Try and persuade our children to make the good choice for themselves by exposing them just as much as possible to that which is a true product of divine inspiration and honest human craftsmanship... In the end, those able to see and look for themselves will then make the right decisions and because they will do it of their own volition, it will be a lasting one." --Unknown

"Those who have used human reasoning to supersede divine influence in their lives have diminished themselves and cheapened civilization in the process." --Dallin H. Oaks

Letter to the Boys and Girls from Charles Kingsley

My dear boys and girls,

When I was your age there were no such children's books as there are now. Those which we had were few and dull, and the pictures in them ugly and mean, while you have your choice of books without number, clever, amusing, and pretty, as well as really instructive, on subjects which were only talked of fifty years ago by a few learned men, and very little understood even by them. So if mere reading of books would make wise men, you ought to grow up much wiser than us old fellows. But mere reading of wise books will not make you wise men; you must use for yourselves the tools with which books are made wise, and that is—your eyes and ears and common sense.

Now, among those very stupid old-fashioned boys' books was one which taught me that, and therefore I am more grateful to it than if it had been as full of wonderful pictures as all the natural history books you ever saw. Its name was *Evenings at Home*, and in it was a story called "Eyes and No Eyes," a regular old-fashioned, prim, sententious story; and it began thus:

"Well, Robert, where have you been walking this afternoon?" said Mr. Andrews to one of his pupils at the close of a holiday.

Oh, Robert had been to Broom Heath and round by Camp Mount, and home through the meadows But it was very dull. He hardly saw a single person. He had much rather have gone by the turnpike road.

Presently in comes Master William, the other pupil, dressed, I suppose, as wretched boys used to be dressed forty years ago, in a frill collar and skeleton monkey-jacket, and tight trousers buttoned over it and hardly coming down to his ankles, and low shoes which always came off in sticky ground; and terribly dirty and wet he is; but he never, he says, had such a pleasant walk in his life, and he has brought home his handkerchief (for boys had no pockets in those days much bigger than keyholes) full of curiosities.

He has got a piece of mistletoe, and wants to know what it is; and he has seen a woodpecker and a wheat-ear, and gathered strange flowers on the heath, and hunted a peewit because he thought its wing was broken, till, of course, it led him into a bog, and very wet he got. But he did not mind it, because he fell in with an old man cutting turf, who told him all about turf-cutting and gave him a dead adder. And then he went up a hill and saw a grand prospect, and wanted to go again and make out the geography of the country from Cary's old county maps, which were the only maps in those days. And then, because the hill was called Camp Mount, he looked for a Roman camp, and found one; and then he went down to the river and saw twenty things more, and so on, and so on, till he had brought home curiosities enough and thoughts enough to last him a week.

Whereon R. Andrews, who seems to have been a very sensible old gentleman, tells him all about his curiosities. And then it comes out—if you will believe it—that Master William has been over the very same ground as Master Robert, who saw nothing at all!

Whereon Mr. Andrews says, wisely enough, in his solemn, old-fashioned way:

"So it is. One man walks through the world with his eyes open, another with his eyes shut; and upon this difference depends all the superiority of knowledge which one man acquires over another. I have known sailors who had been in all the quarters of the world, and could tell you nothing but the sings of the tippling-houses and the price and quality of the liquor. On the other hand, Franklin could not cross the Channel without making observations useful to mankind. While many a vacant thoughtless youth is whirled through Europe without gaining a single idea worth crossing the street for, the observing eye and inquiring mind find matter of improvement and delight in every ramble. You then, William, continue to use your eyes. And you, Robert, learn that eyes were given to you to use."

So said Mrs. Andrews; and so I say to you. Therefore I beg all good boys and girls among you to think over this story, and settle in their own minds whether they will be Eyes or No Eyes; whether they will, as they grow up, look, and see for themselves what happens; or whether they will let other people look for them, or pretend to look, and dupe them, and lead them about—the blind leading the blind, till both fall into the ditch.

I say "good boys and girls;" not merely clever boys and girls, or prudent boys and girl; because using your eyes or not using them is a question of doing right, or doing wrong. God has given you eyes, and it is your duty to God to use them. If your parents tried to teach you your lessons in the most agreeable way, by beautiful picture-books, would it not be ungracious, ungrateful, and altogether naughty and wrong, to shut your eyes to those pictures, and refuse to learn? And is it not altogether naughty and wrong to refuse to learn from your Father in heaven, the Great God who made all things, when He offers to teach you all day long by the most beautiful and most wonderful of all picture-books, which is, simply all things which you can see, and hear, and touch, from the suns and stars above your heads, to the mosses and insects at your feet? It is your duty to learn His lessons, and it is your interest likewise. God's Book, which is the Universe, and the reading of God's Book, which is Science, can do you nothing but good, and teach you nothing but truth and wisdom. God did not put this wondrous world about your young souls to tempt or to mislead them. If you ask Him for a fish, He will not give you a serpent. If you ask Him for bread, He will not give you a stone.

So use your eyes and your intellect, your senses and your brains, and learn what God is trying to teach you continually by them. I do not mean that you must stop there, and learn nothing more: anything but that. There are things which neither your senses nor your brains can tell you; and they are not only more glorious, but actually more true and more real, than many things which you can see or touch. But you must begin at the beginning in order to end at the end; and sow the seed if you wish to gather the fruit. God has ordained that you, and every child which comes into the world, should begin by learning something of the world about him by his senses and his brain; and the better you learn what they can teach you, the more fit will you be to learn what they cannot teach you. The more you try not to understand things, the more you will be able hereafter to understand men, and That which is above men. You begin to find out that truly Divine mystery, that you had a mother on earth, simply by lying soft and warm upon her bosom; and so (as our Lord told the Jews of old) it is by watching the common natural things around you, and considering the lilies of the field, how they grow, that you will begin at least to learn that far Diviner mystery—that you have a Father in heaven. And so you will be delivered (if you will) out of tyranny of darkness, and distrust, and fear, into God's free kingdom of light, and faith, and love; and will be safe from the venom of the tree which is more deadly than the fabled Upas of the East. Who planted that tree I know not, it was planted so long ago; but surely it was none of God's planting, neither of the Son of God: yet it grows in all lands, and in all climes, and sends its hidden suckers far and wide—even (unless we be watchful) into your hearts and mine. And its name is the Tree of Unreason, whose roots are conceit and ignorance, and its juices folly and death. It drops its venom into the finest brains, and makes them call sense nonsense, and nonsense sense; fact fiction, and fiction fact. It drops its venom into the tenderest hearts, alas! And makes them call wrong right, and right wrong; love cruelty, and cruelty love. Some say that the axe is laid to the root of it just now, and that it is already tottering to its fall; while others say that it is growing stronger than ever, and ready to spread its upas-shade over the whole earth. For my part, I know not, save that all shall be as God wills. The tree has been cut down already, again and again, and yet has always thrown out fresh shoots, and dropped fresh poison from its boughs. But this at least I know, that any little child who will use the faculties which God has given him, may find an antidote to all its poison in the meanest herb beneath his feet.

There—you do not understand me, my boys and girls; and the best prayer I can offer for you is, perhaps, that you should never need to understand me; but if that sore need should come, and that poison should begin to spread its mists over your brains and hearts, then you will be proof against it, just in proportion as you have used the eyes and the common sense which God has given you, and have considered the lilies of the field, how they grow.

Joy is Everywhere

Using the Arts to Increase Our Capacity for Joy

"The whole world is full of unworked joy-mines. Everywhere we go we find all sorts of happiness-producing material, if we only know how to extract it." --Orison Swett Marden

How Do We Grow Our Capacity for Joy?

I see something extraordinary on the horizon and, as I have said, women and especially mothers play a key role. Now that you understand the difference between mind and heart, let me begin to unfold what I see by opening with an impression of contrasts.

I was flying home from speaking at a conference and as I was looking down at the cities below, I was thinking how tiny they looked from where I was. And for whatever reason, I tried to picture the Tower of Babel down there, maybe because I was trying to imagine a really big building. I pictured how massive the tower looked to the ones who were building it. I could imagine them standing at the base of it, looking up and going, "Wow! Look what we have built by the workmanship of our own hands! This is magnificent! We can see it must surely reach right up to heaven. We can just climb up there ourselves. And bring on the flood waters again. We've got it covered this time. We'll just climb our way to safety."

Then I tried to imagine it from God's perspective. I was just a couple of miles up, but even from my vantage point, the tower was small and insignificant. Then the tower switched to another tower in my mind's eye—some of the tallest towers in the world are bank towers. And I pictured all the money in the banks piled up in gold bricks around the tower. From my point of view, it was just a little speck down there. Then I tried to imagine how big the country was. I was maybe taking in 50 or 100 square miles. How far did the country go—for that matter, how big was 25,000 miles around the world! It was huge! And that little bank tower and all its gold bricks became even more of a speck.

Then I thought of the earth which seemed so huge and imagined it next to the sun and the earth became a dot. Then the whole solar system was put against the Milky Way and our Solar System became a dot. Then the Milky Way was put against the universe, and the Milky Way became a dot. And that bank tower and the Tower of Babel became a tiny particle of nothing.

Then came the impression of the contrast. As I looked around, I saw light as far as the eye could see. And I thought of how we're taught the Light of God fills the immensity of space. Think of the comparison between the little tower of gold and this Light. We use different words for this Light: Spirit of the Lord, Truth, Inspiration, Living Waters that when we drink this water, we never thirst again.

The effect of this Light upon us, the fruits of this spirit are Peace, Love, Joy and Understanding. These are its gifts. The Light is a pearl of great price, that the merchant would sell all he had to possess it.

In earth's economy, the richest person is the one with the most money. In heaven's economy, the richest person is the one with the greatest capacity for this endless Light and thereby the greatest capacity for Peace, Love and Joy.

So the question at hand is how do we increase our capacity for Light so that more of it can be released in the world? We see forces combining together to do works of darkness and destruction. Where are the forces that combine together to release light?

Helping our children to live lives of maximum joy is the purpose of this heart-based method of learning. So understanding the answer to this question is critical.

I believe those two forces are Heart and Mind working in combination, or in other words, the more the heart desires that which is good and beautiful and true, and the more the mind is willing to comply with true principles and laws, the greater the release of light in our lives. Take away either half of the combination, and the light is blocked. Let me try and build my case.

As I have stated before, we are a very mind-focused, academic-based culture. We lean heavily towards the Mind side of the combination. Let's do a quick review.

Remember how you can tell if you are in the realm of the mind? You can test and measure it. How far away is the sun? What is the population of New York? The mind feeds on facts and information. We associate Reason and Science with the mind which is concerned with discovering the laws, principles and rules by which the universe operates. The mind demands proof and hard evidence. Science and Mind are good.

The Heart on the other hand is immeasurable. How wide is joy? How deep is love? The heart is the place of desires, dreams and visions. The Arts—Music, Imagery, Poetry and Story—warm and open hearts and travel to a place deep within us that words alone cannot reach. Hard-heartedness blocks Light.

There is an order to this combination. Notice the heart develops before the brain within the womb and emotions develop before the intellect outside the womb. It appears Nature has reserved childhood for making impressions on the heart while it is open and uncluttered. And mothers are divinely gifted for this heart work.

As simple as the combination of Heart and Mind appears, the world has had a really hard time holding on to the balance. We lean towards one side or the other. Yet, history shows us that when Heart and Mind, Faith and Reason, Art and Science combine together in balance, there is a burst of light on the world. We call these Golden Ages.

Let me show you what I mean as I take you on a brief tour through history.

Let's first go back to 5th Century Ancient Greece which is known as the Golden Age of Greece. Here you find Socrates going around teaching people to think and question, functions of the mind. We see great dramatists such as Sophocles, Euripides, Aristophanes keeping the hearts of the people warm. Pericles is a wise ruler who has given the people wise rules to follow. But he is also a lover of the arts and he commissions buildings such as the Parthenon and the Acropolis that are built to the highest standards of math and engineering, but also crafted by artisans who love beauty. Heart and Mind. Even their ruins inspire us.

The Ancient Greeks are known for their love of beauty and truth and they continue to influence the world 2500 years later. Following a series of wars, the Greeks could sense their Golden Age was slipping and they started leaning towards the Mind to solve their problems. They reasoned that what they needed to do was to build large academies and teach the young men how to think and reason and persuade others. They hoped the academies would produce great leaders to lead them back to their Golden Age. But in the process, the heart was left behind. Not only did these academies fail to produce a single leader of note, the Greeks slipped into slavery, never to rise again.

Fast forward several hundred years. Now things have swung the other way and you find a people who are ruled by their hearts. The power players of the time are the storytellers and bards who know they can sway the people any way they want with their stories and songs. The people are driven by their fears based in superstitions and false traditions. We call it the Dark Ages. Only half the combination so the light is blocked.

Now go forward a few more hundred years to the 14th century when the intellectual writings of the Greeks made their way to Europe by way of Italy, and there is this wonderful rebirth which is what Renaissance means and another Golden Age where, for a time, Mind and Heart, Faith and Reason, Art and Science combine together. Look at the shining stars of the 1400s and 1500s: Michelangelo, Leonardo da Vinci, Shakespeare, Galileo, Copernicus, Kepler, Martin Luther. We see Columbus and all the explorers out looking for new worlds and possibilities. Light began to burst forth upon the earth.

And then, man looks around and says, "Man is magnificent! Look what we have accomplished by the workmanship of our own hands!" And they leave God and the heart behind and enter a new Age of Reason.

It was in this Age of Reason of the 18th Century that a tender-hearted, kind man arrives on the scene named Johann Heinrich Pestalozzi. He looks around and notices that for all the learning going on, it's not making anyone's lives any better. The people are miserable. Especially the children. The adults are so anxious for them to get into the Greek writings that they start hammering Greek into them almost as soon as they can talk.

And so a great desire grew in his heart. He wrote: "I wish to wrest education from...cheap, artificial teaching tricks, and entrust it to the eternal process of nature herself, to the light which God has kindled and kept alive in the hearts of fathers and mothers... Love is the sole and everlasting foundation in which to work."

He continued: "The primary law is this: the first instruction of the child should never be the business of the head or of the reason; it should always be the business of the…heart. It is for a long time the business of the heart, before it is the business of reason."

He was given charge over a classroom of orphans and started incorporating the tools of the heart—Story, Song, Pictures, and Rhymes even though he didn't have much to work with. Even then there were school administrators who stopped by. "Mr. Pestalozzi. Where are your test scores?" And Pestalozzi would say, "Look around! The children are happy! They're engaged in learning! They're teaching each other!" Yet he would be given the stern look of disapproval.

Through his work, Pestalozzi came to realize that the mother is the most effective educator of the heart. He wrote: The eternal laws of nature lead me back to your hand, Mother." He faced bitter opposition to the idea his whole life.

One of his followers was a man name Friederich Froebel who also understood it was the mothers who were the most important teachers of the heart. The problem was the mothers were overworked and exhausted just trying to keep their families alive. He knew they weren't likely to add one more thing to their lives. But he noticed it was usually the oldest daughter in the family who had charge of the younger ones. So he thought, "What if we open a school and invite these older girls to bring their younger siblings and teach them together so that when they become mothers, they will be prepared." He felt it may take three generations to implement the idea. So he created the Kinder-garten or Child-garden—a place to grow children, and the first classes were formed to train future mothers.

Love was to be the keystone. Froebel described the activities of this kindergarten: "Free play, several sorts of handiwork suited to little children, going for walks, learning music, both instrumental and vocal, learning the repetition of poetry, storytelling, looking at really good pictures; aiding in domestic occupations, gardening."

The years went by and the little mothers had children of their own, and these children were the ones that formed the first, actual kindergarten. Also these were the mothers who formed the first mothers' clubs. And it was the success of these clubs that attracted the attention of the authorities, who could not imagine any other purpose for a club than to hatch a plot against the government.

Officials thought, here comes a man who thinks he knows more than all the priests and scholars who ever lived, and fills the heads of fool women with the idea that they are born to teach instead of to work in the fields and keep house and wait on men.

If this thing keeps on, men will have to get off the earth and women and children will run the world and do it by means of play! This thing has got to stop before Germany becomes the joke of mankind. And so, in 1850, an interdict was placed on Friederich Froebel, making Kindergarten a crime.

His ideas were spreading—success, at last, was at the door. He had interested the women and proved the fitness of women to teach—his mothers' clubs were numerous—love was the watchword. And in the midst of this flowering time, the official order came, without warning, apology or explanation, and from which there was no appeal. It crushed the life and broke the heart of Friederich Froebel.

The chapter I gleaned this from closed with these words: "Men who govern should be those with a reasonable doubt concerning their own infallibility, and an earnest faith in men, women and children. To teach is better than to rule. We are all children in the Kindergarten of God."

I like that.

So here we are again, trying to convince mothers that they possess God-given gifts to do what no one else can do better. And that learning is best begun in play, in poetry, in story, picture, singing and music, and spending time in nature. And it may yet take three more generations to get the idea firmly planted because it seems we have to keep starting over! Pestalozzi said it may take 300 years to get his idea to take hold. Can we be the generation that finally gets it right?

Although Pestalozzi and Froebel felt like failures in their lifetimes, their writings continued to influence other educators into the 19th century, like Charlotte Mason who wrote, "We allow no separation to grow up between the intellectual and spiritual life of children, but teach them that the Divine Spirit has constant access to their spirits, and is their continual helper in all the interests, duties and joys of life." She taught that True education is between a child's soul and God.

Maria Montessori was also influenced by Pestalozzi. On the opening day of her school in one of the poorest sections of Rome, she read from Isaiah: "Arise, shine, for the Light is come and the glory of the Lord is risen upon thee." At the conclusion of her speech, she added, "Perhaps it may be that this children's Home may become a New Jerusalem, which, as it is multiplied...will bring *light* into education." She was criticized and asked what she meant, and she replied that she scarcely knew.

Pestalozzi also influenced Rudolf Steiner who created the Waldorf methodology and schools, still popular today.

And then something wonderful happened.

There was a group of intellectual giants—men and women—who were scholars in history, literature, nature, art and music. These are the great souls who have been my mentors. As they came to understand the importance of stories to warm and open children's hearts, they wrapped their great knowledge into stories for young people and loaded them with principles for happy living and fed children's hearts with desires for the love of the good and the beautiful and a faith in God. It's not uncommon to read in their prefaces things like: Dear boys and girls. I love you. I want you to be happy.

The years from 1880 to 1920 are known as a Golden Age of Children's Literature that you have heard me talk about—the balance of Heart and Mind, Faith and Reason, Art and Science.

Then something else wonderful started to happen. The mothers started doing what mothers do—they started gathering and organizing and forming study groups to re-learn the lost arts of storytelling in their homes and there was a great storytelling revival in the early 1900s. Then, realizing the importance of educating a woman's heart for her important role as heart educator, and recognizing the difficulty for her to go away to college, the Delphian Society was formed in 1910 with the intent to bring college home to busy mothers who could only study a few minutes a day.

The Delphian Reading Course was the equivalent to a bachelor's degree in Classic Studies and included a study of History, Literature, Philosophy, Poetry, Fiction, Drama, Art, Ethics, Music,

Nature Study and more. As women studied the great civilizations of the world, it included a look at home life and education. The focus was on culture—'To know the best that has been thought and said in the world' with the aim of personal improvement of each member, who, in turn, would lift all of society. It was about making of the mind "a mansion of all lovely thoughts."

Women formed study groups and met once a month to have conversations about what they were learning and they became a cultural uplift to their communities. Within a few years, over 2000 groups dotted the nation and were found in every major city.

Is it a coincidence that the generation that followed is known as The Greatest Generation?

Continuing with the tour of history, then came the 1920s and 30s and once again Man said, "Isn't Man magnificent" and an educator named John Dewey changed the course of education for decades to come. His intentions were revealed in a document to which he affixed his name in 1933: the Humanist Manifesto which declares, "Reason and intelligence are the most effective instruments that humankind possesses. There is no substitute." And by the way, there is no God.

We have entered another age of reason, of facts and information, scientific proof and evidence, test and measure. And something has happened that Hans Christian Andersen warned would happen if the mind ruled. Remember the story of the Snow Queen I shared earlier? Our world has turned upside down—that which was bad is now seen as good and that which was good is now seen as bad; every fault is magnified and every good is mocked.

I hope you can begin to see why the call for more Math and Science, more rigorous academics, more focus on STEM subjects, the introduction of academics at earlier and earlier ages and our obsession with test scores is actually fueling our problems.

We are trying the failed solution of the Greeks.

But here's what I can't stop thinking about. This is the extraordinary event I can see just over the horizon. What if we can hold on to this height of intellect? They tell us knowledge is doubling every 72 hours! What if we can combine this height of mind with a proportionate depth of heart? Would we not expect to see a new burst of light upon the world and the entrance into a Golden Age unlike the world has ever seen?

Look at what technology has gifted us in just the last fifteen years to make this combination of Heart and Mind possible.

We have been gifted the finest literature that has ever been written, written by the greatest souls who have ever lived.

In the 10th century, a princess gave 200 sheep, a load of wheat, a load of rye, a load of millet and several costly furs for one copy of a German monk's writing.

In 1999, Internet Archive was formed for the purpose of digitizing every book that has ever been written and posting it online for anyone to read for free. There are now over 25 million books available in the online library and they are adding a thousand books a day which gives us instant access to the thoughts and ideas of the greatest men and women who have ever lived.

Part of that great harvest of books includes the children and young adult books included in Libraries of Hope and the writings of the heart educators I share in the Mother's University. The recent availability of their writings is enabling us to re-learn the lost arts of educating hearts of children which have disappeared in our obsession with the mind. Along the way, technology gifted us with a tablet to make the reading of these treasures convenient and portable.

We have been gifted with access to fine art.

In the 15th Century, when the great Florentine artist Cimabue completed his Madonna, the shops were closed, workmen dropped their tools, farmers left their tasks, the soldiers were released from the camp, all the people assembled in the streets; the artist was borne on the shoulders of the multitude, the picture was lifted up and carried at the head of a procession that marched with music and banners and tumultuous shouts toward the church, where the canvas was hung that all might feast their eyes upon its loveliness.

All that for one painting.

Today I can do a Google search and pull off hundreds of thousands of masterpieces of art that have been hidden away in private estates, museums and palaces around the world.

We have been gifted with the Masterpieces of Music.

YouTube has only been around since 2005, but now I can pull up just about any great masterpiece of music and watch it performed by the finest musicians around the world. I get front row seats to the Bolshoi Ballet and the Metropolitan Opera. When I get ready to do my dishes, I can invite Leonard Bernstein into my kitchen, along with his entire symphony orchestra and give him a playlist to play for me. In surround sound. Without charge. And if he plays something I really love, I can ask him to play it again.

The kings and queens of yesterday, with all their wealth and power, could not have had the kind of heart education now delivered to the humblest home, for free. This is an education fit for a royal generation of a Golden Age.

I see just one missing piece for this combination of heart and mind to happen. And for that missing piece, I need to go back to the Golden Age of Ancient Greece. Scholars attribute the opening of this age to a poet named Pindar who awakened a desire for beauty in the hearts of the Greeks through his poetry. But who awakened that desire in Pindar? I found the answer in an old children's book. Pindar's teachers as a youth were two women—Clyrtis and Myrna—two renowned singers who sang songs into his heart.

What we need now is a generation of mothers who can sing songs into the hearts of their children and awaken their desire to feast on this great harvest of the ages that has just been delivered to their homes, free for their use. But who will sing the songs into the mother's hearts for it will be out of the abundance and treasures of their hearts that the children will be fed.

Tending to mother's hearts is what is behind the Mother's University at The Well-Educated Heart. We have everything we need to cultivate our hearts and the hearts of our children. I see mothers picking up the work where it was left off a hundred years ago while we took a detour. But we needed this little detour. We needed this reign of the mind for technology to thrive and make it possible for the work to continue.

Look at the labor-saving devices given you to free up your time for this work of cultivating hearts. You can put your dirty clothes in a washing machine, push a button and walk away. You can put your dirty dishes in a dishwasher, push a button and walk away. You can put dinner in the microwave and 5 minutes later, you're ready for dinner. Our great grandmothers must look upon our generation with envy.

But where much is given, much is expected.

You are the first generation of mothers to arrive on the scene when all things have been prepared to usher in the next stage. I believe angels are standing by ready to assist you in this important work. A little leaven, a little salt, even a single candle in a dark room can make a difference. By small and simple means, great things will come to pass.

Music

"Music makes people more gentle and meek, more modest and understanding." --Martin Luther

What a glorious gift music is to our souls. It's the great awakener of feelings; some call it the 'quickening art.' Music is the first language we can use to communicate with the hearts of our children, long before they understand words. It's a universal language that speaks directly to the heart because it is pure emotion. It travels to a place in our souls where words alone cannot reach. The ancient Greek orators understood this so they always had musicians who played while they spoke because they knew the music would carry their messages deeper into the hearts of their listeners. Those who make movies know how important music is to stir emotions. What would the movie Jaws be without the soundtrack?

In days past, the music on the battleground was necessary to keep the hearts of the soldiers stirred up and filled with hope. Throughout much of history, music was used as medicine. Today, doctors are rediscovering music as a pain reliever when prescription drugs fail.

Music requires no middle man to explain it as demonstrated by an experience shared by Dr. Karl Paulnack, Director of Music at Boston Conservatory. He and a violinist friend opened a performance at a nursing home in Fargo, North Dakota, with a piece written by Aaron Copland who had dedicated it to a young friend of his, a young pilot, who was shot down during World War II. They played the number with no explanation. Midway through the piece, an elderly man in a wheelchair near the front of the hall began to weep.

Before they started to play their second number, they stopped to tell a little about the piece they had just played and explained the circumstances under which Copland wrote the music and how he had dedicated it to a downed pilot. At the mention of this, the elderly man broke down in sobs and needed to be taken out of the hall.

Later the man was brought backstage, tears and all, to explain himself, as he shared:

"During World War II, I was a pilot, and I was in an aerial combat situation where one of my team's planes was hit. I watched my friend bail out, and watched his parachute open, but the Japanese planes that had engaged us returned and machine gunned across the parachute chords so as to separate the parachute from the pilot, and I watched my friend drop away into the ocean, realizing that he was lost. I have not thought about this for many years, but during that first piece of music you played, this memory returned to me so vividly that it was as though I was reliving it. I didn't understand why this was happening, why now, but then when you came out to explain that this piece of music was written to commemorate a lost pilot, it was a little more than I could handle."

This is the powerful language of music.

I think we have no greater example of the great gift of music to the human soul than among our former slaves. The degradation and suffering of our African brothers and sisters fills us with sorrow and remorse that they had to pass through such an ordeal. Yet, in their day of great trial, they showed the world that God can plant songs in the heart that make the unbearable, bearable.

The slaves sang while they worked in the fields and while they cooked their food over their fires. They sang to their babies in the cradles and over the graves of their dead. They sang their joy and their sorrow.

I came across a couple of old books written by people who interviewed the slaves themselves and recorded their thoughts and impressions in regards to their music. One writer wrote that singing so filled them with the spirit, "that they forget they are working if they just keep singing all the time." Their music was their life saver.

Their music linked their souls to God, as expressed by another writer who wrote, "In questioning great numbers of ex-slaves, I have yet to find one who does not implicitly believe that God himself inspired the words of all their religious hymns." Down in old Kentucky was an old uncle who everyone respected. When he was asked where the songs came from, this is what he said: "Us old heads used ter make 'em up on de spur of de moment after we wrastled wid the Spirit and come 'thoo,' but da tunes was brung from Africky, by our own granddaddies...Dese days dey call em ballotts, but in de old days dey calls 'em spirituals; case de Holy Spirit done teached 'em ter us."

They said that the memory and knowledge of the Bible among the slaves was simply miraculous; that if for some reason the Bible was lost to us, we could look to these old "spirituals" to restore much of its content.

As further evidence of heavenly inspiration, in all the slaves' songs, there is not the tiniest trace or even a hint of hatred or revenge. Their music appears to have been a divine gift to their race as a means of enduring the refiner's fire they were called upon to endure. As a side note, interestingly, their music is even played on a unique scale. While most songs today are built on a scale of do, re, mi, fa, so, la, ti, do, their music was built on just a 5-note scale, meaning all their songs can be played using only the black keys on the piano. It was, in every way, music of their very own, yet it has enriched all of us.

So why am I telling you all this? The answer is simple. The song of the heart that gave joy to the slave in the middle of so much sorrow can lift and bless the lives of all children. We, too, can make work lighter by singing. We, too, can plant truths in the hearts of our children with song. And we can trust that if we should ever have to endure hardships, God has the power to plant songs in our hearts to see us through, if our hearts are soft enough to hear.

Music not only awakens emotion, it creates a sense of order and well-being through its rhythm. Why else do we rock babies? Our hearts beat thousands of times every day. Its steady beat allows us to go about our business without ever thinking about it. It's only when it occasionally skips a beat that we even pay attention to it. The rhythm of day and night, day and night helps to bring order to life. Mothers who establish the rhythm of routine generally have children who are more content. People who have had strokes have had memories restored by applying the ordering properties of music. I'm a pacer when I think. When I have an idea I'm trying to work through, I pace all over the house. I'm afraid my family makes fun of me for it. It wasn't until I thought about this idea of rhythm as the great organizer that it hit me why I naturally do this. The pacing helps me bring order to my thoughts.

We are all deeply and profoundly musical in this way. If you question that, try walking across the room out of rhythm. Try applauding out of rhythm. For that matter, try to say anything arrhythmically. I bet you can't do it even with great effort and concentration. You'll always fall back to the rhythm.

If the rhythm of music is separated from melody and harmony, however, instead of feeling depth of emotion, it has the opposite effect: it shuts down feeling. A loud steady repetitive beat can even shut down thinking. I read the story of a young boy who was forced to become a child-soldier in the Sierra Leone conflict a few years ago. He described how they blasted loud rock music over the speakers in their camp twenty-four hours a day because it kept them from thinking or feeling anything. That's the only way they could stir them up to kill which they never would have done in their right minds. You see the same thing happening among primitive tribes on the warpath who worked themselves up to a frenzy with the steady strong beat of their war dance.

In contrast, the great composers of the 18th and 19th centuries were called Master musicians because they discovered and mastered the rules of music that made it possible for us to feel emotions we had never felt before. And their greatest desire was to reveal to the human heart the very glory of God. I'm afraid music has gone downhill since then to where more often than not, it's been reduced to three chords and a beat, and sometimes we don't even bother with the three chords. Often, instead of feeling deeply, we feel nothing. Classical music is too rich for the average man's taste; to a large degree, he has become desensitized to its language. The objective of music education in a well-educated heart is not to help your child score better on his SAT or get into medical college, although it's been proven to do that; it's to help children feel at home with the rich and beautiful language of music because a love of fine music offers a lifetime of joy and a depth of feeling.

And it starts the day your baby is born.

When you hold a little baby in your arms, you may think to yourself, "I can hardly wait until he gets old enough to teach him." Usually that means you can hardly wait until he starts talking so you can communicate with him. But the impressions on the heart start from the day of birth. Music is the first language your baby will recognize and through music, you can start communicating truth and beauty from the day you first hold him in your arms. In fact, singing is one of the most effective means of communicating with little children. Babies are born into a chaotic and noisy world and your singing gives him a first sense of order and well-being by the rhythm and a sense of calm by the melody. Even newborns can discern between harmonic chords and dissonant chords. Dissonance makes them fussy.

So we quite naturally start with lullabies. If the only lullaby in your repertoire is Rock-a-bye

Baby, expand it by searching online for more lullabies or get hold of the Wee Sing Series Lullabye book. Learn them by heart—they're not hard. The digital sounds from your swing may be soothing, but they aren't the same as the vibration they feel when you sing or hum them yourself. Singing to your baby is your first bonding experience. If you have older children, teach them lullabies to sing to their new brother or sister.

We learn the language of music much as we learn the language of words: by exposure. If you want to make sure your children don't get stuck in the Dick and Jane equivalent of music, let them hear the best of classical music from the days of their birth. Your objective is to make the finest music feel familiar.

Let them listen to the real thing. I have a problem with well-intentioned programs like Little Einstein intros to classical music because, to me, it cheapens the music. Now when I hear a certain beautiful classic piece of music, my mind immediately inserts, "Little plane, little plane to the rescue." The same thing happened in my childhood. A lot of the old cartoons used classical music and it's still hard to dis-associate them from Bugs Bunny or Elmer Fudd and let the music speak directly to my heart.

For the first four years or so, look for music for the Familiar years—songs about home and family, bunnies, eyes and hands. Toddlers enjoy classical animal music like Peter and the Wolf or Saint Saens Carnival of Animals. Let singing be a normal course of day—sing while you get your baby dressed or change his diapers; while you're driving in the car; while you're feeding him. Don't ever make it a formal, "Now, I'm going to teach you a new song." Young children have amazing memories, and as you sing the songs, they'll pick them up very naturally. Remember, toddlers fall in love with the musicality of the words before they pick up the meaning, so silly songs that don't mean anything are extremely pleasurable at this age. Wee Sing has a great selection of silly songs to learn.

Another wonderful free resource for children's songs is the Children's Songbook at lds.org. There are a few songs in there that are particular to my faith, but most of the selections have universal appeal. Besides songs of faith, you'll find songs about helping mommy, enjoying nature and being happy. I have such a fun memory of 5-year-old Madison skipping down the street on a first sunshiny day of spring, singing, "I think the world is glorious and lovely as can be...I sing, and sing, and sing, and sing my thanks to God above." What a wonderful gift we give our children when we give them a way of expressing what their hearts feel. Words just wouldn't have been enough.

There are also many songs in there that will start planting truths in their hearts. We use music to teach the ABC's because we know it will stick; why limit it to memorizing state capitals and multiplication tables when we can plant truths that will teach them happy living? When children are little, you can't explain with words concepts like loving and sharing. But they can readily feel them with music. And a lot of the truths you plant with song at this young age will remain lifelong companions; phrases like these will suddenly float through their minds at just the right moment, even when they're very, very old:

Jesus said love everyone, treat them kindly, too; when your heart is filled with love, others will love you.

Give said the little stream, Give oh give, Give oh give.

Whenever I hear the song of a bird or look at the blue, blue sky...I know Heavenly Father loves me.

In fact, it may be these songs planted in childhood that will bring moments of re-connection if dementia should set in in older years.

Another wonderful feature of the children's songbook at lds.org is that you can listen to the songs online so you know how they go. They're all free. Many of the songs are even sung in Spanish, French or Portuguese if you want to expose your children to foreign languages when they're little, which is a good idea because, again, they pick up on the musicality of words which makes learning foreign languages much easier.

Just one more thought before I move off these familiar songs of home and family; when I was taking piano lessons, I remember my teacher taught me that all music has a home chord and that I wouldn't feel satisfied until I was back home again. My daughter who plays the piano beautifully sometimes still teases me by leaving the final chord off a piece she is playing and walking away from the piano because she knows I will come from wherever I am in the house to play that final home chord. We are born with a longing for home…like Wordsworth wrote, "Trailing clouds of glory do we come from heaven, which is our home." Lately, I've noticed a lot of recent songs leave you hanging in the air...they just end. They never go home. Is that reflective of a culture that devalues home and family? Just thinking out loud.

You might want to check out a wonderful TED talk given by Benjamin Zander that demonstrates this idea of music going "home." I've linked it in the resources.

The Imaginative Years, around ages 4 to 8, are great for introducing musicals. If you play the music around the house so that it's familiar to them, they'll enjoy the movies so much more when you show them to them. Play the music from musicals while kids are doing chores or doing copy work or just as background music in the house. The music from most musicals is lighthearted and energizing.

Also, as you tell them Fairy Tales, introduce them to the opera, ballet or symphonic versions such as Rossini's La Cenerentola based on Cinderella or Tchaikovsky's Swan Lake, Sleeping Beauty or Nutcracker. Their attention span may not be long enough to take in the whole thing, so pick out a part you think they'll like and after they watch it, let them dance to it. Expect repeat performances...many of them! As they watch ballet, you are not only giving them a pleasurable experience, you're giving their hearts an impression of grace and elegance.

Start telling them the stories of operas at this age. I've gathered several of them in the Stories of Operas book in the Nature, Art and Music Series. Mozart's Magic Flute is a favorite even of little children or they might enjoy Hansel and Gretel or Amahl and the Night Visitors. As you tell them stories from Arabian Nights, let them listen to the music from Sheherezade. Again, don't force it. If they're not interested yet, keep finding opportunities to play the music in the background and try again later.

Continue singing songs with them from the Wee Sing Series and Children's Songbook. You may well have hundreds of songs ready-to-go, but if your song bucket is a bit empty, try and learn at least one new song a week and soon you'll have dozens to draw from. Time passes fast in the car when you're singing.

And now on to the Heroic years, around ages 8-12 or 14. These are the years you'll be learning about countries all over the world, so what better way to start preparing than learning folk songs. Folks songs truly convey the spirit of a people. Very few of them can be traced back to a single person; they just seem to spring up in hearts and get passed around until everyone is singing them and as your children start singing the same songs, they'll get caught up in the spirit of the country they're studying. Wee Sing Series has a book dedicated to folk songs around the world. Also, YouTube makes it possible to immerse yourselves in the musical flavor of each country. I've linked several options to start with on the Enrichment pages. You can play balalaika music from Russia or guitar music from Spain. This would also be enjoyable background music while they're working on notebooking or other projects. Many of the YouTubes I've linked have slide shows attached to them with scenes from the various countries.

I've also linked YouTubes of favorite classical pieces in the Music section on the Enrichment pages. Sometimes it's linked to a certain country because the composer was from there and other times I linked it because it had something to do with that country's culture or history. For instance, although Dvorak wasn't an American composer, his New World symphony was all about America, so it's connected to America. I'll continue to update these. I try to find world renowned symphonies or conductors and either choose YouTubes that bring children up close and personal to the musicians and conductor or that attach fine art or appropriate images to the music.

Learning the folk music of our own country will bring many of the events to life. American Folk Songs for Children by Ruth Crawford Seeger is probably one of the best modern collections. I've also linked some older books online in the library where you will find stories of hymns, folk songs, and other music. Telling the story behind the music helps your children love the music even more.

Now more than ever, our children need to learn and sing our national songs and know the stories behind them. National anthems are not meant to be performed. They are meant to provide a way for a people to unite their voices together. What other activity can a large group of people all participate in at the same time? Anthems can be a powerful unifier when the song expresses a feeling of the heart. Look up The Singing Revolution and see how a people freed themselves from fifty years of Communist rule by uniting their voices together in their national songs.

Shakespeare warns us:

> The man that hath no music in himself,
> Nor is not moved with concord of sweet sounds,
> Is fit for treasons, stratagems and spoils.

At this age, you might want to spend time learning hymns. I believe hymns link us to heaven like nothing else can. As you read the stories behind many of the most favorite hymns, you'll learn how often hymns came as a gift; that composers hurried to write down the words and melody that flowed through them. A couple of our daughters had a friend who passed away as a young husband and father. Before he died, he requested that a particular hymn be sung by the congregation at his funeral. At the services, his widow explained that he told her this was the hymn the angels sang to comfort him as they surrounded his hospital bed in his final days. On the tragic night the Titanic sank, the ship's musicians tried to calm the panicked passengers by playing hymns. They volunteered to remain on board, playing their music to the end. It is said "Nearer My God to Thee" was their final offering just before they sank with the ship. And as Jesus led his disciples to Gethsemane, they sang a hymn. Hymns can bring great comfort, courage, hope and strength to the hearts of our children, if they know them. And they can bind the hearts of families together as they sing them together.

The heroic years is the time to start telling the stories of the lives of the great composers. Younger children will enjoy listening to stories of them when they were children, like themselves. I've especially looked for stories of great composers when they were young to include in the Stories of Great Musicians volume. As your children learn their stories, you can select music that corresponds with the musician they're studying about. I'm sure much of the music will already be familiar to them because you will have been playing it for years. But now they'll connect it to the composer who wrote it. I've linked many additional biographies for young and advanced readers in the online library. When they're a little older, they will appreciate Kavanaugh's Spiritual Lives of the Great Composers and at the end of each chapter are recommendations of music to listen to.

Children this age are old enough now to start learning the secrets behind the magic of music—the rules. Years ago, Leonard Bernstein presented a number of Young People's Concerts that were televised and were very popular. These programs can help your children enjoy learning about the orchestra and help them have a greater understanding of fine music. There were over fifty of these programs and half of them are linked in the Mother's University when you study music. The entire series is available on DVD and, in my opinion, is a worthwhile investment. Or I'm sure you can find them through interlibrary loans. These classic videos are highly recommended.

If you have teenagers who have already developed a deaf ear towards classical music, you might enjoy a classic article from 1955 in the Reader's Digest which I've linked in the Mother's University. It's written by a journalist who disliked classical music, but after a chance encounter with Albert Einstein, became a big fan. It's been a popular article for a long time.

Age 8 is usually when children are admitted to live performances. Many local symphonies put on children's concerts on a regular basis that will especially appeal to a younger audience. If you've spent time telling opera stories and listening to the music, your children might enjoy going to a Fathom Event at your local theatre where the Metropolitan Opera broadcasts live performances. Unless, of course, you happen to be in New York where you can take them to the real thing. These are lavish productions with beautiful costuming and scenery. Many of these performances are also available on DVD or can be viewed through YouTube.

Also, as you start to learn the history of countries, you can tie in a study of the history of music in your rotation schedule.

As your children's love of great music grows deeper, some of them will want to study and will now be willing to pay the price to discover its secrets and its rules in greater depth.

And now I want to spend a couple of minutes talking about music lessons. Should all children take music lessons? I think so. But I personally would never force them. I have too many scarred friends who associate music with a very painful experience. And even more, I see too many music students who walk away from their instrument as soon as they leave home. They never connect playing an instrument to an inherently pleasurable experience or as a lifelong companion. Furthermore, they can't see the use of it if they never reach performance level to which I emphatically say, if you are the only one who ever hears yourself play, the lessons are worth it. Playing an instrument can be one of life's greatest joys.

Warming the heart up to the idea is the most important first step and one way you can do that is to make playing an instrument up close and personal. If you have a college or university nearby with a music department, visit the department and see if they would be willing to recommend students who may be willing to come to your home and give mini-performances. Or ask some local music teachers if they have some advanced students who would like an opportunity to perform. Invite a couple of other families over and have a pot-luck dinner. Warm home-cooked meals can be pretty enticing to college students! Have your performers keep it relatively short so your children don't get bored and ask them to play selections with children in mind. It's better to have your kids ask for more than to wonder when it is ever going to end. Over time, invite singers, violinists, harpists, trumpet players, guitarists and flutists and combinations of all the above. Show your children that music is shared among friends and not always performed on a stage. Keep it informal and friendly. Chances are, one of them will ignite a passion for an instrument. And who knows...maybe in some future day you will find you've entertained a future performing star unawares.

Or you can contact local music teachers and find out when their recitals are.

Consider making the learning of an instrument a family affair. As your children watch mom or dad practicing an instrument, you are communicating its value. You are demonstrating it's not just for kids. You are showing them what practicing looks like. And your home will be filled with music.

I like the idea of everyone starting on a keyboard instrument because it's like being a one-man orchestra where you can create your own harmonies. Also, just by pressing the key, you produce a pleasing sound. It may be awhile before you can make a sound anyone but your mother would enjoy from a violin or oboe. So a piano is a nice place to start. I play the piano but I wish I had also learned an ensemble instrument for the thrill of joining with others to create beautiful music.

Unfortunately, traditional piano lessons have a tremendous failure rate—they produce far too few children who stick with it long enough to have music as a lifelong companion or a means of expressing one's self musically. I have come to believe the problem lies in the fact that most traditional music methods are reading based. Reading music is complex and most children quit before they become proficient. It's like trying to teach the mechanics of reading books without the benefit of stories beforehand. Which is why I am happy to see many new programs emerge that are play-based rather than reading-based. In my mind, they fit more in the Pattern for Learning.

Another problem with traditional reading-based lessons is the student usually ends up only being able to play music that is written by someone else rather than music of their own creation. Take away the sheet music, and they can play nothing. I like a method where a child is able to explore and discover before he is immersed in the rules and scales.

In a heart-based education, learning to share talents with others is as important as learning to play the instrument. Helping a child find informal ways to share the gift of music rather than making it purely a performance art would spread music wider in our world and would better integrate it into our culture. Musicians are heart healers.

The story I told you earlier of the WWII vet was part of a welcome speech to a new class of musicians at the conservatory. I really like this message that was delivered in the same address: "Someone is going to walk into your concert hall and bring you a mind that is confused, a heart that is overwhelmed, a soul that is weary. Whether they go out whole again will depend partly on how well you do your craft."

That's good advice for a well-educated heart.

And now I'll let Confucius have the last word: “Harmony has the power to draw Heaven downwards to the earth. It inspires men to love the good, and to do their duty. If one should desire to know whether a kingdom is well governed, if its morals are good or bad, the quality of its music shall furnish forth the answers.”

How do you think we're doing?

The Power of Music

A young woman was dying. Her baby had died at birth a few weeks previously, and since that time the mother had steadily failed. The doctor had just left her room saying emphatically that there was no hope and to give her anything she wanted.

She looked up at her agonized husband and said: "Music. I want music. I know that will cure me." The nurse thought it to be a foolhardy and useless errand, but the husband went in search of it.

The first day old familiar tunes and some of the Chopin that she had always loved, were played softly to her. Her body relaxed under the soothing influence, her nerves became less tense, her breathing deeper and more rhythmical, increasing the circulation. That night she slept. With the shutting out of the senses to the outside world the harmonic reaction brought about by the music continued its work of healing all through the night. The next day she was visibly stronger.

Halfway through World War I, music began to be used on a large scale "to help organize victory." How the men craved music. A victrola was carried lovingly from front lines to hospital. Music was used in every conceivable form as a comfort, as a relaxation from the horrors of war, and as a stimulus to the morale of the men. It acquired all the sacredness of a ministering angel.

Music was used to unite the soldiers in the Civil War. Isn't it telling that both sides were singing the Battle Hymn of Freedom?

Florence Nightingale requested music for hospitals in the Crimean War. The mind blurred by contact with unspeakable horrors was quieted and made normal again.

"There is something wonderful in music. Words are wonderful enough, but music is more wonderful. It speaks not to our thoughts as words do; it speaks straight to our hearts and spirits, to the very core and root of our souls. Music soothes, us, stirs us up, it puts noble feelings into us; it melts us to tears, we know not how. It is language by itself, just as perfect in its way as speech, as words, just as divine, just as blessed."

This "heavenly Maid" is a chief restorer of our mental and physical equilibrium. Music has the power to solve many of our problems for us.

Sadly, it is being misused. Music has become a performing art. Ask someone if he or she is musical, and if that person does not play a musical instrument or sing, the answer will be no. Yet, every one of us is deeply and profoundly musical. If you don't believe me, try walking to your next class out of rhythm. Try saying something arrhythmically—it's practically impossible. We involuntarily sense the home or keynote of music. Without the last note, we would feel incomplete, almost like we're left dangling out there. We long for home.

> God is its author, and not man; he laid
> The keynote of all harmonies; he planned

All perfect combinations, and he made
Us so we could hear and understand.

Certain combinations of notes make us feel sad, others hopeful, others give us longing. Music cheers, comforts, refines and elevates. Music is a means by which we can turn chaos into calm. Think of that next time the noise level of your home climbs to an unbearable level. Music can instantly change our moods.

One of the heart educators wrote: "It seems extravagant to claim that, if everyone could be shown how to follow a tune and remember it, the world's unrest would be ameliorated, but this would seem to be a fact, nevertheless. Because, by doing so, each individual would become conscious of the harmony within himself.

"Yet we have worked many centuries to squeeze all the joy out of listening to music by making the means of enjoyment more and more complex, until now, when we find ourselves starving in spite of the abundance about us... After starving our music sense, and trying our best, by wrong methods, to transform our reaction to it into a lifeless, analytical and empty thing, instead of the warm, glowing healthful reaction it should be, it is time we start working to put it all back again into its rightful place as a joy giver.

"Through music, the mind is stilled to outside influences and becomes a reflector for the inner light which comes only through stillness. Faith comes when the chaotic thoughts of the outside world are stilled. Music can do that."

But not all music. Some music relies so heavily on beat, that while it may get our toes tapping and our heels dancing, it does not have the power to stir our souls and in its coarseness, causes us to dull those refined sensitivities that bridge heaven and earth. Music is made up of melody, rhythm and harmonies and causes us to feel things deeply. But repetitive beat without melody has the opposite effect—it shuts down thought and feeling.

An interesting experiment was done with plants. One group of plants were placed in a room filled with classical music. The other group of plants were placed with heavy rock. Go Google it and you can see the outcome. Show it to your kids.

Music is vibration. It affects us at a deep level, because at our deepest level, we are vibration. Helen Keller loved listening to music even though she was completely deaf. She felt it through the vibration. She was being interviewed for a magazine article in her home and Helen took her interviewer into the room where her radio was. She turned it on and placed her hand on it and smiled—Ahh... Beethoven's Moonlight Sonata. And she said, "Isn't that interesting that a man who was deaf composed this music so a blind woman could see the moonlight?"

The intention of many of the great music masters was to reveal the very glory of God to the human heart—but many of our youth—and adults—have closed their ears. May I offer a couple of suggestions for opening those ears as illustrated in an article that appeared in the Reader's Digest over 50 years ago. It was written by a young journalist who had been invited to the home of a wealthy philanthropist. After dinner, the guests retired to a large room for an evening of chamber music. This young man said he was tone deaf and music meant nothing to him. It was almost painful. So, as the music started to play, he closed his ears and thought about other things.

After the first number, the man next to him asked, "You are fond of Bach?" He hadn't noticed that he was sitting next to Albert Einstein himself! He admitted he knew nothing of him upon which Einstein took him by the arm, led him out of the room, upstairs to a study. "Now then," he said. "Tell me a song you love." He named a Bing Crosby song and Einstein found the song on a record which he played and when it was done, said, "Now. Sing it back to me," which he did to the best of his ability and Einstein's warm eyes lit up. He continued doing the same with song after song until Einstein played a record of music without words and told his young friend to hum it back, which he did. Einstein smiled and said, "Now we're ready for Bach." He led him back down to the hall and whispered, "Just allow yourself to listen. That's all."

The writer said to this day, Bach's Sheep May Safely Graze is one of his favorite pieces of music as he heard it for the first time that night, and which became the gateway to a great love of music.

Notice the two take-away lessons here. #1: Familiarity with music helps us love it. And #2: If the realm of music is to be entered through hearing, one must begin by being able to focus on the melody. One way is to draw a pitch picture, either in the air or on paper. As you practice paying attention to melody—the habit of attention—it will be etched in the memory and can be recalled and reimagined at will, protecting us from feelings and thoughts that are destructive.

Afterwards, the hostess apologized that Einstein had missed so much of the evening's performance. Einstein replied, "My young friend and I were engaged in the greatest activity of which man is capable. We were opening up yet another fragment on the frontier of beauty."

You can open up yet another fragment on the frontier of beauty by engaging in the same activities. Make classical music familiar to your children by playing it in your homes from the days of their birth. Play it because you want to hear it. And then, find those moments to help them practice focusing on the melody. I included a lot of classical music children will love in the Enrichment sections. And you will see some that has a story with it. Most of these stories are linked to old North Carolina Symphony Children's Concerts notes. It's just a paragraph or two of something interesting about the composer or the piece that will add delight to the music as your children listen to it. You'll find other books to further music appreciation on the Music Appreciation page. And I love Leonard Bernstein's Young People's Concerts, as mentioned previously.

I often hear moms regret that they can't afford music lessons for their children. To them I say music is a free art. Your children are gifted with their first and most important instrument—their voices. Don't underestimate the blessing that song will add to their lives. It's that connection between mind and emotion. It will open pathways to the heart. The hard heart can't sing. Remember Captain Von Trapp in the Sound of Music? When he discovered his song again, he reconnected with the joys all around him, especially his family. But maybe the reverse is also true— singing keeps us from growing hard hearts.

Don't make it a lesson—be a singing mother. Be a singing family. How many activities can people join together at once? Not many! But singing is one of them. It will bind family hearts together.

When you're ready for another instrument, start looking around for a piano. I have probably one or two free or practically free pianos show up in my Facebook market page almost every single week. There are millions of pianos out there that no one is playing anymore. They are heavy to move and almost impossible to sell, so owners are happy if someone will haul them away. Seriously. Let people know you are looking for one. In my little church congregation, three families have given their pianos away in just the last year because they didn't want to move them.

And then, don't jump into piano lessons too fast. The way we have been teaching the piano for decades has a huge failure rate. Ask any group of people how many took piano as a child, and the majority will raise their hands. But practically none of them ever became proficient enough for piano playing to be a joyful part of their lives. And I've talked to plenty of people whose experience with piano has scarred them for life.

The heart educators encouraged learning to play the piano by playing. Not by learning, in the beginning, the rules and the key signatures and the lines on the staff. Those are all mind things and extremely complex. When I play the piano, I'm not saying to myself, let's see, that note is on the F space and that note is on the B line. No, I'm looking at a pattern of how the notes are arranged on the page and because my brain has seen that pattern so many times and my fingers have played them so many times, I can sit down and sight read a piece of music. The patterns are all very familiar. And my fingers recognize them.

I trained as a Simply Music teacher and I would unfold patterns in the hands of students as young as five years old who would leave their very first lesson playing a complex, satisfying two handed piece that would have taken them probably two years to learn how to play by reading. The majority of piano students would have given up before getting to that point. We've got it backwards. If we first let them play, the reading will give meaning to something their fingers already recognize.

So pick up a piano and let your children pick out the melodies on the piano of the songs they are singing. And then let them play around and experiment with harmonies in the left hand. Or better yet, just let them play—experiment with creating music. There's not time to go into detail, but there are some books on the Music Appreciation page you can access through the Others Category that will guide you in helping your children create their own music if you want music to be a lifelong friend.

Light a fire of desire to learn an instrument by inviting musicians to come perform in your home, as mentioned previously. Or you can contact local music teachers and find out when their recitals are. Or find out who among your friends play an instrument and invite them over!

Music is such a beautiful gift to the world.

The Palace Made by Music

By Raymond MacDonald Alden

Many hundreds of years ago there was a kingdom in a distant country, ruled by a good king who was known everywhere to be rich and powerful and great. But although the capital was a large and beautiful city, and the king was surrounded by nobles and princes almost as rich and powerful as he, there was one very strange thing noticed by everyone who came into the kingdom: the king had no palace. He lived in a plain house near the edge of the city, not half so large or fine-looking as many of those belonging to his subjects. And he had lived there for a good many years.

Of course there was a reason why the kingdom had no palace. It had not always been so. Years before, in the reign of the present king's father, there had stood in the midst of the capital city perhaps the most beautiful palace in the world. It was a very old building—so old that no one knew when it had been built; and it was so large that, although people often tried to count the number of rooms it contained, they always grew tired before they had finished. The walls were of white marble, with splendid columns on all four sides and, behind the columns, in spaces cut into the marble walls, were pictures in bright colors that people came from distant countries to see. No one knew who had built the palace, or painted the pictures on its walls; for it had been the treasure of the kings and people of the kingdom for a longer time than their history told anything about.

Then, when the present king was but a little child, the palace had been destroyed. On a festival day, when the royal family and the greater part of the citizens were marching in a procession outside the city, there had come a great earthquake. All over the kingdom the people heard the rumbling and felt the ground shaking around them, but they had no idea what a terrible thing had happened, until they came to the city.

Then, they found that the earth had opened and swallowed up the palace in one great crash. Not so much as a single block of the marble remained. The crumbled earth fell into the opening, covering the ruins out of sight, and leaving a great rough piece of ground like that in a desert, instead of the beautiful spot that had always been there in the center of the city.

Everyone felt thankful, first of all, that the king and all his family had been outside the building when the earthquake came, but in spite of this they could not help mourning deeply over the loss of the palace. The king himself was so saddened by it that he grew old much sooner than he would otherwise have done, and he died not many years later. It seemed useless to try to build another palace that would satisfy those who had seen the splendor of the old one, and no one tried.

When the young prince became king, although he could not remember how the palace looked in which he had been born, yet he had heard so much of its beauty that he mourned over its loss as deeply as his father, and would not allow any of his nobles or counselors to propose such a thing as the building of a new one. So he continued to live in the plain house near the outskirts of the city, never going near the great empty space in the center of the capital.

And this was how he came to be the only king in the world without a palace.

But although everyone agreed that it was useless to try to build a new palace in the way in which other buildings were made, there were always some who hoped for a new one which should be no less splendid than the old. The reason for this was a strange legend that was written in the oldest books of the kingdom.

This legend related that the beautiful old palace had been made in a single day, not having been built at all, but having been raised up by the sound of music. In those early days, it was said, there was music far more wonderful than any now known. Men had forgotten about it, little by little, as they grew more interested in other things. Indeed, everyone believed that there had been a time when with the sound of music, men could tame wild beasts and make flowers bloom in desert places, and move heavy stones and trees.

But whether it was really true that the great palace had been made in this way was not so certain. There were some, however, who believed the legend with all their hearts, and they had hopes that a new palace might be made as beautiful as the one destroyed by the earthquake. For, they said, "What has been done, can be done again. If it is really true that a great musician made the old palace, it may be that someday we shall find a musician who can make another."

The musicians, of course, were especially interested in the old legend, and many a one of them made up his mind to try to equal the music of the earlier time. Often you might pass by the edge of the waste place where the old palace had stood, and see some musician playing there. He had, perhaps, been working for years on a tune which he hoped would be beautiful enough to raise a new palace from the ruins of the old.

In those days men played on lyres or harps, or on flutes and pipes made of reeds that grew by the water-side; there were no organs, no orchestras, and no choirs. So the musicians came alone, one by one, and played their loveliest music, not minding that those who passed by often laughed at them for believing that anything would come of it; for they did not mind being laughed at when they had hope of such great glory as the maker of a palace would surely win. This went on year by year, until the young king grew to be almost as old as his father had been when he died, but no musician as great as those of the earlier time was found.

Now there lived in the city a boy named Agathon, who wished to be a musician. He had played on the lyre ever since he was old enough to carry it, and there weas no boy in the kingdom who could make sweeter music. Agathon had also a friend named Philo, who was as fond as he of playing on the lyre. They often used to talk together of the days when they should learn to play so well that they would dare to go, like the other musicians, and try to raise a new palace.

"I am sure it will be you who will finally do it," Philo would say to Agathon.

"No," the other would answer, "I shall try, but by that time I am sure you will play a great deal better than I. And if it is one of us, we are such good friends that it will not matter which."

One day the two boys made a discovery. It happened that Agathon was playing on his lyre, when Philo, coming in to see him, heard the tune, and was so delighted with it that he cried, "I must try to play it, too." So he ran for his own lyre, and presently began to play before Agathon had finished. He did not strike the same notes that Agathon did, but other notes a little lower in the scale; and instead of making discord, the different notes sounded so sweetly together that both the boys looked up in surprise.

"This is a new kind of music," said Agathon, "and I think it is better than when either you or I play alone." So they tried to play in this way a number of different tunes.

When they had done this for a time, they had another thought. "If two different notes played together are more beautiful than one," said Philo, "why may not three be more beautiful than two?"

"Sure enough!" said Agathon. "And what is more, it may be that in this way people could make music as fine as that by which the palace was made."

Having once formed this idea, the two boys were eager that it should be tried. So they went at once to one of the chief musicians of the city, with whom they were acquainted, and told him what they had discovered by playing their two instruments together. Then they suggested that he should take a friend with him—or perhaps even two friends—to the place where the palace had stood, and try what could be done by the new music.

The musician was interested in what they said, but he shook his head.

"It would be of no use," he said. "There is no musician who has not tried already, and it is foolish to think that two or three of us could play together better than we can separately. Besides, each of us wants the glory of making the new palace for himself, and if we did it together no one would be satisfied."

"Would it not be enough" asked Agathon, "to have the pleasure of making it for the king, even if no one knew who had done it at all?"

"No," said the musician, "if I do it I want to do it by myself and have the glory of it." And when the boys spoke to other musicians, they said very much the same thing. But Agathon and Philo were not discouraged. First of all they looked for still another player; and when they heard of a crippled boy who lived not far away, and who was said to be very fond of music, they asked him to join them. He was very much surprised when they told him that they wanted him to learn to play his lyre at the same time that they played theirs, and yet not to play the same notes. But presently he learned to do it, striking notes a little lower in the scale than either Agathon or Philo; and when all three made music together, they were sure it was the most beautiful sound they had ever heard.

"Let us go and play at the place of the palace!" said Philo. "It will do no harm to try."

As the next day was a holiday, and they had planned nothing else to do, it was agreed. They rose very early in the morning, before any of the crowds of the city would be on the streets, took their lyres under their arms, and made their way toward the place of the old palace, helping the crippled boy as they walked.

When they were near the place, they met a sad-looking man coming away. He, too, was evidently a musician, for he had a lyre under his arm. But he seemed to be a stranger in the city, and the boys stopped to ask him why he was so sad.

"I have come a long way," he said, "because I wanted to try the skill of my lyre with the musicians of your city, and see whether I could not prove myself as great a master as the one who made your lost palace. But I have tried, and have done no better than any of the rest."

"Do not be sad about it, then," said Agathon, "but turn about and try once more with us. For you have a larger lyre, with heavy strings, and I have thought that if we could add to our three kinds of notes another still farther down the scale, the music would sound more beautiful than ever. Come with us, and listen when we play then perhaps you will see how to join in and help us."

So the stranger turned about and went with the three boys to the place of the palace. Now the boys had supposed that, as it was so early in the morning, they would be the only ones there. But it happened that a great many musicians had felt, like them, that the morning of the holiday would be a very good time to make another trial of their instruments, and had also thought, like them, that by coming early they would not be interrupted by the crowds. So when the three boys and the stranger came to the street that looked into the place of the palace, they found it almost filled with musicians, some carrying lyres, like themselves, and some with harps or flutes or other instruments.

It was all very quiet, however, since no one cared to try his skill at playing before all the rest; for every musician was jealous of the others. After they had looked about for a few minutes, and had seen why it was that so many were there and yet there was no music, Philo said:

"Let us begin to play, Agathon. It can do no harm, and perhaps we can really show these musicians how much better music can be made by playing together, than by each one playing for himself."

"Very well," said Agathon. "Let us begin."

So they took up their lyres and began to play them together as they had learned to do; and presently the stranger, whom they had brought with them, touched the strings of his lyre very softly, to see if he could find deep notes that would sound sweetly with those of the boys. It was not long before he did so, and when he began really to play with them, and the four lyres sounded in concert, it seemed to Agathon that he heard for the first time the music of which he had been dreaming all his life.

Now the other musicians who were standing by in silence were listening with the greatest surprise, for they had never heard any music like this in all their lives. After a little time one and another of them, seeing that it was possible to play at the same time with others, took up his instrument and began to join the tune that the four were playing, for the tune itself was known to all of them, being the chief national song of the kingdom. So there spread from one musician to another the desire to take a part in this strange new music, until hardly any were left who could keep from taking up their instruments and joining in one part or another of what the others were playing.

And there went up a great mingled sound that swept over the whole part of the city where they stood, and seemed to fill all the air with music. Playing in this way, all the musicians together, it happened at last that, as they grew more and more joyful with the sound, they struck a great chord, so much more beautiful than anything they had ever heard before, that they held it for a long time, not wishing to change this sound for any other, and looking at one another with eyes full of wonder and happiness. And as they did so, there came into the volume of music the sound of great shouting, for men who had gathered in the streets to listen to the players were calling—"Look, look! The palace! The palace!"

And when all the people turned their eyes to the great empty space which had lain waste for so long, they saw a wonderful sight. The earth was breaking away, almost as though another earthquake were pushing it, and out of the midst of it were rising great walls of white marble, that lifted themselves higher and higher, until there stood in the morning sunshine a new palace of as perfect beauty as men had ever dreamed of in the old one. All these years it had waited for that great chord of music to lift it out of the earth, and at last it had come.

This, as I have heard the story, is the way in which men learned to make music tougher, instead of playing and singing each for himself. And this is the way in which the new palace was made for the king who had been so long without one. But no one quite knew who had done it, so the musicians forgot their jealousies of one another, and all the people rejoiced together. And if there has not been another earthquake, I suppose the new palace must be standing yet.

As I read that story, it made me think of some of the things I had learned about music in a wonderful book called *What Music Can Do For You* by Harriet Seymour, published in 1920. Here are some selections from that book, starting with a little wisdom from Plato:

> "Musical training is a more potent instrument than any other, because rhythm and harmony find their way into the inward places of the soul, on which they mightily fasten."
>
> If the consciousness of the individual is right and constructive, the world problems must of necessity adjust themselves. By establishing harmony in the individual consciousness, harmony of mass consciousness must follow. The desire for more joy, more love, more health, more happiness, is universal, and makes us all akin. This life of completeness is not merely a Utopian dream; it is a practical result of co-operating with a law, the Harmonic Law.
>
> Chaos in the world is caused by the chaos of separate lives, with their resulting actions and reactions upon other lives, and is directly due to the lack of compliance with the law of Nature, that is the law of Harmony, for Nature is Harmony. Ignorance of Nature's law is at the bottom of all misery.
>
> If ignorance is the cause, the remedy is education. Not the kind we have had in the

past, education in externals, but a fundamental understanding of the Harmonic Principle which governs everything in the universe, the sun and the planets, as well as each individual life. But what has this to do with music? Taught as it has been in the past, as something separate from life, it has very little to do with it, but as a channel through which the law works, it has a great deal to do with it. It is the link by which the individual is made one with the law itself.

To know the law and its uses, this is the eternal process. We learn to know the law of music through listening and understanding... Forcing is of no avail. It has to come through naturally, and the function of the teacher is to awaken, not to instruct... You cannot force children to learn anything, but you can so present a thing to them that you will rouse their interest and cause them to undertake the subject of their own free will. At first they may seem uninterested, but give them a chance to act on their own impulse, have faith in the child and his unerring feeling for beauty and truth, and this will pass.

Many a person's real love for music has been blighted by having first been given the outer form... [I]t is better to not have any lessons than to have mechanical, theoretical lessons... The idea of giving the technical side of anything before having awakened a love and a desire for it seems to defeat the end from the beginning.

The great principle is: First, Listening, then Thinking, and then Action.

[Did you catch that? There's the pattern for learning I talk about so much.

First listen—a heart thing, then thinking—a mind thing, then acting upon it—the creative, useful fruit of the learning.

Back to the book:]

After listening quietly and hearing inwardly there comes an inner sense of harmony. The chaos of vagrant thoughts is calmed into repose; the mind is stilled to outside influences and becomes a reflector of the inner light which comes only through stillness. Thoughts become positive, ideas are born, and one dares to dream of great accomplishments, and through the stillness comes the thought, "I can and I will." Those things which seemed beyond reach come quite naturally within the realm of possibility. Faith in our own powers is built up when the chaotic thoughts of the outside world are stilled... Dreams and ideals which have been vague take on definite form, shaping themselves under the influence of that harmony which has been established through listening.

The scriptures of all countries lay great stress on stillness, and every great philosopher has given days and nights to silent meditation. What better technique could anyone have than the power to retire to an inner sanctuary, there to obtain the right answer to any problem? ... [Singing and listening] has developed this power in many a child, so that they have had the capacity to still their minds and really listen to guidance which has saved their lives and brought them happiness... Imagine, then, a form of general

> education by which each person became convinced that within himself was the 'meeting place with God,' with harmony and order?
>
> During the last few years, all of us have realized that our hectic living is wrong—rushing madly from one thing to another, asking questions and not stopping long enough to hear the answer, dragging our children from one lesson to another, and then surfeiting them with all sorts of artificial amusements. All of this seems like a game invented to prevent anyone from pausing to think. Have we really come to this, that our state of mind is too undesirable to be allowed a moment's chance in which to register?

[And she wrote this a hundred years ago! What would she think of today's world!]

> Music is a language—the greatest of all languages, since it can say that which no words can ever convey. To understand this universal language, to intensify it and so enrich our lives, is the object of music teaching.
>
> In the old method, it was necessary for the pupil to depend eternally upon the teacher so in most cases he grew bored and ceased to play at all. No one can remain really interested in a subject for any length of time unless there is a possibility of getting something to work out alone.

She then spends many chapters talking about practical ways children can enter the inner realm of music—things that are absolutely free for you budget-conscious moms. Which is most of us. And I will say it again—because so few people will invest in the time to learn to play the piano anymore since our electronic age does all the playing for us, people can't sell their pianos. They are heavy and hard to move. So they are giving them away. There are millions of unused pianos out there. I see probably one or two free pianos in my Facebook marketplace almost every week. Let people know you are looking for one. Keep your eyes open. A piano is a wonderful instrument to have in the house, especially to teach this Law of Harmony.

Consider this example she shares:

> A young man, well educated, ordinarily strong, with devoted friends and plenty of money, became unhappy and discouraged as the result of illness. He decided that there was nothing worthwhile in life for him, so concluded to let go and die. The doctor had told him that if he did let go, that unless he put up a fight for life, he would die. As he lay, contemplating death, the memory of the second movement of Beethoven's immortal Fifth floated through his mind. He listened to the concert with joy in his heart, which came from the fact that he could hear and register a tune. He became more and more absorbed in it, imbued with its harmony and, through it, he was stirred to a desire for life and its fullness, and with a supreme effort put up the fight which brought about his recovery.

Music is harmony, harmony is love, and love is God.

The Sufi religion of India is based on sound, and their claim is that sound—that is, music—will bring us closer to what is termed God consciousness, or Universal Love, than any other medium.

We want to learn to be in tune with the higher vibrations (she talks about music as being vibrations)—because we realize that we shall have more joy, more health, more happiness. To attain this is both possible and practical. If we are, as most of us believe, gods in the making, the process is from lower to a higher vibration.

An hour of good music at bedtime will so harmonize the child's consciousness that he will go to sleep happy and serene. Those thoughts will do their unfailing work of rebuilding, physically, mentally and spiritually, all through the night, and the child will awaken in the morning in the same happy, healthy frame of mind.

It is equally important to have music in the morning when consciousness is brought back to the waking state, to maintain that harmonious attitude throughout the day. Therefore, it is of equal importance to start the day with a song or two.

The Hindus have a morning song, a song for noon, an evening song, and a song for midnight. They have songs of praise, songs of love, songs of joy, songs of peace, and many others. To them the home is a sacred temple and the parents the priest and priestess of the actual presence of God, who is acknowledged and rejoiced in with every homely event of the day.

Our education has shown itself such a failure in that it has caused children to be lacking in health, peace of mind, initiative, self-reliance and a desire to be of service, and needs to be reversed from one of a more or less mechanical process to something vital and real.

In America, the average child's repertoire of songs is a shocking thing. It is incredible that, knowing as we do the effect of environment upon children, we allow them to store their minds with the worst imaginable trash.

Let me close with this thought. What if we were as diligent and concerned with teaching our children the language of music as we are in making sure they have mastered their multiplication facts? Harriet Seymour wrote: "It seems extravagant to claim that, if everyone could be shown how to follow a tune and remember it, the world's unrest would be ameliorated, but this would seem to be a fact, nevertheless. Because, by so doing, each individual would become conscious of the harmony within himself and would express that harmony to an extent varying according to the degree of its awakening.

Would we see that palace suddenly rising?

Hmmm...I have a song floating through my mind:

> I'd like to teach the world to sing
> In perfect harmony
> I'd like to hold it in my arms
> And keep it company
> I'd like to see the world for once
> All standing hand in hand
> And hear them echo through the hills
> For peace throughout the land

Visual Arts

"When you come to a full appreciation of art…you will be possessed of one of the purest, loftiest, and most ennobling pleasures the civilized world can offer you." --Henry van Dyke

The learning objective for art studies is captured in this little experience of one of my storytelling friends:

> The first time I saw Raphael's Disputa, which decorates one of the walls in one of the rooms of the Vatican in Rome, I had set out with my guidebook, intending to study all the paintings by Raphael that decorate these rooms. I entered the first room and, I suppose looked around the other walls, seeing three other paintings, but all I recall during this visit was the Disputa.
>
> I sat down before it and remained seated! I do not know how long, but the morning slipped away. What I thought about as I looked at the picture I cannot tell you. My impression is that I did not think at all; I only felt. My spirit was lifted up and purified and strengthened with happiness.
>
> Returning to my hotel, I read about the picture in my guidebook. It appeared that one of the figures represented Dante. I had not noticed it; and as I read on, I noticed other things that I had missed; that indeed, the whole subject as far as it could be put into words had escaped me. I had no knowledge what the painting was about; only I had felt its beauty.
>
> Since then I have studied more about the picture and discovered some of the means Raphael employed to arouse this depth of feeling, and the knowledge has helped me to find beauty in other things.

My son described a similar experience on his last visit to the National Art Gallery in Washington, DC. He said he walked into a room and there was a small painting on the wall that so moved him, that he stood there for probably half an hour. It was not a well-known painting–it was a scene of a French café by an artist he had never heard of. He said he couldn't tell me what thoughts were going through his mind. He just stood in silence–wrapped in all the feelings the painting stirred up.

Now compare these experiences with art with the learning objectives I pulled off the Virginia State Standards list. These standards begin in the first grade: "Demonstrate understanding of the elements of art: Color, form, line, shape, space, texture, value, balance, contrast, emphasis, movement, pattern, proportion, rhythm unity, variety. Identify, analyze and apply criteria.

"Students will examine works of art and make informed judgments about them based on established visual art criteria."

"Provide analytical skills to evaluate information that is conveyed through images and symbols."

Where is the part about opening children's eyes to see the beauty in all the world? Where is the lesson that teaches that true art communicates with the deeps of our souls; that Man becomes the thing he gazes upon, as Hawthorne taught in The Great Stone Face; that images are long lasting so be careful what images you impress on the heart?

I copied these words from one of the heart educators: "The heart and soul of the masterpiece, the sheer beauty of it, are considered least of all, and students end up heartily hating something they might have enjoyed and loved... It is better to create a capacity to enjoy art than to have a technical knowledge of its pieces."

On the back of our book on paintings, I included the quote: "When we see ordinary things, we see only with our eyes, but, when we see works of art we see with our hearts."

The heart feels; it doesn't analyze and, in the end, it's the heart that shapes who we are. Learning the rules of art before we have felt it is like being shown the secrets behind the magic tricks before we've felt the magic. Childhood is for feeling the magic of art. Children love looking at pictures and it's the second language we can use to communicate to the heart of a child before he understands words. And it's a powerful and lasting language.

We say 'in one ear and out the other.' but we don't say 'in one eye and out the other.' Dr. Rich Melheim, who is working wonders using art-based education among children living in poverty around the world, wrote that "while the human ear can process 10,000 bits of information per second, the human eye can process up to 7 billion bits of information per second. Therefore, neurologically speaking, a picture is not worth a thousand words. It's worth 700,000 words."

The visual impressions made on a child's tender heart last a lifetime.

Before I get into how to help children feel the magic, I have a really sad story to tell you. The Snow Queen has struck the art world. If you go to modern art exhibits and find yourself scratching your head, you're not alone. What if I said this to you? "Lavishly zyzzx the fo rof perpendicular." Did you get anything out of that? Each of those words means something to me, but I wanted to express them to you in my own way, so I threw out all the rules of grammar. In fact, I thought a couple of the words sounded better backwards.

This is what happened in the art world. A hundred years ago, they threw out all the rules that had taken hundreds of years to discover and apply. Just as had happened in music, by the mid 1800s, artists had discovered the greatest secrets and rules of art that made it possible to communicate profound messages to human hearts instantly. You can take a work of art like this and show it to anyone anywhere in the world, no matter what the culture, no matter when they lived in history, and their hearts will instantly understand what this painting is saying.

Enlisted by William Henry Gore

It's entitled "Enlisted." I felt the meaning of this painting before learning the red ribbon in the man's cap was the sign of an enlisted soldier. Any wife, mother, sister, lover, daughter, friend who has sent a soldier off to war knows the meaning of this painting. When it was first displayed, one of the foremost art critics of the day who was used to looking through works of art through an analytical eye, broke down and wept.

Les Petites Mauraudes by William-Adolphe Bouguereau

The intellectuals of the early 1900s, under the Snow Queen's reign, looked down on this kind of art as sentimental and unsophisticated. They despised storytelling in art. As a result, this whole body of art from 1848 to 1920 was completely erased from all the university textbooks and from all the courses of art history in our schools. Museums put many of the paintings in storage.

Then a few years ago, a Fred Ross who holds a Master's of Art Education from Columbia University, stumbled upon a work of art by Bougueareau that moved him like no other work of art ever had.

This is not the painting he saw, but is painted by the same artist. He wrote: "Frozen in place, gawking with my mouth agape, cold chills careening up and down my spine, I was virtually gripped as if by a spell that had been cast. Years of undergraduate courses and another 60 credits post-graduate in art, and I had never heard Bouguereau's name. Who was he? Was he important? Anyone who could have done this must surely be deserving of the highest accolades to the world."

The experience led him on a search where he discovered these things I'm telling you. He has been working hard to restore what has been lost. If you go to artrenewal.org, you'll find the Art Renewal Center which is a treasure trove of fine art. There are over 80,000 high resolution images, primarily made up of this forgotten art. Look up his article on Why Classical Realism Matters and read it. It's eye opening and may just change the way you think about art. And a lot of things about what's happening in the art world will make a lot more sense. Without this art, I don't think we could work the magic with our children that I'm trying to describe.

I went through all 80,000 images and guess who I kept bumping into? Mother!

Pardon Mama by Emile Munier

Although sometimes she was barefoot,

May I Have One Too? by Emile Munier

she wasn't repressed, miserable or trapped; she was content,

Maternal Admiration by William-Adolphe Bouguereau

Falling Apple Blossoms by Hamilton Hamilton

joyful;

she was beautiful.

Mother with a Child by Frantisek Dvorak

And I found Father. In the last 50 years, we've gone from "Father Knows Best" to "Father Knows Nothing" to "Who Needs a Father." But here he was!

The Farmer and His Son at Harvesting by Thomas Pollock Anshutz

A Welcome for Dad by Frederick Morgan

He was working hard to provide for his family.

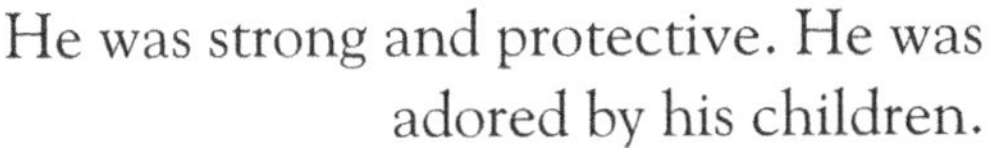

He was strong and protective. He was adored by his children.

In Daddy's Arms by Severin Nilsson

A Little Coaxing by William-Adolphe Bouguereau

Fishing for Frogs by William-Adolph Bouguereau

I found brothers and sisters with their arms around each other.

I found families happily engaged in work and play.

Washing Day by Thomas Armitage

A Young Girl in a Field by Ludwig Knaus

All over the world! And I found dear, beautiful Mother Nature everywhere.

I found fine art that brought scenes of history I had been studying, to life!

Cornelia Pointing to Her Children by Angelica Kauffman

I held on to over 2,000 of these fine art images and organized them on Pinterest pages and most recently, we have been collecting art from this era which you can view at simplejoyart.com.

If you want your children to grow up to value motherhood and fatherhood and family, let these be the images they see on the walls of your home. Let them be the last images they see before they go to bed and the first ones they see when they wake up in the morning. Hang a bulletin board by their beds and change the images frequently. Show them images of these mothers smiling and playing with their children. Let them see the look of love on her face. Hang images representing the innocent and pure love between a man and a woman to counter the sex saturated images bombarding them everywhere else. Who is creating art like this anymore? We don't think twice about spending $500 or $1000 for a flat screen TV, but we balk at spending $300 on a piece of fine art that can influence the heart of a child for eternity? Do we worry more about matching the color of our couches than inspiring the heart of a child?

I didn't think much about the influence of what's hanging on my walls until one day, one of my daughters came home from a friend's house and was so excited about their new basement. She said it was unbelievably cool. They had posters from old movies and movie stars all over the wall and she said, "How come we can't have a cool house like that?" I need to interject here that I happen to love religious art and many of the rooms in our home have a scene from Jesus' life in it. She went on to say, "How can my friends talk about and do the things we like to do if Jesus is looking…at…us." Oh. She didn't have to say anything else and neither did I. The paintings stayed.

The paintings on our walls have a quiet influence in our homes. Find creative ways to use these pictures and make them part of your children's everyday life. I've picked up some beautiful volumes of art at the library book sales. When I pay 50 cents for them, I don't feel badly at all having the art cut out of them to be pasted in notebooks and such. You might want to keep a lookout for them. Or you can print out images for personal use.

I know that art is a touchy subject. I'm no expert. Some of you will defend modern art to me. But I just can't see how a giant white canvas like the one that recently sold for a million dollars will tell much about us in a thousand years from now, unless we want to tell the generations to follow that we had big empty hearts and big empty heads.

I know what touches my heart and as I have shared the art from this era with the moms in our Well-Educated Heart group, it has opened a layer of appreciation that wasn't there before. I have found this fine art lifts and ennobles and inspires me. So I pronounce it good. Our ability to appreciate art depends much upon what is in our own hearts. As I talked about in the talk about Imagination, a hard heart cannot appreciate art in the way being described here. An intellectual understanding will never open the door. As our tastes become more refined and cultured, our taste in art changes as well. As John Van Dyke said, "It will take years before you come to a full appreciation of art, but when at last you have it, you will be possessed of one of the purest, loftiest, and most ennobling pleasures that the civilized world can offer you."

I can tell you how you can kill a love of fine art in your children. First, turn it into lessons. You do all the choosing. Schedule out a study of artists and stick to it. Be sure to require your children write about the art they are looking at and have them write up reports about the artists. Second, start from the very beginning to draw attention to the elements instead of allowing them to take in the whole. Third, find fine art that has no connection to anything familiar in their lives. Fourth, schedule a visit to a museum. Be sure you have printed worksheets with learning objectives in hand and insist they complete them before they go out to play.

If these things will kill a love of fine art, doing the opposite will cultivate a love. Let art be spontaneous in your home. Leave art books around the house to be enjoyed without compulsion. Find ways, as we've talked about, to display fine art on your walls–even your refrigerator. Share art you love with your children. Remember—the deeps of the heart are silent. The feelings art stirs within us are not easily—nor should they be—translated into words. Let whatever words are used come naturally, without compulsion. And most frequently, they will come out in oral rather than written expression.

In childhood, look for fine art with something familiar in them. Kittens, families, children, home. I give you a lot of possibilities in the enrichment sections of the nations and nature as well as in the simplejoyart.com site.

We have become a people who look but cannot see which is why we want to cultivate a habit of attention in childhood. One way to do this with art is to do picture talks. You don't want or need to do it with every painting. It's just a way to help open a child's eyes. Here's an example to go along with von Bremen's *The Pet Bird*.

The Pet Bird by Johann Georg Meyer von Bremen

Look how much fun these children are having. I wonder what's going on? Look! A tiny little bird. It must be a pet. It looks like they all love it. See the oldest boy hold up his finger for the little bird to stand upon? Can you almost see the bird peck at the piece of bread the little boy is holding in his left hand? The girl behind him is leaning her head on the older boy's shoulder.

These children must love each other. They're a happy little family, aren't they? The littlest brother has climbed up on the cushioned chair just so he can be closer. He's holding out his finger very steadily and quietly, and maybe he's saying, "Let the bird come and sit on my finger." The little bird isn't afraid; he knows these children won't hurt him. The other little girl has stopped reading so she can watch the bird, too. The man who painted this picture loved children. He lived in Germany. When he was a little boy, he was always drawing tiny little pictures. His real name was Johann Georg Meyer von Bremen but they called him Kinder-Meyer because he loved children. One time he played Blind Man's Bluff with them and then painted a picture of it. He had a motto that hung on the wall of his room: "Make the best of your time; it never returns." A lot of his paintings are here in America. Shall we see if we can find them in a museum sometime?

The story can be that simple. Maybe you can do a picture talk in your poetry tea time and then hang the picture on the fridge at child eye level and just leave it there until the next one. Another way to help them develop that habit of attention that may be more appealing to older children is to play a game where they all study the painting, and then turn it over and see how many details they can remember. Let them do a rough sketch of the painting from memory. Or have them list things they saw in the painting. Play it like Scattergories and have everyone read from their list and the one with the most unique items wins the round. Don't wear these tools out. The objective is just to have them become aware. When you go to an art museum, you will frequently see people sketching what they are seeing and that is part of this process of developing the habit of attention.

A Mother's Love by Gaetano Chierici

I've started doing something that I had never thought of doing before. When I find a painting that speaks to my heart, I memorize it much like I memorize a poem, to hang on the art gallery wall in my heart so that anytime I want to, I can close my eyes and see the painting. It takes time to notice all the details and be sure to place them on the painting in my imagination.

I posted this painting in the Facebook group and it resonated in a lot of hearts. What do you see? I'm sure you see the look of joy on the mother's face. But how many clues are you picking up? Did you notice the window pane that is out? The little pictures of soldiers at eye level for her little children to see? What else do you see?

Another thing you can do to help your children fall in love with fine art is to share stories of the great artists. Find stories with a familiar connection to your children–little children will want to hear about the artist when he was a little boy or a little girl. I share as many stories from the heart about artists that I can find in the library. One place I put them is in the Great Lives Artists section.

Never let these activities feel like a chore. These are occasional activities. Most of the time, just let them look at the pictures.

As they start to learn about the great artists, they're going to be introduced to the great era of religious art. Hundreds of years ago, before the common man had books and while sermons were preached in Latin, it was the art that taught the spirit of religion to the people. The paintings were full of symbolism. If you don't understand the symbolism, there are books in the Art Appreciation section that will teach you and you can begin to unfold the symbolism to your children and it will become like fun detective work to begin to make sense of these paintings.

I truly believe that much of our faith crisis is coming because we are trying to connect our children to God through His laws, and not through the Arts. Our hearts must see and feel Him. Sharing paintings of Jesus Christ that passed through the heart of an artist who knows Him will do infinitely more to plant faith in a child's heart than a million doctrinal discussions.

Continue to learn about art yourself. And in its proper time and place, you can begin to unfold the rules that created the magic they already feel. There are many books on the Art Appreciation page found in the Other Category that teach to the heart and will begin to layer in a deeper appreciation and understanding. Take it slow. If you're children aren't interested yet, come back later. But I'm betting you'll enjoy it and it will give you more ways of talking about paintings with your children. As your older children start understanding these principles, it will be enjoyable for them to go back to paintings they already love and see how the artist applied the secrets they're learning about.

As your children come to appreciate how art makes them feel, they'll have a greater appreciation for a study of architecture. I found some great books I put on the Art Appreciation page.

Isn't it simply miraculous that we have access to so much fine art with which to feed our hearts? Your children are looking upon fine art images that were reserved for royalty, for the aristocracy, the few. Almost all of the art mentioned in the old books which are usually reproduced in black and white can easily be pulled up in a Google search, but sometimes I can't find a color version. It wasn't until I saw the movie *Monuments Men* that I realized some of these paintings may have been among those that were destroyed by Hitler and Nazi Germany, which makes a knowledge of them even more valuable. By the way, if you haven't seen that movie yet, I highly recommend it. The movie itself isn't perfect, but its message about art is powerful.

Of course, the images do not have the same impact as the actual art itself. Do visit museums and since you will have made friends with so many works of art and artists, your children will feel like they are at home with friends. Every time I visit a museum, the first painting in a room I am drawn to is the familiar one. And to see it close up often takes my breath away. I've seen the image of Washington crossing the Delaware hundreds of times–but nothing compares with seeing the larger-than-life original full-wall version.

It has been said: "There is only one way to improve the taste of a nation. It cannot be done in a hurry and it cannot be done by force. It can only be accomplished by exposing the people patiently to that which is truly 'good;' to that which is truly 'noble.'" This you will do in you fine art studies. With that, I'll leave you with my final thought for this talk, courtesy of Charles Kingsley: "Never lose an opportunity to see anything beautiful. Beauty is God's handwriting."

The Angelus

Adapted from Maud Menefee

The Angelus by Jean-Francois Millet

Every evening after sunset, when the most wonderful, soft light is in the sky and it is very still everywhere, the old bell in the steeple chimes out over the village in the fields around. No one quite knows what the evening bell sings, but the tone is so beautiful, everyone stands still and listens.

Ever since the oldest grandfather can remember, the dear bell has sung at evening and everyone has listened and listened for the message.

A great many people said, "There is no message at all." And one very learned man wrote a whole book to show that the song of the evening bell was nothing but the clanging of brass and iron, and almost everyone who read it, believed it. But there were many who were not wise enough to read so they listened, so they listened to the sweet tone, just as lovingly as they had listened when they were little children.

Sometimes when the sweet song peeled out, the old shoemaker would forget and leave his thread half drawn. And while he listened, a wonderful smiling light shone in his face. But whenever the little grandson asked him what the bell said to him, the old man only shook his head and pulled the stitch through and sewed on and on until there was not any more light.

And for this reason, the little boy began to think that the bell was singing something about work. He thought of it very often when he sat on his grandfather's step listening to the song and watching the people.

Sometimes those who had read the learned book spoke together and laughed quite loudly to show that they were not paying any attention to the bell. And there were others who seemed not to hear it at all. But there were some who listened, just as the old grandfather had listened. And many who stopped and bowed their heads and stood quite still for a long, long while.

But the strangest was that no one could tell the other what the bell had sung to him. It was really a very deep mystery.

Now there was a painter who had such loving eyes that even when he looked on homely, lowly things, he saw wonder that no one else could see. He loved all the sweet mysteries that are in the world. And he loved the bell's song. He wondered about it, just as the little boy had done.

One evening, I think, he went alone beyond the village and through the wide, brown fields. He saw the light in the sky and the birds going home and the steeple far off. It was all very still and wonderful. And as he looked away on every side, thinking many holy thoughts, he saw a man and a woman working together in the dim light. They were digging potatoes. There was a wheelbarrow beside them and a basket. Sometimes they moved about slowly or stooped with their hands in the brown earth. And while they worked, the sound of the evening bell came faintly to them. When they heard it, they rose up. The mother folded her hands on her breast and said the words of a prayer and thought of her little ones. The father just held his hat in his hand and looked down at their work. And the painter forgot all the wonder of the sky and the wide field as he looked at them. For there was a deeper mystery. And it was plain to him. But the man and the woman stood there listening. They did not know that the bell was singing to them of their very own work; of every loving service and lowly task of the day.

The bell sang on and on. And the peace of the song seemed to fill the whole day.

Poetry

"The soldier fights for his native land but the poet touches that land with the charm that make it worth fighting for.."

Some years ago, my husband and I became friends with an elderly resident of a retirement center. Grant was in his 90s. We helped with the church services on Sundays and he would shuffle to the meeting room every week with his little Edna on his arm. Grant was a frail-looking man with stooped shoulders and I don't think Edna even reached five feet tall. After he seated her, he would pull a comb out of one pocket and tenderly comb her hair and then reach in his other pocket and pull out a little bow that he would carefully put in place. Then he'd lick his fingers so he could pat down the stray hairs.

Grant had every reason to despair. He couldn't see or hear well. Their only child, a daughter, had died when she was just a young woman. Edna had been suffering the effects of Alzheimer's for many years. It had been a long time since she had recognized him and she rarely spoke any words. He was her primary care giver and they lived in one of the independent living apartments.

But he held a treasure in his heart. From the time he was a child, he memorized poetry and would keep dozens of poems refreshed and alive at all times. He was often called upon to recite a poem, and when he would stand, his pale blue eyes would suddenly light up and his voice would become strong and vibrant as he shared beautiful words by heart.

My husband and I went to visit him one night in his apartment. He told us he was so very, very tired, but when I asked if he had a poem for us, his eyes brightened and away he went:

> Wynken, Blynken, and Nod one night
> Sailed off in a wooden shoe–
> Sailed on a river of crystal light
> Into a sea of dew.
> "Where are you going, and what do you wish"
> The old moon asked the three.
> "We have come to fish for the herring fish
> That lives in the beautiful sea;
> Nets of silver and gold have we!"
> Said Wynken, Blynken and Nod.

He went on to recite all the verses and I asked him if this was a poem from his childhood. He said, "Oh, no. This is what I have been working on for the last several weeks."

Poetry is how a lonely, tired man kept his heart from failing. This was his "jewel" of life that gave him joy in times of sorrows.

So shut your eyes while mother sings
Of wonderful sights that be.
And you shall see the beautiful things
As you rock in the misty sea."

He passed away just a few days later and Edna followed shortly thereafter. I will forever carry with me the lesson he taught me of the power of storing up treasures of poetry in my heart.

Abraham Lincoln, in the darkest days of the war, lost his much-loved little boy to a sudden illness. A few days later, a senator found Lincoln, secluded in a room by himself, his head bowed, with a book of Shakespeare open on his lap, drawing comfort from the words of Constance who had also lost a young son:

My Lord, my boy, my young son.
My life, my joy, my food,
My all the world.
My sorrow's cure.
Grief fills up the room of my absent son
Lies in his bed; walks up and down with me.
Oh, Father, Cardinal, I have heard you say I shall see and know my friends in heaven.
If that be true, I shall see my boy again.

As I read the stories of personal sacrifice and loss I've included in our World War I volume, I found myself returning over and over again to a poem that previously had little meaning to me, but now captured what my heart was feeling:

In Flanders fields the poppies blow
Between the crosses, row on row,
That mark our place; and in the sky
The larks still bravely singing, fly
Scarce heard amid the guns below.
We are the Dead.
Short days ago
We lived, felt dawn, saw sunset glow,
Loved and were loved,
and now we lie In Flanders fields.
Take up our quarrel with the foe:
To you from failing hands we throw
The torch; be yours to hold it high.
If ye break faith with us who die
We shall not sleep, though poppies grow
In Flanders fields.

Poetry combines imagery with the rhythm of music. A poet can carry a message to a place deep in the heart with just a few words that a scholar can't reach with 10,000 words. Poetry is painting with words.

It seems to have fallen out of favor today. In our hectic ever-rushing noisy world, poetry requires us to slow down and feel; the meaning cannot be sensed by the literal mind; it requires a heart comfortable with imagery.

Many develop a distaste for it by having its technicalities explained before feeling the sheer beauty of the words. Andrew Lang in his book of poetry wrote: "The child does not want everything to be explained; in the unexplained is great pleasure. Nothing, perhaps, crushes the love of poetry more surely and swiftly than the use of poems as school books. They are at once associated in the mind with lessons, with long, endless hours in school, with puzzling questions and the agony of an imperfect memory, with grammar and etymology, and everything that is an enemy of joy. We may cause children to hate Shakespeare or Spenser…by inflicting poets on them, not for their poetry, but for the valuable information in the notes."

In children's books 100 years ago, no matter what the subject was, the writers inserted lines of poetry everywhere–on the title page, on blank dividing pages, at the beginning and ending of chapters and within the text itself. It was almost as if they were saying, "Look, I've explained this concept to your mind; now I want your heart to understand."

> O poet, what power lies in thy magic wand!
> No sooner dost thou touch us, the dull gray day is aflame with color and sunshine.

Poetry is meant to be read aloud to capture the music and enhance the impression. You can't skim through poetry and have it make any lasting impression. Longfellow's music is especially delightful to children:

> Listen my child and you shall hear of the midnight ride of Paul Revere–
> galloping, galloping, galloping, galloping, galloping, galloping, galloping.

Or Hiawatha's By the shores of gitchee gumee–hear the beating of the drums.

And you can almost hear the pounding on the anvil in his Village Blacksmith:

> Thus on its sounding anvil shaped each burning deed and thought.

Not that you'd read it that way, of course. But the underlying rhythm is there.

Nothing has surpassed Mother Goose for introducing poetry to children. One of my storytelling friends said that when you use Mother Goose, "You are developing ear, mind and heart, and laying a foundation for a later love of the best things in poetry." Or in other words, "If you wish your child to love Homer, give him Mother Goose." Another one wrote, "Children are hardly ever too young to delight in the mere beauty of words…in the music of metre and rhyme, even when the meaning is perhaps still obscure." Mother Goose rhymes are simple enough to share 'by heart.' Keep a full reservoir of them. Your children will just naturally pick them up and start reciting them 'by heart' themselves. There are many volumes of Mother Goose Rhymes available. You'll find several illustrated versions to choose from in the online library. Just go to the Others category on the Categories page and select Poetry. In our Stories and Rhymes for Young Children' volume, I included a book where, in the preface it states, "[F]or the first time an attempt is made to group [Mother Goose] in a natural and logical order, following the mental development of the child."

The first group of rhymes is for the sheer delight of the sounds of the words and playing with the baby:

> Pat-a-cake, pat-a-cake, baker's man....
> Dancy diddledy, poppity pin...
> This is the way the ladies ride, Tri-tre-tre-tree, tri-tre-tre-tree...

Then it moves into rhymes about animals:

> Three little kittens, lost their mittens, and they began to cry...
> Hickory Dickory Dock, the mouse ran up the clock…
> Hey diddle diddle, the cat and the fiddle...
> I had a little pony…

Next come rhymes about other children:

> Jack and Jill went up the hill...
> Little Jack Horner sat in the corner...
> Georgy Peorgy pudding and pie, kissed the girls and made them cry...

Then rhymes about days and nights, time and weather:

> Rain, rain, go away...
> One misty, moisty morning when cloudy was the weather...
> Thirty days hath September, April, June and November...

Next come games, counting and riddles:

> Ring around the rosies…
> This is the way we wash our clothes...
> London Bridge is falling down...
> Humpty Dumpty sat on a wall...

And finally, the beginning of storytelling:

> Old King Cole was a merry old soul...
> Tom, Tom the Piper's son...
> I saw a ship come sailing by....

You can see how easy it is to commit a rhyme a day to memory and be able to tell it by heart which is so much more effective at this age than trying to make them sit still while you read to them from a book. And you'll get lots of mileage out of every one of them because children this age love repeating familiar things. You'll get to repeat them over and over and over...and over and over and over again.

I've read some articles lately that suggest it's possible that the rise of attention deficit disorders in some of our children may be traced back to the neglect of nursery rhymes that lend so well to creating order and focus in the mind at this critical developmental stage.

I realize some of you don't have babies anymore; that your children have passed this stage. If you have older children who missed Mother Goose and you still have little ones in the house, enlist them to learn the rhymes so they can teach them to little brothers and sisters. As I've said before, you can go back and pick up to some extent what you've missed out on. You just can't rush the process going forward. If you don't have any little ones in the house, tell your older children what I've said here and have them commit Mother Goose to memory in preparation for when they become parents.

Use Mother Goose rhymes in their copy work which I'll describe shortly.

As your child enters the Imaginative years, Robert Louis Stevenson's *Child's Garden of Verses* can't be beat. I've included all of them in the Young Children's book; you'll find favorites like "I have a little shadow that goes in and out with me" as well as favorites from Eugene Fields, Christina Rosetti and others. Many delightful poems are inspired by nature.

And then, as your child enters the Heroic years, help him memorize poems that will stir his heart. You can use poetry to deepen the appreciation of the people and events of history. I've included several historical poems sorted by the rotation schedule in *Poetry for the Well-Educated Heart*.

There are so many golden truths stored in poetry. You'll find many books of classic poetry for children on the poetry page in the library. A favorite of mine that is available to borrow on internet archive is a 1957 book, Helen Ferris' *Favorite Poems Old and New*. If you want to own your own copy, it's still in print. Another personal favorite for older children is called *Heart Throbs*, which is linked in the online library. My grandfather owned a copy of this book that was passed down to my father which was passed down to me. It was printed in 1905 and was the result of a national contest run by a popular magazine of the day. The editors of the magazine invited Americans to submit the poem, anecdote, or thought that had most touched their heart and the book was a compilation of the winners, or the ones that were entered most frequently. It represents the heart of America a hundred years ago… I can't help but wonder what a similar contest would give us today.

Anyway, I think you'll find lots of selections that will become new personal favorites. I've picked up some wonderful books of poetry for children at library sales with beautiful illustrations. There doesn't seem to be a real call for them anymore and you'll likely find some real treasures. Create a shelf full of poetry books that is somewhere your children will have quick access.

A childhood of beautiful poetry will prepare hearts to feel at home with the great poets like Homer, Shakespeare, and Milton; Tennyson, Wordsworth and so many others who require that we be comfortable with imagery and who offer us one of the highest forms of literary experience, with multi-faceted layers of rich meaning and understanding. And what that translates into is more joy and satisfaction for you and your children.

I read a recent study where volunteers agreed to sit in a room, alone for fifteen minutes. The room was stark bare; no pictures to look at, no magazines lying around. They also had to agree to not take any electronics in the room with them–they had to leave their iPhones and iPads behind. Can you guess how many minutes it took before they started going absolutely stir crazy?

The average time was 5 minutes. They kept reaching for phones that weren't there. It was just them, alone, with their thoughts. And for most of them, there weren't many thoughts to keep themselves company.

Now contrast that with a group of prisoners Victor Frankl observed in the Nazi death camps. At peril of losing their lives, they gathered together to recite poetry, improvise plays and sing songs, which were forbidden. It was how they survived.

How true are these words of Marie Antoinette, who knew loneliness as few of us will ever know: "What a resource amid the casualties of life is a well-cultivated mind! One can then be one's own companion and find society in one's own thoughts." How would you or your children fare, left alone with your thoughts?

The objective is not to see how many poems we can pour through our children; it's to see how many we can help them hold on to. Our brains have a tremendous capacity for memorization. Prospective students at a leading university in Turkey hundreds of years ago were required to demonstrate that they had memorized the entire Koran to even be considered for admittance. For hundreds and even thousands of years, before written language, the history of nations was passed from generation to generation in ballads committed to memory. Their genealogies were kept the same way. Were it not for the ballads, awareness of many of the people and events of the olden days would have vanished long ago.

But most of us have allowed our brains to become very flabby. We know we can look up anything on the internet, so we don't train ourselves to remember. Helping our children memorize poetry strengthens that memory muscle. Our memory skills diminish as we age. Take advantage of this prime time for memory work. These days I forget what I'm saying right in the middle of saying it, but I can still recite you this poem I memorized for a talk in church before I was ten:

> I knelt to pray when day was done
> And prayed, Oh Lord, bless everyone.
> Lift from each saddened heart the pain,
> And let the sick be well again.
> And then I woke another day
> And carelessly went on my way.
> The whole day long I did not try
> To wipe a tear from any eye.
> I did not try to share the load
> Of any brother on the road.
> I did not even go to see
> The sick man just next door to me.
> Yet, once again when day was done,
> I prayed, Oh Lord, bless everyone.
> But as I prayed into my ear
> There came a voice that whispered clear,

"Pause now, my son, before you pray.
Who did you try to bless today?
God's richest blessings always go
To those who serve Him here below."
And then I hid my face and cried,
Forgive me, Lord, I have not tried.
But let me live another day,
And I will live the way I pray.

Little children need to be taught concentration and poetry is one of the best means. Memorizing poetry fosters the habit of attention that will reach into all other aspects of learning. And remember what I said about the vital importance of oral expression? That the secret of the Greek's artistic nature lie in the fact that they had their children spend their time in poetic recitation rather than in writing exercises. Although you can certainly kill a love of it by assigning and forcing it.

The imagery and rhythm of poetry are the secrets behind its long-lasting and staying power. When you help your young children memorize poetry, first let them take in the whole poem before you start breaking it down for memorization. Listening to the rhythm of the words will give the words something to organize themselves by, so let it be oral work rather than giving them the written words to memorize from. Then maybe work on just a line or two a day, not in a formal, sit-down, "Let's memorize this poem session," but rather in the course of the day—while you're driving to the store or making a bed together or picking up toys. Be sure you're breaking it up by complete thought or image rather than by end of lines. If you were learning Wordsworth's Intimations of Immortality, it would be confusing to say, "Trailing clouds of glory do we come" and then "from God, which is our home." You would want to give the entire thought as one: "Trailing clouds of glory do we come from God, which is our home."

Or look what happens to In Flanders Field when you break it down line by line:

In Flanders fields the poppies blow
Between the crosses, row on row,
That mark our place; and in the sky
The larks still bravely singing, fly
Scarce heard amid the guns below.

Doesn't it make more sense to unfold the poem, thought by thought, like this:

In Flanders fields the poppies blow between the crosses, row on row, that mark our place; and in the sky the larks still bravely singing, fly scarce heard amid the guns below.

If you go to the Poetry section in the young children's online library, I've linked to a couple of books that will give you ideas for helping children learn poetry. But it's really not rocket science: choose poems suitable to their age level and interest. Start with simple ones that will help build confidence. Give them opportunities to share them with family friends or grandparents. Keep the images in mind over the words. Clarify images that may be unclear or confusing to children. Read poetry every day. Invite your children to choose favorites they want to work on memorizing.

In one of the books I just referenced about how to help children love poetry, the top suggestion was to encourage them to create their own anthology of favorite poems. That goes for you, too. You can call Poetry notebook whatever you like, but I like the word "Gem" because it describes something that is very small, but is very valuable and lasts a long time. Poems are small but are of great worth. The first notebook you should organize, if you don't have one already, is your very own. Let your children see you copying favorite poems with cursive handwriting and decorating the pages to add to its pleasure, if you like. Read to them from your book of Poetry Gems. For your child, the Poetry anthology he creates not only will become a lifelong treasure, it serves as a first reading book and also a means of practicing, first printing, and then cursive handwriting in a meaningful and enjoyable way. They will want to include their very best work and it will become a source of pride to show grandparents and aunts and uncles and others. A 3-ring binder is a good first option because a child can create individual pages and add them as he goes along. If he makes a mistake, it's not hard to throw the page away and create another one as opposed to starting with a bound journal or a bare book where the pages are all intact.

Nursery Rhyme Gem Page

For a toddler who isn't reading yet, you could glue pictures from Mother Goose rhymes that will trigger a rhyme he's familiar with. You can shop thrift stores to look for illustrated Mother Goose books that you won't mind cutting up. Or you can print out images from the old Mother Goose books we've linked online in the online library for young children. So now, when he sees the picture of a clock with the mouse running up it, he recites the rhyme associated with it.

Little Bo Peep Gem Page

I started a Poetry Gem book with a little granddaughter who is just learning to read while I was helping my daughter with a new baby. I had her pick a nursery rhyme and then had her show me where she wanted me to write it on the page. I wrote the words as she dictated them to me, and then I had her read them with me as I pointed to each word. Then she took the page and illustrated it. We punched three holes in it and put it in her 3-ring binder. After a couple of days, her little 4-year-old sister wanted to do the same thing with Little Bo Peep, so we started hers as well. The power of the heart seeing something happening. If I had required her to color a page, I doubt she would have been interested.

Not only was she feeling the delight of the poetry itself, I accomplished several lessons with this simple little activity: I demonstrated that words can be written out. I showed left to right. I was giving her heart a chance to watch the act of writing play out. I could tell that Emma, the 4-year-old, was watching carefully how I drew circles and lines to form the letters. I was giving her something to imitate.

A book of poems like this can become a very personal first 'reading' book. One of my daughters had a first-grade teacher who taught them to read entirely from poetry pages they recited and illustrated. As a child starts learning to write, copying poems that she is memorizing can provide copy work to practice handwriting, even if she just starts with just one or two words a day. The pages can continue to be illustrated or decorated with designs or stickers. Little children love

Poetry Gem Page

cutting paper, so why not have them cut out pictures from old magazines to keep in a box that can be used to decorate their poetry pages. Cutting out pictures is one of the activities you can have your children do while you're reading stories to them to keep their hands busy and thereby hold interest longer.

Eventually, as your child matures, encourage the use of cursive handwriting to copy all the poems they are memorizing or are including in their anthology of favorite poems. Yes, it may be easier to print them off the computer. But the very act of cursive writing connects parts of the brain and deepens the whole process that wouldn't happen if you just type in the words.

Encourage your children to memorize scriptures or passages of Shakespeare or great quotes as they get older and add them to their Gems notebook. And how do you encourage them? By letting their hearts see you do it.

As I said before, these poetry books can become a lifelong treasured possession–sort of a scrap book of worthy thoughts. I was reading poetry before I went to bed the other night and ran across a poem I hadn't seen for more than fifty years. But as I read the first lines, a whole scene opened up to my memory of my childhood room, and the dusky sunlight that filtered across my bed as I heard the poem as a child. And my mother was there. I don't even have words to describe to you the experience, except to say that it was pure joy. This was the poem, called Velvet Shoes:

> Let us walk in the white snow
> In a soundless space;
> With footsteps quiet and slow,
> At a tranquil pace,
> Under veils of white lace.
> I shall go shod in silk,
> And you in wool,
> White as a white cow's milk,
> More beautiful
> Than the breast of a gull.
> We shall walk through the still town
> In a windless peace;
> We shall step upon white down,
> Upon silver fleece.
> Upon softer than these.
> We shall walk in velvet shoes:
> Wherever we go
> Silence will fall like dews
> On white silence below.
> We shall walk in the snow.

Definitely a poem worthy of my poetry gems book.

Poetry Tea Times have become popular with families where you put a nice tablecloth on the table, pick some flowers if you have some, and pull out your nicest china teaset. Enjoy some delicious treats and some hot cocoa or other drink while you share poetry with each other, preferably poems that are being memorized, but certainly reading them aloud from books works, too. I've had some moms say, but I have boys! You'll be surprised–poetry isn't just for girls. And especially consider how many of the great poets were men!

Did you watch the *Dead Poet Society* with Robin Williams? You will probably remember the words from this scene: "We don't read and write poetry because it's cute. We read and write poetry because we are members of the human race and the human race is filled with passion. Medicine, Law, business and Engineering–these are noble pursuits necessary to sustain life, but poetry, beauty, romance, love, these are what we stay alive for."

And now we're to the end of another talk. So let me end with this thought: The stories of history teach us that when a people have lost their heroic spirit; when their hearts have grown cold; it's not the scholar or the scientist who fans the flame again. It's always the poet–a Thomas Moore in Ireland or a Lord Alfred Tennyson in England–who rises up and breathes new life and plants new hearts in nations. So I'll leave you with a question I jotted down from my readings: Art thou the poet that shall save the world?

William Jennings Bryant: Poet of Nature

Edited by James Baldwin

Do you know what is meant by "the love of Nature"? Yes? But are you quite sure? Think a little. It is not an easy thing to understand, and many older people than you do not know what it means.

Bryant was the great American poet of Nature. His poetry is best understood and enjoyed by those who have first learned to love Nature as he loved her. To all such it appears to be very simple and grand.

In order that we may come by easy steps to a true appreciation of Bryant's poetry, let us take a lesson in the love of Nature.

"Man made the city; God made the country," is the old saying. Look at the long rows of city houses: how ugly they are! How dirty are the streets, from which on windy days clouds of dust sometimes rise and almost choke you as you walk along! Even the sky above is not often clear and blue as it ought to be, but it seems filthy with smoke and soot. And what sounds you hear! The noise of the cars as they buzz and jar along the street, the monotonous roar of human traffic, and the rough words of teamsters and hackmen as they try to crowd by one another—all these grate upon the sensitive ear.

How different is everything in the country! What a clear, brilliant blue the sky is; and what a vast variety of color the surface of the earth presents!

Here is the light, fresh green of the grass, and over there are the darker greens of the pines and cedars. In the autumn we observe the gorgeous hue of the males and the oaks as their leaves change with the frost from green to crimson and gold. Think, too, of the flowers! Here are fields white with daisies, and there are other fields filled with yellow buttercups or red clover blossoms! Farther away are fields of the graceful, slender-staled wheat, or of the tall, rustling corn!

Have you ever been in the woods in June? Instead of the harsh sounds of the streets, you hear the tumultuous but harmonious songs of birds; instead of the steady roar of traffic, you hear the deep note of the wind through the trees, or the murmur of a little brook flowing over stones or dashing down a waterfall. All around you the trees rise, like columns in a cathedral, but more beautiful and majestic; and the air is filled with a sweet scent fit to be used for incense in the churches.

Now read what Bryant has to say in his *Inscription for the Entrance to a Wood*. There are many hard words in it, and you must read very carefully and thoughtfully; but it will make you feel that on entering such a wood you are indeed going into God's own natural church, a place even more magnificent and wonderful than Solomon's temple:

Stranger, if thou hast learned a truth which needs
No school of long experience, that the world
Is full of guilt and misery, and hast seen
Enough of all its sorrows, crimes, and cares
To tire thee of it, enter this wild wood
And view the haunts of Nature. The calm shade
Shall bring a kindred calm, and the sweet breeze
That makes the green leaves dance, shall waft a balm
To thy sick heart. Thou wilt find nothing here
Of all that pained thee in the haunts of men,
And made thee loathe thy life. The primal curse
Fell, it is true, upon the unsinning earth,
But not in vengeance. God hath yoked to guilt
Her pale tormentor, misery. Hence these shades
Are still the abodes of gladness; the thick roof
Of green and stirring branches is alive
And musical with birds, that sing and sport
In wantonness of spirit; while below
The squirrel, with raised paws and form erect,
Chirps merrily. Throngs of insects in the shade
Try their thin wings and dance in the warm beam
That waked them into life. Even the green trees
Partake the deep contentment; as they bend
To the soft winds, the sun from the blue sky
Looks in and sheds a blessing on the scene.
Scarce less the cleft-born wild-flower seems to enjoy
Existence, than the winged plunderer
That sucks its sweets. The mossy rocks themselves,
And the old and ponderous trunks of prostrate trees
That lead from knoll to knoll a causey rude
Or bridge the sunken brook, and their dark roots,
With all their earth upon them, twisting high,
Breathe fixed tranquility. The rivulet
Sends forth glad sounds, and tripping o'er its bed
Of pebbly sands, or leaping down the rocks,
Seems, with continuous laughter, to rejoice
In its own being. Softly tread the marge,
Lest from her midway perch thou scare the wren
That dips her bill in water. The cool wind
That stirs the stream in play, shall come to thee,
Like one that loves thee, nor let thee pass
Ungreeted, and shall give its light embrace.

This is one of the hardest things in Bryant's poetry. When you can see all its beauties, and take pleasure in reading it, you will have learned to love both Nature and Nature's poet-priest.

It is not uncommon to hear young people say, "I don't like poetry at all. It is dry, horrid stuff, and I don't understand it." No doubt some of you will say or think this about Bryant's poetry. It is true that he used a great many long, hard words; and his poems are sometimes rather solemn. What is more, they are not musical like Longfellow's. It is said that Bryant had no ear for music. For this reason you cannot read his poetry as you do Longfellow's, swinging along from line to line. Young people who read in the sing-song style will find that they cannot do that when they come to Bryant. At first you may think his poetry is, for this reason, not good poetry at all. Perhaps it would be better to call Bryant a prose poet instead of a musical poet. But when you get used to his prose-like poetry, you will like it if you have in you the least love of nature or natural beauty.

Take some one poem that you like and read it over and over again, until you have it almost if not quite by heart. Take one, and read it until by very force of habit you learn to love it; and then the next poem you take up will reveal beauties which you ever suspected when you first read it.

There is a city poem of Bryant's, "The Crowded Street," well worth learning to love:

Let me move slowly through the street,
Filled with an ever-shifting train,
Amid the sound of steps that beat
The murmuring walks like autumn rain.

How fast the flitting figures come!
The mild, the fierce, the stony face;
Some bright with thoughtless smiles, and some
Where secret tears have left their trace.

Story

"Storytelling is an ageless and beautiful art. When the lights are low and your child is in a quiet, reflective mood, the stories told him will never be forgotten and their influence will follow him the rest of his life."

Mary King threw the strand of pearls on her bed, her eyes blazing with anger. "My mother! My stupid, stupid mother! How can she do this to me?" Tomorrow was her graduation from high school and she had spent the day at the lake with her friends. They had each told about the presents their parents had bought them for graduation. How could she face them and tell them she had been given this old string of beads? And that wasn't the worst of it. While her friends had all been out shopping with their moms for new outfits to wear, her mom had handsewn a plain, simple dress and now she expected her to wear this necklace with it. It was just humiliating.

As Mary dressed for bed, she noticed an envelope on the top of her dresser. It was from Mr. Morse. Mr. Morse had been like a father to Mary. She and her mother had lived in his home for as long as she could remember. He had often given her gifts. "At least I bet there's a check in here," she thought to herself.

But as she tore open the envelope, there was no check. Just a long letter… She sat on her bed and started to read.

Dear Mary, I had planned on giving you a check for your graduation, but that can come later. I was at the lake a couple of days ago when you were there with your friends and I couldn't help but overhear what you were saying to them. You wished your mother's face was pretty like your friends' mothers instead of all red and cross looking. You wished her hair was thick and curly like theirs instead of thin and stringy. And you complained about how embarrassing it was to go anywhere with her because her one foot dragged a little when she walked and you thought it made people stare. That's when I knew that what you needed more than a check, was a story.

Mary rolled her eyes. "Has everyone gone crazy around here?" But she continued to read.

Many years ago, a young couple moved into town. Everyone loved them and they could tell how much they loved each other. The bride was so pretty and had such a bright smile that everyone was drawn to her. But being in a small town, it wasn't long until the townspeople came to know their story.

The husband was the son of a wealthy mill owner in a nearby city in eastern Pennsylvania. His father had picked out the girl he thought his son should marry. She was from one of the other prominent, rich families. When his son refused and insisted on marrying this other girl, the father disowned him; told him he'd never get another cent from him.

The two moved to a nearby town to start a new life. The husband hadn't ever had to work before and wasn't used to hard labor, but he willingly grabbed any job that would take him. And she worked hard, too. Bit by bit they saved enough money to build a little house on the hill, and they were very happy.

Then one day there was an accident. The scaffolding the husband was standing on collapsed beneath him. His coworkers carried his bruised and bleeding body to their little home and laid him on the bed. That very night a little girl was born to them. Oh, how he fought to live for that little girl, but after a short time, he was gone.

The father-in-law, still bitter at the girl because he blamed her for taking his son away from him, sent word that he would take the child and raise her as his own. She would lack for nothing, only the mother was never to have contact with her again. The mother sent back word: "I love her too much. I will find a way to provide for her." And she did.

She continued to work every job that came her way. Eventually she was offered a position as a teacher of young children. The job included room and board at the school for her and her little daughter. And they were very happy there.

Then, one day, when the little girl was about 3, the mother was downstairs reading a book when she heard a cry that struck terror in her heart. "Fire! Fire in the west wing!" That's where her little girl was! She threw down the book and flew up the stairs, two and three stairs at a time. By the time she reached the third landing, the smoke was curling down the hall from the bedrooms. She dropped to the ground and felt her way through the smoke.

Minutes passed when firefighters on the main floor saw a figure stumble down the stairs. Her face, hands and feet were badly burned. All her hair was gone. In her arms she was carrying a bundle wrapped in a quilt, and from her hand dangled a strand of pearls. "I'm badly hurt," she whispered, "but I have rescued my two greatest treasures. Please keep them safe for me," and she collapsed to the ground.

For weeks she writhed in agony. No one expected her to live. But she was fighting to live for that little girl. Slowly, she started to heal. And then one day word came to her again from the father-in-law: "Give me the child and I will raise her as my own. She will lack for nothing." Again word was sent back: "I love the child too much. I will find a way."

Mr. Morse continued. "That's when I stepped in. I built a large home far enough away from the town so that no one would know what had happened and you and your mother have lived here ever since. I have watched your mother find work to do with her hands, even though they were stiff and painful to use. Many a time I passed her room and found her on her knees pleading for strength. I watched her carefully save every penny so that you could go to college. I wanted to tell you these things, but she made me promise to never tell you. She said it would kill her to have your pity. She wanted you to love her just for who she was. But when I heard you talking to your friends like that, I just couldn't keep silent any longer. Now you must never tell her that I have told you. Sincerely, A.E. Morse"

Mary sat in stunned silence. And then hot tears started flowing down her cheeks. How could she have been so selfish? All this time, she thought it was Mr. Morse that was sending her to college. No, it was her mother. All those times that she was embarrassed that her mother always wore the same homemade dress...she was saving for her. "Dear God, please forgive me", she whispered.

She now heard her mother's familiar shuffle coming towards her room. Somehow it didn't annoy her this time. Her mother knocked on the door. "Mary, is everything OK?" Mary remembered her promise to not let her mother know she knew, so she hurried to wipe the tears from her face. "Oh, come on in! I guess it's just the excitement of the graduation and everything tomorrow.... Mother...the pearls...they're beautiful. Have you had them long?" "Oh, yes. I've had them for many years. Your father gave them to me. He had to work so hard to earn them. I love every pearl on that string. I saved them for you once in the long ago because I wanted you to have something that he had earned for us."

Mary could hardly speak. She gently wrapped her arms around her mother and held her close as she whispered, "Truly, I have the most beautiful mother in all the world."

It was more than 50 years ago that I heard this story. I couldn't have been more than 7 or 8. It made such an impression on my heart that every time I saw a pearl necklace, it made me think of this story. I remember clearly the little book my Sunday School teacher read it from. In fact, every time I saw a little book of stories, I would open it up looking for the story again.

I'm going to come back to this story of the pearls, but I want to push a little pause button to share an experience I had while I was working on the Forgotten Classics Family Library. I learned so many things I had never known before and was anxious to share them with families. But I ran into a problem. How do you make old books with no pictures appeal to children who aren't reading so much anymore; who are used to flashy video games and entertainment? I knew the rich, beautiful language they used could be a barrier to many children.

I pondered over this for many months. And then one day when I was out in Utah visiting my mother, I was heading out the door to go out to dinner when I had a feeling that I can best describe as how you feel when someone walks up to you and says, excitedly, "Come here for a minute... I want to show you something."

So I slipped downstairs to get on to the computer for a minute and went on Internet Archive where I spend most of my time. I said out loud, "I don't know what I'm looking for!" and then a keyword came into my mind that I entered in. A long list of books came up and I started scrolling through them until I came to one title that seemed to jump out at me. It wasn't a particularly interesting title; it was *The Use of Story in Religious Education* by Margaret Eggleston.

I started reading and immediately knew this was the answer I was looking for. Before I went to bed that night, I discovered there had been a revival in the art of storytelling about a hundred years ago for the very purpose I was looking for–to warm and open up the hearts of children so they want to learn more. I found a whole circle of warm-hearted storytellers and educators who started teaching me how to reach the hearts of children.

Opportunities started coming to me to share what I was learning and as I taught about restoring the art of storytelling in our homes, I found the stories that I most often told and that made the deepest impressions were Margaret Eggleston's, such as this one:

One day Margaret went to visit a friend and when she walked in the front door, she could hear her friend's 6-year-old son, John, upstairs kicking, and screaming and throwing things. The mother explained that he had disobeyed her one time too many and had been sent up to his room without his supper. Margaret asked if she could go upstairs and see if there was something she could do. The mother didn't think it would do any good but agreed to let her try.

As she entered the bedroom, she found John curled up in a heap at the foot of the bed. He didn't even look up at her. She sat herself down on the floor and proceeded to say, "I think I'll tell you a story. You needn't listen of course. Away up in the far north where it is very, very cold, there lived a little boy who had a sled. Now, he didn't pull this sled with a rope. Oh, no. He hitched it up to four little dogs and how they would fly over the snow."

By this time, John was facing her and had stopped kicking. Slowly and quietly, the storyteller unfolded the story of little Jimmy Standby of Labrador who had stood by the dogs all through the night and the day in the bitter cold because he had promised Dr. Grenfell he would stand by.

As the story progressed, John crept closer and closer to her until he had crawled up in her lap, his face eagerly looking into her face as he followed Jimmy Standby to the very end. When Margaret stood up to leave, John said, "Please, will you ask my mother if I can come downstairs for just a moment? There is something I need to tell her." After some coaxing, the mother agreed and John, with his dirt-streaked little red face, came down the stairs and walking right up to his mother said, "She has told me a nice story and I want you to know I'm going to have a name like his. I'm going to be Jimmy Standby, too." And he walked upstairs like a man.

When Margaret was asked if storytelling really made a difference, she answered the question with this story:

One day she told a story to a group of adolescent boys among which was a sort of rebel. She didn't think he was paying any attention to the story. It was a story of a young boy who had a job sweeping up a bank at closing time. As he went to empty one of the trash cans, he noticed a large roll of money that had accidentally been thrown away. As he held it in his hands, he thought how much this money would mean to his family. His father was a drunk who spent most of what he earned on drinking. The little bit of money this boy brought home went toward food for his little crippled sister and his mother who was very ill. The doctor had told him that if he didn't find a way to get medicine for his mother and move her out to the country where she could get fresh air, she probably wouldn't live past the fall.

He looked around and saw that no one had noticed him, so he slipped the money in his pants pocket and headed home. Along the way, the money felt heavier and heavier in his pocket. He moved it first to his outside jacket pocket and then to the inside pocket. But the closer he got to home, the heavier the money felt until he at last realized he just couldn't keep the money.

He headed back to the bank where a security guard let him in. He marched straight to the bank president's office, knocked on the door, walked in and threw the money across the desk to the president, explaining how he had come by it. The president looked surprised. "Son," he said, "I know how much this money would mean to you and your mother. No one knew you had it. Why did you bring it back?" Without hesitating, the boy leaned across the desk, and looking straight into the eyes of the president said, "Sir, as long as I live, I have to live with myself and I don't want to live with a thief."

That was the story. There had been no particular reaction to it and Margaret lost contact with this young man until years later when she received a letter from him. He was now a soldier fighting on the war front in France. As she opened it, she read, "Years ago on a wet and rainy day when the ice was dangerous on the sidewalk, you came and told a story to a group of boys. I don't remember the details of the story, but I remember how it ended: "As long as I live, I have to live with myself and I don't want to live with a thief." That one story has kept me from lying and stealing and from being a coward. And here in France, it has kept me true to my manhood. I have a class here in the barracks–I know that may be hard to believe–some of my men need that story. I want it for all of them for all that I am, I owe to that one story and I thank you from the bottom of my heart."

There was another story Margaret told that I loved, but there was something about the story— I couldn't put my finger on it...something I was understanding just wasn't right. She had reluctantly included it in the final chapter of her book. Although she had told the story several times, it was of such a personal nature that she didn't feel comfortable putting it out there for just anyone to read. Yet, she felt she should include it.

She had happened to step into a Sunday School class one day where the young men in the class had been grilling the teacher – Does anyone really know there is a God? He had exhausted all his answers but had not satisfied them. Margaret looked into their sincere and eager faces and said, "Boys, yes, I do know there is a God. If you'll come back next week I'll tell you how I know."

The next week all the boys were there plus a few extra as she unfolded this story:

Some years previous, her father, as I understood, had been diagnosed with a serious illness. The doctor said he needed to be out in the fresh country air, undisturbed by anyone or anything. He needed quiet. It was decided that they would head to a campsite in Maine where she had already spent several summers. They took with them "a little girl of 7." I wasn't sure who she was...maybe a little sister or a helper.

Over the next several weeks, the father seemed to be doing a little better. The flowers were in full bloom and they picked fresh blackberries that grew in abundance in the hills around them.

And then one day, he took a turn for the worse. The doctor was sent for from the nearest town 20 miles away. He left them with some medicine and went on his way. It seemed to give some relief and they had all gone to sleep when Margaret heard some noise at the flap of the tent. The doctor had returned. He quickly explained that the blood work had shown there was a poison that had spread throughout the system of the sick one and the medicine he had left wouldn't do any good. It was a very serious situation. The doctor gave her new medicine and told her she would have to administer it every 15 minutes throughout the night. But even with that, he said death could come at any moment. He could only stay a little while because he had other patients to tend to. Margaret stood at the opening of the tent and watched his lamp fade away into the forest. And she was alone again.

She began to administer the medicine as she had been instructed. In between dosages, she tried to write letters, but her hands were shaking too much. She tried to read, but she couldn't concentrate. It was now the middle of the night. She stood at the opening of the tent, wrapping both hands around the pole, bracing herself against the night breeze. For the first time in her life, she was afraid. Really afraid.

The moon shone on the lake before her and reflected on the hills on the opposite shore. As she looked out into the stillness of that scene, the same words that came to the Psalmist came to her mind: "I will lift mine eyes unto the hills from whence cometh my help. My help cometh from the Lord who made heaven and earth. The Lord is thy keeper. The Lord shall preserve thee." The words came again, only this time she repeated them softly, aloud. "I will lift mine eyes unto the hills from whence cometh my help." But this time as she spoke the words, a peace and a comfort filled her whole soul and the fear completely left her. She felt strengthened to face the hard things.

Finally, the morning broke and death had passed them by. After a pause, she quietly said, "Boys, that's why I know there is a God."

And they were satisfied.

Well, remember how I said I have been looking for the story of the pearls for over 50 years? A couple of years ago I happened to be in a thrift store and I found a little book of stories. I opened it, and there it was! I was so excited to find it that I stood in the aisle and read it right there. It was exactly as I had remembered. What I didn't expect and what caught me completely by surprise was that at the end of the story, it said, "by Margaret Eggleston."

Shortly after I had found the story again, I was invited to our Stake Girls Camp. They wanted me to come after dark when the girls were gathered around the campfire and tell them a story. You can guess the story I told them. It got me thinking about Margaret Eggleston again and after I told the story, I wondered if she had any other books of stories. I looked and found she had another book published in 1921–the year after her first book. It was called *Fireside Stories to Tell to Teenage Girls*. And then I glanced through the titles of stories and there was my story of the pearls! I smiled at the coincidence that I had just told a story in a campsite to teenage girls that Margaret had specifically written to be told at the campsite to a group of teenage girls.

Well, more months passed by as I continued working on my project. And I had one of those moments when you've been working hard on something and you pause for a minute and reflect on what you have accomplished. I had now filled nearly 60 volumes of stories of all sorts from this wonderful Golden Age of children's literature. I had also selected and organized an online library for families from the same literature and had over 2000 books available. I had spent several months going through my stacks of notes, trying to organize what I had been learning about reaching the hearts of our children so I could share it with others and had recorded over several hours of audios that we posted online. I thought about how much my own life had been enriched by spending so much time with all these stories and storytellers. I can't even begin to describe the joy that has come into my own life and I have been filled with so much hope.

And my thoughts turned to Margaret. And I thought, "Margaret, you are the one who opened the door to all of this for me and introduced me to all your friends." I was so grateful to her. I pulled her book from the shelf—her *Use of Story in Religious Education*—and started to re-read it. Knowing what I now knew, I appreciated even more the depth of her wisdom. I could feel the goodness of her soul. And I found myself wondering, "Margaret, who are you? What do you look like?"

I searched and searched online to learn anything about her and couldn't find anything at all. Only a birth year–that she had been born in 1878. I told my husband how disappointed I was that I couldn't find anything about her, and he suggested I get on a site that has a lot of public records available. He does a lot of family history and thought I might find out something about her that way.

I never knew before how many Margaret Egglestons there are in the world and I didn't know how I was going to find her. I went back to her book for clues. On the title page, it said she was a teacher at Boston University and she dedicated the book to her little daughter. In 1920, when she wrote it, she would have been 42 so I assumed she must have had only one child because you wouldn't single out one child if you had others, would you?

Using those clues, we found her in Boston in the 1920 census. She was living with her widowed mother, Elizabeth White, age 72 and her 13-year-old daughter who I noted would have been born around 1907. What I was sad to learn was that Margaret was also a widow. What happened?

We found her again in the 1910 census. She was living in Brooklyn, Kings County, New York. Her husband, Gurdon Eggleston, was a clergyman and they had a little 3-year-old daughter. So now I knew I was looking for a death certificate of Gurden between 1910 and 1920. We found one in 1914, but it said that he died in Stoneham, Oxford. I told my husband that I didn't think that was him because, wasn't that England? My husband said to hold on and he said, no, Stoneham, Oxford is in Maine.

I pulled out a map and found Oxford. It sits at the northern tip of a lake, about 20 miles from the nearest large town.

Suddenly I realized what I had missed in the previous story. She had worded it so that I wasn't clear who the people were in the story. She referred to the father of her family, and I assumed it was her father. Now I knew it wasn't her father at all–it was her husband. The little girl of 7 was their little girl. This was the story of how she faced the loss of her own husband and the story became even more meaningful to me because I, also, had a husband who faced a serious illness. I wasn't alone out in the wilds of Maine, but I felt just as alone. I knew well the fear that overtakes you in the dark hours of the middle of the night. I, too, had felt that comfort and peace pour into me that gave me the strength to face the hard things. Only my husband had been restored to health. She had to say good-bye to hers.

In the story, it said death passed by for the time, but evidently not for long as the death certificate said he passed away in the middle of the summer on July 31, 1914, just before his 36th birthday. The cause of death was a cerebral hemorrhage from a brain tumor. His occupation was still clergyman.

What more could her stories teach me about her, I wondered. I returned to the *Fireside* book I had only quickly scanned through before. Now I read carefully. The first story was about May–with an M—who had been told by the doctor in the spring that her father was very ill and she needed to take him somewhere it was quiet and they wouldn't be disturbed. She took him to a little cabin in New Hampshire. As winter approached and she became fearful, she went to the lake and was strengthened as she looked to the hills from whence cometh her strength. The details of the story had been changed, but I clearly recognized it as her own true story.

Then it hit me. What I had learned from Margaret was that the stories that will make the deepest impact and will leave the most lasting impressions are those you draw from personal experience. Was it possible that the story of the pearl necklace, that for all these years I had assumed was a good story but purely fictional, was actually based on true events in the life of this woman who has come to have such great influence on my life? I certainly knew she was a practical woman; I couldn't imagine her making up a sensational story just to stir emotion. She would have grounded it in true events and I started looking for evidence to back it up.

I discovered that her mother, Elizabeth White, immigrated from England in 1870 when she was 22 years old. In the Fireside stories, I found several stories about an Elizabeth who had come from far across the ocean. The only work she could find was working in a factory and she couldn't afford to live anywhere but a boarding house. One story told how lonely she was and how she longed for a friend. Some of the rich people in the town snubbed her, but she caught the eye of one of their most popular and favorite sons who was attracted to her goodness.

In the story of the pearl necklace, the wealthy mill owner lived in eastern Pennsylvania. When the young couple married, they moved away to a nearby town. Margaret was born in Walton, NY. It was a small town then and is a small town today and it lies just over the north-east border of Pennsylvania.

After the fire, Mr. Morse took the little girl and her mother to a place far enough away that no one would know what had happened to her. In the story, Margaret describes how they loved to play at the lake. There's a lake about 100 miles north of Walton. Not far from the lake is a little college town: Kirkland, NY. In the 1900 census, I found the name of a college student there: Gurdon Eggleston.

Now I found a story about May–with an M—about to graduate from college. Several young men are interested in her. Should she choose the rich one so she would always have financial security? Or should she choose the football star who always made her laugh. Or maybe she should choose the scholar. She didn't know what to do and sought the advice of a favorite professor who told her she should look at them through the eyes of who would she want to be the father of her children.

She had gone back to her room and found bouquets of roses from her suitors. But there was also a plain lunch box. She opened it and found it filled with forget-me-nots which she loved. But who were they from?

She placed a few of the flowers in her hair and tucked some in her belt and left for the ceremonies. On the way, she saw her friend, Gene, with a G. "Oh, I see you got my flowers!" He said that he had left very early in the morning because he wanted to pick up his mother to meet her. Along the way, he spotted the forget-me-nots, which he knew she loved, emptied his lunch box and filled it with the flowers, and put them on the mail train that was just going by. He had hoped they would get to her.

She had met Gene in her Geology class and they had spent many happy hours combing the hillsides looking for rocks and wildflowers. He was always so courteous and cheerful and good natured, even when things weren't going right. And here he was being so sweet to his little mother. Yes, Gene was the one she would choose to get to know better.

One more little piece of evidence that would seem to back up the story. In 1921, Margaret applied for a passport. It had a picture of Margaret in it. She was beautiful! As part of the application, she had to include an affidavit of someone who could vouch they knew her. The writing was the same as whoever had filled out the application, which I would assume was Margaret. But the person vouching for her was her mother, Elizabeth White, who had only signed her name. Clearly, the signature was made by a hand that wrote with great difficulty, which the story of the pearl necklace would have explained.

I can't say for sure that the story of the pearl necklace is true. Details of the story were likely changed. But I believe the evidence suggests it was based on true events in Margaret's life and the life of her mother and somehow that makes the story even more meaningful to me.

As I mentioned, my husband loves to do family history and he likes to see if people are related to him. So he searched on the Family Tree Search and found someone had already placed Gurdon Eggleston's name in their family tree. He didn't have to go back very many generations before he found that Gurdon's family line merged with one of my husband's family lines. But what was missing on the record–what was left blank because it was unknown–was that Gurdon had a wife and a little girl.

But it's not left blank anymore. Almost exactly 100 years from that sorrowful parting in a lonely camp on a lake in Maine, the names of Margaret White Eggleston and Gurdon Eggleston with their little girl have been re-united, always and forever.

So why have I spent your time telling you about Margaret Eggleston? Well, I have lots of reasons. First of all, I wanted you to feel the difference between a story and information. What if I had introduced Margaret this way? Margaret White was born in Walton, NY in 1878. She married Gurdon Eggleston, a clergyman, who died in 1914. In 1920, while teaching at Boston University, she wrote a book, *The Use of Story in Religious Education.* Would you have cared about her? Would you have any pictures of her in your mind? Would she have any personality? Notice how each story revealed different facets of her personality.

The function of story is to stir feeling and awaken emotion. We use words like *dry*, *cold* and *hard* to describe facts, but stories breathe life into them. Stories help us to care. They fire up desire and passion. If you find the right story, you can create an interest in any subject. Stories help us to see clearly and to understand things in our hearts that our eyes alone cannot comprehend and that facts, alone, cannot reveal. Stories are one of the most important tools you have in teaching your children and are best used in that first step in the pattern for learning.

My grown-up son recently finished reading a story for a second time–Charles Dicken's *Tale of Two Cities*. He was home when he finished reading it and I happened to be in the kitchen when he said, "Wow." And again "Wow." If you've read a book like that, you know exactly what was going on inside of him. To borrow the words of someone else, it was enlarging his heart, enlightening his mind and it tasted delicious to him. It was good fruit. The deeps of our souls, like the deeps of the ocean, are silent and I didn't want to intrude on the work that was taking place inside of him with mere chatter. In ways I don't fully understand, that story was making him better and wiser and thereby, happier.

Not all books have that effect on us. What gave this book that power? And my answer is that it has everything to do with the heart through which the story flows. Charles Dickens had a happy childhood. He was a voracious reader and loved to spend time out in nature. But that season of his life came to an abrupt end when he was just eleven and his father was thrown into a debtor's prison. Dickens was left to wander the streets and fend for himself. He ended up working 10-hour days at a rat-infested, tumble-down shoe blacking factory. Over the next while, he experienced a cold, bleak winter of life where he knew hunger, loneliness, poverty and despair. As miserable as it was, the experience enlarged his heart and carried into his writings.

But there's another heart through which *Tale of Two Cities* flowed. Thomas Carlyle had been encouraged by his dear friend, John Stuart Mills, to write on the French Revolution. After five months of painful toil, he gave his one and only manuscript of Volume One to Mills for suggestions before sending it on to the publisher. Weeks passed and Carlyle hadn't heard anything from his friend, so he paid him a visit and found that his friend had loaned the manuscript out where it had carelessly been left on the parlor floor. The housekeeper thought it was trash and used it to light the hearth fires. Mills was absolutely beside himself with grief. He could think of no way to repair the damages, although he offered monetary compensation. To Carlyle's credit, he confided to his wife, Jane, "Mills, poor fellow, is terribly cut up. We must endeavor to hide from him how very serious this business of life is for us." And serious it was. The Carlyles had no money. They had hoped this work would help lift them from their poverty. And he had already destroyed his notes. Carlyle wrote, "I remember and can still remember less of it than of anything I ever wrote with such toil. It is gone." He had no hope of recovering it. But that night, he had a dream in which his father and brother begged him not to abandon the work. The next morning, he accepted enough money from Mills to buy some paper and he started writing again. First he wrote volumes 2 and 3, then he went back to recreate Volume 1, writing the entire manuscript from memory, using words, as Carlyle himself described, that came "direct and flamingly from the heart." He said, "It is as if my invisible schoolmaster had torn my copybook when I showed it, and said, "No, boy! Thou must write it better." The result was a masterpiece that has remained in print to this day. He wrote as though he was a participant to all the events of the French Revolution, bringing it to life in such a way that the reader feels like he, too, is there.

It was this work that Charles Dickens read and re-read and that inspired him to write his *Tale of Two Cities*. My son simply had to pull the book off a shelf, open and read and the souls and understanding of both Carlyle and Dickens poured into him.

Just as the wisdom and experience of Carlyle and Dickens was preserved within the covers of a book my son only had to pull off a shelf and read, so has the wisdom and experience of all ages been preserved and is now being made available to us in miraculous ways. A single book may contain an entire lifetime of someone's toil and effort. Today, we're not limited to the narrow view of our own experiences. We can see and experience life through thousands of eyes. And history has preserved the best of the best for us.

We have instant access to the greatest literature of all time. When we come to a word we don't understand, we can simply click and learn its meaning. We owe a great debt to Noah Webster who spent his life mastering 28 languages so that he could take each word, one at a time, and look at it through its roots and pass that knowledge on to us.

When our children come to a word they can't pronounce, just click and there it is. *Niebelingenlied*....who would have thought. Where is this place again? Click away and it takes you to a map. Click again, and you can view it. Can you not remember who a certain person was? Click and find. Forget a fact? Click and find.

This is an education fit for royalty. We have the potential to raise the noblest, most cultured, most refined, the wisest and happiest generation in the history of the world. The eyes of those who have suffered, sweat, sacrificed and starved to bring forth truths are upon us. But here we are with a field that is white and already to harvest...but we're faced with a generation that has little desire to reap. It is your privilege and upon you rests the responsibility to light the fires of desire within their hearts. No one can do it better than you.

Nothing opens the heart like a good story. And some of the works of the greatest storytellers that have ever lived are preserved in the Libraries of Hope Library. Just as I brought Margaret Eggleston to life through her stories, these storytellers bring the great men and women of history to life so that they can have a real and personal influence on the lives of your children. Through stories, they can become some of their best friends.

All these wonderful stories were wrapped in love. These storytellers didn't shy away from sharing their love for the children. Dearest boys and girls–I love you. Signed, your loving friend; your affectionate friend. You'll feel the warmth.

So let's talk about using Story in your everyday life. I strongly believe that our ability to maintain hope in the days ahead will be in direct proportion to how broad and how deep our reservoir of stories is from which we draw. There's an old saying that says, "What's down in the well comes up in the bucket." You cannot draw from a story that's not there. What happens when we try to operate our lives from a puddle of stories? We see the answer to that question every day in the news of people who take desperate measures because they find themselves locked in raw emotion for which there is no story to help find a way through.

It doesn't mean you need to read stories all day long. Even if you only have time for one story a day, 1 story a day is 365 stories a year and in 18 years when your children leave home, they will have heard over 6500 stories! That's a pretty good start, I'd say.

And if you want to instill a love of faith, freedom and family, you must find stories that reflect these values. I happened to be looking for something on the secular humanist site and landed on the "Frequently Asked" page. A parent asked for recommendations of books for his children that he could pick up at the library that would be free of any reference to religion or spirituality or faith. The response was: if the American Library Association recommended a book, he could be confident it would be safe for his family.

Dr. Paul Fitz, Professor of Psychology at New York University, did a study of 90 of the most widely used reading and social studies texts used in our schools at the time. Keep in mind–this was back in 1986. In social studies, which was supposed to reflect American life to children in younger grades, not one of the texts examined–over 15,000 pages–had any reference to any word of any type of religious activity, such as attending church or worshiping or praying. Not one text mentioned marriage as a foundation of the family. Not one text used the words "marriage, husband, wife, homemaker." In upper grades, there was not a single reference to any patriotic theme after the year 1780. Only one story focused on traditional male/female romantic love. No stories supported motherhood or showed any woman or girl with a positive relationship to a baby, a young child or even a doll. However, stories of sex-role reversal was common as well as stories of feminism.

We are seeing, truly, that what is in the well comes up in the bucket. Libraries of Hope exists to give you another choice. Children and adults are naturally drawn to stories, so it is one of your main tools in cultivating hearts. And the music in your voice is an important part of relaying those stories. So pay attention that you don't allow the words to come out as a monotone. Let your voice reflect the emotion of the story. The music in your voice is the reason why read-alouds are so vital in childhood especially.

Their hearts need to be well stocked with stories and if the only stories they can get to are the ones where they have to work so hard to decode the words, it's a great loss of opportunity. Listening to audio recordings is a wonderful option as well. And having your children read aloud, too, opens that thought and emotion connection we talked about earlier.

One thing I hope you'll consider is recording yourself as you read aloud and submitting the recordings to Librivox. Librivox is well equipped to store recordings and then your labors will benefit so many others. I hope you'll start recording some of the heart books that are in public domain in the site. Choose the ones that touch your own heart, because that will reflect in your voice. Do bring the stories to life with the music in your voice! There are too many Librivox recorders who forget to do that one simple thing and it's almost impossible to listen to them. Let me know which books you have recorded and I'll link them in the site.

Use stories to awaken interest in any and every subject. Even huge corporations are beginning to turn to stories.

Rudyard Kipling wrote, "If history were told in the form of stories, it would never be forgotten."

And don't forget to tell family stories. These family stories have the power to bind the hearts of generations and give children such a sense of belonging.

Work towards being able to put the book down and sharing stories heart to heart. We are a story-deprived generation, so we have some work to do to fill our own reservoirs. But many of you are familiar with scripture stories. Start there. You cannot measure the impression of a well-told scripture story told in the dark from the heart of one who loves it just as a child drops off to sleep.

Once upon a time, I listened to a story of a strand of pearls–that story has lifted me up and changed my life forever. Lifting up and changing lives *is* the power of a story. Stories can heal our hearts. Stories can heal our world. Don't underestimate the power of a story.

Using Stories in the Grieving Process

We took in a stray cat and named her Juliet. Actually, it turned out we took in three cats, because she was already expecting. My granddaughter, Kayleigh, who was seven years old at the time, immediately claimed her as her own. She took her to bed at night, fed her, played with her and loved her. She even cleaned out the kitty litter. When the mama cat was ready to deliver the babies, she delivered the first one in Kayleigh's hair in the middle of the night. Now, that's a bonding experience.

We usually kept Juliet in the house, but one night she ran out the front door. If you've ever owned a cat, you know you don't coax a cat home if she's not willing. We kept opening the door and calling to her, but finally had to go to bed, hoping she'd come back when she was ready.

The next morning my husband left early before the sun came up, and there was our little Juliet, laying by the side of the road. He said it was apparent she hadn't suffered. But our hearts hurt at the thought of having to tell Kayleigh.

Soon, I could hear Kayleigh's footsteps upstairs as she anxiously ran around looking for Juliet, calling her name. She came running into the kitchen. "Where's Juliet?" My daughter put her arms around her, and with lots of tears, told her what had happened.

Kayleigh didn't say anything, but ran into her bedroom where she drew a picture of Juliet lying on the foot of her bed, nursing her two little babies. She glued it to a simple paper picture frame and hung it next to her bed. There were tears on the picture.

Later that night, she created a little book by stapling some papers together. The first picture was Juliet on the back patio when she found her. There was a drawing of the night the kitten was born in her hair. And then came the hardest drawing of all—drawing a car with headlights and Juliet running towards it. The final picture was out under the trees with the leaves falling all around where Juliet was buried.

Within a few days, Kayleigh's dad came home from a deployment and the family moved back on the army base. Dad said, "No more cats." He's not heartless. Just practical. And Kayleigh became quiet and withdrawn.

She continued to draw cats—hundreds and millions and billions of cats. But in the busy-ness of life and moving, the stories had stopped.

One day I suggested to her dad that he take time to ask Kayleigh to share the stories about Juliet and they started flooding out of her heart. She told him about the time Juliet left a 'gift' of a dead mouse on the basement floor. And how, one time, Juliet carried one of her baby kittens upside down—by her bottom. She always told that story with a giggle. And, of course, how the baby came to be born in her hair in the middle of the night. And in so doing, once again moved along the process of healing a broken heart.

Kayleigh started smiling and laughing again.

Without the stories, raw emotions can be unbearable. Stories help us sort through feelings and provide a means of releasing them.

Stories are a powerful heart-healer.

The Influence of a Story

In a season of major storms and worries of approaching storms, we had a "storm" come through our lives.

One day, we started having difficulties accessing our website to make changes. We were assured by our hosting company that they were aware of the problem and had technicians working on it. But after several frustrating weeks, we were delivered the bad news. Our host server had decided to not renew the license with the company through which we had built our website, but failed to let the users know. What that meant was that we were completely locked out of it. Not only could it not be accessed, it couldn't be copied and pasted or transferred. The code would work with no other server.

Furthermore, because it was no longer being supported, the site was "disintegrating" before our eyes and there was not one thing we could do about it. We were warned we were likely to completely lose everything there, and I was referred to the small print in our contract that the host owned our property and we had no recourse for damages done.

We contacted several experts who looked at the site and they all came back with the same discouraging news. Our only option was to completely rebuild the site.

So let me try and give you a sense of what that would mean. There were 341 pages on the site and thousands and thousands of links. I had personally searched every image, handled every book, sifted through countless YouTubes, researched hundreds of movies. This had been a labor of love on my part. I could never have paid someone to build what I had built. It had taken years to build and thousands of hours. The thoughts of transferring all the information one piece at a time just made me cry.

It was like someone stole my baby.

I kept holding on to hope that there would be a more simple fix. But no simple fix had surfaced yet. We had managed to save the data, but re-entering it would be a massive job.

Around that time, I had been spending quite a bit of time with Professor Laurence Jones who had been mentoring me in faith and courage and not giving up. Like most of my friends, he died long ago, but he was teaching me through his story.

He was an African-American who had the privilege of being educated in the North. He could have had a very comfortable and successful career. Instead, he traveled to one of the poorest sections of Mississippi to help lift the lives of families who were struggling to survive in the aftermath of slavery.

He knew a school would bless their lives, but he had no means to do so. A school existed only in his dreams. Doors were slammed in his face everywhere he went. Although his intentions were pure, people were suspicious of him. He went hungry and suffered much, but he persisted.

Finally a strange event opened the doors and he began his school on a tree stump with one student who brought a couple of friends the next day who brought more the next day until he was teaching a hundred students out under the trees.

Eventually, they started building a school. They didn't have money to do it. But by now the parents had caught the vision of educating their children and they shared what they had—a chicken, a board, helping hands. They celebrated every step along the way.

And then, just as the school was nearly ready to open, a tornado roared through Piney Creek. It took off the roof and twisted the building off its foundation. The trees were ripped out. All their hard work was undone.

Laurence said this was the most discouraging moment in his life. He couldn't fathom that these people who had already given all they had would be willing to start again. He didn't even know if they had survived the tornado. He stared at the walls, not knowing what to do.

And then a couple of days later, he heard the sound of a horse coming his way. And then voices. The people were coming back to rebuild. They had all survived. And the dream grew and prospered and eventually blessed the lives of thousands.

I read the part about the tornado the night before our "tornado" blew through. There were tears. Lots of tears. I couldn't fathom starting over. And I started questioning the very worth of what I was doing. How many families were really even using the site? Was I doing all this work for 25? 50? 100? I had no idea. Did the work really matter? If I shut down, I could plant flowers in my yard. I could take up painting and read all these beautiful books I've been lining my shelf with. I love to notebook. I could spend more time doing that. I could spend more time with my grandchildren.

But then came your posts and letters. You told me what a blessing these resources have been in your lives. And one of my daughters called: "Mom, what would I do without it? I turn to it ten times a day." And I asked myself, would it be worth it if my grandchildren were the only ones using it? And the answer was a definite yes.

But that wasn't the only thought process. I looked at what was going on in the world; how history is being erased and distorted before our eyes; how hearts are growing colder; how mothers are searching for help to navigate this upside-down world.

I don't know all the answers, but I felt like I had been entrusted with knowledge of great worth, gleaned from the writings of a hundred years ago. How could I throw that all away?

I felt your love and concern. I appreciated your offers to help that came in many ways.

So the decision was made to roll up our sleeves and rebuild, just like Laurence's Piney Creek friends did. And if I were to play the Pollyanna Glad Game, I would say that our storm had a silver lining. The new site is much more user friendly. We were able to completely redesign it and add even more books to the library. If you, for some reason, don't have access to books through your public library, I wanted you to have somewhere to come. I wanted you to have a Library of Hope.

Laurence stopped by at just the right time when I needed that extra push to not give up. Thanks, Laurence, for inspiring me with the example of your life. Thank you for giving me hope.

Did you tackle the trouble that came your way
With a resolute heart and cheerful?
Or hide your face from the light of day
With a craven soul and fearful?
Oh, a trouble's ton, or a trouble's an ounce,
Or a trouble is what you make it,
And it isn't the fact that you're hurt that counts,
But only how did you take it?

You are beaten to earth! Well, what's that?
Come up with a smiling face.
It's nothing against you to fall down flat,
But to lie there—that's a disgrace.
The harder you're thrown, why, the higher you bounce;
Be proud of your blackened eye!
It isn't the fact that you're licked that counts;
It's how did you fight—and why?

And though you be done to the death, what then?
If you battled the best you could,
If you played your part in the world of men,
Why, the critic will call it good.
Death comes with a crawl, or comes with a pounce,
And whether it' slow or spry,
It isn't the fact that you're dead that counts,
But only how did you die?

--Edmund Vance Cooke

Building Character

A question I am asked frequently is, "What books do I recommend to build character?" My reply is always the same—the objective of the writers of the older books was almost always to build character in young people so they are loaded with character-building examples and even direct references to the character lessons they are portraying. The books I post in the Libraries of Hope library are all character building books.

But then that request is taken one step further and I find moms who want stories with specific traits, like honesty or kindness or courage. Some have even gone so far as to organize their monthly learning around a character trait—the Benjamin Franklin method, I would say. But my opinion is a caution against that. It is a subtle form of compulsion. Children may thereby understand the traits with their minds, but it may not have gotten deep enough in their hearts for them to desire to acquire the trait for themselves.

The best way of instilling character—as taught by the heart educators—is to immerse your children in a variety of stories and allowing them to draw the lessons out for themselves that they are ready to. A child who has been caught being dishonest may not benefit from a story about honesty in the very moment because dishonesty is serving some kind of purpose or benefit to him, much like if I am about to eat a warm, delicious chocolate chip cookie fresh out of the oven, that it's not the time to tell me about what it will do to my waist. I need that desire planted before I ever put the cookies in the oven.

You can have several children listen to the same story, and one child will connect to the lesson of kindness, another to honesty, another to courage according to what he or she is ready to take in. A child can listen to the same story at a different time and derive an entirely different lesson. That is the power of stories on individual hearts.

In the introduction to a little guide book on using stories to teach character, I found this advice: "Some say, 'By the direct method: tell the children with unfailing plainness of speech, and with proper penalties following, what they ought to do and to be.' That is, no doubt, a part of it. It is the general opinion of teachers, however, that the larger and better part is indirect: Provide the children with materials out of which they may construct their own sermons, and preach them to themselves. For that is how human nature works. Children form their convincing ideals from the heroes and heroines of the stories which they read..."

Through immersing your children in fairy tales, mythology, epic heroes, legends, fables, folk tales, fine literature and especially encouraging them to spend much of their time with the stories of great souls, this process of character building will happen very naturally, over time, and in the best way. Somewhere along the way, help them begin to notebook what they're learning and applying.

Exploration and Discovery

I love that we begin with Exploration and Discovery each year because that pretty much sums up a heart-based philosophy of learning—encouraging our children and ourselves, for that matter, to explore and discover. The whole world is filled with so many things to explore and discover. Like Robert Louis Stevenson wrote, "The world is so full of a number of things, I think we should all be as happy as kings."

By the way, there is no need to tell the story of Columbus every single year. There are so many other adventurers to follow with their stories of daring and danger and courage.

For centuries, sailors hugged familiar shorelines and didn't dare venture out into the unknown deeps. And then, finally, one came along who felt compelled to brave it and once he showed the world it could be done and there was a new world out there, hundreds followed. It doesn't matter to me that Columbus never saw the United States mainland.

You would think such a courageous and brave act would be celebrated. Well, it appears it's human nature to envy and malign the explorer who leaves the safety of familiar things. You may have gotten a little taste of that when you stepped outside the norm and decided to homeschool your children and then ventured even further and stepped outside a set curriculum to discover new paths of learning for yourself.

Take whatever scoffs and scorn of the doubters you may be experiencing, magnify it a hundred times and you have a tiny taste of what Columbus endured. 500 years later, the contempt towards him is just getting hotter. Ironically, it's the explorers and discoverers who are turning up the heat. For years Columbus was held up as a hero in schoolbooks, and then some intellectual explorers, if you will, started questioning and digging around and found all sorts of unsavory things about the man.

One problem is, these intellectual explorers are accepting that if it is in writing—if it appears to be an original source document, as they call it, it must be true. They fail to take in the whole picture that all kinds of people were writing all kinds of things about Columbus out of jealousy and other selfish reasons and making it appear true. Might future generations discern the truth about us from the National Enquirer?

Scholars admit they are having difficulties sorting fact from fiction in the case of Columbus.

Which isn't really where I'm trying to go with this. I fully accept Columbus may have done atrocious things. I'm not here to convince you one way or another.

But here is what I am trying to say.

Columbus isn't the only one falling from grace. I'm in a Facebook group where there was a thread about the book *Les Misérables*. An intellectual explorer amongst them had discovered that Victor Hugo in no way resembled the beloved Jean Valjean. In fact, he was a self-admitted womanizer—he kept company with prostitutes and kept diaries of his sex exploits and there were other unsavory things about his character that they had discovered which were repulsive to them. The person who started the thread felt herself to be in a dilemma. "How can I keep reading this book, knowing it was created by such a despicable man." And in the comments that followed, others felt the same way. They felt they could no longer trust the book because it came out of the heart of such a sinner.

Other heroes who have recently appeared on the chopping block are Abraham Lincoln who was listed as one of nine presidents who messed up our country. Thomas Jefferson with his alleged slave mistress and slaves, Robert E. Lee for fighting on the side of slavery and owning slaves himself which also knocks down the pedestal under George Washington and most of our founding fathers. And I almost forgot the Pilgrims—America's first terrorists.

Helen Keller and Mother Theresa have even made the list of despicable human beings! Helen for her views on socialism and abortion and Mother Theresa for allowing people to suffer when she had the funds to relieve more suffering than she did.

It doesn't surprise me, though. We are living in a peculiar age that Hans Christian Andersen saw over 200 years ago; an age he captured in his story of The Snow Queen that I have talked about before. When the mind and the age of reason rules and the heart is neglected, the world turns upside down. That which was bad is seen as good and that which was good is seen as bad. Every fault is magnified and every good is mocked.

Isn't that us today? Of course, we're trying to correct that by paying more attention to the heart.

So how do you deal with these things that you are bound to discover if you are a true explorer? I am reading more and more mothers who are refusing to even tell the story of Christopher Columbus to their children.

Which is problematic because if we will only tell our children about Saints, there will only be one story left to tell. Although it's a very, very good one. And we'd do well to spend a whole lot more time telling that story.

Well, I was pondering the dilemma not long ago when I glanced up and noticed the painting of Van Gogh's Sunflowers that's on my wall. When I look at that painting, the whole story of Van Gogh flashes before my eyes. On the outside, there isn't much to like about him. He was a bit of loner. Couldn't hold down a job. Well, he didn't try much. He lived and slept with prostitutes. He was depressed and eventually went insane. But in the midst of his darkness, he painted Sunflowers. And the thought struck me: God grows sunflowers out of manure. That is one of His wondrous powers.

I can keep my nose stuck in the manure, inhaling the stink or I can step back and look for the flowers. And in every one of the examples I just listed, I found lots of flowers to gather.

Mother Theresa has inspired the world with compassion. Helen Keller has given hope to those who live in sightless and silent worlds, both physically and figuratively. She has shown the world the joy of an inward light—that is what she wants the world to know about her.

While we abhor slavery and are sad it ever happened, I rejoice in the fact that we abolished it. And there were those who were willing to sacrifice their lives to do so. And while I love the story of Harriet Tubman and how she led over 300 slaves to freedom, the part of the story not being told is that it had taken decades before Harriet to establish the Underground Railroad. And who established it? In large measure, hundreds of white Quaker families who risked their lives, homes and livelihoods so that Harriet would have a means by which she could conduct her charges safely to freedom.

There is a whole bouquet of sunflowers right there.

And speaking of slaves, I can dwell on the horrors of it, or I can step back and see what God grew out of the manure of slavery. I am first reminded He allowed His own chosen people to dwell in slavery over 400 years—twice as long as it was an institution in America's early history. And I am reminded that Joseph was sold into slavery in Egypt, yet God used him to save a nation.

I shed tears at the horrors endured by some of the slaves. But I rejoice at the gifts they brought—the leaven of their childlike faith preserved in their songs, their patient endurance, the moral stories they planted in the hearts of the children of plantation owners and the inspiring stories they have supplied to all of us by their examples of overcoming the direst of circumstances—stories like that of George Washington Carver and Booker T. Washington and Mary Bethune and so many, many others.

They labored to build a new nation by their blood, sweat and tears. They planted our crops and helped the United States grow and prosper. There were those who served faithfully to defend liberty although they, themselves, were not free.

Those are all sunflowers that grew out of the manure. And I thank God for them. And I pray that as a nation we will continue to open the doors for them to bloom and grow. That won't happen if we keep our focus on the stink.

Abraham Lincoln preserved a Union despite opposition from all sides. Anyone who cannot be inspired by an Abraham Lincoln has been smelling smelly fumes way too long. Robert E. Lee was a man of honor who is due our respect and who humbly acknowledged at the end of the war, we are not south and north. We are all Americans.

Our founding fathers pledged their lives, their fortunes and their sacred honor to secure our freedom. Only ingratitude and ignorance is blind to the gift they gave us.

And where are the sunflowers of Vincent Van Gogh's life? Deep in his heart of love that is so rare, I can't think about it without tears.

As the song says,

> Now I understand
> What you tried to say to me
> And how you suffered for your sanity
> And how you tried to set them free

They would not listen, they did not know how
Perhaps they'll listen now.

And the Victor Hugo dilemma? I look for that which inspires me to be better, less selfish and to do good. *Les Misérables* qualifies. The characters of the Bishop and Jean Valjean do that for me at a deeper level than just about any other work of literature. If these beautiful souls grew out of manure, so be it. I am unwilling to let go of the sunflowers.

Columbus opened a new world at just the right time when freedom needed a home and that beacon of freedom and hope has spread out over the whole world. I can't help but wonder—Have the Columbus bashers read any of the stories of what was going on in the world at the time? I cheer that there was a Columbus who never gave up; who stood up to all the opposition and the naysayers and opened up a new world of which you and I are the beneficiaries.

Is that not worth sharing with your children and celebrating?

I love these wise words that would serve you well as you embark on a new year of exploration and discovery.

"Don't be gloomy. Do not dwell on unkind things. Stop seeking out the storms and enjoy more fully the sunlight. (And I would add the sunflowers.) 'Accentuate the positive.' Look a little deeper for good. Go forward in life with a twinkle in your eye and a smile on your face, with great and strong purpose in your heart. Love life!"

There is so much to love! Happy Exploring and Discovering!

The Art of Storytelling

The discovery of the story is probably the most important discovery of all my work. I had been studying principles of education for some time when, in the middle of the night, I sat straight up in bed and said to my husband: "It's story!" It was my *Eureka!* moment. The key to everything was story. Which may sound so simple, but do you know what? I didn't even really know what a story was.

But I do now.

And I cannot begin to describe the change that would come to our world if just one generation of mothers put down the books and became storytellers.

When I first started doing presentations ten years ago or so, I taught on the subject of restoring the art of storytelling in the home. I had stumbled upon a book—*The Use of Story in Religious Education* by Margaret Eggleston—and it changed my life. Because from there, I learned about the revival in the art of storytelling in the early 20th century, especially among mothers. I dug up every book I could find written during that storytelling revival to help mothers learn the art—there were about 25 books that I found. I read and underlined every one of them and it was these storytellers who introduced me to all the other heart educators of the day and it is these mentors who have taught me the things I share with you.

They taught: "With the great storehouse of classical and folk-lore stories within easy reach; stories of brave deeds well done; of self-sacrifice; of love and duty and other high ideals, the mind of the child is easily guided into channels of right thinking, and if mothers only realized it more fully, it is in their power through the medium of these stories to fill the little mind with ideals, which will have a most important bearing through life in the development of character. Through the simple art of storytelling the mother possessed the key to the hidden nature of the child if she could only be made to appreciate and understand the value of the story influence."

I compiled the highlights of what I learned from these original storytellers in a book called *Restoring the Art of Storytelling in the Home* and I included a collection of their stories—mostly classic stories—that were given to the mothers to practice the art. At the back of the book, I list all the books I learned from and you can read them yourself in Internet Archive. There is also a large list of books with an endless supply of stories to tell. A free digital copy of my book is found on the Forgotten Classics page.

I still love to go back and peruse their writings and they continue to teach me. But I discovered that, even though telling a story by heart is one of the most powerful tools you have to shape the character and souls of your children, it was too big of a leap for mothers in this generation. I came to see for myself how terribly story depleted we are as a people; how fact-based and academically minded we are; how undeveloped our imaginations are; how our very personalities have been stunted by neglect and too much screen time.

And so the focus of my work shifted and I've been working on trying to fill up reservoirs of stories so that they can begin to be in hearts to be told.

I am so excited to now start to see mothers who are catching on; who are discovering the difference between reading a story—which still has value—and telling a story by heart. And I hope the enthusiasm will spread. Maybe some of your Mothers of Influence groups will decide to take storytelling on as one of your focuses of study in a much bigger way. And that you will find ways to take your talents out into the community and be a voice of influence through your stories.

Story Clubs were formed in this revival of storytelling a hundred years ago for the purpose of practicing and perfecting the art. You can do the same.

I think few understand the benefit it will have on their own lives.

Let me share some of those benefits as they appeared in an article from one of the Storytelling magazines of that time:

The Psycho-Therapeutic Value of Story Telling by Frances E. Foote

> Many writers have voiced many opinions as to the benefits to be derived from the exercise of the Art of Storytelling, but there is one which I have never seen in black and white, about which I feel impelled to write. It is the Psycho-Therapeutic value of Storytelling.
>
> Pain is a real thing, and will hold us in his clutches and claim all our attention if allowed to do so.
>
> Sorrow is absorbing, and will bow our heads and break our spirits if unhindered.
>
> Upon what, then, may we concentrate our attention, that pain may grow weary of pressing his claim?
>
> With what may we so absorb our minds that sorrow will fade away?
>
> One of the fundamental principles of Storytelling is that the oral interpreter of Literature, must so vividly see the pictures described in the story, that he will cause his hearer to feel that they, too, see.
>
> He must feel the impulses and emotions of the characters in the story so truly that the hearts of his hearers will thrill with the same feeling.
>
> Since this is true, that the mind must be absorbed in the distant scenes of Story Land, pain in due course of time must grow tired of urging his claim and will ultimately depart.
>
> The emotions dominant in stories which we tell are altruistic for the most part. We prefer to dwell upon themes in which evil is overcome by good; those in which sorrow flees away and joy comes with the morning.
>
> Isn't it true that the person who, day after day, creates these altruistic emotions in the hearts of his hearers will find his sorrow, deep-seated though it may be, growing dimmer

day by day as he brightens the lives of his hearers?

There are many cases which I could give you to prove my point. One, of a little child with spinal trouble, who was treated by a great surgeon. He would call upon her two or three days out of the week and each time tell her a story. He required her, meanwhile, to make up similar stories. For instance, he would tell her the story of "little Green Cap." Then he would say, "Now, by Tuesday I want you to have a story ready for me. It must be about a poor little girl, a princess and a magic ring." So absorbed did the child become in such work that the pain in the poor little back grew less and less insistent until she ceased to be an invalid and was able to attend school. She was one of the happiest children I ever knew. She said she didn't mind the pain any more, she had such lovely things to think about.

Another was the case of a young woman upon whom sorrow laid a heavy hand. Prostrated by grief, she lay for several days in a darkened room. Then rousing herself she went to a hospital and secured permission from the superintendent to visit daily the friendless patients who seemed lonely. For months she reported daily to the superintendent, was given directions as to which patients to visit, and for three hours she would go from one to the other telling humorous stories. The morning hours she spent hunting for artistic, mirth-provoking stories and her afternoons in bringing smiles to sad faces. The result was inevitable. People everywhere welcomed her as a ray of sunshine.

One more case—that of a young woman who, while making a brave struggle to recover from one serious operation, suddenly found herself facing another even more serious. With nerves racked by persistent pain, courage well nigh gone, pursued by that dread foe insomnia, she turned to her one accomplishment, Storytelling. Though able to sit up but a few hours at a time, she held large audiences in many cities two or three times a week, until she once more went under the knife. Then within two months she was on the platform again, bringing herself back to health by compelling her mind to dwell in Storyland. I knew all the particulars of this case, the physical torture she endured for two years, the struggle she made to live, and knowing what I do, forces me to believe that if Storytelling did not save her life, it certainly saved her reason.

It is a law of life that the only thing which we may always keep, is the thing we give. If then, the prime function of Storytelling is the giving of Joy the Joy is the thing which the Storyteller may have.

To those who "travail and are heavy laden" I commend the Art of Storytelling.

Searching for Hope in a World that Seems to be Crumbling

There is a lesson for us in the final scene of the movie, Camelot, where a weary and sorrowful King Arthur is standing in the early morning fog, dreading the battle of the day. The two people he has loved the most have both betrayed him. Knight is fighting knight. His beloved kingdom is crumbling around him.

Suddenly a young boy appears. "I wish to become a knight and to fight the battle."

Arthur looks perplexed. "A knight? Why do you wish to be a part of this extinct profession? What do you know about knights? Have you seen a knight? Did your father serve as a knight? Was your mother rescued by a knight?"

"Oh no, me Lord, I've heard their stories. I know all about them—Might for right, justice for all—everything!"

"And from these stories you wish to be a knight?"

"Oh yes, me Lord, a knight of the Round Table."

Suddenly Arthur's face brightens. He commands the boy to kneel and with the sword Excalibur, he knights him. And then he commands him to not fight in the battle, but to run behind the lines and to live so that he can spread the stories far and wide of what he sees and knows.

A trusted companion appears. "Your Majesty. It's time. You have a battle to fight."

Arthur looks at him. His face beaming with joy, his eyes brimming with tears. "Oh no, Pelle, I have already won my battle and here is my victory: What we did will be remembered."

Nature

"If the trees and flowers, the clouds and the wind, all tell wonderful stories to the child he has sources of happiness of which no power can deprive him." --Flora Cooke

One day, Helen Keller who could neither see nor hear, was visited by a very dear friend who had just returned from a long walk in the woods. She asked her friend what she had seen, to which she replied, "Nothing in particular." Helen exclaimed, "I might have been incredulous had I not been accustomed to such responses for long ago I became convinced that the seeing see little.

"How was it possible, I asked myself, to walk for an hour through the woods and see nothing worthy of note? I who cannot see find hundreds of things to interest me through mere touch. I feel the delicate symmetry of a leaf. I pass my hands lovingly about the smooth skin of a silver birch, or the rough, shaggy bark of a pine... I feel the delightful, velvety texture of a flower, and something of the miracle of Nature is revealed to me.

"At times my heart cries out with longing to see all these things. If I can get so much pleasure from mere touch, how much more beauty must be revealed by sight. Yet, those who have eyes apparently see little. The panorama of color and action which fills the world is taken for granted. It is human, perhaps, to appreciate little that which we have and to long for that which we have not, but it is a great pity that in the world of light, the gift of sight is used only as a mere convenience rather than as a means of adding fulness to life."

This section is dedicated to raising a generation of children who will never walk through the forest and see "nothing." Many of the ideas I'll talk about have come from a little book written in 1904 called *How Nature Study Should Be Taught* by Edward Bigelow. You might enjoy reading it. I included sections of it in the Mother's Learning Library book on nature.

The objective of Nature Study is not the same as science. "Nature study is not a systematic study of nature, for that is science. Nature study is emotional. Science is intellectual."

Professor Bailey of Cornell University said, "Nature study is a revolt from the teaching of mere science in the elementary grades... Nature study is not science. It is not fact. It is spirit. It is concerned with the child's outlook on the world... Nature study is not to be taught for the purpose of making the youth a scientist. Now and then a pupil will desire to pursue a science for the sake of the science, and he should be encouraged. But every pupil may be taught to be interested in plants and birds and insects and running brooks, and thereby his life will be the stronger. The crop of scientists will take care of itself."

Longfellow understood the objective of Nature Study:

"And Nature, the old nurse, took

The child upon her knee,
Saying, "Here is a story book
Thy Father has written for thee."

Wordsworth knew:

"To know Nature is to know God.
The world is too much with us; late and soon,
Getting and spending, we lay waste our powers,
Little we see in nature that is ours. "

Shakespeare knew about the: "...tongues in trees, books in the running brooks, Sermons in stones and good in every thing."

Nature is God's university. John Burroughs, the great naturalist, said, "I would, by all means teach the young people the elements of the great sciences... I would also inculcate the scientific habit of mind, accuracy of observation, care in reading conclusions... But I would not encourage the young people to think they can dissect their way into the mystery of Nature, or reach her through the laboratory."

The objective of nature study for the well-educated heart is pure and simple joy. This is what nature study looks like: First, from the life of the great painter, Jean Francois Millet: One day little Francois stood at his father's side. They were watching the setting sun sink into the waves. The western sky was all aglow with purple and deep crimson. Great bars of golden light were stretched across the horizon. The boy felt the glory of the scene. The father lifted his hat and bowed his head, saying gravely, "My son, it is God." The boy never forgot.

Second, from the life of Arthur Henry King, an Oxford trained professor, whose writings have inspired me greatly: "My first real discovery of nature in life came one morning in April 1916. My father put me on the back of his bike where I had a little seat and said, "Off we go." And then he turned in the wrong direction, for I thought he was taking me down to Quakers' meeting–it was Sunday. "No," he said, "we are going somewhere else today." And we rode for about eight miles, and we stopped at a wood... We went into the wood, and there, suddenly, was a great pool of bluebells stretching for perhaps a hundred yards in the shade of the oak trees. And I could scarcely breathe because the impression was so great. The experience then was just the bluebells and the scent; now, when I recall it, it is also the love of my father who chose to do that that morning–to give me that experience. I am sure he had been there the day before, found it, and thought, "I'll take my son there." As we rode there and as we rode back, we heard the distant thud of the guns at the Battle of the Somme, where thousands were dying every day. That overwhelming experience of a natural phenomenon, a demonstration of beneficent creation, and at the same time hearing those guns on the Somme–that experience has remained with me almost more clearly than anything else in my life."

This next experience is related by Lucy Maud Montgomery who gave us *Anne of Green Gables*: "I had always a deep love of nature. A little fern growing in the woods, a shallow sheet of Junebells under the firs, moonlight falling on the ivory column of a tall birch, an evening star over the old tamarack on the dyke, shadow-waves rolling over a field of ripe wheat–all gave me 'thoughts that lay too deep for tears' and feelings which I had no vocabulary to express. I was very near to a kingdom of ideal beauty."

And finally, my most memorable nature study lesson took place on a Saturday night when I was a young girl. I had just gotten out of the shower and my hair was still wrapped in a towel. As I walked past the front door, I noticed my dad out on the front porch sitting alone in the dark. I went out and sat next to him. He smiled at me but didn't say anything. He was just staring up at the sky. I looked and looked to see what he was looking at, but all I could see were the stars on a warm summer night. Finally he sighed a deep sigh and said, "Do you ever wonder what's out there?" And then the two of us sat there together for the longest time in silence–just wondering.

From my notes: "To teach young people or old people how to observe nature, is a good deal like trying to teach them how to eat their dinner. The first thing necessary in the latter case is a good appetite; this given, the rest follows very easily. And in observing nature, unless you have the appetite, the love, the spontaneous desire, you will get little satisfaction. It is the heart that sees more than the mind. To love nature is the first step in observing her."

"I would have the boys and girls rush over to the apple tree, pick up handfuls of apples, putting some in pocket and munching the rest. That is nature study. I would have those same boys and girls sit at a table and make cross sections and vertical slices of some of those apples, noting the structure, the relation of seeds, cases, pulp and epidermis. That is science. I would have them climb on the ledge, stand near the boulder, and have a general good time in fun. That is nature study. I would tell them a little of the history of this ledge, its relations to the surrounding country, its geological structure and perhaps its chemical composition. That is science. Enjoy the beautiful moonlight; note the bright stars and planets, and construct the fanciful pictures of the constellations. That is nature study. Tell of the surface of the moon, the distance of the stars, the various physical characters of the planets. That is science."

The learning tools for a successful nature study program are: "fresh air, sunshine, trees, flowers, birds and all the other happy life of the fields and forests. Weave in generous proportions. Do not skimp and carve, and trim, and minimize, and scrutinize too much. Pour in the generous cupfuls, hours rather than minutes... Let them have them in their fullness of enjoyment."

Loving nature is as simple as loving your mother. And happens just as naturally when a child spends time with her. "Oh no," Edward Bigelow says with tongue in cheek, "some scientific appreciator of a mother may say, that is crude; it flavors of the Middle Ages, of the amateur, of those who love their mother from the heart. This is an age of scientific spirit, an age of the intellect rather than of the affections. Do nothing so simple as that; learn really to know your mother, and then you can love her with solid, intellectual appreciation.

"First collect some pictures and drawings of all the mothers you can find; arrange them side by side and compare your mother with them. That will add to your knowledge of the comparative merits of your mother's appearance. Devote a half-hour at a certain time every day to the study of mothers. Draw pictures of them; make a detailed list of color of hair, number of eyes, nostrils, ears; length of chin, height, weight, number of fingers on each hand; state the age, past history and a hundred or more other facts. Arrange these details under a few heads, draw a bracket before each, and collocate these in line under one big brace, with the word Mother written in capital letters. Make a drawing of your own mother standing erect, and also bending down to kiss you as you start for school in the morning. Sketch in detail her eyes, fingers and nose. Write a list of nouns, adjectives, verbs and adverbs that will apply to your own mother, and from these compose ten sentences each day from 10:15 to 10:45 a.m. in connection with your drawing work, and if the task is completed before the time has expired, we will fold our arms and sing about our mothers.

"Bear in mind that you must never really go to see your mother for the enjoyment of seeing her, nor only for the enjoyment of her loving presence, but you must learn to love her, and to let her influence permeate every fiber of your life, by noting down with pad and pencil, all possible details of her physical structure."

A love of nature? Too much detail, too much method, too much correlating kills it.

At the turn of the 20th century when schools were feeling like they needed to add nature study to their curriculum, and adding it the only way they could justify it, by presenting it with measurable outcomes, which means facts and testing, this little interchange was posted in a local New York daily paper.

The principal of a large grade-school in that city was sitting in his office intently poring over reports and excuses, when the janitor swung open the door and announced: "A lady to see you, sir."

A German woman of ponderous size and waddling gait strode into the room. Both sleeves were rolled up to her elbows. In her right hand, by her side, she carried a huge lobster, just touching the floor, and swinging in accompaniment with her every pacing step. Her appearance indicated that it was indignation which had separated her from the wash-tub.

She swung the lobster over her head, and slapped it down on the table near his desk with a bang that made the absorbed mind of the principal leap from mental to physical matters.

"Vat ish dat?" shouted the belligerent visitor.

"Why-wh-y, that, madam is a lobster, but—"

"How many leegz has it?"

"Strictly speaking there are ten, but only eight are—"

"How many claws has it?"

"The first pair of the ten legs have large claws, the next pair have small claws, and the other two have only—"

"How many eyeez has it?"

"The lobster has two eyes—"

"Vat color is—"

"But wait, madam; before I answer any more questions, please explain why—"

"Dat's vat I vant to know–vat for ish dat our teacher ask my Shonny all dese fool questions. I vork so hard at mine vash-tub all day long, send my boy Shonny here to larn, and your teacher tell him all dat shruff, and ax him all dese fool questions. Vat for ish dat?"

That is a good question. What for is that when children are little? Too much lobster spoils their appetite. Save the systematic unfolding of facts and information for when they're ready for science and they've got a deep emotional base to plant it in.

Charles Kingsley observed, "No amount of book learning will make a man a scientific man; nothing but patient observation and quiet and fair thoughts over what he has observed." Nature study is all about patient and quiet observation. And a generous dose of wonder and curiosity.

So the number one method of teaching Nature Study is direct immersion. Translation: Outdoor play and discovery without making a lesson out of everything.

I took a couple of my granddaughters to a little park here in Appomattox a little while back. It wasn't long until they got tired of the swings and slide and one of them had gotten some dirt on her hand, so we found a little stream to wash it off. Then the real fun begun. I just sat and watched over the next hour as they dug in the mud with little sticks and raced leaf boats down the stream and watched the dragonflies landing here and there. Lesson objective achieved: Pure and simple joy.

Little children love naming and learning the names of everything, so that's a second natural part of Nature Study. My father loved flowers just like his father. He taught me all their names when I was a little girl. I loved the hydrangeas that grew by my father's office, the gardenias by the back door, the hibiscus by my bedroom window. I looked forward to the johnny-jump-ups that popped out each spring with the apricot blossoms. I cut pyracantha berry branches with my mom every Thanksgiving to decorate the Thanksgiving table.

By the way, fairies definitely do not dance on zucchini–they only dance on rose petals and hollyhocks. I can still feel the excitement of running out to the backyard in my pajamas because my dad told me the Pink Lady had opened up. And I remember clearly feeling God's love while lying in the grass beneath the camellia bush.

On May Day we used to make little paper baskets and fill them with flowers from the garden. Then we'd hang them on the doors of some of the older neighbors in the neighborhoods, ring the doorbell and then run and hide in the bushes so we could watch their reactions. My oldest daughter emailed me a picture of the little Mayday baskets she made with her little girls this year. She told me that while she was combing little 6-year-old Madison's hair that night, Madison said, "I feel so happy inside! I just love doing things for other people and I was thinking to myself, 'I'm so glad my mom made up this plan.'" I call that a successful heart-based education nature lesson plan.

You can also help open eyes by sharing Nature stories. They don't necessarily have to be told while you're out in nature. Your children will carry the impressions made by the stories with them while they're out in nature. As I've read the books I've been gathering to our Nature Library, I've been astonished at how my eyes have been opened as I'm out walking in our neighborhood. I notice things I've never noticed before. Even the songs of the birds have taken on new meaning.

For the familiar years, start with stories of how mother birds, insects and animals take care of their children; the homes they build for them; how they feed them. Those are the stories I've tried to start each of our nature books with in the Nature, Art and Music Series.

Many young children thoroughly enjoy Thornton Burgess' nature stories or the Clara Dillingham Pierson books, all found in the Nature Bundle. These stories are much different than the facts and information books so common for children today. The facts books will continue to feed the fire that's already burning. Right now we're trying to get the fire started.

From my notes: "If the trees and flowers, the clouds and the wind, all tell wonderful stories to the child he has sources of happiness of which no power can deprive him."

We've become accustomed to associating nature and science studies with experiments for children. But can anything reveal the wonder and mystery of nature more than watching a beautiful flower grow from a tiny seed? Don't make your children measure and record the growth in the beginning. Let them enjoy and be amazed. We've become so practical, I see lots of mothers grow vegetable gardens with their kids. But I have yet to see the 4-year-old who laughs with delight at the plate of freshly grown spinach on his plate. Let them grow flower gardens when they're little! The more the better.

The flower industry is as huge as it is because flowers speak to our hearts. Is there anything more exquisite in color or texture or fragrance than a flower? In the Nature, Art and Music Series, I dedicated a whole book to growing flowers. The writers speak to the children directly, instructing them how to take some dirt and transform it. Nothing fancy. Very basic. But highly rewarding. Corrie Ten Boom in her book, *The Hiding Place*, wrote: "People can learn to love, from flowers."

Eventually keeping a Nature Journal will deepen their connection with Nature. Unlike a Science Journal where you might draw plants and diagram its parts and add Latin names, the Nature Journal is purely emotional. John Ruskin, when the camera arrived on the scene in the mid 1800s, warned people to keep sketching; that if they stopped, they would lessen their ability to see the beauty in the world. Sketching nature will open that part of the heart and will help us remember what we see.

What will you sketch? Flowers in fields, a butterfly on a flower, sunsets and sunrises, trees and the bark on trees, birds, squirrels, ponds, clouds, bees, ants. When you recreate a leaf, you notice the shades of color, the intricate vein work, the fringe designs around the edge that might all bypass you when you just look at a photo. By sketching and later coloring, you start noticing the panorama of color all around and the beautiful contrasts.

The worst thing I would suggest is to give your children a journal and say, "Draw." The way to inspire them is to let them see you keeping yours. They may watch you for months before they finally say, "I'd like to try that." And that's perfectly fine. You may be saying that you can't draw. That's common. But the truth is, everyone can draw. It's a skill like learning to write.

I can't recommend John Muir Laws enough. He offers so many free videos to help us learn to sketch from nature. I love his passion for it. He wrote: "When we see with clear eyes, we know that we are surrounded with beauty. Let yourself fall in love with your life by paying attention."

As David Steindl-Rast says: "It is not happiness that makes us grateful. It's gratefulness that makes us happy."

As you record what you see in your journal, give thanks for what surrounds you. When you celebrate the world through the ages of your journal, every stroke of your brush or pencil can be a song of gratitude for the opportunity to be alive. "Love can be defined as sustained, compassionate attention. Nature journaling will slow you down and make you stop, sit down, and look again. Engaging in this process helps you to organize your thoughts, piece together answers and ask richer questions. Once you slow down and look long enough to record observations in your journal, mysteries will unfold before you… I draw to see."

Keep in mind–the objective is love of nature, not perfect journals. Edward Bigelow said he was once asked to judge a nature journal contest. As he looked over the entries, he found beautiful, perfect handwriting and beautiful drawings in all eighty of them. But all eighty of them were all alike.

This is how he described the winning entry: "Next I picked up an unattractive letter written on the leaves of a pocket note-book. The drawing that accompanied it was crude and the paper was soiled by finger marks. With difficulty I read it, but was fascinated as I deciphered the story of a boy's seaside investigation of the fiddler crab.

"He wanted to know how they lived underground; what they did; what food they ate; what kind of quarters they occupied. He made inquiries of the fishermen. No one knew. He said, 'I'll find out if it takes a week.' He borrowed pick, shovel and crowbar. He went to work and he found out. Then he wrote the story, as he sat beside the hole that he had dug after several hours' hard work. He made the drawing after careful watching of the living object.

"I was sorry that I had not a basketful of prizes to give that boy, because he wrote his letter for the love of it."

For the love of it. That's the most critical component.

So how will you know if your children have successfully passed the objectives of Nature Study?

The following test questions are suggested in the little book I've been quoting from:

Q: Do you enjoy going on rambles across the fields, through the woods and down the ravines to the meadows and swamps?

Do you like to pick the flowers, hear the birds sing, and watch all forms of life?

Do you read outdoor books that tell of nature's interesting plants and animal life?

A yes to these 3 questions earns a 100%. And I would say the child is now ready to move on to

Science.

John Burroughs said, "Unless science is mixed with emotion and appeals to the heart and imagination, it is like dead, inorganic matter."

The child who has successfully passed a course in Nature Study will be well prepared for his next studies in Science. One of my daughters just returned from the Amazon Forest in South America. She told me that just prior to venturing into the forest, a teacher in the group shared a pattern in nature for them to watch for. And then turned them loose to discover the pattern for themselves which stirred up all kinds of questions—naturally. She was amazed at how many practical lessons she walked away with when she asked her own questions and paid attention to her own observations. It was a much different experience than the usual lecture on species and facts. She loved it.

A couple of closing thoughts: I've been re-reading the Four Gospels and this time through, I noted how much Jesus loved being out in nature. He taught by the seashore, retired to the mountain, prayed in the garden. The biggest troublemakers were in the crowded cities! He frequently sought the solitude of nature to restore His soul. His earthly ministry was just three years, and what did He leave us? A handful of stories, and so many of them tied into nature: Consider the lilies of the fields; if you have faith the size of a mustard seed; even a sparrow does not fall unnoticed; the fields are white and ready to harvest; a sower sowed seeds that fell on the wayside; He spoke of wheat and tares and living waters. There is an important lesson in His example to us.

Louisa May Alcott wrote: "My wise mother turned me loose in the country and let me run wild, learning of Nature what no books could teach, and being led—as those who truly love her seldom fail to be—'through Nature up to Nature's God.'

"I had an early run in the woods before the dew was off the grass. The moss was like velvet, and as I ran under the arch of yellow and red leaves I sang for joy, my heart was so bright and the world so beautiful. I stopped at the end of the walk and saw the sunshine out over the wide 'Virginia meadows.'

"It seemed like going through a dark life or grave into heaven beyond. A very strange and solemn feeling came over me as I stood there, with no sound but the rustle of the pines, no one near me, and the sun so glorious, as for me alone. It seemed as if I felt God as I never did before, and I prayed in my heart that I might keep that happy sense of nearness all my life."

To that entry there is a note added, years later: "I have, for I most sincerely think that the little girl 'got religion' that day in the wood, when dear Mother nature led her to God."

That's Nature Study for the Well-Educated Heart.

HECOA Presentation on Nature Study

If you have come to this presentation looking for a systematic way to teach all the facts of nature to your children, you'll probably be disappointed. There are many great curriculums out there to help you do that. I have much loftier intentions. Let me set the stage with this little journal entry of Louisa May Alcott, who, of course, wrote Little Women. "The Alcott children were encouraged to keep diaries where they wrote down their thoughts, feelings and desires, and even at an early age, Louisa's journal was a record of deep feelings." Here's the entry:

"I had an early run in the woods before the dew was off the grass. The moss was like velvet, and as I ran under the arch of yellow and red leaves I sang for joy, my heart was so bright and the world so beautiful. I stopped at the end of the walk and saw the sunshine out over the wide 'Virginia meadows.'

"It seemed like going through a dark life or grave into heaven beyond. A very strange and solemn feeling came over me as I stood there, with no sound but the rustle of the pines, no one near me, and the sun so glorious, as for me alone. It seemed as if I felt God as I never did before, and I prayed in my heart that I might keep that happy sense of nearness all my life."

To that entry there is a note added, years later: 'I have, for I most sincerely think that little girl 'got religion' that day in the wood, when dear Mother Nature led her to God."

Charles Darwin had a similar experience as a young man. He recalled standing in the middle of a Brazilian forest and looking up at the majesty of the trees and feeling there must be a higher power. In his later years, he regretted that he hadn't taken time from his scientific studies to read a little poetry and listen to some music every week because his heart had hardened and he no longer was capable of feeling such things. It had happened gradually, he said, so he had felt no alarm.

That which we don't use atrophies from disuse. The truth is, we feel God, and the hard heart cannot feel Him.

We are living in an increasingly godless world and I trace the root cause to hard-heartedness. The heart develops before the mind and childhood is the time when the heart is most open to feelings and impressions. In our rush for academic excellence which depends upon that which we can test and measure and is centered on the mind, we are starving the hearts of our children and thereby hardening them.

The approach to Nature Study that I'll present today is centered on warming hearts and the way we warm hearts is through the Arts—story, music, poetry and pictures. I know many of you are anxious to instill faith in your children. And while turning to scripture study is vital, sometimes we forget that God has revealed His heart and His intentions in many places. He is found in inspired works of art and music, in inspired literature. He is found in the pages of history. And one of the best places to learn about the Creator is through His creations.

Nature is God's University.

A hundred years ago, educators understood the connection between spiritual matters and a study of nature. This spiritual element is missing in most of today's nature study for children which tend to focus only on the facts and information. To me, the facts are the shallow part. If they remain unconnected to the heart, they'll fade away with time. A deeper layer of nature study is the science part where the laws and principles by which all of nature operates are revealed. But the deepest lessons can only be understood by the heart, which often cannot be expressed in words, but are as real or even more real than the facts gleaned by sight, sound and touch.

I believe we've got learning turned upside down. We usually start with facts and information, but they are dull and barren by themselves. They can sometimes be so cold and hard, a child develops a complete distaste for the subject. And then we turn to what we call a study of science. But most science curriculums I see are nothing more than a systematic unfolding of the facts with some contrived experiments. Have we forgotten that a sense of wonder and questioning is at the heart of all true scientists? That a true scientist has learned to rely upon his own ability to closely observe and draw conclusions and form questions and theories from those observations? I see little of that in most science textbooks.

I am in awe at the things man has figured out throughout history without the aid of computers or special equipment. They relied upon their power of observation and reasoning. I read an article recently that talked about how there have been relatively few scientific discoveries in the last hundred years. Technology has flourished, but not scientific discovery. Blame was placed on the lack of curiosity and the diminished power of observation, which I believe is the result of not tending to the heart first.

Curiosity or desire and the powers of observation are the two gifts a mother can give to her children in Nature Study. "What you make a child love and desire is more important than what you make him learn." --Alice O'Grady

All the ideas I will present today for a study of nature are for tending to desire—which is a function of the heart—and for giving children eyes to see. Then you can add in the next layer, the science layer which reveals the laws upon which everything operates. Heart first, then mind.

I've spent the last ten years immersed in the writings of great men and women I call the heart educators of a hundred years ago who understood the art of educating hearts of children first. I want to help you feel the difference, so I'm going to share samples from their writings. Let me start off with an excerpt from a letter Charles Kingsley wrote to children in the beginning of his Boys and Girls Book of Science written in 1881.

> Dear Boys and Girls:
>
> So it is. One man walks through the world with his eyes open, another with his eyes shut; and upon this difference depends all the superiority of knowledge which one man acquires over another. Settle in your own minds whether they will be Eyes or No Eyes;

> whether they will, as they grow up, look, and see for themselves what happens; or whether they will let other people look for them, or pretend to look, and dupe them, and lead them about—the blind leading the blind, till both fall into the ditch.
>
> God has given you eyes, and it is your duty to use them. If your parents tried to teach you your lessons in the most agreeable way, by beautiful picture-books, would it not be ungracious, ungrateful, and altogether wrong to shut your eyes to those pictures and refuse to learn? And is it not altogether wrong to refuse to learn from your Father in heaven, the great God who made all things, when He offers to teach you all day long by the most beautiful and most wonderful of all picture-books, which is, simply all things which you can see, and hear, and touch, from the suns and stars above our heads, to the mosses and insects at your feet? It is your duty to learn His lessons, and it is your interest likewise. God's Book, which is the Universe, and the reading of God's book, which is Science, can do you nothing but good, and teach you nothing but truth and wisdom.
>
> So use your eyes and your intellect, your senses and your brains, and learn what God is trying to teach you continually by them. I do not mean that you must stop there, and learn nothing more; anything but that. There are things which neither your senses nor your brains can tell you; and they are not only more glorious, but actually more true and more real, than many things which you can see or touch. But you must begin at the beginning in order to end at the end; and sow the seed if you wish to gather the fruit. God has ordained that you, and every child which comes into the world, should begin by learning something of the world about him by his senses and his brain; and the better you learn what they can teach you, the more fit will you be to learn what they cannot teach you. The more you try now to understand things, the more you will be able hereafter to understand men, and That which is above men. You begin to find out that truly Divine mystery...by watching the common natural things around you, and considering the lilies of the field, how they grow, that you will begin at last to learn that far Diviner mystery—that you have a Father in Heaven. And so you will be delivered (if you will) out of the tyranny of darkness, and distrust, and fear, into God's free kingdom of light, and faith and love;
>
> For that thirst to know why was put into the hearts of little children by God Himself; and I believe that God would never have given them that thirst, if He had not meant to satisfy it.

Isn't that a beautiful introduction to Nature Study?

A masterpiece can only be painted one brush stroke at a time and while we want our children to take in nature as a whole, it is best revealed a little here and a little there.

If you go to welleducatedheart.com, and select Nature in the online library, you'll see that I've created a 12-month rotation schedule for the study of nature designed primarily for children 12 and under. But I promise there's a lot to captivate the interest of your older children, as well. The first 8 months have topics, and the last 4 months fall in spring and summer when, hopefully, you'll be able to take your children to mountains and oceans and deserts to begin to apply the lessons they've learned in the previous 8 months.

The topics generally follow the order of Creation in the Bible. I say generally, because you'll notice it falls apart in the very first month. The first order of business was "let there be light," but the sun and moon and stars weren't created until the fourth day in the Creation story when it was time for seasons to start growing things. But there's a lesson—all creation begins with a spiritual light, a spark of life, that the eye cannot see. Still, I think Month 1 is the perfect time to start instilling a sense of wonder at the expanse of the universe and our place in it. Then comes the Ocean and a study of water. When you look at a map of the world and see the rivers and streams, it's almost like looking at the circulation system. Water delivers life and it makes me think of the Living Waters of Jesus Christ. Where there is no water, there is barren desert where nothing grows. Water is also the force that is wearing down the hard rocks to create the soil in which plants and living things can begin to flourish and grow. Then came other life forms that I unfold from the smallest to the largest—the insect, the bird and the animal. As the creation is unfolded like that, you get the sense of the preparation; how one thing needed to be prepared in order for the next stage. And the purpose of all creation is to provide a home for God's crowning creation: His children.

These topics are not meant to be rigid. It's perfectly acceptable to study a beautiful bird in your yard in Month 1 even though birds don't come until Month 7. The only reason for these topics is to help bring a little order to your teaching so that you will eventually introduce all the topics. It gives you a focus each month to build around. Because you'll come back around the next year and the next year, you can adapt the study to the ages and developmental and interest level of your children. You don't have to cover everything in one sitting.

I'm going to take you through a little sampler tour of these 8 months to show you the kinds of resources you have to draw from and to begin to plant ideas of how you might use them. We're warming hearts, so you'll find a lot of story, poetry, music and art.

For our first stop, listen to Arabella Buckley's introduction in *The Fairyland of Science* written in 1879 that may be something you'll want to share with your children.

> There are forces around us, and among us, which I shall ask you to allow me to call fairies, and these are ten thousand times more wonderful, more magical, and more beautiful in their work, than those of the old fairy tales. They, too, are invisible, and many people live and die without ever seeing them or caring to see them. These people go about with their eyes shut, either because they will not open them, or because no one has taught them how to see.
>
> There is only one gift we must have before we can learn to know them—we must have imagination—the power of making pictures or images in our mind, of that which is, though it is invisible to us. Most children have this glorious gift...which enables us through the temporal things which are seen, to realize those eternal truths which are unseen.
>
> You must wish to see them. You ask yourself why things happen, and how the great

> God above us has made and governs this world of ours; if you listen to the wind, and care to learn why it blows; if you ask the little flower why it opens in the sunshine and closes in the storm; and if when you find questions you cannot answer, you will take the trouble to hunt out in books, or make experiments, to solve your own questions, then you will learn to know and love those fairies.
>
> We learn to see that there is a law and purpose in everything in the Universe, and it makes us patient when we recognize the quiet noiseless working of nature all around us… [W]hen we realize that all is worked with fixed laws, and that out of it (even if sometimes in suffering and pain) springs the wonderful universe around us. And then say, can you fear for your own little life, even though it may have its troubles? Can you help feeling a part of this guided and governed nature? Or doubt that the power which fixed the laws of the stars and of the tiniest drop of water—that made the plant draw power from the sun, the tiny coral animal its food from the dashing waves; that adapted the flower to the insect and the insect to the flower—is also moulding your life as part of the great machinery of the universe, so that you have only to work, and to wait, and to love?
>
> We are all groping dimly for the Unseen Power, but to one who loves nature and studies it can never feel alone or unloved in the world. Facts, as mere facts, are dry and barren, but nature is full of life and love, and her calm unswerving rule is tending to some great though hidden purpose.
>
> Even the little child who lives with nature and gazes on her with open eye, must rise in some sense or other through nature to nature's God.

So let's start with Month 1: The Stars. Remember, your job is not to supply all the facts of nature and the answers to every question you can anticipate. Rather, your job is to awaken desire, primarily by using stories that will begin to plant ideas in your children's hearts of things they'll look for when they get out in nature. We want them to fall in love with her! Isn't it awesome that the most glorious university in the world is free?

You don't have to do Nature Study every day, although it's good for children to be outside as much as they possibly can. Most of what your children will learn about nature will be by exploration and discovery and finding answers to their own questions. You're just priming the pump by planting ideas.

If you go into Month 1's topic of Stars, you will find links to old books that can be read online for free. The selections I will be sharing in this presentation come from the Nature Series in our Forgotten Classics Family Library. Then there are suggestions for classical music, and even craft ideas. It's not that the craft ideas in themselves are necessarily instructive, it's that they can occupy little hands so that their little ears can be open while you read nature stories to them or play classical music. At least that's one use. Mostly, it's to engage in a pleasurable activity in association with the topic.

One of the important activities of childhood is naming things—naming stars and flowers and animals. I can recreate the home of my early childhood by the names of flowers—the hibiscus by my bedroom window, the gardenia out the back door, the hydrangea, bounganvilla, camellia, pyracantha berries, hollyhocks, the magnolia tree in the front yard. There were no formal lessons, but I knew them all by name and I knew my mother's favorites were the gardenias and the magnolia tree.

Begin to name the stars and constellations and tell the stories the Greeks told of the stars, not all at once. A little here and a little there. Wrap up in blankets and go lay out in the grass after bedtime and gaze up at the stars together. Sometimes silence is the best teacher. Recite poems—did you know Twinkle Twinkle Little Star has a lot of verses? Play Mozart's Variations of Twinkle. Or Holst's Planets. Or recite Wordsworth.

> Our birth is but a sleep and a forgetting,
> The soul that rises with us, our life's Star,
> Hath had elsewhere its setting
> And cometh from afar;
> Not in entire forgetfulness,
> And not in utter nakedness,
> But trailing clouds of glory do we come
> From God, who is our home;
> Heaven lies about us in our infancy!

Share stories of scientists who loved the stars—Galileo, Maria Mitchell or the story of Van Gogh's Starry Night. Study the Space Program. Watch *October Sky*. Read science fiction where imaginations paint pictures of what may be out there. So many possibilities for the heart.

Here's a little book I found that I love: *Among the Stars or Wonderful Things in the Sky* by Agnes Giberne (1885).

Let me share the beginning:

> "Dormer, I can't think where my star is gone... My own beautiful star! O Dormer, it was always there before I was ill every evening for a whole week. And I meant to go on watching it always. Every evening it was there over the poplars and you wouldn't let me go to look until today. And now it is quite gone."
>
> Dormer replied, "I wouldn't mind, if I was you. There's hundreds of other stars just as good. One doesn't signify, more or less."
>
> "Wouldn't anybody care if a star was lost?" asked Ikon wistfully.
>
> "I shouldn't," Dormer replied.
>
> "I think I should. I did love that star so," murmured the child. 'I used to think...'
>
> Ikon stopped short. Dormer was a most excellent and affectionate nurse, and he loved her dearly.
>
> She had cared for him with motherly tenderness from his earliest babyhood. Still, there was a certain something wanting between them. Ikon never found that his little innermost thoughts and feelings and fancies met with a response from Dormer. He was

a delicate and dreamy child, and he often longed for somebody to whom he could speak freely, somebody by whom he could be understood.

Ikon was always wondering about this and that, wishing to ask questions of somebody. He was tired of asking his teacher. She never would allow any break in her regular plan of teaching, and at the beginning and end of the time she was always in a hurry.

It was a lonely life that he led. He had no little sisters and no little friends. His chief pleasures were found in the companionship of his pet dog, and of the birds and plants and trees in the garden. But Ikon had one pleasure greater than even these; and that was in the companionship of the stars.

This seems an odd word to use about the stars and a little boy, yet in a sense it is the right word.

For Ikon loved the stars. He could not have told the time when first he began to love the stars. The feeling seemed to have grown upon him slowly, as he grew up out of babyhood. Even as a tiny child he had delighted to gaze on the glittering sky, and had often clapped his little hands with joy at the sight.

He could not have told why he loved that star so much. It was only about a week or ten days before his illness, that he had first noticed it, shining over the distant line of poplar trees, low down near the horizon. But now it was quite gone—a lost star. There were many other stars over the far-off poplars, but not one so bright and soft and shining as this particular favorite.

Tears came into Ikon's eyes. He was really grieved, really distressed. For somehow that dear star had seemed to his little heart to smile upon him out of heaven, and made him think of the mother whom he had never known. And this was the fancy which he could not tell to Dormer, for Dormer would not have understood in the least what he meant.

"Dormer, do the stars die? ... I want to know where the stars all go every day. They don't all die because they are all right again next evening. I want to know where they go. I do want to know what the stars are. What they really are. I want to know why they twinkle so; and why some of them don't. And I can't think why they should be so bright. I wish I knew what made them shine. "

Could you feel how many ideas were being planted in just that small passage? As the story unfolds, Ikon's father brings in a friend, a wise and kind professor who begins to answer Ikon's questions about the stars. Yes, the book teaches all about the stars and the planets, but the book itself is a tutorial in teaching for you. Notice how the teacher carefully unfolds the layers and allows Ikon time to digest and ponder.

At one time, the professor tried to provide illustrations to answer a question Ikon had and Ikon wondered which was the best illustration. The professor replied,

"Whatever helps you to see most clearly the wonderful power of God. His power is shown in His works."

In these old books, you'll frequently find God woven into the stories in a quiet, gentle way.

"Are the stars His works?" asked Ikon.

"He made the stars, child."

"The heavens declare the glory of God, and the firmament showeth His handiwork."

It's a beautiful interchange between a wise, loving older friend and a child.

Now let's on to Month 2: the Ocean.

Maybe you don't live anywhere near the ocean. Search YouTube—you can find hours of ocean images and sounds of waves and seagulls that can be played on your TV as a background. Or look for flowers or birds or mountains—whatever you're studying that month. That's how you can bring nature indoors even when the snow is deep. How about playing The Moldau while your children are working on a craft, where they can hear the little stream at the beginning that combines and grows bigger until it forms rapids and finally settles into the quiet sea. Month 2 is a good time for stories of explorers and adventurers who sailed the oceans of the world. Introduce your children to Jacques Cousteau and his undersea adventures.

I love this little 1904 book of *Sea Stories for Wonder Eyes* that starts with this little chapter on: A Little Girl Who Wondered

> A little girl sat on a great rock by the sea looking out over the water.
>
> As far as her eye could reach she saw only crested waves that came from far beyond; and every wave was wreathed with foam that flashed like a coronet of jewels.
>
> She had never heard what people say of the strange ebb and flow of the tides, but she knew that twice every day the waves crept up to the rock on which she sat, and that twice every day they receded, leaving a stretch of sandy beach.
>
> "I wonder who calls the waves back into the deep," she said softly to herself, and a strange awe came into her heart.
>
> "I wonder if a Voice tells them when they may come back and play upon the sand," and as she spoke the tide of awe that rose in her heart gave deep colors to her eyes, like the colors of the sea.
>
> "O wonderful Sea, do tell me some of your secrets!" she exclaimed.
>
> For answer a great wave with a crest of foam rose up from the green and purple currents and broke with a roaring sea laugh almost at her feet.
>
> When the surf was gone she saw that the wave had left bits of seaweed on the sand, and shells, and queer creeping, wriggling little sea things.
>
> "So this is the way you answer me!" she exclaimed, "and I have to find out everything for myself!"
>
> At first she saw only the shells and coarser wrack that lay exposed, but as her eye grew accustomed to the search she found countless treasures that had been left on the sand,

> in coves, and imprisoned in tide pools.
>
> The longer and the closer she looked the more she was rewarded.
>
> The more she saw of the little sea things the more she loved them; and the more she loved them, the more she was able to find.
>
> Slowly again the tide crept up the sand.
>
> "So, old Sea, you are coming back after your treasures, are you?" said the child, "and I must go away. I love your roar, and your sea songs make me glad; but I wonder what you are singing about. I wonder where your bright waves come from.
>
> "Oh, I wonder and wonder so many things!"

For this little girl who sat by the sea and who wondered—and for other girls and boys who wonder—these sea stories have been written.

Month 3: Rocks

There's something about rocks that children love. I can never take my little grandchildren on walks without them filling their pockets with rocks. Let them bring them home and start learning their stories and building a rock collection! Collecting and sorting and identifying rocks and leaves and flowers all help children love nature more. My dad and one of my brothers loved to go rock hunting together. Today, my brother's yard is filled with rocks and he can tell you the story of every one of them. Our dad has been gone for many years, but when he's out in the desert looking for rocks, he feels close to him. Grinding and polishing rocks has become a fun hobby that gives him much happiness and satisfaction.

Have your children choose some rock crafts to do while you read to them and help them begin to learn the stories of the rocks such as are found in this 1899 book, *Stories of our Mother Earth* by Harold Fairbanks.

It begins:

> The earth is our home. As we climb the hills, or follow the rippling streams or wander along the beach, we feel that this is a very pleasant place in which to live. We enjoy seeing the mountains and the plants and the trees and by and by we begin to wonder about them, and to ask questions. (There's an idea being planted again.) The world becomes to us something more than a mere playground made for our especial benefit.
>
> We question the mountains, and the rivers, and the ocean. We wonder if they have always been where they are now. The mountains look so firm and solid it seems as if they must always have stood where they do now. But some day we find shells upon a high ridge far from the ocean. This puzzles us, for these shells must have lived in the ocean once.
>
> We finally come to the conclusion that before we can know all about the plants; why one kind grows on the hillside, another by the brook; why the animals are distributed where we find them; why cities grow up where they do; and why in one part of the

> country people till the ground, and in another dig deep for the minerals, we must know a little more about the foundations of our home.
>
> We must know how the rocks and the soil were made, how the mountains grew, and why the rivers run as they do. We must understand how Nature is shaping the earth for us.
>
> In order to do this, we shall study what the rain and the frost are doing upon the mountain tops. We shall trace the river's course, and find where the mud which it carries to the ocean comes from. We shall try to understand how this mud is spread over the floor of the ocean, and what the waves are doing as they continually beat against the land.
>
> We shall go beneath the rich soil upon which our grain grows, and find out what is going on within the earth. We shall want to know about many things which are dug from the earth.

Nature has many forces at work, some great and some small. They have worked a long time getting this home of ours ready for us. If we can understand how Nature works, our home will be more dear to us, and we shall be happier.

Another idea is to listen to the Grand Canyon Suite with images from the Grand Canyon. Then read Brighty of the Grand Canyon together.

If you're looking for a rock scientist, I love Louis Agassiz who loved reading the story of our world in the rocks. As I read in one of the older books, it said the story of the creation told in the Bible and the story told in the rocks are simply two versions of the same event. One account didn't discount the other. Faith and reason, mind and heart worked together in these old children's books. Agassiz was a teacher of great renown at Harvard who taught his students to learn by using their eyes.

One biography I read of him said of him that he never knew a dull hour in his life and thought it an incredible joke that any person could 'kill time in a world so full of interest.' In a letter to his brother, he wrote, "Write me about what you are reading and about your plans and projects, for I can hardly believe that any one can live without forming them: I, at least, could not." His friends wanted to send him to Europe—he turned them down because he said there was too much he hadn't seen yet in his own back yard and spent the next 9 months in joyful discovery. Agassiz is a good friend for a child to have.

Longfellow wrote him a poem on his 50th birthday:

> It was fifty years ago
> In the pleasant month of May,
> In the beautiful Pays de Vaud,
> A child in its cradle lay.
> And Nature, the old nurse, took
> The child upon her knee,
> Saying, "Here is a story-book

> Thy Father has written for thee."
> "Come, wander with me," she said,
> "Into regions yet untrod;
> And read what is still unread
> In the manuscripts of God."
> And he wandered away and away
> With Nature, the dear old nurse,
> Who sang to him night and day
> The rhymes of the universe.
> And whenever the way seemed long,
> Or his heart began to fail,
> She would sing a more wonderful song,
> Or tell a more marvellous tale.

If your children are little, here's the story of a little boy who grew up to be a great geologist—Hugh Miller. Here's how the story goes:

> Many, many years ago there lived in a fishing town on the north-eastern coast of Scotland a boy who afterwards became a very famous man. When he was only 5 years old, his father, who was a sailor, was lost at sea. His mother, though very poor, managed to send little Hugh to school, and there he learned a good deal from books; but if he had learned no more than to read and to write, he would probably have still been a great man, for in the meantime he had found something else worth more to him than many books. He had learned to read another language. He had found out that he had two eyes, and how to use them.

Notice the ideas being planted in your own children's hearts about learning! And then the book goes on to describe how Hugh read the clues in the rocks. Soon your children will read the clues in the rocks for themselves.

Month 4: Plants and Trees

Is there anything more beautiful than a flower? What has man ever created that can even slightly compare with the color, the scent and the texture of a flower? In month 4, introduce your children to Beethoven's Pastoral Symphony. Beethoven loved to take long walks out in nature and he translated what he felt and saw into his music. And what better time to read *The Secret Garden*? Here's some flower crafting they can do while they listen to you read from an 1898 book, *Plants and Their Children* by Mrs. William Starr Dana.

And now a sample:

> Is there a nicer place in which to play than an old apple Orchard? Once under those favorite trees whose branches sweep the ground, you are quite shut off from the great, troublesome, outside world. And how happy and safe you feel in that green world of your own!—a world just made for children, a world of grass and leaves and birds and flowers, where lessons and grown-up people alike have no part.

> That you children long to be out of the schoolroom this minute, out in the orchard so full of possibilities, I do not wonder a bit. But as the big people have decided that from now on for some months you must spend much of your time with lessons books, I have a plan to propose.
>
> What do you say to trying to bring something of the outdoor places that we love into the schoolroom, which we do not love as much as we should if lessons were always taught in the right way?

She then goes on to describe the life of an apple blossom leading up to a surprise for me! Have you ever cut an apple horizontally? Where did the apple blossom go? It's right there, imprinted right there in the middle of an apple! Nature is full of surprises like that.

And I loved this little interchange as she poses the question of what is the purpose of a plant's life.

> There is one especial thing which is really the object of the plant's life. A great many people seem to think that the object of all plants with pretty flowers must be to give pleasure. But these people quite forget that hundreds and thousands of flowers live and die far away in the lonely forest, where no human eye ever sees them; that they so lived and died hundreds and thousands of years before there were any men and women, and boys and girls, upon the earth. And so, if they stopped long enough quietly to think about it, they would see for themselves that plants must have some other object in life than to give people pleasure.
>
> But let us go back to the tree from which we took this apple, and see if we can find out its special object.
>
> 'Why apples!' some of you exclaim. 'Sure the object of an apple tree is to bear apples."
>
> That is it exactly. An apple tree lives to bear apples.
>
> And now why is an apple such an important thing?
>
> Why is it worth so much time and trouble? What is its use?
>
> "It is good to eat," chime all the children in chorus.
>
> Yes, so it is, but then, you must remember that once upon a time, apple trees, like all other plants and trees, grew in lonely places where there were no boys and girls to eat their fruit. So we must find some other answer. Think for a moment, and then tell me what you find inside every apple.
>
> "Apple seeds," one of you replies.
>
> And what is the use of these apple seeds? "Why they make new apple trees!"
>
> If this be so, if every apple holds some little seeds from which new apple trees may grow, does it not look as though an apple were useful and important because it yields seeds?
>
> And what is true of the apple tree is true of other plants and trees. The plant lives to

> bear fruit. The fruit is that part of the plant which holds its seeds; and it is of importance for just this reason, that it holds the seeds from which come new plants.

And now I'll just leave the story there and let you ponder the layers of its meaning.

Learning about flowers and trees is a perfect month to introduce nature journaling. I really love John Muir Laws. He has a lot of free videos online that teach you how to draw from nature, but he came out with a book that is just the best called: *The Laws' Guide to Nature Drawing and Journaling*. John assures us anyone can learn to draw.

Here are a few excerpts from his book:

> When we see with clear eyes, we know that we are surrounded with beauty. Let yourself fall in love with your life by paying attention. As David Steindl-Rast says: "It is not happiness that makes us grateful. It's gratefulness that makes us happy." As you record what you see in your journal, give thanks for what surrounds you. When you celebrate the world through the pages of your journal, every stroke of your brush or pencil can be a song of gratitude for the opportunity to be alive.
>
> Think how often you have said to yourself, "I will never forget this moment." Sometimes the moment sticks, but although it can be hard to admit, we forget many experiences and ideas that were once meaningful to us; it is possible to skip through this life with only dim memories of even our most major life events. In every instant, we consciously process only a fraction of the data we get from our senses, and we remember only a tiny piece of that. But the process of journaling is enough to burn a moment into your memory. Every day, you can fill your mind with wonder and fill your journal with a record of the beauty you have experienced.
>
> Love can be defined as sustained, compassionate attention. Paying sincere attention to another person helps us build understanding and kindness. Similarly, I feel understanding, care and compassion when I journal and turn deep attention to nature.
>
> Journaling is a skill for anyone who wishes to live life more deeply, a skill that you can learn at any age and that will develop with intention and practice. Observing and journaling will slow you down and make you stop, sit down, look and look again. Engaging in this process helps you to organize your thoughts, piece together answers and ask richer questions. Once you slow down and look long enough to record observations in your journal, mysteries will unfold before you.
>
> At the heart of science are insatiable curiosity and deep observation, qualities that lead to the best kind of learning, learning motivated by your intrinsic wonder, hunger to understand and ability to observe.
>
> I draw to see, to remember and to stimulate curiosity; you move through the world with joy.

Doesn't that make you want to grab a sketch pad and some paint and start drawing? And by the way, there's no better way to inspire your children to start nature journaling than to watch you do it.

Since Month 4 falls in December and Christmas time, which is busy for most families, I continued the study into Month 5 and added gardening as part of it. Now, you may say that would definitely be taught in Spring. But not so! January is exactly the right month to start dreaming and planning of what's going to be in that garden and going through seed catalogues and ordering seeds, many of which can be started indoors.

I can think of no more important activity in a child's life than growing a flower garden of his very own. And I love two little books by Frances Duncan written in the early 1900s that makes the process simple and at a child's level. *When Mother Lets Us Garden* and *Mary's Garden and How it Grew.* It opens with:

> The very nicest kind of fathers and mothers will always let you make a garden. If there isn't a small piece of ground that you can have, then take a box; if you can't have a box of earth, then take a flower-pot or even a tin can.

What better way to teach children the lessons of patience and waiting, of sowing and harvesting.

And like Corrie Ten Boom taught in *The Hiding Place*, "People can learn to love, from flowers."

Month 5 is when we're going to take a look at Insects and Bugs.

What child doesn't love Rimsky-Korsakov's *Flight of the Bumblebee?* And Month 5 could be a good month to read *Charlotte's Web* or *A Cricket in Times Square*. Let them craft bugs while you read *Cecil's Book of Insects* by Selim H. Peabody written in 1868. Here's a preview:

> Do you ever find yourself, some dreamy summer day, with nothing to do? The hot, dense rays of the July sun scorch the dry grass, glow in the burning sand, and almost hiss in the water of the idle stream. The birds hide in the dense thickets, the cattle pant in the shade, and the very dog wishes he could take his jacket off. The boy has exhausted all his own plans for fun, and in despair asks his mother, "What shall I do?"
>
> I'll tell you what to do. Find an ant hill in some shady place, where the sun will not burn your back, lie down upon your face, and watch it. You have passed such a thousand times, without knowing what curious things could be seen there. The little fellows worked all the morning, and brought up out of that hole in the middle, all the grains of sand that you see piled around in a tiny circular fortress. One by one they brought them out and laid them in their places. Now they are thoroughly warmed by the sun, and they are carrying them back again, into the rooms which they have excavated below. If there is a flat stone near, turn it over, and you will quite likely find a much busier crowd. A large chamber, with many winding passages running hither and thither, and connecting with each other, and with other passages underneath, has been made, like the public square and the thronged streets of an old fashioned city… Scattered all along the thoroughfares of this stone-canopied town are many long, round, white somethings, a little like grains of wheat. People have mistaken these things for food of the ants, and so have written, The little ant, for one poor grain, Doth tug, and toil and strive.

> But the ants lay up no food. They need none; for as soon as the hard frosts of autumn chill them, they lie down to sleep till the spring wakes them again. If they did lay up food, it would not be grain, for the ant can no more eat grain than a man can eat gold, and the ant is not so big a fool as to hoard what he can not use.
>
> Others have thought that these little white sacks are the eggs of the ants; but eggs do not grow, and surely ants can not lay eggs that are larger than themselves. Whatever they are, the ants evidently think them very valuable.
>
> These sacks contain the young ants. The eggs were laid by the queen, and hatched by the warmth of the hot grains of sand. The grubs were fed, and grew, and finally shut themselves up in the sacks, as the caterpillar spins a cocoon. Then the ants take great care of these sacks. They are very precious to them because they contain their children.

I'll let you think on that.

Insects are the smallest of creatures, but when you consider the complex and intricate makeup of their tiny little bodies and the instinct to organize and colonize and build and care for their young, it's astonishing.

And here's a good parenting lesson from the world of insects and tiny creatures:

> A twig where clung two soft cocoons
> I broke from a wayside spray,
> And carried home to a quiet desk
> Where, long forgot, it lay.
> One morn I chanced to lift the lid,
> And lo! As light as air,
> A moth flew up on downy wings
> And settled above my chair!
> A dainty, beautiful thing it was,
> Orange and silvery gray,
> And I marveled how from the withered bough
> Such fairy stole away.
> Had the other flown? I turned to see,
> And found it striving still
> To free itself from the swathing floss
> And rove the air at will.
> "Poor little prisoned waif," I said,
> "You shall not struggle more";
> And I tenderly cut the threads,
> And watched to see it soar.
> Alas! A feeble chrysalis
> It dropped from its silken bed;
> My help had been the direst harm—
> The pretty moth was dead!

I should have left it there to gain
  The strength that struggle brings;
'Tis the stress and strain, with moth or man,
  That free the folded wings!

Moving onto Month 7, we're ready to take a look at Birds. Are there any other creatures that seem to know the meaning of Joy like they do? Have you ever just sat and watched them? And what would the world be without their songs?

Listen to Stravinsky's *Firebird Finale* or Tchaikovsky's *Swan Lake*. Introduce them to Audubon and his beautiful drawing of birds. Read a children's classic like *Trumpet of the Swan*.

Find a branch from a tree and set it in a pot in your house and see how many birds you can identify and sketch and hang on your little tree. You may need some binoculars. And can you recognize them from their song?

Make some bird feeders, and while their hands are busy, tell them a story like this from Olive Thorne Miller's *True Bird Stories* written in 1903:

> I want to tell you about a wild bluebird, who knew enough to appreciate the comforts of home.
>
> The bird was found in a store in a very bad condition, having been caught in a trap and beaten herself against the wires till her wing feathers were broken so that she could not fly. She was put into the cage of another bluebird, who had been so injured that he could never fly.
>
> The stranger showed herself to be rather ill-mannered. She grabbed the best of everything, and drove the owner of the cage about as if it were hers and not his. In fact, she was so greedy that the mistress thought he would be very glad when she had gone. So as soon as she had moulted and had come out with new plumage and perfect wing feathers, the cage door was opened and away flew Madame Blue and disappeared.
>
> Then the bird who was left began to call to her. All day he called, but there was no sign that the runaway heard.
>
> The next day, twenty-four hours after she had been set free, one of the family found her back, and trying with all her might to squeeze into the cage between the wires, while her old cage mate was greatly excited, calling in the sweetest voice, welcoming her, and encouraging her to come in.
>
> The cage door was opened for her and she flew right in, plainly delighted to get home. Then came the most lively chatting between the two. One could not help feeling that she was telling how uncomfortable she found it having to hunt up food and water, and how much nicer it was to have a whole family of people to wait on and care for one.
>
> She ate and drank, and appeared as if she could not get enough, and was evidently perfectly happy. Open doors were no temptation to her.

I'll let you ponder on that story, too.

And now Month 8: Animals. Are there any stories that are more delightful to children or of which there is an endless supply? *Black Beauty*, *Lassie Come Home*, all the Marguerite Henry books, *Bambi*—not like the Disney movie at all. The list is long. And so are the lessons as children learn how carefully animal mamas care for their babies, how they build their homes, how they teach their children to be independent. Introduce them to James Herriot's writings—a vet who loved animals.

This is a little book I found written in 1911 by Harry Brearley called *Animal Secrets Told: A Book of Whys*.

Here's an excerpt from the intro.

> *Animal Secrets Told* is intended much less as a means for conveying information, than for suggesting, and if possible stimulating the use by the reader of those original powers of observation and deduction by which he may gain knowledge at first hand.
>
> These powers are natural and active in the mind of the child. He is surrounded by a world of crowded wonders which must at first produce the sense of confusion, but the innate orderliness of his mental action soon manifests itself in his commencing to ask "Why?" In other words he perceives this is a world of Reason—that there is a Law behind these phenomena—and it becomes at once a keen, intellectual pleasure to find these reasons, and then by applying straight-forward childish logic to uncover the law.
>
> No parent need be told how active is this phase of childhood, nor how the rapid fire of 'whys' from little lips is accompanied by the rapid expansion of the little mind. But the grown person is apt to become mentally lazy and to wish to receive his knowledge in predigested form, whereby it happens that the fascinating glamour of those early 'golden days' passes swiftly away.
>
> One's arm will shrivel if he never uses it, one's teeth will decay if he neglect to chew. One's eye was intended for seeing not for looking, put steadily neglected for years in its higher function it becomes at last a mere dull looker upon a leaden-colored world, where the truer-visioned child finds light, color and enchantment.
>
> As a matter of fact the world is as fascinating a place as ever. It has not changed its capacity during the few years since childhood. The dreary, unimportant phenomena which seem to fall into a heavy-footed procession of endless repetition, are in reality dancing forth alive with interest and almost bursting with significance as the seeing eye would at once perceive.

Animal Secrets Told asks the question "Why?" Why are the eyes placed on a fish one way and on a bear another and other similar questions. My grown son formatted this book for me and was so curious he could hardly wait to go to the National Zoo to see for himself. As was written: "Grown people as well have come easily under the spell of doing what so many adults have hardly grasped as possible to them: Learning things for themselves instead of waiting to be told." Isn't that so true?

Now notice something else. After you've been through the rotation a few times, it's time to start layering in the Science layer. In essence, your children have felt the magic, and now you're going to take them backstage and start helping them see how the magic is done. This is a time for simple experiments that demonstrate laws and principles. Notice how the first three months lend themselves to a beginning study of Earth Sciences: Light and Physics, Chemistry, and Geology. The last months lend themselves to Life Sciences: Biology, Botany, Zoology.

As you continue to layer in understanding, by the time your children reach high school, they will have rich and fertile soil in which to begin a systematic academic study of science, all of which will continue to reveal the workmanship of a Creator who pays attention to the minutest detail and who loves us and who is a God of order, beauty and purpose. We are His crowning creation.

And you will have laid the foundation for a lifetime of interest, with endless discoveries to be made, and lessons too deep for the heart to be revealed in any other way.

As Anna McGovern wrote:

"The value of Nature Study should not be measured by the acquisition of knowledge, but rather by the love and the profound reverence for the design and the protecting care revealed in the works and sky by an all-wise Creator."

I hope I have helped you feel the difference between a heart education and a mind education. Heart and mind need to work in concert, but heart first, and then mind if you want to do your part in turning the tide of hard-heartedness. Again, all these nature selections came from the books found in our Nature Series in the Forgotten Classics Family Library. There are free digital copies available, or you can buy hard copies in our store.

If you have high schoolers that missed this heart phase, I always start my study of anything by finding a children's book. Let your high schoolers know these children's book really are not beneath them and may open a whole world they didn't know existed even though it was right there all the time.

One of the commonalities among many of the great lives I have studied is the time they took to walk in nature. There's an ordering property that happens when you take walks in nature. Part of it may lie in the rhythm of walking, but I think more importantly, there are instant messages made on our hearts that clarify our thoughts, clear our brains and renew our spirits. We associate recreation with the great outdoors. Well, it is truly a place of re-creation, as is expressed in this little poem with which I will close.

> The little cares that fretted me,
>   I lost them yesterday,
> Among the fields, above the sea,
>   Among the winds at play;
> Among the lowing of the herds,
>   The rustling of the trees;
> Among the singing of the birds,
>   The humming of the bees.

The foolish fears of what may happen,
  I cast them all away
Among the clover-scented grass,
  Among the new-mown hay;
Among the rustling of the corn,
  Where drowsy poppies nod,
Where ill thoughts die and good are born
  Out in the fields with God.

More Thoughts on Nature Study

This quote is found on the back of the Mother's Learning Library Nature Study book:

"The value of Nature Study should not be measured by the acquisition of knowledge, but rather by the love and the profound reverence for the design and the protecting care revealed in the works and by an all-wise Creator."

When the heart educators of a hundred years ago suggested nature studies, they had their eye not just on the acquisition of knowledge, but on the underlying spiritual truths. You find this throughout their writings, which differentiates their writings from modern ones.

For instance, in the teacher notes of a book written by Dallas Lore Sharp who I will talk about in a future Take 5, he gave this advice to the teacher:

> Go yourself frequently into the fields and woods, or into the city parks, or along the water front—anywhere so that you can touch nature directly, and look and listen for yourselves. Don't try to teach what you do not know, and there is nothing in this book that you cannot know, for the lesson to be taught in each chapter is a spiritual lesson, not a number of bare facts. This spiritual lesson you must first learn before you can teach it—must feel, I should say; and a single thoughtful excursion alone into the autumn fields will give you possession of it.

For most of us, when we being to study something, we do it through the eye of knowledge. So, for instance, this month we are studying the Stars. You might be inclined to have your children make a chart of the planets in order and maybe even memorize them. Study their relative size and the distance between each other. There is no end of facts you can accumulate about the stars and the universe. But facts are cold and hard. One day you may need a use for them—or a desire to know them to satisfy your own questions. But handed out as assignments, they don't serve much of a purpose on their own, although they can keep kids busy.

I don't know about you, but as many times as I had to put the planets in order, I still can't do it.

And not knowing that really hasn't posed a problem so far. Maybe if I were on Jeopardy and the Final Jeopardy question had something to do with the 4th planet from the sun I would wish I had paid closer attention. But overall, not knowing it hasn't been an obstacle. If I'm home and care to know what that 4th planet is, I'll just ask Alexa. She knows everything.

Let me share a few words from the great American naturalist, John Burroughs:

> What knowledge I possess of her creatures and ways has come to me through contemplation and enjoyment, rather than through deliberate study of her. I have been occupied more with the spirit than with the letter of her works. In our time, (*which, by the way, he is writing a hundred years ago and it has only gotten worse*) it seems to me, too

much stress is laid upon the letter. We approach Nature in an exact, calculating, tabulating, mercantile spirit. We seek to make an inventory of her store-house. Our relations with her take on the air of business, not of love and friendship. The clerk of the fields and woods goes forth with his block of printed tablets upon which, and under various heads, he puts down what he sees, and I suppose loots it all up and gets at the exact sum of his knowledge when he gets back home. He is so intent upon the bare fact that he does not see the spirit or the meaning of the whole... Of that sympathetic and emotional intercourse with nature which soothes and enriches the soul, he experiences little or none.

The knowledge of nature that comes easy, that comes through familiarity with her, as through fishing, walking, farming—that is the kind that reaches and affects the character and becomes a grown part of us. We absorb this as we absorb the air, and it gets into the blood. Fresh, vital knowledge is one thing; the desiccated fact is another. Do we know the wild flower when we have analyzed it and pressed it or made a drawing of it? Of course this is one kind of knowledge and is suited to certain minds, but if we cannot supplement it with the other kind, the knowledge that comes through the heart and the emotions, we are poor indeed.

I recently had a letter from the principal of a New England high school putting some questions to me touching these very matters: Do children love Nature? How shall we instill this love into them? How and when did I myself acquire my love for her? Etc. In reply I said, "The child, in my opinion, does not consciously love nature; it is curious about things, about everything; its instincts lead it forth into the fields and woods; it browses around; it gathers flowers—they are pretty; it stores up impressions."

... I hunted, I fished, I browsed, I wandered with a vague longing in the woods, I trapped, I went cooning at night, I made ponds in the little streams, I boiled sap in the maple woods in spring, I went to sleep under the trees in summer, I caught birds in their nests, I watched for the little frogs in the marshes... I was not conscious of any love for Nature, as such, till my mind was brought in contact with literature. Then I discovered that I, too, loved Nature, and had a whole world of impressions stored up in my subconscious self upon which to draw. (*May I just insert here Pestalozzi would have called that Anschuang or sense-impressions if you've been reading* A Mother's Influence. *Back to Burroughs.*) I found I knew about the birds, the animals, the seasons, the trees, the flowers and that these things had become almost a grown part of me. I have been drawing upon the reservoir of youthful impressions ever since.

Anything like accurate or scientific knowledge of nature which I may possess is of later date; but my boyhood on the farm seems to have given me the feeling and to have put me in the right relation with these things. Of course writing about these subjects also deepens one's love for them. If Nature is to be a resource in a man's life, one's relation to her must not be too exact and formal, but more that of a lover and friend.

So did you catch the key points? Let your children play in nature. They are accumulating sense impressions that will serve them later. Don't make nature an assignment or a worksheet to be completed.

You must first feel the beauty yourself. You can't fake it. And then, don't separate great literature and the poets from a study of nature. In the same section of the Nature Study book, you'll read: "The teacher who earnestly desires to lead children to see, to enjoy, and to love nature, must dwell with the poet and the artist as well as with the scientist; she must learn to appreciate something of the beauty they saw in forest and stream and the joy they felt in its portrayal.

"When the teacher recognizes clearly the power of literature as a spiritualizing element in her own life, she will earnestly endeavor to bring the child under the influence of writers who will touch his heart, quicken his perception of beauty and give him great and beautiful thoughts as a permanent possession."

As Burroughs said, "Unless science is mixed with emotion and appeals to the heart and imagination, it is like dead, inorganic matter; and when it is mixed and transformed, it is literature... This power to beautify and transform the most commonplace objects...is caused by literary artists."

In the Nature Study book, you'll find a book in the last half called *Type Lessons for Primary Teachers in the Study of Nature, Literature and Art*. It is divided by Fall, Winter and Spring—I guess the teacher figured the kids were out of school for the Summer so there is no summer section. And you will find a lot of poetry and stories to connect to what you see in Nature. Feed yourself first.

But since we're talking about Stars this month, let me share a story to go along with their study.

Notice how much it has to do with being rather than just knowing. I can't help but think of the Native Americans who attached stories of being to everything their children saw in nature so that they were constantly reminded of lessons on how to live life that their parents wanted to instill in their hearts.

After you hear this story, can you look at the Big Dipper without the impression made by the story?

And by the way, if all this talk of tying literature and poetry into nature study feels so far over your head—I know it does mine!—it is simply an ideal to reach towards. Small and simple steps are good enough. Like just letting your kids play in nature is a giant step upward for many of them. Go spread a blanket out under the stars this month—and if all you do is stare, you've provided a wonderful lesson on the stars this month.

A Legend of the Great Dipper

The faces of the stars shone so brightly one night that the earth-children thought the moon was telling a pretty story. And so she was, and this is the story:

The great Dipper which you, my dear children, love to see has a deep meaning which you are not to forget as long as the stars shine. I will tell you the story.

In another world than ours, said Lady Moon, there was once great trouble and sorrow. No, it was not in the earth world, my dear, she said to a small star who always asked questions, it was not in the heaven world either, but in another far-away world, where many children lived.

For some good reason, which only the Father knows, the people and children, the animals and every living thing, were suffering great thirst; and no water, nor dew, nor a drop of moisture could they find anywhere. A little child of that world went out alone in the dry, dark night, carrying a small tin dipper, and prayed very earnestly for just that little cup of water, which would not spill, though she ran rapidly, her hand trembling with her faintness; for she did not taste the water, having prayed for another's need. As she ran, she stumbled and fell, for she was very weak; and when feeling about, trying to rise, she touched a little dog that seemed to be dying of thirst, and the good child poured a few drops of the precious water in the palm of her hand and let the dog lap it. He seemed as refreshed as if he had drank from a river.

The child could not see what happened to her cup; but we saw and sang for joy. The cup turned to silver, and grew larger the water not having become less, but more, by her giving.

She hurried on to give the water to one who was quite unable to come to meet her—none other than her own dear mother, who took the water eagerly, as one in a deadly fever, but without putting it to her lips; for she heard just then a weak moan which came from the faithful servant who tried to raise her mistress's head, but found she had not the strength. The mother pressed the dipper into the hands of the maid, and bade her drink, feeling her own life so wasted that one little cup of water could not renew it. And neither servant nor mistress noticed that the dipper changed from silver to gold, and grew larger than before.

The good servant was about to give each member of the family one spoonful of the precious water, when a stranger entered, dressed in a costume unknown in that country, and speaking in a strange tongue, but showing the same signs of thirst and distress as themselves. The servant said, "Sacred are the needs of the stranger in a strange land," and pressed the dipper to the parched lips of the fainting man.

Then the great wonder was wrought! And the golden dipper flashed forth incrusted with the most precious diamonds, containing a fountain of gushing water, which supplied the thirsting nation, as freely and surely as it had quenched the thirst of the little dog.

And the Stranger stood before them, a glorious, radiant Being; and as He faded from their sight, a silver trumpet tone was heard to proclaim: "Blessed is he that giveth a cup of water in My name."

And the possession of a dipper blazing with diamonds is in that country a sure badge of royalty; for no one can buy or receive one as a gift, nor can fathers bequeath them to their children. Each child is given a tin dipper at its birth, and only by purely unselfish acts can a diamond one be wrought.

Some of the foolish people have not yet learned its secret, and they go about trying to exchange their tin for silver by doing kind deeds. Sometimes they accuse the Father of All very bitterly because they grow old possessing only the tin dipper; for the secret of the exchange can no more be told than the beautiful, flashing, sparkling diamonds can be purchased. Sometimes there are great surprises, when people give up the hop of such a possession, and forget themselves; for then they often find the castaway tin bearing evidence in silver, gold, or even diamonds, that they have become royal; but by that time they have no vanity because of their fortune. Only modest, thankful, brave, happy feelings possess the owners of diamond dippers.

The Lady Moon now lifted a white finger toward the east, which was growing rosy, and the baby stars all knelt a moment, looking like white-robed nuns at prayers. Then the morning wind swept aside the great blue silken curtain of the sky, and the Moon followed her children into Heaven, to do whatever the Father had planned for them while they were out shining for His earth children.

The Garden

In the beginning was a garden—a wonderful, beautiful garden wherein the first man and woman were placed. In a state of purity and innocence, that garden was an endless feast of sights, sounds, textures, scents and tastes, in which they were allowed to discover and explore for themselves. Everything within the garden was intended to gladden the heart and offer pure joy.

The child who learns about the world through books alone is like the person who is given a menu to read but is never actually served the food to taste and enjoy. Nature is a child's first and most important classroom and his most important tools for learning are his eyes, ears, nose, fingers and mouth. The most important thing you an do is get out of the way. There is much that Nature has to teach that cannot be expressed in words or taught directly.

Don't bypass the garden years of your child's life.

> Every child should know a hill,
> And the clean joy of running down its long slope
> With the wind in his hair.
> He should know a tree—
> The comfort of its cool lap of shade,
> And the supple strength of its arms
> Balancing him between earth and sky
> So he is the creature of both.
> He should know bits of singing water—
> The strange mysteries of its depths,
> And the long sweet grasses that border it.
> Every child should know some scrap
> Of uninterrupted sky, to shout against;
> And have one star, dependable and bright,
> For wishing on.
>
> --Edna Casler Joll

Thoughts on Cultivating Souls

There's a small patch of dirt in front of my porch where I have been wanting to plant some flowers. We have a hard, red clay soil here in Virginia that is hard to grow things in. It needs to be cultivated before planting. The last few years have been crazy busy and I couldn't get to it, but last fall I was determined to make it happen. So I slowly started making my way through it, bit by bit, digging up the dirt one shovelful at a time, adding top soil and potting soil and peat moss and nutrients, but by spring, I was only half way through.

My son knew I wanted flowers, so for my Mother's Day gift, he went out in the hot sun and finished digging up and breaking up the soil so I could plant my flowers. You can see that the little flower garden all looked the same when we planted. But keep in mind, only half of it had been properly cultivated.

Well, several weeks into the season, you can see the difference. In the cultivated soil, the flowers are blooming! I love their colors and beauty. But in the uncultivated side, all that's left is a wasteland of stems.

When we focus on training the mind without first cultivating the heart, our learning doesn't bring color and beauty into our lives or our world.

We push for academic excellence and focus on STEM subjects, leaving the cultivation of the heart behind. And we can see the results all around us. Instead of color and beauty, we see a growing wasteland where lewdness and vulgarity are reaching new lows and the use of profanity new highs reflected in the movies we watch, the books we read, the music we listen to and in our everyday walk of life. I even see it in the greeting card section at Walmart! We see a rise in hopelessness and despair.

The world has been here before. And the corrective measure has to do with well-educated hearts.

But how?

In the fourteenth century, a skilled workman who lived near the city of Venice, created an instrument with one of our first keyboards. He was the one who gave it the name 'key' board. The name came from the word *clavis* which means something which gives its owner power to open a closed door. He wrote, "These small bits of wood give me the power to unlock the sound which is in my organ, and so I shall call them keys"

Well, there are keys to unlock the power of beauty and love and goodness within the heart of each one of us. And these keys are called the arts—music, pictures, poetry, and story. The arts are the tools for cultivating hearts.

Light and Warmth

To continue with my thoughts on balancing heart and mind, if you live where it gets very cold in the winter, you know that you can step outside on a January morning and see the sun shining just as brightly in the middle of winter as it does in the middle of July. Yet, without its warmth, nothing grows.

Warmth starts the growing process.

John Dewey who is recognized as the father of modern educational philosophy added his name to a document known as the Humanist Manifesto back in the 1930s. What I draw from this effort is that a group of 'smart' people decided if we can learn to be guided by our intellects, we can stop the cycle of repeating humanity's dumb mistakes. From an intellectual standpoint, who would ever think war is smart? This line of reasoning here carried into today's current focus on critical thinking skills and scientific facts in our schools. What I see happening is while the school's attention is placed on the mind (light), they're ignoring the heart (warmth). And our schools are failing.

Just like plants in winter, human beings don't grow on light alone. We need warmth.

The danger of light without warmth is pointed out in the following thoughts of Oliver deMille.

> As Allan Bloom pointed out in his classic bestseller, *The Closing of the American Mind*, the last society to be highly trained [light] and as poorly educated [warmth] as the current U.S. was Germany in the 1930s. A significant number of German engineers were highly enough trained to build cutting-edge weaponry, submarines, missiles, airplanes and so on, but not well-read enough of history to vote against Hitler or refuse to do his bidding.
>
> Same with German scientists, who understood chemicals and genetics enough to experiment on their neighbors when they were thrown immorally into prison camps, but not learned enough in ethics, morals, history, psychology or basic politics to not elect Hitler or refuse to torture their countrymen.
>
> Critics could say that by the time submarines were being launched and people were being tortured, it was too late for anything. But only the combination of top technical training [light] and poor Leadership Education [lack of warmth] could have allowed this all to happen. A less highly-trained people could not have done it, and a truly educated people would not have done it.

Put one more way, knowledge is knowing a tomato is a fruit. Wisdom is knowing you don't put it in a fruit salad.

Light *and* warmth; mind *and* heart; knowledge *and* wisdom; reason *and* faith.

Joy in the Tornado

One Wednesday afternoon, I was sitting at my computer working when my cellphone started beeping and tornado warnings started blasting outside. Tornados are rare here in Appomattox, Virginia, but I quickly learned a massive tornado was heading our way and we were warned to seek shelter immediately. Our power went out as we gathered in the basement and waited for the wind and hail to pass.

A little while later, my friend, Traci, texted me. "Are you OK?" I texted back, "We're all fine. How about you?" She responded, "Pray for Grace's family—they lost half their house." I asked again, "Are you OK?" And we lost communication.

My husband and I tried to drive to Traci and her husband John's house to check on them, but the emergency crews wouldn't let us get anywhere near their street. It wasn't until after 9:00 at night that the roads were clear enough to drive to their house. It was nearly pitch black. All the way over I kept thinking about our friends. They had dreamed for a long time of leaving the big city and moving out to the countryside. Thirteen years ago after their children were grown, they found a little five acres property with an old fixer-upper farmhouse here in Appomattox. It was dubbed The Itty Bitty Farm. They wanted to be self-sufficient and so they planted a big orchard full of fruit trees and tilled the garden beds. They shunned debt and patiently made improvements on the house only as fast as they could earn the money to do so. A couple of years ago, Traci put the scaffolding up herself and spent the hot summer days painting the house sky blue. Just a few months previous, they excitedly showed us their new beautiful wood floor they helped install. They had been saving for that for a very long time. John put the finishing touches on the crown molding in their bedroom the morning of the tornado. You could feel the sense of pride in every project they undertook. It never bothered them that there was no air conditioning in the house.

I asked her once if the noise of the train that sped past the front of their property several times a day bothered her. She laughed and said she and her husband were like a couple of kids. When a train came by, they'd run out on their porch and wave at it. They loved the trains. The front porch had old-fashioned Christmas lights strung across it which they turned on clear into February. She told me how happy the bright colors made her. When they were out of town, we'd go over and take care of the chickens and they'd give us fresh eggs in exchange. On one side of the house, there was a picnic table under a giant pecan tree where they regularly invited friends over to visit and eat.

As we neared their property, the moonlight was just bright enough to see that the giant pecan tree had taken out the back half of the house. The attic was now in the kitchen. We saw a flashlight shining on the back side of the property and called out. It was John surveying the damage with another mutual friend and his young son. As he showed us around the property with his flashlight, we saw all the big shade trees lying on the ground. A few chickens huddled under the collapsed chicken coop. The garage and other outbuildings were gone. Completely gone. Most of the barn had blown away. There were debris everywhere.

We asked if they had somewhere to sleep that night. He said they weren't going anywhere. This was home. Their bedroom was in the front half of the house and he had determined that part of the house was still safe. "We'll be just fine," he said. I wouldn't have expected him to answer any other way.

There is a good chance the house will be bulldozed, but I know John and Traci are going to be 'just fine' because they possess the same characteristics and traits as the pioneer stock who laid the foundation of America. They have that same spirit of independence and rugged self-reliance that will see them through all the challenges ahead. That first night when John gave us a tour of the damages, he kept saying that it was all just 'stuff.' Losing it didn't matter to him. It was the relationship with his wife that mattered and he still had her. And the reason Traci wasn't there that first night was because she was off doing what she always does—she was comforting and tending to the needs of someone else.

While most people are looking to the elections in November to solve our nation's problems, I'm looking to people like Traci and John. They remind me of the wise words written by David Starr Jordan, the first president of Stanford University, over a hundred years ago:

"If the experiment of government by the people is to be successful, it is you and such as you who must make it so. The future of the Republic must lie in the hands of the men and women of culture and intelligence, of self-control and of self-resource, capable of taking care of themselves and helping others. If it falls not into such hands, the republic will have no future... The problem of life is not to make life easier, but to make men stronger, so that no problem shall be beyond their solution... The remedy for oppression is to bring in better men who cannot be oppressed."

Maybe the most useful question isn't, "Who is the best president the people can have?" but rather, "Are we the best people a president can have?"

I've said it before and I'll say it again. You mothers are our hope as you raise a generation who value relationships over 'stuff' and self-reliance over entitlement; who find more joy in giving than in receiving and who can find happiness in as simple things as passing trains and colored Christmas lights.

When I saw Traci the morning after the tornado, she wasn't discouraged in the least. She said that she hadn't expected this chapter of her life to end so abruptly, but she had dreams in storage and was already forward thinking to their next great adventure. She was irritated at the Condemned notice they posted on her door, so she countered with a sign of her own which she taped next to the Condemned sign. It was a declaration of all the things she cherished, written in 2003 when they moved into the house.

The list began with, "Hope for a better, brighter tomorrow" and ended with "...knowing that families are forever" and "courage to endure to the end."

She had not lost one single thing on that list.

*The final toll of damage was that over 70 homes were completely destroyed and over 200 severely damaged. Sadly, their next door neighbor was one of the fatalities.

Anchored in Faith

I had been down in bed for several days with the flu when my daughter called. I was already feeling physically miserable and exhausted. "Mom, the baby is really quiet today."

"Maybe he's just resting up for the big event," I said, which was just a couple of weeks away. I had bought my plane tickets months earlier and had been looking forward to cuddle time with this new little grandson—a boy— a rarity in our family of girls. But I agreed with her that she should check with her doctor.

A few hours later she called again. "Mom, there's no heartbeat. I've lost the baby."

I've heard the question posed—which is more painful? A broken bone or a broken heart. I know how I would answer that question. I cried gallons of tears, not only for that little baby I wasn't going to get to hold, but more so for my sweet daughter who loves being a mother and my son-in-law who so loves being a dad. And now, not only did she have to deal with that pain of loss, they were going to induce her right away and she would have to go through all the pains of labor, knowing there would be no baby's cry at the end.

It was a sleepless night. She was 2000 miles away. There was nothing I could do. I listened to the clock chime 1:00, 2:00, 3:00. I finally got out of bed to continue my prayers in the living room. I was miserable and exhausted, but through my tears, I heard the words, "Believest thou that I can heal this little baby?" I immediately replied, "Lord, I know all things are possible to thee." And I allowed myself to consider the miracle. Yes, it had been several hours since the last time his little heart had beat. But hadn't Lazarus lain in the tomb for three days? If the baby was born whole and well, the doctors would just think they had been mistaken, but I would know of the miracle.

Then came the words, "But you don't know what you are asking… Look." And it was as if a curtain was pulled back and I could see my daughter in her hospital bed, tears on her cheeks. It's too sacred an experience to share here, but what I saw next changed me. And the question was posed to me again: "Wouldst thou still have me work the miracle?" And I replied, "How can I? Thy ways are so much greater than our ways." Then came the words, "Then be at peace."

My daughter called just after noon the next day. "Mom, he's so warm and soft—a beautiful baby boy. Practically perfect in every way." And he was beautiful. There is no medical explanation as to why his little heart stopped beating.

I caught a plane as soon as I could and when I got to my daughter's home, I told her of the experience I had had in the night. I didn't know if it was just the imagination of a wishful mind, but then my daughter told me she had almost the identical experience and it would have been at about the same time.

The healing of that little baby would have been a great miracle. But is it any less of a miracle to experience the peace that passeth understanding in such a time of sorrow and loss? My daughter and I have had several conversations over the years where she has said she couldn't imagine getting through the loss of a child. And yet here she was. It was as though she was born up on angels' wings. A few days later, she and her husband both stood before a chapel full of loved ones at a memorial service and bore testimony of the love of God just before we took that tiny casket and buried him next to my little brother and my father.

So why am I sharing such an intensely personal experience to a group dedicated to educating children? I hope you see the connection. This is what this kind of learning is all about—the fruits of peace and joy and love. When I talk about well-educated hearts, I am talking about preparing hearts that will not fail when life hands us unwelcomed and unexpected events.

I am home now, but I have been reflecting on the events of the last couple of weeks and how it has been the languages of the heart that have been so healing.

So much comfort has come through shared stories and experiences. It has come through poetry. Late at night, in the hospital after my daughter had delivered the baby, she was trying to process all that had happened. Mere words weren't enough—they needed the music of poetic language and she wrote a beautiful poem that captured her feelings and which she shared at the memorial service.

I thought of all the beautiful flowers that were sent to their home. Some people find sending flowers to be impractical—they don't last long. It seems to them there are better ways to spend money. We forget the importance and power of beauty to heal our souls and is there anything more beautiful than a flower? It has been said that beauty is God's handwriting. "Beauty is a quality of divinity, and to live much with the beautiful is to live close to the divine." It's true—flowers don't last as a reminder that beauty has to constantly be refreshed in our lives. We were so grateful for the beautiful flowers.

We were grateful for the power of images and our imagination. It was a cold, dreary day when we buried little Dawson. They had to clear the snow to dig the little grave. If our minds dwelt on that tiny grave, it would have been unbearable. But my daughter turned the page of her calendar to March which happened to be a painting called 'Stairway to Paradise.' It was a painting of a stone stairway bathed in heavenly rays and beautiful gardens. That is where we picture him. And it is comforting.

We also were grateful for the power of symbols. Some months ago, my daughter gave her husband a tie with anchors on it, symbolic of being anchored in faith. When they went to shop for a little blanket to wrap around the baby, they found a blanket with anchors on it. And then, one more tender mercy is that my 96-year-old mother had also gone shopping for a baby blanket a few weeks earlier. She can hardly see and her hands are so arthritic, but she has been working for months on crocheting one last baby blanket. It's been frustrating for her as she has mostly had to feel her way and kept pulling out the mistakes. She was afraid it wouldn't be finished so she had one of my daughters take her shopping for a blanket just in case she didn't get it done in time. It just happened to be a soft little blue blanket covered with anchors.

This has been the blanket my daughter's little 4-year-old has wrapped himself in. It's been comforting to him. He's been so excited for a little brother. He has two little sisters. When they were brought to the hospital and he could sense his mommy and daddy's sadness, he asked if they could pray to Heavenly Father. My daughter thought maybe he would pray that his baby brother would be made all better. Instead, with the faith of a little child, he prayed: "Dear Heavenly Father, please help my baby brother be happy in heaven." He told us in the days following that it was like he could feel his brother near. He was anchored in faith.

Music also played a big role in healing our hearts. All the cousins sang Families Can Be Together Forever at the memorial service. A couple of days later, when he could sense his mother's sadness, he said, "Can we sing that forever family song again?"

I was also so grateful for my daughter's Mothers of Influence group. They have only been meeting for a few months, but what a blessing of comfort they have been as they have reached out and put their arms around my daughter—truly what these groups are meant to be. Prior to forming this group, my daughter felt so isolated and alone. No more. Her MOI group has been such a tremendous blessing.

Story, Music, Poetry, Art and the beauties of nature—these are the healing forces for our hearts. Facts and information would have been of little service to us.

One last tender mercy. I am the organist at church. It falls on me to select the hymns the congregation will sing. In early January, I sat down to select and submit all the hymns for January and February. I had just one intermediate hymn left for the last Sunday in February. As I flipped through the hymn book, I stopped at a hymn that was rarely if ever sung. I knew my congregation strongly disliked singing unfamiliar hymns, so I was going to find something else, but a strong impression came to me: Someone is going to need the words of that hymn that day.

I had forgotten about the hymn until I went to play it just before flying out to be with my daughter. There are only a couple of hymns in our hymn book that are in the language as though the Lord is speaking to us. Most of the hymns are singing praises to Him or singing of some gospel message. But the words of this particular hymn are as though the Lord is speaking in a personal way.

I will close with the words of this hymn which flowed through my mind constantly in the days that followed. I know many of you are going through trials that try your heart; that break your heart—may you find comfort in the words of this hymn as well.

> Lean on my ample arm, O thou depressed!
> And I will bid the storm cease in thy breast.
> Whate'er thy lot may be On life's complaining sea,
> If thou wilt come to me, Thou shalt have rest.
> If thou wilt come to me, Thou shalt have rest.
>
> Lift up thy tearful eyes, Sad heart, to me;
> I am the sacrifice offered for thee.

In me thy pain shall cease, In me is thy release,
In me thou shalt have peace Eternally.
In me thou shalt have peace Eternally.

The Art of Christmas

My daughter is a Relief Society President. Relief Society is the women's organization of the church I belong to. A couple of weeks ago, it was her turn to teach the Sunday lesson to the ladies and she decided what she wanted to do was to help them feel the glow of the Christmas spirit. She wanted them to feel it the second they walked into the room. So the plan was to set up a small Christmas tree, covered with lights. There was going to be beautiful Christmas music playing in the background and a plate of warm cookies and milk on the table to greet them. Then she was going to read them parts of a Santa Claus story that actually tied in perfectly with Christ and then close by reading a poem followed by playing a recording of the spirit of the poem set to music. She pictured the room filled with that wonderful, magical Christmas spirit.

Well, she got to the church early to set up the room, got the lights on the tree, plugged it in, and found out the lights didn't work. Then she started pouring glasses of milk to go with the cookies and another woman who was in the room said, "Uh, did you remember today is Fast Sunday?" For those of you who aren't familiar with this practice, we go without eating the first Sunday of each month and then donate the money we would have spent on food to those in need. OK. Scrap the milk and cookies. So she went to pull out her phone so that she could at least have some music playing and realized she had left her phone at home, which meant she wouldn't have the closing song she had planned either. It was time to start, so she asked someone if they would look for the song on their phone so she would at least have that to end her lesson.

She said, although they were surprised at first to hear a story about Santa Claus at church, it ended up being a nice discussion. When the time was up, she set up the beautiful song they would end up their meeting with by first reciting the Christina Rosetti poem:

What can I give Him
  Poor as I am,
If I were a shepherd,
  I would give Him a lamb.
If I were a wise man,
  I would do my part.
But what can I give Him?
  I will give Him my heart.

Cue the song. It was the wrong one. Instead they listened to Sissel sing an upbeat song in Norwegian about the winter solstice.

My daughter and I laughed as she told me about her disaster. But I thought, that pretty much sums me up at Christmas time. Every year, I anticipate creating that magical glow of Christmas I read about in magazines or see in movies and somehow it never goes according to my plans. It has taken me a lot of years to make peace with Christmas. Christmas is so magical in childhood, isn't it? Oh, how I loved Christmas as a child. I loved the music and the sparkly tree—we had one of those aluminum trees with the color wheel that would go round and round and I'd lie beneath it, watching the colors change. I loved the lights and the whole feeling of the season. My brothers teased me less, it seemed. And were much nicer to me. But it was Christmas morning I could barely wait for. I could never sleep on Christmas Eve. I'd call out every few minutes to my parents or go in my brothers' rooms and whisper, "Is it morning yet? Is it morning yet?" My parents had the Santa custom that all the presents were placed under the tree in the night so we never knew how many presents would be there until we woke up Christmas morning. And it never disappointed! All night I'd play out the scene of presents spilling out all over the room—wondering if they could top the year before—and my brothers saying, "Wow, Marlene this big one is for you!" And I'd rip it open! What could it be?? I could scarcely contain the excitement and anticipation.

So when we started having children, I wanted to give them the same excitement of Christmas morning I had as a child. Only we had some pretty lean years and we had a lot of children. Christmas soon became my most dreaded time of the year as that knot would grow in my stomach that we didn't have a way to give them Christmas. At least the Christmas as I envisioned it to be. There were several Christmases I locked myself in a room to at least try and make them some presents so they would have something to open on Christmas morning. I'd finally drop into bed at 4:30 or 5:00 Christmas morning, presents finally finished and wrapped, and I could hardly wait for the day after Christmas when I could pull down the tree and put Christmas behind me for another year.

One Christmas was the year of the Cabbage Patch doll. Every little girl wanted a cabbage patch doll. Even if we could have afforded them—which we couldn't—they were hard to come by.

People paid ridiculous prices so their little girls wouldn't be disappointed Christmas morning. I didn't want to disappoint my little girls so I learned how to make them and I spent the month of December sewing and stuffing little bodies and painting faces and making yarn hair late into the night, My mother helped by sewing lots of little dresses and little bags to hold them in. I don't remember much about that Christmas morning, except that one of my daughters threw hers across the room because her doll had brown hair, not yellow and she hated it.

She tells me now that she feels really badly about that and loves her doll. Funny thing...nearly all the other presents they were given over the years have long gone to landfills or thrift stores, including the store-bought cabbage patch dolls that came later. But they all have kept their homemade cabbage patch dolls.

Even when money was no object and we could have given our kids anything they wanted, that knot in my stomach was still there because I was afraid the presents I bought would be disappointing and they would miss that magic of Christmas morning of my childhood. Even on those Christmases when the presents were piled high and filled the room, after all the paper was ripped off, there was always, always a hollowness in my heart. The presents themselves never satisfied. Even if everyone got everything they asked for.

I remember one Christmas when all the presents were handed out, and there wasn't a single present under the tree for me. And I felt guilty that I hurt—mothers are supposed to give and give, aren't we? And not expect anything in return? It wasn't that I needed anything or wanted anything especially, it just hurt. I think my kids were all so busy with the fun of the morning they didn't notice me fighting back the tears that I couldn't quite explain but that flowed freely. So I stuffed the garbage bags with the wrappings and went to the kitchen to start cooking Christmas dinner. Reflecting in a more mature mind now, I've thought maybe that's a little taste of what our Lord feels on the day that is meant to be the celebration of His birth. He doesn't need us to give Him anything, and yet there is something about being remembered that matters.

When my husband and I became empty nesters and spent our first Christmas in a home away from family, I didn't put up any Christmas decorations. I think I may have put the nativity set up that year, but that was all. I actually started to hate Christmas. That was the year the thought hit me, you know, Christmas isn't a commandment. It's not a sin to not celebrate Christmas.

Like I said. It has taken me a lot of years to make peace with Christmas and to love it again. And I do love Christmas. Now. The lessons I am learning apply to what we are talking about here at the Well-Educated Heart about learning and education. Let me share insights that have helped. Although you may all love Christmases and can't imagine what I'm talking about!

My daughter and her husband took a little trip this week and I agreed to watch my little 4-year-old granddaughter. She asked if she could watch something on my husband's iPad. And I couldn't believe what held her attention. They were stupid little videos of people opening presents. That's it. There were mermaids that would swim and find a present and open it and children that would open presents and even adults opening presents. She was mesmerized and would have watched it all night long if we had let her and never lost interest.

And then it struck me. We have built an entire holiday around this basic human desire to unwrap a present and see what's inside. And no matter how many presents are around the tree, when a child unwraps the last one, he looks around for just one more. Usually, no matter what's inside, even if it's something he has really wanted, he's on to the next one. Oh! The anticipation of what's inside! And we parents live for the moment of watching their reactions when the gift is open. Parents stand in long lines in the middle of the night on Black Friday just in anticipation of watching that present be unwrapped on Christmas morning. The whole frenzy of the Christmas season revolves around the thrill of that moment of unwrapping the present. And then there's that nagging doubt—what if they hate the presents? What if we have failed to satisfy that longing for something and 'ruined' their Christmas?

Think about it—when we say a family won't have Christmas, what we are saying is they won't have the thrill of that moment when their children unwrap a present. So we collect Toys for Tots and set up angel trees in churches and stores for that single moment of the thrill.

And come the morning after Christmas, the stores will open to the long, long lines of people returning those gifts. And Christmas will disappear almost overnight.

That thrill is momentary, it has no lasting effect. If Christmas revolves around that moment, it can never satisfy.

There's an inscription in the stone entryway of Chicago's Fine Art building that says: "All passes; art alone endures."

I've been thinking about that phrase as it relates to Christmas time and the thought hit me, as I look at Christmases past and Christmas present, everything that I love about Christmas the most is tied to art—the beautiful Christmas music, the heart-warming stories, the glow of candles and the colorful lights; the Christmas scenes, the smells of cinnamon and baked goods, the memories of experiences together. Yet I somehow allowed the Christmas morning event to take over the season.

I've even taken a closer look at the art of gift giving. A whole stack of stuff doesn't compare with the one single gift that connects to a desire of the receiver and is the expression of the thoughtfulness of the giver. We may use the gifts of the magi as our excuse for giving gifts, but I've thought how practical and needed those gifts were. Joseph, Mary and the babe were about to become refugees in a strange land. Joseph was a carpenter; not a wealthy man. How would they survive? Enter the gifts of the Magi. I think they were inspired to bring the gifts. I'm still working on that one—the art of giving and receiving gifts.

But I think I am realizing what I've gotten wrong. As I take the time to enjoy the season as a whole and savor each moment, and not allow the Christmas morning event to be the crowning moment, the knot inside me is gone. And the spirit of the arts and the spirit of Christmas—of peace on earth, goodwill toward men—stay with me and are renewed in different forms all through the year.

These same lessons apply to the learning going on in your home. The instinct of anticipation isn't a bad thing. It's the same thing that makes us hold on to a story—we want to know what happens. It's the anticipation of the unknown. That anticipation drives us to learn something new—to unwrap some new piece of knowledge or understanding or insight.

But if the learning is all geared towards the one culminating event—receiving the college acceptance letter, opening the report card and seeing the A's or seeing the high test score get posted—when it's over, it will feel hollow.

The learning with staying power and deep satisfaction is the learning that happens all along the way. There is no final destination. It will go on into the eternities, with different shapes and forms.

The mother that takes on the responsibility of making the learning 'magic' for her children will burn herself out. All the fancy programs and visual aids and learning materials we think we need to spend money on—we really don't need them. The lasting kind of learning is within the child and can only be appreciated and created by him and is connected to music, pictures, poetry and story in a heart-to-heart learning environment. Simple really is best.

The learning that they'll hold on to, that will have the greatest meaning, is that which connects to the desires of their hearts. Which is why we spend so much lime learning about how to awaken those desires.

So I wish you a Happy and Joyous Christmas Season whether there are a million presents piled under the tree, or no presents. May it be filled with warm memories of love and music and joy; of savored moments of togetherness.

I'll close with a favorite Christmas poem found some years ago by Debra Crevelli.

The rush of Christmas traffic blurs
  The days that we prepare
To celebrate the birthday of
  A babe so sweet and fair.
In all the rush did we neglect
  A place for Christ to stay—
A tiny manger in our hearts
  Where He may spend each day?
For once within His presence grows:
  The love that will unfold
Will be enough to reach and warm
  A world confused and cold.

Pebbles on the Seashore

Once a child played on the sea-shore. The waves sang and the sand shone and the pebbles glistened. There was light everywhere; light from the blue sky, and from the moving water, and from the gleaming pebbles.

The little one, in its happiness, sang with the murmuring sea and played with the stones and the shells that lay about. Joy was everywhere and the child was filled with it.

But the day passed. And the little one grieved in its heart to leave the beautiful place. Delight was there and many rare things that one could play with and enjoy.

The child could not leave them all. Its heart ached to think of them lying there alone by the sea. And it thought:

"I will take the pebbles and the shells with me and I will try to remember the sunlight and the song of the sea."

So it began to fill its little hands. But it saw that after as many as possible were gathered together there were yet myriad left. And it had to leave them.

Tired and with a sore heart it trudged homeward, its hands filled to overflowing with the pebbles that shone in the sun on the sea-shore. Now, however, they seemed dull. And because of this, the child did not seem to regret it so much if now and then one fell. "There are still some left in my hands," it thought.

At length it came near to its home; so very tired, the little limbs could scarcely move. And one who loved the child came out smiling to welcome it. The little one went up close and rested its tired head; and opening its little hand, soiled with the sea and the sand, said:

"Look, mother, I still have one. May I go for the others some day?"

And the mother said:

"Yes, thou shalt go again."

And the child fell asleep to dream of the singing sea and of the sunlight, for these were in its heart.

--Thomas Tapper

The Treasure of the Wise Man

by James Whitcomb Riley

O the night was dark and the night was late,
And the robbers came to rob him;
And they picked the locks of his palace-gate,
The robbers that came to rob him—
They picked the locks of his palace-gate,
Seized his jewels and gems of state,
His coffers of gold and his priceless plate,—
The robbers that came to rob him.

But loud laughed he in the morning red!—
For of what had the robbers robbed him?—
Ho! Hidden safe, as he slept in bed,
When the robbers came to rob him, —
They robbed him not of a golden shred
Of the childish dreams in his wise old head—
"And they're welcome to all things else," he said,
When the robbers came to rob him.

Heart Before Mind

Heart-Based Education

"The world is so full of a number of things, I'm sure we should all be has happy as kings."

--Robert Louis Stevenson

"Look at homeschooling as primarily an opportunity to educate yourself and bring the kids alongside." Show them—don't tell them. Be a light, not a hammer.

To visualize a heart-based education, compare a child with a seed planted in the ground. Its not the light of the sun that activates the life force within the seed; it's the warmth. As the warmth starts the growth process, the seed starts building a strong root system. The soil needs to be nutrient-rich because the plant will draw from the nutrients in the soil to feed itself. You can't see this root system growing from above the ground. You just have to trust it is happening. If you pull it up to take a look, you'll kill the plant. Likewise, there are things going on inside our children's hearts that we just have to trust are happening. Then, when the shoot reaches above ground and opens up its leaves, now there is a surface area to catch the light. If you shine intellectual light before there are leaves to catch it, it's not going to do much good. As the plant grows, the more surface area there is to capture intellectual light as the roots continue to take in nutrients and in the end, you'll have the beautiful flower. And why is it important your seed flowers? Because it is only within the flowers that you find the seeds to multiply and replenish the earth.

The Royal Gallery of Poetry and Art (from the Introduction)

By W.H. Milburn (1886)

Our life is mystic, unfathomable—open to manifold subtle influences which help to make or mar us. Who needs be told that we are embosomed in Immensity, when beneath the nightly heavens the eye is greeted by the light of stars, which, notwithstanding the speed of its flight, has been journeying for ages from its source to reach our planet. If sunrise could be witnessed but once a year, who would be abed on the morning of that more than imperial pageant; yet is the splendor less, because almost every day it streams along the sky? In our impatience of the commonplace, in eager search of beauty and inspiration, we cross the sea to Britain, France, or Italy, and come back no richer than we went, because the beauty and inspiration must go with us or we shall not find them anywhere.

The fault of spiritual poverty is in ourselves, not in our surroundings. The heavens by night or day are as beautiful, grand and sacred over the humblest home in America as over the greatest gallery or cathedral in Europe; and he who cannot find the treasures of life here, will discover no treasures there.

Doorways to the infinite knowledge, glory and blessedness of the universe are near the path of every "traveler betwixt life and death"—the humblest as well as the highest; the latchstring is always on the outside, and whoso wills it may enter and find riches, "where moth and rust do not corrupt, nor thieves break through and steal."

At school or college, at the handles of the plow, or with a hoe in the fist, at the carpenter's ben, on the bricklayer's scaffold, in the blacksmith's shop, behind the tradesman's counter, in the merchant's office, in the wife's and mother's round of ceaseless toil and care, wherever our appointed task is to be done—and woe to him who has not found his task, or shrinks from doing it—there must the secrets of the world be learned and the power gained, by use of which we enter into and possess the estate of the soul.

Few in this land are so bereft, so desolate, that visions of ineffable beauty, messages from a world above matter, are denied to them; but the eye must be clarified to see the vision, the ear opened to hear the beatific tidings.

We are so immersed in the life of the senses, so cheated by the shows of things, occupied by greetings in the market-place, trifles in the street, fashions of dress; we give such time and attention to gossip of newspapers and society, that the eye becomes dull and we see not, the ear heavy and we hear not, and the soul forgets its nobleness—is defrauded of its heritage.

We delude ourselves that happiness is to be found, and only found, at the winning-post of life's race. We like the haste and din of crowds, the shuffle of feet and clapping of hands; the ear loses its sense of harmony, and noise becomes music; the eye its discretion, and we mistake paste for diamonds, and fancy that gas-light is better than sunshine.

The world is too much with us, late and soon:
Getting and spending we lay waste our powers.

God deals with us as with sons, and the blows of affliction fall, not to punish, but correct. There are few hearts that have not known the discipline of sorrow. Silence and solitude are appointed to us for seasons, that they may do what the bustle and the crowd cannot; and they bid us open our minds and hearts to the ministry of healing, the consolation of higher influences, and persuade us that while on one side we are of the earth earthy, on the other we are His brethren, who is the lord from Heaven. Religion, philosophy, science, the arts and letters, are friendly guides to lead us away from the deceit and allurements of our own hearts to the palace of the Great King in whose courts and gardens we may find health, sanity, strength, and so come back to the working-day world as giants refreshed.

What power is found in books! A well-chosen library, though small and inexpensive, may introduce us to the best company the world has known, bring us upon terms of intimacy with the kingly spirits of our race, admit us to their confidence so that they tell us the secrets of their hearts, show us the weapons with which they conquered the world and themselves, breathe upon us the spirit of their courage, enthusiasm, faith, hope and love; teach us the secret of their nobleness, heroism, divinity, until in the wrapt communion we grow into their manners, aims, achievements, and make them our own.

The value of a book depends upon the use we make of it; it is little worth except to the good reader. If its true office be performed for us we must eat, drink, digest, assimilate it so that its nourishment becomes part of our own being, recruiting our life with its intelligence, wisdom, inspiration.

When books were rare and costly, chained to columns in monasteries, borrowed with pledges that might have been the ransom of princes, men studied, devoured them, and so appropriated their virtue. Now, when books may be bought for a song, when Homer, Dante, Shakespeare, Goethe, Wordsworth, may be had for the asking, we glance at, caress with compliments and pass them by as fish swim among pearls and know not of their value.

A wise man once said of a omnivorous reader, "He read so much he came at last to know nothing." "A good book," said Milton, "Is the precious life-blood of a master spirit, embalmed and treasured up on purpose to a life beyond life:" and he who by devout and constant reading of a few such will realize in his spirit all that is claimed for the transfusion of blood in the veins; recover him from disease, cause the languid eye and pallid cheek to glow and sparkle with the health of immortal youth, lend the voice the music and accents of courage and joy. Through well-chosen books we become heirs of the ages, and when the pencil of the artist and burin of the engraver embody in living form the writer's thought, we have the presence and the glory of a sacrament—"an outward and visible form of an inward and spiritual grace."

Oft, in lonely rooms, and 'mid the din
Of towns and cities, I have owed to them,
In hours of weariness, sensations sweet,
Felt in the blood, and felt along the heart:

And passing even into my purer mind,
With tranquil restoration, feelings too
Of unremembered pleasure; such, perhaps,
As have no slight or trivial influence
On the best portion of a good man's life,
His little, nameless, unremembered acts
Of kindness and of love: nor less, I trust,
To them I may have owed another gift,
Of aspect more sublime: that blessed mood,
In which the burthen of the mystery,
In which the heavy and weary weight
Of all this unintelligible world
Is lightened:—that serene and blessed mood,
In which the affections gently lead us on—
Until, the breath of this corporeal frame
And even the motion of our human blood
Almost suspended, we are laid asleep
In body, and become a living soul:
While with an eye made quiet by the power
Of harmony, and the deep power of joy,
We see into the life of things.

--William Wordsworth

Homer's Iliad wrought itself into the soul of Alexander, and became the brain and sword with which he conquered the world. A young man walking one day on the river's bank saw something floating in the current, drew it ashore, found it to be a parchment Bible which had been thrown into the flood by command of the apostate Emperor Julian. The youth dried the volume, read it until its contents took possession of him, winning him from the study of Greek Philosophy, and he became the "Golden-mouthed" John of Antioch, afterwards Archbishop of Constantinople, known to the world as St. John Chrysostom, the most powerful preacher the East has known since the days of St. Paul. A young African, who had run a course of intellectual and animal excess, paced to and fro, one pleasant summer afternoon, in a Roman garden, and heard a child in the next garden reading aloud; he paused to listen, heard words which took hold of his conscience and heart, for they were words of the Holy Scriptures. He got the book and studied it, and became the most renowned Doctor and Father of the Christian Church—St. Augustine.

If the men and women, young or old, will "read, mark, learn and inwardly digest" [the contents of great books] until each day "memory have its fraught," they will find it a treasure beyond price, attuning the ear to the melodies of our noble speech, refining the taste, purging the eye to behold the things most real but invisible to mortal sense, informing the mind with "thoughts that wander through eternity," and storing the recollection with truths and images which cannot die; making them to hear

Oftentimes
The still, sad music of humanity,
Nor harsh nor grating, though of ample power
To chasten and subdue, and they may feel
A presence that disturbs them with the joy
Of elevated thoughts; a sense sublime
Of something far more deeply interfused,
Whose dwelling is the light of setting suns,
And the round ocean and the living air,
And the blue sky, and in the mind of man:
A motion and a sprit, that impels
All thinking things, all objects of all thought,
And rolls through all things.

Educating the Mind Without Educating the Heart is No Education at All

I believe our reliance on facts and the testing of them is deadening the hearts and starving the souls of our children. For all our testing and concern about reading comprehension, the majority of our students will never pick up another book and read it after graduation.

And if, by chance, they do, I can almost guarantee it will not be a book of history, poetry or classic literature. The very mention of these words stirs up an intense dislike they've developed for the subjects.

For all our testing and concern over proper spelling, grammar, composition, vocabulary, and MLA form, most students will settle into short texts of "brb" and "lol." They have little in their hearts they care to write about.

Because they have spent twenty years answering someone else's questions, by the time they leave school, they have lost the desire and even the ability to ask their own questions. For all our academic worrying, studies suggest that students will lose 90% of what we force feed them. Because practically every day of their lives has been scheduled and assigned by someone else with little time to dream, to lie on the grass and watch the clouds go by, they lack self-control and self-motivation. After graduation, they finally enter a world, as someone has said, "surrounded by all stirring things, unmoved." They can't tell a birch from an elm, a peony from a primrose. They know nothing of the meaning of the songs of the birds or the stars in the sky. Studies are revealing high levels of depression, hopelessness, anxiety, and dissatisfaction with life and relationships.

If something is to be judged by its fruit, this is not good fruit.

We need to seriously look for a new path.

Awhile back, an elderly gentleman who lived down the road from me passed away and I went to his estate sale. Evidently, he had been a school teacher and I came home with some of his textbooks from the 1920s and 30s. One of the sets I have kept next to me by my desk: *Treasury of Life and Literature: Reading and Living in 5 volumes*. It's a series of readers for the middle and upper grades. Listen to what is written in the Preface:

Good Books Help Us to Live Together

"At home or at school, at work or at play, we spend most of our waking hours with other people. Happiness depends largely upon our success in getting along with companions. Indeed, a successful life is chiefly the result of living well with other folk."

And then it goes on to say that the selections of literature were chosen to portray life and present ideals of right living.

Somewhere between then and now, we separated learning from happy living, didn't we? This path less traveled that we are on is an attempt to join learning and happy living back together.

I want to use the study of history as a means of helping our children learn the art of joyful living. We'll use the men and women of history to "portray life and present ideals of right living."

Or some of them will allow us to see the consequences of wrong living.

In the world's economy, the richest person is the one who makes the most money. The graduating class that commands the highest salary is deemed the most successful. But in heaven's economy, the richest person is the one with the greatest capacity for joy which is closely tied in to the person's capacity to love. Both joy and love reside in the heart. The writers of the 1920s texts clearly understood the everlasting value of the riches of the heart.

I would consider that good fruit. And I want our children to be very, very rich.

Hungry hearts, finding nothing within for nourishment, turn to outside pleasures—endless video games, non-stop shopping, excessive eating, alcohol, recreational drugs, pornography, the pleasures of sex without relationship or responsibility, and obsession with looks and clothes. And truly neglected hearts derive a sick pleasure by inflicting pain; they feed on the miseries of others. They are consumers—not producers. And they are never satisfied.

Lacking roots in the heart, they bear no fruit.

I saw, for myself a few summers ago, what happens when a plant has a shallow, weak root system. I planted a square foot garden and was so excited when all the stems started popping up, but then nothing happened. The plants withered and died before they ever bore any fruit. A friend told me that I hadn't given the plants enough water and nutrients so that the plants could grow a rich and deep root structure. Without a strong root system, a plant can never produce fruit.

And neither can our children. I am suggesting to you that the reason our current educational system is not producing good fruit is because we are neglecting the roots of our children's hearts. Without a strong root system in the heart, learning withers and dies on the vine before bearing fruit. All our attention is on academic stems—the academic establishment doesn't even try to hide the fact that it values STEM subjects over ROOT education.

But mothers, in the home, can change that. Because no one has the access to the heart of a child that a mother has.

Educating hearts of children—growing strong root systems in the heart—is a lost art that this generation of mothers needs to re-learn if we want to raise a generation of children who are fluent enough in the languages of the heart to access the treasure so recently delivered to them.

The heart educators of a hundred years ago taught that a child must progress through three developmental learning stages, each one serving a specific purpose. To some extent, you can go back and pick up what was missed, but you can't rush the process going forward. Nor would you want to. As I walk you through these developmental stages (see Vol. 2, p. 61), you'll notice the layering process. Heart-based education is very much a line upon line, layer upon layer, here a little, there a little process which is very different from acquiring facts and information.

Math

So, you may be saying, that's great about all this story, art, poetry and music stuff. But what about Math? I find it interesting as I observe homeschool moms that they are careful and troubled about many things, and Math seems to be at the top of the list. Never mind is your child happy? Is he kind? Do you have a good relationship with him? No, it's, "Oh my goodness, my son or daughter is in the 3rd grade and hasn't mastered multiplication tables" and it sets off a panic attack.

I think the reason we place so much emphasis on Math is because it's one of those clearly defined benchmarks. Many moms who choose to homeschool feel a lot of pressure to 'measure up' to the outside world looking on, and math is one of those measurable subjects. If a child can do math above grade level, she sighs a sense of relief that she's not ruining her child and maybe even has a gifted one on her hands. But heaven help the child who is running below level in math. "I'm a failure! Maybe I should just give up and put my child back in school."

But it's just math. And although today's world would have you think that the whole future of civilization rests upon our kids' math scores, it simply isn't true.

Now, you may be one of the moms who has it all under control. Yay for you! But for you other moms who are trying to navigate the waters, let me try and widen some perceptions here. I encourage you to spend some time in the Math section of the Mother's University. At the top of the list of questions we should be asking, I would choose, "Why study math at all?"

First, let me insert here some inspirational words from Galileo: "Mathematics is the language in which God has written the universe."

If you had a bad experience with math in school, you are now free to see it with new eyes and a sense of wonder right along with your children. That's the heart part of studying math. I recommend, if you haven't watched it yet, watch the TED talk posted in this section given by a High School math teacher where he addresses our question of why study math at all.

Then move to the articles I've posted, starting with *Why Johnny Can't Add*. This was written by the son of an aerospace engineer. Because his dad worked on top-secret projects, he had no idea what his dad did. He found out later that his dad had designed the first anti-ballistic missile in the U.S. and he was involved in other space projects. The tinkering his dad would do at the kitchen table or out in the garage late at night was how he was solving complex issues that involved precise mathematical computations.

Surely his brilliant father must have had an intense math program growing up! Actually, no. His family was dirt poor and he attended a small one-room school that didn't have enough money to even supply the students with books. So the full extent of math instruction consisted of memorizing addition and subtraction, multiplication and division facts through drill and practice. He didn't even hear the word 'calculus' until he got to college.

He said that that was the education of most of the engineers of that early space program. There was no PhD in physics or advanced mathematics. He got a bachelors in Ceramic Engineering and took as many math classes as he could because he had an interest. Arithmetic wasn't some mysterious subject that was difficult to comprehend–it was presented as a tool. There's lots of good food for thought in that article.

Then take a look at *Just Do the Math*. Dan Greenburg is a co-founder of the Sudbury school. There's another interesting topic for another day. But the simple premise behind the teaching of subjects is: Wait until a child asks for it, and has a use for it, even if it is just college admission. He wrote a book about a little experiment, claiming he could teach students the entire K-6 math portfolio in just 20 contact hours. He had a dozen children, ages 9 to 12 and there was one rule: Be on time. 11 am sharp, twice a week, for half an hour. If anyone was 5 minutes late, class was cancelled. If it happened twice, no more teaching. Using just an old 1898 math primer, in 20 hours, every single student knew the material. Every single one. He said math isn't a hard subject. What's hard–virtually impossible–is beating it into the heads of youngsters who hate every step.

Then follow it up by reading the Benezet experiment, which also showed that it's not necessary to spend years pounding math into kids. This particular teacher suggested an experiment in which the teacher waited to start math instruction until the 6th grade. The principal got nervous and he had to end the experiment a little earlier than that, but his students not only passed up the kids who had been drilled since kindergarten, they easily surpassed them going forward.

Then I linked a great article by Heidi Nash on how to inspire a love of math. There's the heart part of math–creating the desire. And then teaching the facts, as these previous articles show, can be done without tears and in a much shorter amount of time than we tend to make it. You'll find a lot of heart-based math resources in the Mother's University math section. I'll let you make your way through that.

But start becoming aware of natural ways to make numbers and math a useful part of life. When you play games with your little kids that require rolling of dice and moving their little figures on the board, they get lots of practice counting and adding up numbers in a useful way. That's math. When you cook, you're introducing fractions with your quarter cup measures and your teaspoons of measurement. Same as when you cut a pizza into six pieces and give one-sixth of it to your brother. How long will it take a child to learn to count by 5s if you pay him for some work with nickels in anticipation of saving up for something he really wants? Math is useful! And that is the impression little children need.

I think that's enough said for now. Have fun exploring some of the resources and articles I linked. I'll close with a little poem I remember clearly from my 5th grade math class.

A Mortifying Mistake by Anna Maria Pratt

I studied my tables over and over, and backward and forward, too;
But I couldn't remember six times nine, and I didn't know what to do.

Till sister told me to play with my doll, and not to bother my head,
"If you call her 'Fifty-Four' for a while, you'll learn it by heart," she said.
So I took my favorite, Mary Ann (though I thought 'twas a dreadful shame
To give such a perfectly lovely child such a perfectly horrid name),
And I called her my dear little 'Fifty-four' a hundred times, till I knew
The answer of six times nine as well as the answer of two times two.
Next day Elizabeth Wigglesworth, who always acts so proud,
Said, "Six times nine is fifty-two," and I nearly laughed aloud!
But I wished I hadn't when teacher said, "Now, Dorothy, tell if you can."
For I thought of my doll and –sakes alive!–I answered, "Mary Ann!"

The Whole Apple of Learning

My mother will turn 97 in a couple of weeks. Although her eyesight and hearing are failing and her hands are crippled with arthritis, the doctors tell her she is the healthiest 97-year-old they have seen. Her mind is sharp. She is pretty amazing.

She regularly calls me and tells me all about some new advertisement she's gotten in the mail that announces a new miracle cure to fix what ails her. Usually this miracle cure is some vitamin or mineral that has been extracted out of a fruit or vegetable, put in a capsule and sold for a lot of money. And yet, every time I do the research, I find that the vitamin or mineral isn't nearly as effective without the rest of the apple; that for optimal usage, it needs to work in concert with the other minerals or the fiber or some other property of the apple.

I see that a lot in education today where the pieces are extracted from the whole. Examples of this are working on vocabulary and spelling lists, isolating a reading comprehension skill, doing map work as an isolated study, analyzing the parts instead of taking in the whole.

While this may be a common and familiar education method, how is it working for us? We are told we can judge something by its fruit. For all the time spent on reading comprehension skills, how many students will continue to read after they graduate? And what will they read? Will they choose to read great literature or history, for example? Studies say no. A hundred and fifty top scholars entered a nationwide contest where they were to be awarded a cash prize. Because they all had perfect scores, the committee awarding the prize had to find some other way to differentiate. So they asked the contestants to tell of one book they had read in the past year that wasn't assigned to them. If I remember correctly, only one had done so.

It seems the more we try to isolate pieces of learning, the more we tend to get in the way. I was reading from my daughter's college children's literature textbook and it said that children who are taught to read with basal readers with controlled vocabulary learn to read much more slowly than children who are taught to read with quality literature.

One study was conducted in New York's West Side. 92% of the children came from non-English speaking homes. 96% were below the poverty level and 80% spoke no English when entering school. The study began with 225 kindergarten children who were allowed to read in an unpressured, pleasurable way–in other words, no basal readers and no workbooks. They were simply immersed in children's literature. By the end of the year, all 225 students were reading, some on a second-grade level.

Another study addressed the problem of 'stalled' readers; those readers who hated reading and who for more than a year made no progress. In the study, teachers abandoned the intensive decoding programs and instead just had them listen to stories from real books. Soon, these non-progress children were off and running.

For all our focus on writing skills–the vocabulary lists and the grammar sheets and the five paragraph essays–how many adults go on to write because it's a pleasurable activity?

The same goes for science and math. Only a few students will have any desire to use this knowledge after graduation. And most of what was learned will slip away.

We don't have to teach our body what to do with an apple. All we have to do is chew on its juicy sweet deliciousness and our body breaks up its parts and makes use of its nutrients.

Here are four examples of eating the whole apple of learning, taken from my daughter's college textbook (*Children's Literature, Briefly*, by James S. Jacobs & Michael O. Tunnell, pp. 319-321):

1. Robert Howard Allen at age 6 was left to be raised by his grandfather, three great-aunts and a great-uncle who all lived in the same house in rural Tennessee. After his grandfather taught him to read, he started reading the Bible to a blind great-aunt. "From age seven he read thousands of books–from Donald Duck comics to Homer, James Joyce and Shakespeare... He began picking up books at yard sales, and by his early 20s he had some 2000 volumes." He never went to school, not even for a day. At age 32 he showed up at Bethel College in Tennessee and graduated three years later, summa cum laude. He then enrolled in graduate school at Vanderbilt University, earning a PhD in English. He went on to be a visiting lecturer in a college in Kentucky.

2. Lauralee Summer and her mother were homeless and moved from one shelter to another. She recalled sitting on her mother's lap and listening to stories when she was a little girl. When she was 20 months old, her mother started reading her the same book every night because it was the only book she owned–a well-thumbed book of nursery rhymes. On her fourth birthday, Lauralee was given enough money to buy a See and Say book and taught herself to read. As they moved from town to town and shelter to shelter, she always visited the libraries. She tried school at age 10, but preferred to remain at the shelter and read. In her senior year, she took the SAT and scored 1460, putting her in the top 99.97th percentile of America's high school seniors. In 1994, she was admitted to Harvard University on full scholarship.

3. Dale Wasserman is best known as the creator of Man of La Mancha. When his parents died when he was 14, he was placed in an orphanage, "undisciplined, secretive, and almost entirely unschooled." One night, in the middle of the night, he ran away and hitched his first freight train ride. For the next five years he rode the rails, never having a home, going to school, or working a steady job. This is how he described his learning: "In the library of a small town, I would select two books, slip them under my belt, read as I rode, and slipped them back into the stack of another library in another town where I'd borrow two more."

4. Cushla Yeoman was born with multiple handicaps, mental and physical. The doctors recommended she be institutionalized. Her parents refused and instead kept her home and read picture books aloud to her, sometimes reading up to 14 books a day, week after week and month after month. By the age of five, Cushla was pronounced by doctors to be socially well-adjusted and intellectually well above average.

You may say these four cases must be exceptional, but I can give you a lot more. In fact, as I read the lives of great men and women, I see the same pattern repeated over and over again–lots of stories in childhood and lots of uninterrupted time alone with books.

Let me throw in just one more example of someone who literally ate the whole apple. Lew Wallace was a general in the Union army, and after the war he wrote a book that was the bestselling American novel of the 19th century, even outselling Harriet Beecher Stowe's *Uncle Tom's Cabin.* It has been called the most influential Christian book of the 19th century–the book is *Ben-Hur.*

I'll let Lew describe his own educational experience: "I had one mainstay: I loved to read. I was a most inordinate reader. In some lines of literature, especially history and some kinds of fiction, my appetite was insatiate, and many a day, while my companions were clustered together in the old red brick schoolhouse, struggling with their problems of fractions or percentages, I was carefully hidden in the woods nearby, lying upon my elbows, munching an apple, and reveling in the beauties of Plutarch, Byron or Goldsmith."

Two more examples of eating the whole apple of learning–vocabulary words are picked up ten times faster within context than when provided as separate vocabulary lists. Also, critical thinking cannot be taught as a separate subject. As was stated in one article I read, "People who have sought to teach critical thinking have assumed that it is a skill, like riding a bicycle, and that, like other skills, once you learn it, you can apply it in any subject." Decades of cognitive research have proven that's just not the case. You learn critical thinking by immersing yourself in rich content of thought.

The best way to learn is to make learning a part of life, not separate. A child will learn fractions much more easily by measuring out ingredients for cookies or cutting pizza into six pieces and giving 1/6 of a pizza to a little sister than by working through a pile of worksheets. See how fast a child learns counting by 5s when he's adding up the nickels he's earned doing chores so he can buy a new toy. A child will learn more about trees spending time outside in nature than reading about them in a textbook and filling out a worksheet. Telling and listening to stories, singing, playing, sharing rhymes, looking at pictures, watching sunsets and stars and chasing butterflies–this is eating the whole apple in early childhood education.

I would say the concept applies to adulthood, too. While most organizations try to solve the problem of poverty and homelessness by focusing on the pieces—helping the homeless acquire job skills or providing housing or teaching them to fill out an application—one group thought entirely out of the box. The Clemente Project offered free college level humanities courses to homeless people with amazing success. The difference was, these courses tended to their hearts and once their hearts could see and feel, they felt empowered and they began to lift themselves out of poverty. I would call that a whole apple approach.

We have so mechanized learning, it is shutting down the desire. A student spends the first twenty years of his life being told, every day, exactly what he will do and what he will learn. The teacher asks the questions. And we see the fruit all around us–apathy, lack of curiosity, narrow mindedness. We as a people, as has been said, are 'surrounded by all stirring things, unmoved.'

I'm not saying that there is not a time for detailed study. There is! Lew Wallace, once the desire was lit to start writing, took it upon himself to put himself through a rigorous course in grammar. Abraham Lincoln did the same. We're just backwards–we work from the outside in. The rule, as was taught by all the heart educators, was: from within, out.

I can't help but think of possibilities when I learned of the Saracen model of education. You'll recall that when the Crusaders finally made it to the Holy Land, instead of finding a barbaric, uncivilized people, they found beautiful fountains, silks, mosaics, universities. As I read of the Saracen model of education, I found it interesting that rather than a teacher driven model, it was student led. There were no tests, no degrees, no requirements, no compulsion. Rather, a teacher would advertise a class and the students would come and sit in on the class. If the student felt like the teacher had something to offer that he was looking for, he would contract with the teacher to continue teaching him. And he stayed so long as it was of benefit to him. When he was satisfied, he left. So many of the things we enjoy had their beginnings in this air of educational freedom from the Saracen world.

Freedom is a vital ingredient in a whole apple style of learning. It is always difficult to find words to describe something you see in your heart and I hope I'm conveying what I am seeing. But let me try one more way to describe this whole apple of learning: My all-time favorite movie is *The Sound of Music*. I'm sure I've seen it dozens of times. In fact, our local theater ran a special screening on the big screen at the beginning of summer and I went and watched it. Twice. And then a couple of weeks later, my family took me to see a live production at the Kennedy Center in D.C. for my birthday. I loved every second of it because everytime I notice something new. Remember that little thing that went around awhile ago–Everything I needed to know I learned in kindergarten? I think everything you need to know about educating hearts can be learned in the musical number, Do-re-mi. Let me show you what I mean.

The first thing Maria did was tap into a desire of the children–Shall we learn a song to sing for your father? And that's when they said they didn't know how to sing, but they wanted to learn because they did want to sing a song for their father because they loved him. And Maria is going to teach them to sing because it's something that has brought so much joy into her life. She wants to share the joy! So step one in the pattern for learning: Awaken desire.

I remember being taught about alliteration in school and then working through worksheet after worksheet, identifying alliteration. Although identifying it was easy enough, I thought, who cares? And I hated it. It was decades later, while I was reading a passage aloud and stopped to re-read it because it sounded so beautiful. Ah! That's why writers use alliteration! How different would it have been if a teacher I loved read beautiful literature first, and maybe paused and said, "Isn't that beautiful? Do you want to know what the writer did to make us feel that way? And then taught the concept. As an isolated subject, it was dead and unappealing.

Then, let's start at the very beginning. A very good place to start. Whenever I want to learn anything, do you know where I go first? To a children's book. Because I know it will clearly lay out the basics of what I need to know. It will likely illustrate them so I can see. There's a good chance it will include a story. Pictures and story feed the heart and continue to feed that desire to want to know more. And then I can layer deep from there.

If you have older kids, even high schoolers, encourage them to not be too quick to pass up or too proud to read the children's books. I remember hearing a very wise and well learned man–a scholar—who said this was his method of learning. And in fact, when he needed to nourish his soul and relax, he would turn to a children's book. The beginning is a very good place to start.

Next: When you read, you begin with ABC. When you sing, you begin with do-re-mi. Here she's tying into the familiar. Learning to read by learning their abc's was an activity they had all experienced, so now they could understand that do-re-mi was simply an alphabet for singing. Providing many experiences to connect to, and then finding ways to connect to that which has been experienced, is a key component of learning success. Always be on the lookout for those familiar connections. The first three notes just happen to be do-re-mi. Sometimes facts are just facts and you just need to accept them for the time being. The first 3 numbers just happen to be 1 2 3. The capital of our nation just happens to be Washington, D.C. Later, they may learn how Washington, D.C. came to be our capital and how the first three notes came to be do-re-mi, but for now, we can move forward by just accepting the fact. Let's not get bogged down.

Then Maria models all the notes in the scale: do re mi fa so la ti — and notices they're not getting it, so says, "Hmm. Let's see if I can make this easier." She thinks for a second, looking for an illustration, and then begins to connect each of the notes to something that is familiar to them. Do, a deer a female deer. Re, a drop of golden sun. And so forth. Notice the joy on their faces as she connects to things that are familiar to them.

First they listen–and then she repeats. Repetition is also a vital part of the learning process. None of us pick up the whole of anything on the very first try. I can read the same book over and over again, and each time pick up something new. Or watch a movie, for instance, over and over again. Even dozens of times. Who would do that, right?

That's why I encourage you to consider using the rotation schedule. It allows you to pass by the same subjects many times, each time gathering something new. So, next time through, Marie lets them take turns saying just the notes, and she sings the part that's connected to that note. As they become more confident, they join in more until she sits back and watches them sing the whole thing on their own.

Pay attention to the fact that they are learning to sing by singing. We learn to do by doing. We learn to cook by cooking. We learn to write by writing. We learn to read by reading. My son-in-law loves to play board games and he's always finding new ones. If he sits down and tries to explain the whole objective of the game and all the rules upfront, I'm totally lost. The way I learn to play new games is that we start playing, and along the way, in the time I need to know, I pick up all the rules and strategies. At first, we take it slow and then after a couple of times of playing, I'm ready. That's a whole apple way of learning. How much of teaching are you trying to do by explaining rather than doing? And, again, notice the joy and variety of the learning process as they march around the hillside and dance around the city as they practice their new skill?

Now they are ready for the next layer, that of tools and rules. "Now, children do-re-mi-fa-so and so on are only the tools we use to build a song." Once you have the notes in your head, you can sing a million different tunes by mixing them up! Here is fruit to the learning. They didn't learn the notes just for the sake of learning the notes, they learned them because now they are going to be able to sing a million different songs! You didn't learn how to read words just so you can read words, you're now going to be able to mix those words up and read a million different stories; you're going to be able to write a million different things! And she begins to model what she's talking about and has them repeat what they hear her sing.

And I can't help but see the looks of love and adoration the children have for Maria. They willingly follow her because she loves them and they love her. Her love for singing is contagious. I see two principles from Dr.Neufeld's talk: You cannot parent a child whose heart you do not have and the young seek for something to attach to, and once it attaches, it grows to be like that to which it is attached. Look at all the smiles! Then, more practice, more repetition in a lot of different settings. Look at the creative process unfold–they've been given raw materials and are now organizing it all in new and endless ways. And the learning continues to layer until by the end of the number, they're singing in harmony and confidence.

What is the fruit of all that learning? Music changes the atmosphere of their home. It touches their father's heart and heals their relationship and heals his heart. They now have a skill that brings opportunity and meaning to their lives with all its variety. Their learning has born good fruit.

Now let's learn Do-Re-Mi curriculum style.

"Children, today we are going to start learning the 8 notes of the scale." Notice, they're not given a reason or a desire. What I see too often are kids showing up and being handed the day's learning assignment. "The first note of the scale is *do*. I will write *do* on the board for you to see. And now, please copy it in your notebooks. Your homework tonight is to copy do ten times in your best handwriting."

Day 2. "The second note of the scale is Re. Will you say that with me? This is how you write Re. I need you to copy it 5 times. Now, tonight, your assignment is to write a story, using Re as your protaganist. You will be marked down for misspelled words."

Day 6. "The 6th note of the scale is La. This is how you write La. Please copy it in your notebook. Your assignment is to write a five-sentence paragraph on how you feel about La." Now, I don't know about you, but other than the fact that La is the note to follow So, I don't know much else about it. Certainly not 5 sentences worth. And I actually have no feelings about it. I couldn't care less. I'm afraid some of the writing assignments we give to kids feels just like that to them. And then we say they don't like to write! Or they can't write.

I was talking to my daughter who had a conversation with another mom who was tearing her hair out over her little boy. He had one simple little assignment he had to do. All he had to do was write a five-sentence paragraph and he balked and pouted and cried all day long and she was so frustrated. It was so simple! Why was he being so stubborn? Well, I suspect it was the La thing.

"Now children. Study these 8 notes you have learned because you will be tested on Friday and you'll be expected to put them in order."

Monday rolls around. Today, children, we are going to begin to learn time signatures.

Be still my little heart!

It's this mechanization of learning that is getting in the way of developing imagination–that thinking of the heart. I know I'm exaggerating, but this is how learning felt to me in my school years. I wish I could find the exact quote, but I read someone say recently that we have built the biggest system of schooling wherein our children spend all their days reading the menu without ever actually getting to taste the food. I think that's a good description.

Learning by heart is a joyful experience. Eat the whole apple of learning.

Let me close with the words of an old 1805 hymn with some good reminders for well-educated hearts:

> Know this, that every soul is free to choose his life and what he'll be.
> For this eternal truth is giv'n: That God will force no man to heav'n.
> He'll call, persuade, direct aright, and bless with wisdom, love and light,
> In nameless ways be good and kind, But never force the human mind.

Learning is a Piece of Cake

Learning the heart-based way is a piece of cake. If your children are hungry, would you feed them a cup of flour or a spoonful of salt or baking soda? Would you offer them a teaspoon of vanilla or a couple tablespoons of vinegar? Do you think they would like you to give them a stick of butter to suck on? And even if they love sugar and chocolate, would you sit them down to a bowlful of sugar or a half a cup of unsweetened cocoa, even if you stirred the two together?

Of course not. But if you take all those ingredients which are totally unappetizing individually, stir them all together in a 9x13 pan and bake them in an oven for 30 minutes, you'll have the most delicious moist chocolate cake to serve them. And I guarantee, they'll ask for more.

It's become the way of education to serve learning by individual ingredients: vocabulary lists, spelling lists, plot, phonics, setting, rules of grammar, alliteration, onomatopoeia, facts to memorize. And it's making our young children lose their appetites. But serve them stories, songs, poetry, pictures and allow generous portions of play time, they're not only going to keep coming back for more, you're going to find their heart and your heart wrapping around each other and attaching to each other. If you are the one who administers the daily dose of vinegar, they're going to run when they see you coming!

When they get a little older and want to bake their own cake, then they're going to want to know all the individual ingredients because they've already tasted the cake and it was delicious.

There is a time for academics, but childhood is not that time.

Three Bears Cake

Put the following in an ungreased 9x13 baking dish:

2 ¼ c. flour
1 ½ c. sugar
4 ½ T. cocoa
1 ½ tsp. baking soda
¾ tsp. salt

Mix well with a fork.

Make 3 holes: a papa size hole, a mama size hole, and a wee little baby hole. In the papa bear hole, pour 1 cube of melted butter. In the mama bear hole, pour 1 ½ T. vinegar and in the baby bear hole, pour 1 ½ tsp. vanilla. Quickly dump 1 ½ C. cold water over it all. Stir quickly with a fork until it is well mixed.

Bake at 350 degrees for 25-30 minutes. Cool and serve from the pan.

Ants and Car Manuals

Ants have always fascinated me. As much as those little black sugar ants annoy me when I see them trailing through my kitchen, I am amazed as I watch them. How does some little scout find his way into my kitchen, find a good source of sugar in my cupboard, and then go back and recruit an army to come and haul it back to their headquarters? I can brush them away, and they'll instantly re-group and re-organize and get back to business. I'm amazed at how ants build complex networks of tunnels underground, hauling out one grain of dirt at a time. I recently read how red ants will scout out a black ant colony, go in and steal their eggs, and bring them back to their own colony where they raise them as slaves. That's terrible, isn't it? But miraculous! Who taught them to do that? How do they know how to communicate, organize, how does each ant know its purpose and role in the colony? People can't even organize as efficiently or work together as cooperatively as ants do in an ant colony.

Yet, look at the size of their little ant brains! If God endowed ants with such power to learn, what powers and gifts for learning must He have placed in His own children?

I'm afraid too many educators look at children as lumps of clay; that if we don't teach them, that if we don't program something in, there's no way they can learn. The more I learn, the more I believe that we are interfering with natural learning processes built within each of us.

Do you remember your first driving experience? I was so excited to learn to drive! And how did I learn? I got behind the wheel in the driver's seat. The instructor told me to turn on the key. I already knew from watching my parents drive that if you pushed the right accelerator, the car would go forward and if you put on the brake, it would stop. I had watched them put it into gear. So I did what I saw them do, and instantly, I was driving. No one had to teach me how to steer.

I instinctively kept the car in the lane. In fact, my driver's ed teacher had me merging and driving on Southern California freeways the very first day! It was thrilling!

And once I got my license, driving meant getting together with my friends and driving to the beach and glorious independence!

Have you noticed how fat car owner manuals have gotten? We bought a new car a few months ago and the manual must be over an inch thick. How many of you have read yours cover to cover?

What? You can operate your car without studying the car manual?

I was glad I had it, though, when we got in our car last week and a light came on the dash board we had never seen before. That's when I pulled out the car manual and found the page that identified it and we took care of it.

But I got to thinking. What if before you got behind the wheel of your new car, you were required to study that entire manual, page by page by page. Maybe write out lists of definitions. Fill in diagrams and charts from memory. Give reports on what you were learning. Be tested on it. Would it make you a better driver?

I think that's what we've done to education and learning. We are so intent on drilling all the mechanical details of learning into our kids that we're squashing their desire to learn, when the truth is, they are already divinely gifted with natural instincts to learn. Children come well equipped.

I love this quote by Herbert Spencer I came across in an old Delphian handbook. I hope you can get past his flowery language to hear what he is saying.

> Who, indeed, can watch the ceaseless observation and inquiry and inference going on in a child's mind, or listen to his acute remarks on matters within the range of his faculties, without perceiving that these powers which he manifests, if brought to bear systematically upon any studies within the same range, would readily master them without help.
>
> This need for perpetual telling is the result of our stupidity, not of the child's. We drag him away from the facts in which he is interested, and which he is actively assimilating of himself; put before him facts far too complex for him to understand, and therefore distasteful to him; finding that he will not voluntarily acquire these facts, we thrust them into his mind by force of threats and punishment; by thus denying the knowledge he craves, and cramming him with knowledge he cannot digest, we produce a morbid state of his faculties, and a consequent disgust for knowledge in general; and when as a result partly of the stolid indifference we have brought on, and partly of still continued unfitness in its studies, the child can understand nothing without explanation, and becomes a mere passive recipient of our instruction, we infer that education must necessarily be carried on thus. Having by our method induced helplessness, we straightway make the helplessness a reason for our method.

Think about that.

I've brought up before the miracle of speech acquisition; that a toddler can figure out how to produce sounds and the meaning behind them just by observation. That he figures out—without direct instruction from us—vocabulary, grammar and syntax and can do it in multiple languages simultaneously. Can you imagine if we took over the job?

"Today, Bobby, we're going to learn to form the letter L. Now. Put your tongue at the top of your mouth just behind your top teeth. Let's practice that a few times." Next day. "Today we're going to practice pushing air out of your lungs. I need you to do that 20 times." Next day. "Now we're going to put the two pieces together. I want you to push the air out of your lungs just before you put your tongue back of your teeth. Tomorrow, I'll teach you how to make a sound in the back of your throat and by Friday, we should have mastered saying the sound of L! Are you so excited!" Pretty ridiculous, right?

Why do toddlers pick up vocabulary so naturally, and then when they hit school age, we think we have to take over the process and hand them vocabulary lists, taken out of context and force them to write definitions and sentences, thinking that's the only way they can learn new words?

Winter

I've talked about the importance of spring's 'warmth' in releasing a vital life force in the process of learning. But I haven't addressed the need for winter.

Winter is the 'chilling time.' And while, on the surface, it appears as though nothing is going on, it's an important phase of learning. In plants, it's a time when growth is temporarily halted while energy is held in reserve, building up for new growth. I just learned that without a sufficient chilling time, a fruit tree will generate fewer and weaker buds and some seeds will just rot.

> Many things are going on while the snow is covering the ground that we do not see but is vital to plants survival… Many plants have a requirement of cold before they will bloom… The cold rest period is when the leaf growth on lawns stop, but the root system is still growing and forming foods to bolster the spurt of new growth in the spring. Without this rest the lawns would not survive. (*Why Winter is Important*, by Glenn Bronner)

When someone is out of control, we tell them to go 'chill out.' Are you allowing your children time and space to 'chill out' in their learning, thereby allowing them a chance to build up their energy reserves and deepen their roots for a next burst of growth?

The Echo of Greece

I picked up a gem of a book at a used book sale: *The Echo of Greece* by Edith Hamilton written in 1957. She wrote: "Fourth-century Athens has a special claim on our attention apart from the great men it produced, for it is the prelude to the end of Greece… The kind of events that took place in the great free government of the ancient world may, by reason of unchanging human nature, be repeated in the modern world. The course that Athens followed can be to us not only as a record of old unhappy far-off things but a blueprint of what may happen again."

At the end of the book, she talks about a crossroads for the Christian faith. The art- and beauty-loving Greeks were open to the message of Jesus—to tend to the kingdom within. They understood it. The New Testament was written in Greek; Paul found willing listeners among the Greeks. But in the end, the Christian church went the Roman way of outward ritual and rule. And it's been a rocky and often bloody road. What might have been different if the Greek way had been chosen?

But what I mean to talk about is this. Mrs. Hamilton describes that the Golden Age of 5th Century B.C. Greece was a time of great freedom because the people themselves were self-governed; they took responsibility for their own lives. Following the great wars, there were those Greeks who longed for the old days. They thought it was their system of government that had made them free and labored to re-establish it. The words of Socrates that had taught them to tend first to their hearts were in large measure disregarded. Plato in his early years sought that ideal, but in his later years succumbed to the practical and by the time Aristotle came along, a large shift to mind had happened. The great schools of Athens—including the great Academy—by which its founders dreamed of producing a philosopher-King, failed to accomplish their goal and Greece never rose again and in fact, slipped into slavery.

"Socrates never conceived, any more than Christ did, of establishing an institution to spread the truth—an Academy or a theological seminary. To both, the truth they knew could not be expressed in statements and taught to others. A man could be aroused to seek it, that was all. He could find it only by seeking it himself."

How to Manage

First, a little observation from a mom who had 9 children in an 11-year span. It's not the things that I did that made me tired; it was all the things I didn't get to that weighed me down. When you are on a facts and information treadmill trying to keep up with 'them,' it's easy to feel overwhelmed and scared you're not measuring up.

In a heart-based education, there's no one to measure up to or compare yourself to. When your children are young, set a goal for yourself that every day, you are going to give your children something to prepare their hearts to be inspired—look at a work of fine art, listen to beautiful music, recite a selection of poetry, read a story together. In the process, you'll be giving them a vision of good things to hope for and will be teaching them the right-use of all things in love. Each story, each poem, each piece of music has a lesson for the heart that all begin to add up over the years. Build life around these four things. Every night you can go to bed feeling satisfied that you have shared something of lasting value with your children.

More Food for Thought

The Gift of a Hungry Soul

(Talk delivered in Stake Conference, Lexington VA)

I was asked to share a time when I felt the greatest influence of the Spirit in my life. Immediately, examples of promptings, warnings, understandings, instruction and comfort came into my mind. But as I tried to focus on those times I felt the greatest influence—the most powerful manifestations of the Spirit—I quickly saw a pattern emerge, because they were all connected to a time of intense personal struggling; of a time of difficulty or hardship.

I asked once, in a prayer, why, if we're supposed to have joy, why is life so hard? I immediately had a simple explanation come into my mind that at least partly satisfies that question. This is what came in my mind: Remember when you ate at the restaurant not long ago that had such good food, you ate and ate until you were so full, you could hardly move? What happened when the waiter brought the tray of desserts by? Didn't you hold your hand up to him and say, "No way. I can't eat another bite. Take it away."

Sorrow and hardship make our souls hungry. And the hungrier we are, the more room we have for spiritual nourishment that we might have sent away if we were full. So being hungry from time to time is actually a great blessing.

The Proverb puts it this way: "The full soul loatheth an honeycomb. But to the hungry soul, every bitter thing is sweet."

I'm afraid if all of my unwise prayers were answered, I would keep everyone in a perpetual state of fulness. No one would ever lose a job. Everyone would have enough money. No one would ever get sick or have an accident or lose a loved one.

I was praying one day for my children and asking for the usual blessings. I asked that they would be watched over and protected from all harm or accident; that they would be kept healthy and strong and be given every blessing they were in need of.

The Spirit gently interrupted my prayer and asked, "Marlene, are you asking me to deny them the very experiences that have taught you to know of the power of God?"

I had been praying to keep them full.

Of course, it didn't seem right to pray for disasters to come into their lives, so I asked what I should pray for. The Spirit said to pray for more trust in the Lord. He loved them and knew what He was doing. I find that is a harder prayer to offer, but I am trying.

I think the hungriest time we find ourselves is when we feel a critical need for guidance and comfort, and we feel we have complied with all the Lord has asked, and the Spirit seems silent.

I have read the Beatitude many times that says, "Blessed are they which hunger and thirst after righteousness." I always took that to mean someone who longs for or desires righteousness, and that may be its primary meaning. But recently when I re-read it, an additional meaning came to my mind: "Blessed are they who hunger and thirst *after* righteousness"—meaning, after you have made sacrifices for the Lord and have placed your heart and soul on the altar; with all your heart, sought to do His will and keep His commandments, and the expected guidance and comfort doesn't come.

That is profound hunger.

I believe the Lord often prolongs that kind of hunger for days and sometimes even months and years because He uses it to stretch and enlarge our capacity to receive His Spirit. His intentions are clear. "Blessed are they who hunger and thirst after righteousness for they shall be filled with the Holy Ghost." Not just a spoonful, but with enlarged capacity, pressed down and flowing over with the fruits of the Spirit which include light and joy and love and peace. And instruction. That is God's promise to the hungry.

And God always keeps His promises.

I am thankful for the supernal gift of His Spirit that delivers the Bread of Life to my soul and satisfies my hunger.

Preparing a Child's Heart

Keynote at American Heritage Spring 2018

Some years ago I had a dream. And in this dream, I was invited to sing a solo in church. Now, I love to sing, but, believe me, I don't have the kind of voice you would want to listen to as a soloist. I knew that. But somehow, I knew the invitation had come from the Lord. So, even though the thought terrified me, I felt that if I could get myself in front of that congregation and open my mouth, I would be given gifts and talents beyond my own. So I accepted the invitation in that faith.

The moment came to sing. I opened my mouth, but all that came out was my own voice. I was mortified because I knew the song I had to sing was very long. Evidently I wasn't the only one in pain. As I looked over that very large congregation, I saw some members with their hands over their ears. Others were looking away from me or down in their laps out of embarrassment. I could hear whispering in front of me—"Who does she think she is? Does she really think she can sing? Why doesn't she just stop and sit down?"

Believe me! No one wanted to stop and sit down more than me. I kept scanning the exit signs for the fastest escape route when it was over. But because I knew the Lord was the one who had asked me to sing, I knew I had to finish the song.

And I did.

When I sat down, I buried my face in my hands and cried. Why had He asked me to do that? It surely hadn't benefitted those who had to listen to me and for me, it was embarrassing and humiliating.

Suddenly the scene changed and I found myself standing in the middle of a choir singing the most glorious music I had ever heard. And when I opened my mouth to sing, my voice was beautiful like theirs! How could this be, I wondered. I can't sing. As if someone had perceived my thoughts, a voice behind me whispered, "Remember when you were asked to sing? A messenger was in the congregation that day whose assignment it was to watch and see if you would finish the song. And you did! Because of that, the Lord has chosen you to sing in His choir and it is He who has given you your voice."

And now I cried again, but this time out of pure joy. I thought to myself what a small and insignificant price I had paid for this magnificent blessing. Truly, "eye hath not seen nor ear heard neither hath entered into the hearts of men what great things lie in store for those who love Him."

And the dream ended.

I believe each of you is here today because you have felt the invitation to sing—and your song is that of teaching your children. When you accepted the invitation, perhaps you expected, because you felt a divine call, that you would be gifted with talents and abilities beyond your own. But as you wake up every morning, and open your mouth, some of you feel your very ordinariness and all your inadequacies. Maybe you hear voices around you—*Who does she think she is? Does she really think she can teach her children? She's going to ruin their lives. Why doesn't she just stop and let someone who knows what they're doing teach them.*

And maybe you've been tempted to stop and sit down before the song is over. I hope I may be able to say a few things today that will help give you the courage to keep singing. Because I believe there are things you need to do that a mother is best equipped to do.

Like Martha, I know you are careful and troubled about many things. How can I get these multiplication facts to stick? My 9-year-old still can't decode words. My 12-year-old hates to read. My high schooler is unable to produce a coherent five-paragraph essay. How can I make sure my children will score well on the tests and get into a good college? How can I teach the periodic table of elements, the timetables of history, the endless list of subjects I feel I am supposed to teach at a developmentally appropriate level to a houseful of kids of all different ages? And there is that endless stream of dishes and laundry to do.

I don't minimize your concerns. But I think of the Savior's response: One thing is needful and Mary hath chosen the better part, which shall not be taken away from her. And what was that one thing Mary was doing while Martha was so very busy taking care of things? She was listening to the spoken word of the Lord.

That phrase: the spoken word of the Lord is used in my patriarchal blessing. I know we hold our patriarchal blessings as sacred and private, but when that particular phrase is used, it is addressed to all those who love the Lord and I believe that is the audience I am addressing. So these words were spoken to you as well as me. The complete phrase is: The day will come that the spoken word of the Lord will be the mentor for you and your family day by day and at times, hour by hour.

It's been nearly 50 years since I was given that blessing and I have often pondered its meaning. I noted that it was given for a day yet to come. Did it describe a time when we will actually hear an audible voice of the Lord guiding us? Did it mean that the day will come when we won't have access to written words and we will have to rely upon that which is spoken? Maybe it meant that the day will come that we will have to rely upon the words spoken through the mouths of His prophets, but I thought how could he direct the needs of individual circumstances worldwide, day by day and hour by hour? None of these possibilities satisfied me.

I was thinking about it again not long ago, and the thought struck me, "Google it." Google it? Really? But I did. And I was astonished at what I instantly learned. The first article that pulled up said that when the New Testament was translated from the Greek, while the English translation used one expression—the word of the Lord, there were two very different Greek words from which it was translated. One was *logos* and the other was *rhema*. Now, people who are way smarter than me have been analyzing and discussing the difference between the two words for centuries. And not always agreeing with each other. But for the sake of having a word to use to describe an experience I believe you'll relate to, let me describe the difference as I see it.

All of you here today will hear the *logos* of my words. The words may pass in and out of you, with no distinct impressions. But for some of you, something I say will 'light up'—it will stir your heart and resonate in your soul. It may have a quickening effect where you will feel a call to action. That is *rhema*.

Rhema, according to the article I just referenced, means: divine illumination; a divinely inspired impression upon your soul; a flash of thought or a creative idea from God.

It is the still, small voice deep within our hearts. And this voice can act as a mentor or guide to us in all we do—surely day by day or even hour by hour. It is a voice spoken to individual hearts.

This explanation of the spoken word of the Lord is consistent with the 45th section of the D&C wherein we learn the five wise virgins had taken the Holy Spirit as their guide. It aligns with the Lord's promise to lead us by the hand; and Isaiah's vision of the day when all our children will be taught of the Lord—I believe that as meaning taught by Him, not just about Him. And it makes me think of the phrase in Charlotte Mason's writings: True education is between a child's soul and God.

Rhema is the one needful thing in education.

And there is one primary thing that blocks it—Hard heartedness; a very real condition wherein we are past feeling and cannot feel that divine illumination; those impressions or flashes of inspiration on the heart. As you study your scriptures, pay attention to how often the heart with its desires and feelings is referred to and especially the caution against hard-heartedness.

Late in life, Charles Darwin, the great scientist, wrote: "Formerly I was led to the firm conviction of God and the immortality of the soul. In my journal I wrote whilst standing in the midst of the grandeur of the Brazilian forest, 'It is not possible to give an adequate idea of the higher feelings of wonder, admiration and devotion which fill and elevate the mind.' I well remember my conviction that there is more in man than the mere breath of his body. But now the grandest scene would not cause any such conviction and feelings to rise in my mind... Disbelief crept over me at a very slow rate, but was at last complete. The rate was so slow that I felt no distress."

He was past feeling. His heart was hardened. What had caused that to happen? By his own account, he wrote: "If I had to live my life again I would have made it a rule to read some poetry and listen to some music at least once every week; for perhaps the parts of my brain now atrophied would thus have been kept active through use."

We all know that music is made up rhythm, melody and harmonies. The beat or rhythm maintains a sense of order while the combination of melody and harmony stirs our feelings. We are seeing a trend in music and in society generally that is heavy on beat and light on melody and harmony and the effect is a shutting down of sensitive feelings. The rhythmic and repetitive counting of sheep shuts down our thoughts and puts us to sleep. The pounding of the war drums among savage tribes had the effect of dulling their feelings so they could go out on the warpath and kill. The Pharisee who lived by the perfect beat of the law lost the capacity to feel the awe and wonder of the healing of a withered hand. The letter killeth.

I would suggest to you that much of the hard-heartedness we are seeing in our generation comes from the steady beat of rigorous academic training in childhood—the endless stream of facts and information; all that can be tested and measured—without the stirring influences of the arts which provide the melody and harmony of learning. What little of the arts we still include are quickly turned into academic exercises that not only squeeze the joy out of them, but leave a distaste for them all together.

Children come to us with hearts that are open and impressionable, but instead of using their childhoods to tend to their finer and nobler faculties through the use of music, pictures, poetry and story, we see a focus on academic training at earlier and earlier ages. It has been said we are "in danger of organizing the soul out of education, of making it mechanical and therefore barren." That which is not used atrophies from disuse. Hearts that are past feeling is a real condition caused from neglect.

So how do we correct the situation?

Louisa May Alcott wrote:

> A little kingdom I possess,
> Where thoughts and feelings dwell

I believe our most important job as mothers is to tend to the inner kingdoms of hearts—where thoughts and feelings dwell— to keep them soft and open to divine impressions. All other learning will flow from this core.

I would like to offer 5 decorating tips for this kingdom. In so doing, we will heed the admonition of Paul and seek for that which is virtuous and lovely, of good report and praiseworthy. Before we go there, though, I need to place credit where credit is due. A hundred years ago or so, there was a group of educators I call the heart educators who understood all about tending to the inner kingdom of the heart. I have been so immersed in their writings over the last several years, their thoughts and words have completely intertwined with my own so that I can often no longer tell where their words leave off and mine begin. I'm afraid it would be a huge distraction if I were to credit their unfamiliar names every time I quote or use their words to teach you as we go forward. So please know, if something beautiful or profound comes out of my mouth, it likely came from one of my heart educator friends and if there is a particular quote you'd like me to give proper credit to, just write to me and I'll try and hunt it down.

Decorating tip #1: Fill the air with worthy music.

A young woman was dying. Her baby had died at birth a few weeks previously, and since that time the mother had steadily failed. The doctor had just left her room saying emphatically that there was no hope and to give her anything she wanted.

She looked up at her agonized husband and said: "Music. I want music. I know that will cure me." The nurse thought it to be a foolhardy and useless errand, but the husband went in search of it.

The first day old familiar tunes and some of the Chopin that she had always loved, were played softly to her. Her body relaxed under the soothing influence, her nerves became less tense, her breathing deeper and more rhythmical, increasing the circulation. That night she slept. With the shutting out of the senses to the outside world the harmonic reaction brought about by the music continued its work of healing all through the night. The next day she was visibly stronger.

Halfway through World War I, music began to be used on a large scale 'to help organize victory.' How the men craved music. A victrola was carried lovingly from front lines to hospital. Music was used in every conceivable form as a comfort, as a relaxation from the horrors of war, and as a stimulus to the morale of the men. Music acquired all the sacredness of a ministering angel.

Florence Nightingale requested music for hospitals in the Crimean War. The mind blurred by contact with unspeakable horrors was quieted and made normal again.

"There is something very wonderful in music. Words are wonderful enough, but music is more wonderful. It speaks not to our thoughts as words do; it speaks straight to our hearts and spirits, to the very core and root of our souls. Music soothes us, stirs us up, it puts noble feelings into us; it melts us to tears, we know not how."

This 'heavenly Maid' is a chief restorer, mentally, emotionally, spiritually and physically. Music has the power to solve many of our problems for us.

Sadly, it is being misused. Music has become a performing art. Ask someone if he or she is musical, and if that person does not play a musical instrument or sing, the answer will be no. Yet, every one of us is deeply and profoundly musical. If you don't believe me, try walking to your next class out of rhythm. Try speaking out of rhythm—it's practically impossible. Worthy music always leads us home.

> God is its author, and not man; he laid
> The keynote of all harmonies; he planned
> All perfect combinations, and he made
> Us so that we could hear and understand.

Certain combinations of notes make us feel sad, others hopeful, others give us longing. Through music, the mind is stilled to outside influences and becomes a reflector for the inner light which comes only through stillness. Faith comes when the chaotic thoughts of the outside world are stilled.

Some music is chaotic in itself or relies so heavily on the beat, that while it may get our toes tapping and our heels dancing, it does not have the power to stir our souls and in its coarseness, causes us to dull those refined sensitivities that bridge heaven and earth. The intention of many of the great music masters was to reveal the very glory of God to the human heart, but many of our youth—and adults—have lost the capacity to feel it.

We have worked for a very long time to squeeze all the joy out of listening to music by making the means of enjoyment more and more complex, until now, we find ourselves starving in spite of the abundance about us... Not only have we starved our music sense, our wrong methods of instruction frequently transform our reaction to music into a lifeless, analytical and empty thing, instead of the warm, glowing healthful reaction it should be. Isn't it time we start working to put it all back again into its rightful place as a joy giver?

May I offer a simple suggestion for opening ears as illustrated in an article that appeared in the *Reader's Digest* over 50 years ago. It was written by a young journalist who had been invited to the home of a wealthy philanthropist. After dinner, the guests retired to a large room for an evening of chamber music. This young man said he was tone deaf and music meant nothing to him. It was almost painful. So, as the music started to play, he closed his ears and thought about other things.

After the first number, the man next to him asked, "You are fond of Bach?" He hadn't noticed that he was sitting next to Albert Einstein himself. He admitted he knew nothing of Bach upon which Einstein took him by the arm, led him out of the room, upstairs to a study. "Now then," he said. "Tell me a song you love." He named a Bing Crosby song and Einstein found the song on a record which he played and when it was done, said, "Now. Sing it back to me," which he did to the best of his ability and Einstein's warm eyes lit up. He continued doing the same with song after song until Einstein played a record of music without words and told his young friend to hum it back, which he did. Einstein smiled and said, "Now we're ready for Bach." He led him back down to the hall and whispered, "Just allow yourself to listen. That's all."

The writer said Bach's *Sheep May Safely Graze* became one of his favorite pieces of music as he heard it for the first time that night, and which became the gateway to a great love of music.

After the concert, the hostess apologized that Einstein had missed so much of the evening's performance. Einstein replied, "My young friend and I were engaged in the greatest activity of which man is capable. We were opening up yet another fragment of the frontier of beauty."

So here is the simple suggestion: If the realm of music is to be entered through hearing one must begin by being able to focus on the melody. The harmonies will begin to play in the background quite naturally. As you practice paying attention to the melody, drawing a pitch picture with your hand may help—it will be etched in the memory and can be recalled and reimagined at will, and can protect us from feelings and thoughts that are destructive.

One writer suggested: "It seems extravagant to claim that, if everyone could be shown how to follow a tune and remember it, the world's unrest would be ameliorated, but this would seem to be a fact nevertheless. Because, by doing so, each individual would become conscious of the harmony within himself." And that harmony would spread outward.

Music should decorate the atmosphere of our inner kingdoms continually.

Tip #2: Line the walls with fine art.

I was talking with my son recently and he told me about a visit to the National Art Gallery. As he walked from room to room, people were always gathered around the familiar, famous paintings. But as he entered one room, he was drawn to a very small painting by an artist he had never heard of. It was a sunset over Paris and he was so captivated by it, he couldn't move.

He said he stood there staring at it for probably half an hour. There are no words to express what it was saying to him. But just by remembering it as we talked, all the feelings of that painting came rushing back to him.

"When we see ordinary things, we see only with our eyes, but, when we see works of art, we see with our hearts." Great paintings are a source of rest, delight and inspiration. The heart that is open to 'feel' art is possessed of one of the purest, loftiest and most ennobling pleasures that the civilized world can offer.

Enjoyment is the first and final purpose of art in the lives of children. "Let pictures be, like the stories we tell, among our children's dearest delights. Above all things else we must avoid mechanical methods of instruction as the most deadly blight to the imagination." And that is of no small consequence for it is through the imagination we unlock the doors of beauty.

We say 'in one ear and out the other' but we don't say 'in one eye and out the other.' The images we take in are long lasting and difficult to erase. So we need to be careful and mindful of the images we allow into our inner kingdom.

Take the time to peruse great masterpieces of art, especially those paintings created by great souls, and when one speaks to your heart; when you find one that uplifts you, ennobles you, stirs your heart with all that is good and beautiful, find a print if you can and hang it somewhere where you can look at it frequently.

Trace it, sketch its parts over and over until every detail is ingrained on the wall of your memory. Love these personally selected paintings until they are a part of you for then this art gallery in the kingdom of your heart will be yours to visit anytime you want. And this ideal that is enthroned in your heart, this you will become.

Tip #3: Furnish the rooms with poetry.

Some years ago, my husband and I were called to serve in a branch at a Senior Center and we became friends with Grant and Edna, both in their 90s. Grant was the primary caregiver of Edna who suffered from Alzheimer's and hadn't recognized him for years, yet they lived in the Independent Living side of the facility. Their only child had died years earlier.

Grant looked old and frail, but over a lifetime, he had furnished his inner kingdom with hundreds of poems committed to memory and when we would ask him to recite one, his eyes would light up and his voice would become strong as he shared a poem he loved by heart.

We visited him in his apartment one night and I asked him if he had a poem for us. He smiled, and off he went:

"Wynken, Blynken and Nod, one night sailed off in a wooden shoe; Sailed on a river of crystal light, into a sea of dew."

When he was finished, I asked if this was a poem from childhood and he said, no, this is what he had been working on the last few weeks. Poetry is how he kept loneliness and discouragement at bay and how he kept his heart from failing. He passed away just a few days later and Edna followed shortly thereafter, but whenever I think of the gift of poetry in our lives, I think of Grant.

David O. McKay was said to have stored over 1000 poems in his heart.

When Lincoln's much-loved young son died while living in the White House, with the Civil War bearing down hard on his shoulders, a Senator found Lincoln alone, one day, a book opened on his lap. It was Shakespeare's King John—the part where a mother, Constance, was grieving over the loss of her young son, Arthur.

> My Lord, my boy, my young son,
> My life, my joy, my food, My all the world, My sorrow's cure.
> Grief fills up the room of my absent son Lies in his bed;
> Walks up and down with me.
> Oh, Father Cardinal,
> I have heard you say
> I shall see and know my friends in heaven If that be true,
> I shall see my boy again.

It was a poet's words that brought Lincoln comfort in his own grief.

Longfellow's dearest love, Fanny, mother to his 5 living children, was sealing packets of her children's curls one day when Longfellow heard screams. He rushed from his office to find her dress on fire. He frantically tried to put the flames out with his own body, but she was too badly burned and she died. This great poet turned to another poet for comfort and immersed himself in the task of translating Dante's *Divine Comedy*. A few years later, he penned the words to our familiar Christmas carol: I Heard the Bells on Christmas Day and could declare, in spite of the sorrows: "God is not dead, nor doth he sleep."

Victor Frankl observed a small group of prisoners in those horrible death camps of Nazi Germany who would secretly gather together to recite poetry and sing songs even though it was forbidden and punishable by death. Poetry was their soul's means for self-preservation.

Keats wrote that poetry should be a friend to soothe the cares, and lift the thoughts of man. "Among earth's wisest teachers, we give the first place to the poets. These are the men of vision, the interpreters of the beautiful...when the clouds stand upon the horizon, they pierce through the darkness, and show us the sweet fields that lie beyond." Poets present the deepest and most vital truths in the most beautiful and lasting forms.

Our first aim with poetry must be to feel, not to know.

Andrew Lang cautions us: "Nothing, perhaps, crushes the love of poetry more surely and swiftly than the use of poems as schoolbooks. They are at once associated in the mind with lessons, with long, with endless hours in school, with puzzling questions and the agony of an imperfect memory, with grammar and etymology, and everything that is the enemy of joy." Rather, associate poetry with joy, and beauty and freedom to choose, with the mystery of faery, the wonderful things of life, and the beauty of nature, if it to them is always a thing of beauty, it may remain a joy forever."

Longfellow gives us simple instructions for poetry appreciation:

> [R]ead from some treasured volume
> The poem of thy choice,
> And lend to the rhyme of the poet
> The beauty of thy voice.

Poetry was written for the ear and not the eye.

If you haven't already, begin, today, to create your own anthology of poems that you love. Copy them. Decorate the pages if you'd like. Always have a poem you are memorizing. Use the 'beauty of thy voice' to share them with your family. And then encourage them to do the same. And soon your palace will be filled with rich furnishings upon which you can find refreshment and rest.

Tip #4: Invite great souls to dine with you.

Gather around your dining room table prophets, statesmen, poets, philosophers, kings and queens, saints, musicians, artists, inventors, scientists, martyrs, writers, holy men and women, humanitarians, brave soldiers, philanthropists, explorers, adventurers. Let them tell their stories. Laugh with them. Cry with them. Rejoice with them. Share their heart-ache and their victories. Pay attention to their wisdom and life lessons. And before they leave, have them sign your guest book so that you can remember what they shared with you.

My guest book is a 3-ring binder. I create guest pages for each one with their names at the top, a brief reminder of their contribution to the world, where they lived, the year they were born and the year they died. I then arrange the pages chronologically by year of birth.

When I hear a name, I want a face to come up in my memory. So I do a Google image search, print the picture out if I can find one and glue it on their page. And I look for a few other images that trigger remembrances of the stories they shared. Also, I make a short description of stories I want to remember from their lives and make reference to where I can find the full story again. And I copy those priceless gems of life lessons and make note of character traits with which I want to adorn my own life.

I use cursive handwriting to copy the words. Neuroscientists have been able to observe the brain while people have keyboarded, printed and written cursive. Only the cursive lights up the whole brain. Writing in cursive will leave a deeper and more long-lasting impression.

Sterling W. Sill created similar guest books of thoughts and ideas. He said, "When in my reading I come to some little nugget of an idea that sends a chill up and down my backbone—I take that out and put it in my [book]." Some of those words he memorized and thus they became a part of him. Over a lifetime, he filled 25 notebooks with over 300 pages each—That's over 7500 guest pages filled with ennobling thoughts and ideas!

One guest taught me that as I immerse myself in the thoughts and feelings, the joys, hopes and aspirations of some of the great men and women who have looked at the world, I can gradually learn to look with their clearer eyes and see the beauty which delighted their more appreciative souls and my own world becomes larger and lovelier through the experience.

In very real ways, these guests become my dear and influential friends. Many friends are found only on the pages of literature and I keep separate guest books for them. Jean Valjean or the Good Bishop, creations of someone's imagination, have no less impact on my life than someone who has actually walked on the earth.

A fifteen-year-old boy was hugging his guest notebook one day and he said to his mom, "If people knew what was inside of this notebook, they would know it is a treasure of great worth."

Who will you invite to dinner today?

Tip #5: Beautify the surrounding grounds with gardens of flowers and canopies of trees.

Nowhere can we feel closer to our Creator—and feel that *rhema*, that spoken word of the Lord, that divine illumination—than among His Creations. The Sioux Indians knew that a man's heart, away from nature, becomes hard. Nature is loaded with music, pictures, poetry and story to stir our souls and heal our hearts. The problem is we look but do not see; we listen, but do not hear. In many ways we walk in darkness at noonday sun.

Helen Keller, who was blind and deaf, thought it would be a good idea for people to experience her world for a brief time. She wrote, "Darkness would make him more appreciative of sight; silence would teach him the joys of sound." She remembered asking a friend what she had seen after a walk through the forest, to which the friend replied, "Nothing in particular." Helen exclaimed, "I might have been incredulous had I not been accustomed to such responses, for long ago I became convinced that the seeing see little."

She continued: "[I]t is a great pity that in the world of light the gift of sight is used only as a mere convenience rather than as a means of adding fulness to life."

The remedy to this sightlessness can be as simple as starting a nature journal and sketching what you see. "Why do we wish to learn to draw? ... In order to develop in us those nobler faculties which God has given for the appreciation of His works in nature. Drawing produces an exactness in thought."

A mother told me of a girl she knew who never took a formal science class in high school, but she diligently kept a nature journal. When she decided she wanted to pursue nursing, she panicked a bit about the college level science courses she would have to pass. She called home in her first semester of Biology, excited to tell her mother she was at the top of her class. She said it was because, as her teacher described things, because of her drawing, she could see exactly what he was talking about and it all came together for her while her classmates struggled.

I love the work of John Muir Laws and there are dozens of his free training workshops you can access online to help you learn to draw from nature. He writes, "We live in a world of beauty and wonder. Train your mind to see deeply and with intentional curiosity, and the world will open before you. The goal of nature journaling is not to create a portfolio of pretty pictures but to develop a tool to help you see, wonder, and remember your experiences."

A nature journal develops gratitude and reverence.

"If the trees and flowers, the clouds and the wind, all tell wonderful stories to us, we have sources of happiness which no power can deprive us of."

The poet William Wordsworth captures this gift of nature perfectly in this poem:

> I wandered lonely as a cloud
> That floats on high o'er vales and hills,
> When all at once I saw a crowd,
> A host, of golden daffodils;
> Beside the lake; beneath the trees,
> Fluttering and dancing in the breeze.
> I gazed and gazed—but little thought
> What wealth the show to me had brought:
> For oft, when on my couch I lie
> In vacant or in pensive mood,
> They flash upon that inward eye
> Which is the bliss of solitude;
> And then my heart with pleasure fills
> And dances with the daffodils.

"Never lose an opportunity to see something beautiful. Beauty is God's handwriting."

As you tend to this little kingdom within by filling the air with worthy music, hanging fine art on the walls, furnishing the rooms with poetry, inviting great souls to visit, and walking among the beautiful gardens, you have created a sanctuary in your heart where the Spirit of the Lord will feel at home and where it will seek to dwell and converse with you day by day and even hour by hour. Beauty is a quality of divinity, and to live much with the beautiful is to live close to the divine. The rich music, art, poetry and story treasures of the ages are our heritage, free for the taking through today's technology. Only we can keep ourselves poor in the matters of heart and spirit.

The last-day prophecies describe scenes of great destruction, sorrow and misery, yet in the midst of these horrible conditions, there is seen a people making their way to Zion singing songs of everlasting joy. Surely they carry their kingdom within that stands independent from outward circumstances and which keeps their hearts from failing. When the scourges have past, the earthly kingdom they will build will be but an outward expression of that inner kingdom of beauty and joy they brought with them.

You may feel the invitation today to sing such a song, but when you get home and open your mouth to sing, perhaps you may feel too inadequate to finish it. The cares and demands of life weigh heavily upon us and you may feel the resistance of your children in our electronic media saturated world. Well, let me share some advice from a guest who dined at my table—he has a page in my guest book.

I met him not long ago when I visited the National Portrait Gallery in Washington, D.C. In one of the rooms, I happened upon a sculpture of a little girl—*La Petite Pensee*—that so captured my heart, I couldn't stop looking at her. What she was telling me, I have no words to describe. But I didn't want to leave her. When I got home, I couldn't stop thinking about her. I wondered who the artist was who could have created such an exquisite work of art.

I learned his name was Thomas Ball and I found an autobiography of him online. At the end of his book was advice that he gave to young artist friends and as I read it, I thought, these words are for you, too, because I see you as artists—creators of children's hearts, caregivers of their inner kingdoms. And sometimes the work is discouraging. We feel ordinary and lacking in the necessary gifts and talents. Sometimes we feel like we aren't doing a very good job. The work isn't turning out the way we hoped it would. So let me repeat his advice:

> My most bitter tears have been shed at the completion of some work, when I felt that I had done all I could do, and yet found it so far from what I had hoped to make it, and that it must go out to the world with all its imperfections. Falling upon my knees in agony, praying for comfort and faith to believe the present disappointment to be for my ultimate good, I have arisen comforted and strengthened in the hope that perhaps I had worked better than I knew...
>
> Imperfect and unsatisfactory as all my work seems to me, I shudder when I think of what they might have been, and what I might have been, without that firm belief that He was ever at my right hand as long as I was true to myself—to bear me up when I would have fainted; to help me when my strength left me.
>
> I write this for the encouragement of my young brothers in art; not those arrogant and proud ones who believe in nothing but their own strength and will, jealous at even a hint of any assistance from a higher power... —But to that sensitive, retiring one who shrinks from the sound of approbation...to him I would say Coraggio! You are stronger than you imagine; be but sincere and conscientious in your efforts; work away with all your might. Strive to live a pure and clean life, and to improve the talents God has given you, and leave the rest to him. He will not let you fail. Keep up a good heart; cultivate a cheery disposition.

The gift of a great choir director is that he can take seemingly ordinary voices and combine and blend them with other voices to create glorious music. The great day of gathering and harmonizing voices is upon us. Your little alto part that may seem so monotonous and uninteresting, is a vital part of that great choir of the Lord's chosen singers.

So, in closing, I echo the words of Thomas Ball: "You are stronger than you imagine...keep a good heart. He will not let you fail. Corragio!: Courage!" Finish the song you have been given to sing and one day you, with your family, will be chosen to sing this new song in His choir:

> The Lord hath brought again Zion,
> And the heavens have smiled upon her;
> And she is clothed with the glory of her God;
> For he stands in the midst of his people.
> Glory, and honor, and power, and might,

Ascribed to our God; for he is full of mercy,
Justice, grace and truth, and peace,
Forever and ever, Amen.

Don't Forget the Broccoli

(Presented to the youth at a LDS homeschooling conference in Nebraska, 2017)

Gladys Aylward was a little woman. She didn't even reach five feet tall, but she possessed a superpower—the greatest superpower of all. When she was growing up, she thought she wanted to be an actress. And by the way, she thought church was pretty boring. But then one day, she went to a meeting that changed her life. For the first time, she felt the love of Jesus Christ pour into her heart and she was consumed with the desire to share it with others.

She doesn't know why—but something inside of her drew her to the Chinese people. She longed to share the love of Jesus Christ with them. People told her she should go to a missionary society and see if they would sponsor her. So she did. After several months of classes, they regretfully told her they didn't think she was smart enough and that she should just settle down and serve where she lived there in England, which she did. For awhile.

But the desire to go to China was like a fire in her bones. She was working as a housemaid, making a pittance, when she was sitting on her bed one day, reading about Nehemiah in her Bible. She said she felt very sorry for him and understood why he wept and mourned when he heard about Jerusalem in its great need and could do nothing about it. He was working as a butler and had to obey his employer, just as she did.

But as she got to the second chapter, she exclaimed out loud, "But he did go! In spite of everything he did go!" As if someone was in the room, a voice clearly said, "Gladys Aylward, is Nehemiah's God your God?"

"Yes, of course!"

"Then do what Nehemiah did, and go."

"But I am not Nehemiah."

"No, but assuredly, I am his God."

She started saving every penny and putting it towards a one-way train ticket to China. And then, at 9:30 on a Saturday morning, October 15, 1932, the train pulled out of the station. She had about $10.00 in her pocket. She waved farewell to her loved ones, not knowing if she would ever see them again. She had been warned that there was fighting going on and that she may not make it to her destination by train, and that proved to be true. So, for the next several weeks, she traveled by train, by foot, by boat and finally a two-day journey on the back of a mule.

At last she arrived in the remote village of Yangcheng. A 74-year-old widow who had been a missionary in China met her, but she died not long after.

And Gladys was alone. Well, not really alone. She had her God.

Home was an old abandoned inn in terrible disrepair. The Chinese thought it was haunted, so no one would live there. The windows were all broken out, but Gladys named it the Inn of the Eight Happinesses. Known as the foreign devil, as she walked the streets, mud was flung at her and she was called all kinds of horrible names. They weren't interested in what she had to tell them.

Now, this inn was on an ancient mule train trail. And you've heard the phrase, stubborn as a mule. Well, Gladys took advantage of that. She went out and pulled the first mule in one of the mule trains into the inn, knowing the others would follow. And once she started feeding them, she knew they wouldn't go anywhere and the mule train driver would have no choice but to come in.

Which is exactly what happened. After they were all fed, she started to tell them stories because they loved stories. Long ago, in a faraway land, lived a carpenter who was gentle and kind. And from these stories, the people started to love this Jesus Christ and one by one, they joined the Christian faith and started gathering together.

By the power of her love, the people came to trust and respect her and they re-named her Ai-Weh-Deh—the virtuous one. Even the great Mandarin was persuaded of the Christian faith.

Well, one day, some shiny silver things were seen in the sky. These remote villagers had never seen a plane before. They ran out into the streets, clapping and laughing and waving at it. And then objects starting falling from them and soon hundreds and thousands of bodies were strewn in the streets. Homes were demolished.

The Japanese had invaded.

Gladys now became mother to over a hundred orphaned children. It was impossible to find food there and it simply was no longer safe. Any day they could be bombed and killed. There was danger everywhere. She learned that Madame Chaing Kai-Shek had set up sanctuaries for children where they would be fed and sheltered if Glady could get them there.

Her friends tried to dissuade her. "It is miles and miles to Sian, and you have no food and no money with which to transport a hundred children."

She replied, "The Lord will provide."

So they set off—one hundred children from ages three to sixteen. The older children carried the little ones on their backs when the little ones grew too tired to walk. There were several mountain ranges to cross, often with nothing more than a mule track to follow. They usually slept by the roadside under the open sky. They had no blankets, so they slept in tight clusters to keep each other warm. They begged food along the way, but often all they had to eat was a thin gruel.

For twelve long, weary days and twelve shivering nights, they struggled on and on until they finally came in sight of the Yellow River. There were still many more days of travel by boat and train and foot and finally one more mountain to climb in spite of their utter exhaustion. This part of the journey was far worse than any they had yet undertaken. They had to scramble over loose rocks and slide down steep slopes. It was a nightmare journey. They slept on the bare ground. Every bone in Gladys' body ached and for days she had been ill.

"Please, God, give me strength to take them where they will be cared for," she prayed.

After 27 days, they at last made it to Sian. But they were rudely halted. The city gates were closed and the gatekeeper refused to open them.

"You cannot come in here," he shouted. "The city gates are closed against refugees. There is no food—nothing. You must go somewhere else."

This last disappointment was almost too much to bear. Then someone took pity on them and told them of a Buddhist temple where children would be cared for. It was a day's train journey away.

By now Gladys was utterly exhausted and too ill to remember much of what happened. But once she knew her children were safe, she bid them goodbye and set out to teach the love of Jesus Christ in other villages. Her next recollection was in a hospital. Evidently she had collapsed. No one knew who she was. She was taken in a cow cart to a mission house. Two days later when a doctor had arrived, he had shaken his head over her. "There is very little hope; she has pneumonia and typhus. Perhaps if we can get her to a hospital, we can save her."

Her bed was loaded in a cattle truck. They scarcely hoped she would be alive by the time they got to the hospital, but she made it and for a month, too ill to talk, conscious of very little going on around her, she began to heal and in time, set off again to share the love she felt in her heart.

And that's how she came to be in a new town. She was penniless, hungry and dressed in rags. A kind missionary couple took her in and fed her and clothed her. There had been a lot of missionary activity in that city and Gladys wanted to go somewhere where she could teach people who had never heard of Jesus. The couple told her there was such a place that hadn't been touched in that city—the prison—the second largest one in all of China.

Gladys was repulsed by the thought. The conditions were deplorable. The inmates were filthy and loathsome. But the Lord told her there were souls that were precious to Him there. Whether she liked it or not, He needed her there.

It wasn't easy to get the Governor of the prisoner to let her in, but she stood on a little mound and began to teach. And started winning hearts to Jesus Christ.

One day, four new prisoners who were chained together entered the prison and were thrown to the ground under heavy guard. Gladys wanted nothing to do with them. She soon found all four were murderers and within a few days, three of them were dead.

The fourth one, Mr. Shan, was young and handsome and arrogant. The Spirit told her to talk to him, and he spit in her face. She said there was something deeply evil about him.

I'll let you hear her own words of what she said happened next:

One day after I had finished speaking, the men formed into their lines to return to their cells. They always had to move at a trot, and not one could speak while moving.

I stood watching them pass, my heart aching for them. By now I knew most of these men. I knew why they were in this place, and though not allowed to speak, I could smile and nod.

Way down the line I saw the man I disliked so much—Mr. Shan, the man who seemed harder to move than the prison walls themselves.

Very clearly a voice said, 'Speak to that man!'

'Oh, no,' I replied. 'He despises me! He actually spat at me. Besides, the law of the prison states I must not speak to him while the line is moving.'

'Nevertheless, you must speak to him.'

What was I to do? A cold sweat broke over me. He was almost up to me. I was so agitated that I leaned forward and let my hand fall on my shoulder, while I burst out, 'Oh, Mr. Shan, aren't you miserable?'

Of all the stupid remarks, I thought immediately.

With a horrible curse he threw off my hand... Mr. Shan passed on, and I realized the awful thing I had done. One of China's greatest unwritten laws is that no woman touches a man in public.

I left that prison depressed and ashamed. Before those men I had defiled myself and with such a man as Mr Shan!

Mr. Shan followed the line and sat on a stone in an inner courtyard, his head bowed in his hands. A few moments later, Dhu Cor, the first man who had been converted in the prison, saw him sitting there.

'Are you going to be ill?' he asked, staring at him closely.

'Did you see what she did?'

'What?'

'She touched me.'

'No. That is a lie!'

'It is no lie. She put her hand on my shoulder.'

'I cannot believe it.'

Another prisoner who had been listening joined in. 'What he says is true. She did touch him.'

'She touched me as if she loved me!' Mr. Shan gasped.

'Perhaps she does love you,' Dhu Cor replied.

'What, a clean woman like her love me, a murderer, who has cursed her and spat at her!'

'Yes, I believe she could because she believes that God loves you no matter what you have done.'

Mr. Shan was converted, not because of a great sermon, but because years ago in London God had taken a girl and asked her to give Him her hands, her feet, her whole body for His use, and that day God had touched Mr. Shan through that poor human instrument.

Mr. Shan's conversion began the real revival in that prison.

And even the governor himself was converted.

Love is the greatest superpower of all. God is Love.

But how important is it that you and I possess it?

Let me put it this way.

One day I asked my husband to go to the store and buy me some broccoli for a casserole I was making. When he came home, he had several bags of groceries on his arms. There was milk and bread and butter, cookies, chips and cereal. Although everything he brought home was good, the one thing I needed wasn't there: the broccoli.

Love is the broccoli of life. Another word for this kind of love is Charity and it means the pure love of Christ.

The Book of Mormon prophets were a little more direct than I am.

Nephi wrote: "Except they should have charity, they were nothing."

Mormon agreed: "Wherefore, if ye have not charity, ye are nothing...cleave unto charity which is the greatest of all."

And his son Moroni, in those final words to us in the Book of Mormon when all his kindred and friends had been killed, felt it important enough to remind us one more time, "Except ye have charity ye can in nowise be saved in the kingdom of God."

Ether said: "Except men shall have charity they cannot inherit the place prepared for them in the mansions of the Father."

And the New Testament prophets said the same.

Peter wrote: "Above all things have fervent charity among yourselves."

And John recorded: "By this shall all men know that ye are my disciples, if ye have love one to another."

To paraphrase I Corinthians, though you should score a perfect score on the SAT, graduate with honors from Harvard, write a New York times bestseller, head up a major corporation, find the cure for cancer or be awarded the Nobel Peace Prize, if you do not have this charity, you are as sounding brass or tinkling cymbals.

On the other hand, though you may never learn to speak a foreign language, fail Algebra twice, cannot compare or contrast two characters in two major works of literature, are never once asked out on a date, live out your life in a small one-room cottage and never do one single notable act in the eyes of the world, if your heart is filled with the pure love of Christ, you will be in possession of the greatest of all God's gifts. And all else will be added unto it.

I remember watching an Oprah Winfrey show many years ago and she had on three guests who claimed that they had died and had gone to the spirit world and then came back to life. I can't verify that that really happened, but I found what they said very interesting. If I remember correctly, two of the three prior to this experience were atheists. They didn't believe in a God. But after this near-death experience, they said not only is there a God, they learned that the only thing that really mattered in this life was how much they loved. And it changed them.

If this love is so important, we probably better find out how to obtain it, right?

If we do it our way, we might set some goals to obtain this love. Maybe I'll do 7 kind acts of service this week and 12 next week. And if I try hard enough, if I just concentrate, I'll teach myself how to love. But I'm afraid that's like trying to cook a piece of toast in the toaster without ever plugging the cord into the power socket.

The Apostle Paul taught us: "And though I bestow all my goods to feed the poor…and have not charity, it profiteth me nothing." Moroni taught, "If there be one among you that doeth good, he shall work by the power and gifts of God."

We can't teach ourselves this kind of love because Charity comes as a gift. And He who offers the gift has told us the only way we may obtain it. We have to do it His way.

This love—this power—this Spirit—fills the immensity of space. It is the Light of Christ that flows from God through Him to us. We're surrounded by it. But it's as though there's a Golden Combination lock on a gateway to our souls—a Sacred Combination. You know how a combination lock works, right?

You have to line up the right numbers and when you do it just right, the lock opens. Well, the Lord has given us the combination to this lock that's within us repeatedly in the scriptures. And when we align ourselves with this combination, this love pours into us along with Joy and Peace and Kindness—all the fruits of the Spirit. This love is also known as Living Waters and whosever drinketh of them shall never thirst again.

Here's the first part of the Combination: Desire. Do you desire this great gift? You may or may not right now. But you can feed and nourish this desire until it begins to grow. Here are some ways I feed this desire.

I spend time in Nature. Nature is God's University and He teaches things to my heart without using any words. I notice how He pays attention to the tiniest detail and when I am in nature, I am surrounded by beauty that fills me with awe and wonder. I can feel His love among His creations.

I treasure up in my heart that which is virtuous and lovely; that which is of good report and praiseworthy. We are taught in the D&C that Light cleaves to Light. I want to give something for the Spirit to cleave to.

I spend time with people who have this Gift. Most of these people I have never met, but I can read their stories like the story I just told you of Gladys Aylward. And, as I read, my heart longs to be like them. My heart wants to feel what they felt. And so with that desire, I seek out opportunities to serve and I continue to nourish that desire as I begin to get a taste of that feeling. I constantly have to nourish that desire. I can't eat one meal and expect it to nourish my body for the rest of my life. Neither can I stop feeding my desire for this gift of charity.

Now, included in the first part of the combination, we have to combine this desire with prayer. Moroni teaches us we are taught to pray unto the Father with all the energy of heart, that we may be filled with this love.

And there is no greater way to feed the desire than to spend time with the One who bestows the Gift. Elder Russell M. Nelson recently gave the challenge to the youth to spend time reading the words and studying the life of the Savior to become close to Him.

Do you remember it was through the stories of Jesus that Gladys opened up the hearts of the Chinese and filled them with the desire to know more?

I know if I desire this great gift, I must spend time with Him—daily—learning of Him and reading His words. As I read them, I am sitting on the Mount as he teaches me how to be happy. I am filled by the loaves and fishes. I am the woman of Samaria—flawed and imperfect, who sits at his feet. I long to drink of the living waters and never thirst again. I am in the midst of the storm and I watch the winds and waves obey his voice; I cast my nets over the side of the boat and they are filled. I am the woman who has touched the hem of his garment and been healed; I am blind and He has given me my sight, I am deaf and He has made me to hear again. I am lame, and now I walk. I am a leper, the outcast of society, and He has made me whole. I hear His voice call to me, though I am dead, "Daughter, arise." I am the woman caught in adultery; He has taken my hand and lifted me up—'Neither do I condemn thee; go thy way and sin no more." I hear his invitation: "Come unto me, all ye that are heavy laden, and I will give you rest."

For I am "the way, the Truth and the Life."

I follow Him into the Garden. I witness His anguish...those drops of blood...they are shed for me. He is mocked and scourged. I follow Him to Calvary and see the nails driven into His hands and His feet—I hear His groans of pain and agony. I fall to the ground and weep. "I tremble to know that for me, He was crucified; that for me, a sinner, He suffered and bled and died."

As I remember all these scenes and more, my heart swells with love and gratitude. Oh, dear Savior, dear Redeemer, Thou hast given me so much, what can I possibly give thee in return?"

And I hear His voice: 'If ye love me, keep my commandments."

Here is the second and vital part of the combination that opens the gateway for the Light to enter: to keep his commandments.

“Yea, Lord, but it seems there are so many of them. Where do I start? I am so weak." And He patiently replies, "Be thou Humble, and I will lead thee by the hand." "By the power of the Holy Ghost, thou shalt know all things that thou must do."

To know what He would have me do becomes my daily quest. I take His name upon me. I want to be His. I hear His voice whisper to me, and I obey because I love Him and want to show Him that love. And somehow, in ways that I cannot explain, in that process of loving and obeying, something begins to happen deep within my soul as His healing Spirit begins to pour into mine. At first, almost imperceptibly. But over time, I begin to notice the peace, the love, the kindness, the Joy, the fruits of the Spirit that begin to adorn my life—a Light that grows brighter and brighter.

He has somehow taken my stony heart and given me a new soft and fleshy one. It is as though I am born again. He restoreth my soul. He leadeth me beside still waters; He maketh me lie down in green pastures. I no longer worry about keeping track of all the ways I may be tempted to sin, for I have lost my disposition to do evil. I am encircled in the warm arms of His love and I never want to leave. He hath purified me and my heart is bound to His eternally.

This is the Sacred, Golden Combination. If you forget it, you'll be reminded every week in the Sacrament prayer. To first, always remember Jesus, which feeds our desire to be near Him. Then, keep His commandments, so that you will have His Spirit—His Love, His Joy, His Peace, His Kindness, His Charity —to be with you always. He invites you to experiment upon this and prove Him herewith.

If you try really hard to keep every commandment, even perfectly, but do not do it from a love of the Savior, the gate remains locked. If you love Jesus, but willfully break His commandments or do not strive to know what they are so that you can keep them, the gate also remains locked. The gift of charity is bestowed upon those who love and obey.

And what a gift it is. In Lehi's vision, the fruit on the tree is the Love of God and is most precious and desirable above all other fruits; yea it is the greatest of all the gifts of God.

It is the pearl of great price that one would sell all he had to possess it. When Aaron taught the father of King Lamoni, who was King over all the Lamanites save a small section and who had been a murderous and idolotrous man—when Aaron taught the king about this great gift, the king exclaimed, "Behold, I will give up all I possess, yea I will forsake my kingdom, that I may receive this great joy."

It is the glad news of the gospel.

And once you possess it, nothing can tear you away from it. Gladys taught the glad news to a hardened general who had been killing and looting and pillaging the villagers. When he tried to share the message with his men and make them stop what they were doing, they took all his clothes and tied him to a mule. For nine months they continued as bandits, burning, looting and rioting. They dragged their general with them and tried in every way to break his faith. He was tortured, starved, kicked, and beaten, but fixed in his mind was the knowledge that he belonged to Jesus Christ.

He finally escaped and wandered for 15 months when he made his way back to Yangcheng where Gladys was and entered the courtyard of the inn as a poor, battered, penniless beggar. As his health improved, the children of the village adored him and hung around him until a year later when he died, still strong in his faith.

Gladys' work brought her to a university where she taught the students and many of them were brought into this gift of the great love of the Savior. When the Communist party took complete control of the university, they did everything they could to break the faith of these students. Exasperated, one day they hauled 200 of them into the market square.

A man had a list of names. He called out the first one—a refined and beautiful girl of seventeen and demanded she renounce her faith. But her voice rang out, clear and strong. "I know Jesus Christ is real."

One after another, those two hundred names were called out, and not one faltered. Every one of them was beheaded that very day in the marketplace.

I read recently of William Tyndale who, in exile, penned many of the words we still find in the King James Version of the Bible. It was a dangerous task and he was finally betrayed by a friend and spent the last year and a half of his life in a cold, dark, damp prison cell before he was burned at the stake. But because of the conduct of his life and his peace and joy, even in prison, the prison guard and his family were all converted.

I read of James, who, by one account, was led by a rope around his neck by the executioner to a place of execution. Along the way, James converted the executioner by the conduct of his life, who was beheaded alongside James for his unwillingness to part with his new-found faith.

And one more—the apostle Paul who at one time had breathed out threatenings and slaughter against the disciples of the Lord.

He wrote: "Who shall separate us from the love of Christ? Shall tribulation, or distress, or persecution, or famine, or nakedness, or peril, or sword?

"Thrice was I beaten with rods, once I was stoned, thrice I suffered shipwreck, a night and a day I have been in the deep.

"In journeyings often, in perils of water, in perils of robbers, in perils by mine own countrymen, in perils by the heathen, in perils in the city, in perils in the wilderness, in perils in the sea, in perils among false brethren;

"In weariness and painfulness, in watchings often, in hunger and thirst, in fastings often, in cold and nakedness.

"Yet...

"I am persuaded, that neither death, nor life, nor angels, nor principalities, nor powers, nor things present, nor things to come,

"Nor height, nor depth, nor any other creature, shall be able to separate us from the love of God, which is in Christ Jesus our Lord."

We are living in the last days; a time when, we are told, we will see commotions and upheaveals and great destructions. And yet, sprinkled throughout these accounts are seen a people who continue to make their way to Zion, singing songs of joy.

These are they who possess this superpower of Love in their hearts.

My dear young brothers and sisters. Your Father in Heaven and your Savior Jesus Christ love you. They want you to enjoy life while you're here on this beautiful planet they have created for you out of their love for you. Do hike the beautiful mountains and ski down their slopes. Go sailing on the lakes and see as much of the world as you can. Play with your friends. Engage in wholesome activities together. Go to dances. Listen to music. Develop your talents. Pursue an education and a satisfying career. Fall in love, marry, have children.

But with all your gettings and all your doings and all your goings, please...

Don't forget the broccoli.

Four Impressions Shared at a Home in Alpine

The first impression. I often hear about leadership education; leadership training; that we need to raise a generation of leaders. It seems good to me. But as I turned to the scriptures to see what the Lord has to say about it, I couldn't find where He taught that. If you look up Leaders, rather than a call to leadership, you find many cautions against leaders who err, leaders who are blind, leaders who lead astray. He reminds us of our weakness—that as soon as we are given a little authority, we tend to start exercising unrighteous dominion.

He teaches, rather, he that is greatest among us is the least; that the last shall be first. He uses the simple and the weak to confound the wise. When Jesus chose His 12 disciples, He didn't go to the learned, wealthy and successful scholars of the Sanhedrin. He chose fisherman. At least 5 and possibly 7 of the 12 were fishermen. His greatest leaders have been reluctant leaders who felt unqualified for the task. Enoch—I am just a lad and am slow of speech and the people hate me. Moses—who am I that thou art mindful of me? David, a shepherd boy. Even in modern days—George Washington felt unqualified, but placed his trust in the strength of Divine Providence and when he was done with his duty, he just wanted to go back home out of the limelight.

Some of the most dangerous figures in history have been those who fancied themselves as leaders. In Ancient Greece, as their Golden Age was fading, the Greeks set up their great Academies of learning in hopes that they could raise leaders—philosopher kings—who could restore their former greatness. Not only did their Academies fail to produce a single leader, they slipped into slavery, never to rise again.

We believe a man must be called of God to lead and He qualifies and prepares those who will fill that role. That's not our job. I believe the Lord, instead of teaching our children to be leaders, would rather have us raise Followers of Jesus Christ who set the example of leading by serving. Consider the image of Jesus, stooped on the ground, cleaning dirty feet. He would have us raise servants, not leaders.

The second impression is tied into the first. We have become a goal-setting world. It is true that we can achieve just about anything we set our sights on in this world by a system of setting and achieving goals. Many people have even mastered admirable character traits through goal setting. Men have accomplished amazing things through vision and goals.

But goal setting is inadequate for the Remnant. That's because "Eye hath not seen, neither hath ear heard, neither hath entered into the heart of man what great things the Lord has in store for those who love Him." There is no vision board for this.

When Lehi was told of a Promised Land, there was no way to map out his journey there because he didn't know where it was. Rather, he and his family spent 8 years wandering around in a wilderness while the Lord taught them that he would give them daily directions according to their righteousness and willingness to follow the Lord.

A person can accomplish great things with his life through goals, but at the end of the day, I imagine the Lord saying, to borrow a little C.S. Lewis, "Yes, you have made of yourself a nice little cottage. But I had intended to make of you a palace." The self-made goal-setting man tends to say, "Look what I have done by the workmanship of mine own hands," not allowing His creator to finish His work.

Years ago I read a statement made by the late Arthur Henry King, one of the legendary BYU professors that struck me because I had never heard anyone say this before: "If setting goals does nothing else, it will tend to occlude the Holy Ghost."

In its place, he suggested this: "If we hold on to one goal in our life—to act righteously at every moment, then all the other goals will fall into place."

Rather than teach our children how to set and achieve goals, maybe we should, instead, be teaching them to, everyday ask the Lord, "Today, what wouldst thou have me say? Today, where wouldst thou have me go? Today, what wouldst thou have me do?"

Often, those instructions don't make sense to us. But as we place our trust in Him, He always leads upward.

I am seeing a trend to get young children to find their personal life mission and set goals in relation to this mission. But many missions aren't revealed until later in life after the Lord has caused a person to pass through many qualifying and preparatory experiences. And many people won't realize they have fulfilled their missions. I thought again of Lehi. How could Lehi have possibly seen or comprehended that it was his quarreling and contentious sons who would launch a thousand year long story that would be condensed down to a small 'seed' by a lonely man and buried in the ground. It would be hundreds of years before it would come forth and bear fruit by instructing and influencing millions of people who would be called to build up the kingdom of God.

The third impression is connected to the second. One of the big goals we often set is to make ourselves financially secure. It's done with the best of intentions. If we can free ourselves from money worries, we can do so much good in the world and serve the Lord. We can go on missions. We can send our children on missions. We can help the poor.

The irony of it is, of all the ways Jesus helped people, there is not one recorded instance where Jesus gave money to help the poor.

He doesn't need our money to serve Him. He's rich and He tells us the riches of the earth are His to give. When we are engaged in His work, He makes us joint signers on His bank account for all we need. But as you do His work, you soon find money often hinders more than helps and that we really don't need very much. He sent His disciples out without purse or script.

There are much more powerful ways to serve than with money. Think of the example of Gladys Aylward.

He has taught me the relative unimportance of money for myself.

When the beginning seeds of Libraries of Hope were being planted, we lived in Alpine. We had a beautiful 6000 square foot home. I loved to sit on my porch and look at the pinks on the mountains and the waterfalls. It was so peaceful and beautiful and there were so many good people around me. I wanted to live there forever.

But over the next few years, our lives turned upside down. There was an illness and then everything we tried to do to earn money, failed. We started selling everything we owned of value to keep afloat. Eventually we literally were facing having nowhere to live and we didn't have a penny in our bank accounts. Our youngest had graduated from high school when my oldest daughter called and said her husband had decided to join the Army and would be away at Officer Training School for several months right when their third baby was due. They had just bought a little home out in the countryside of Virginia. Would we come stay with her while he was away?

When we moved from Denver to Alpine, it took 6 24-foot, jam-packed full moving trucks to move all our stuff. When we moved from Utah to Virginia, everything we needed fit in an 8-foot Uhaul we pulled behind our car cross country. Instead of a 6000 square foot home, I now had my bed on a cement floor in a cold, unheated, unfinished basement, surrounded by storage boxes. I woke up every morning to the insulation hanging down from the ceiling.

My son-in-law deployed for a year and so we stayed with our daughter while he was away. And then they moved away to their first assignment and they let us stay in their home. We moved upstairs. But here we were—out in the middle of nowhere. Church was 30 miles away. The nearest Walmart when we first moved in was 30 miles away. We even lost our only car.

It was in those conditions that the feeling that came to me was, "Well, now that we have all of that stuff cleared out of your life, let's get to work." I was reminded of a charge that I had felt earlier—that I could never let personal profit enter my mind as a motive for Libraries of Hope or He would withdraw His spirit and I would be left to myself. I am often asked, "How do you monetize all this?" I don't. Others have said, "You know, if you developed this into a curriculum where mothers have daily lesson plans, you could make a lot money." I know. But it would all just become an empty shell. That may change in the future, but I'm not the one in charge. And I am content with that.

We went for nearly seven years without an income. But when I quit kicking and crying, I learned for myself that the Lord can and will provide for our needs when we seek to do His work. One day when I was so discouraged, I knelt down and cried, "Oh, Heavenly Father, this would be so much easier if I had money." And the words immediately came into my mind: "If you had money, you would do this your way. I need you to do this my way." Without my husband's technical skills, all of this would just be a picture in my brain. His time, also, needed to be freed up. And so it was. We watched as the Lord inspired hearts to come to our aid—and then watched Him bless the lives of those who helped us who often helped at great personal sacrifice. At times, He provided miraculous means. In some strange way, I came to feel more secure without an income than I did when I had a padded bank account. Mostly He changed my heart. I have come to know that sometimes the Lord breaks our hearts so that He can reach and fill the deeper places. As He started to fill up the treasure within my heart, I lost my desire for 'things.' I felt satisfied. And then, one day, not long ago, one of those miracles came when a business opportunity was dropped in my husband's lap—something he had never done before but is now providing a very comfortable living while yet allowing flexibility of time to continue this work.

I'm not suggesting at all that you run out and sell everything you own or quit your job. It's not wise nor does the Lord expect us to get in line for such an experience. These tutorials are custom designed. They come in many forms, but all for the purpose of learning to trust in Him.

The reason, I think, I felt to share this is because some of you are afraid to do some of the things I talk about because you fear that it may interfere with your child's chances of getting into the right college so that he or she can earn the right income and secure themselves financially. That may be a good strategy for some people. But for some of the Remnant, it won't be right at all.

I have a sense that some of the most important roles in the days to come are going to fall among the artists— that it's the musicians, the painters, the poets and the writers who serve to warm and teach hearts of people who will make the biggest difference. Often our children are steered away from those fields because they can't make any money in them. That's not a new thing. Many of the world's greatest artists, musicians, poets and writers had fathers who wanted them to study law so they could have positions of prestige and financial security. As lawyers, we would never have known they ever lived. But as artists, their contributions are priceless and their names live on. Starving artists and starving musicians are a real thing. Yet, it may be that very process of starving that will break the heart of that individual so that the Lord can reach and fill the deeper places. And artists need to feel deeply.

We tend to want to make our children's lives cozy and comfortable and secure. It will take a special kind of courage to allow some of our children to take different paths. And to trust the Lord's way.

Which leads me to the fourth impression.

Your greatest accomplishment as mothers in this day will not be to make scholars of your children. Your greatest accomplishment will be to teach your children to know and to love the Lord—to attach their hearts to His. And once you do that, you can be reassured all will be well because the young heart grows to become like that to which it is attached. The character traits you try so hard to teach and instill in your children will be a natural outgrowth of that bond and far more effective than specific lessons on character.

We tend to instruct by telling our children from the very beginning all the things they have to *do* to get back to their Heavenly Father—but hearts are not attached through doctrine, words, and rules. We attach hearts through the arts, especially story, first. It gives the why and then the how is embraced.

When Gladys Aylward first went to China, she was called the foreign devil. Everywhere she went, she was shunned and mud was thrown at her. She got nowhere until she started telling stories: "Long ago, and far away, in a land called Palestine, there lived a carpenter who was gentle and kind." From these stories, hearts were converted so thoroughly, when the Japanese occupied their villages and demanded they deny Jesus, these sweet people who felt wrapped in the love of their Saviour, chose to starve, be tortured, lose all their worldly possessions, and even die rather than be separated from that love.

What does this have to do with education? It has everything to do with it because Jesus Christ is the source of light and life and love and He is being cut out of the process of learning.

Brigham Young taught: "Mothers, let your minds be sanctified before the Lord, for this is the commencement, the true foundation of a proper education of your children."

As you purify your life through your love of the Lord, you will be a conduit through which His light will flow to your children and if you have created fertile soil by warming their hearts, they will begin to be taught by Him. Isaiah saw our day when "all thy children will be taught of the Lord and great shall be the peace of thy children." This doesn't mean to be taught *about* the Lord; it means to be taught *by* the Lord. By introducing academics at younger and younger ages, we are hardening the hearts and deadening the spirits of our children and this process of learning is being disrupted.

Let Our Joys Be Known

Keynote Address LDSHE Homeschool Conference, Logan UT (2019)

Some years ago, I was telling the story to my little granddaughter who was 4 or 5 years old at the time, about the time her mommy got married. As part of the story, I told her how much, from the time I was a little girl her age, I wanted to play the harp. Every time I saw a picture of a harp, I'd get so excited and it's like my fingers ached to pluck those strings. I kept begging to play it and my dad finally told me if I did dishes every day for a year, he would buy me a harp. I wish I had taken him up on the offer! Because I was nearly 50 years old before my dream came true and I've certainly done a lot more than a year's worth of dishes! Oh! how I loved playing that harp. Sometimes when I'd walk by our living room and see my beautiful pedal harp standing there, I would pinch myself. I finally had my harp.

And then one day, I told my granddaughter, her grandpa got really sick. And he couldn't work. And some other hard things happened and we lost all our money and we had to move out of our beautiful home and we didn't know how or where we could move. And in the middle of those hard things, her mommy told me that she was going to be married. We were so happy for her! But I was sad, too, because I wanted her mommy to have a pretty wedding dress and I didn't have any money.

And then, I thought, if I could sell my harp, we would have the money we needed. I knew the family next door had girls who were learning to play the harp and I asked them if they would like to buy it. They said they would and told me they would come by the next night to pick it up. All day I cried and cried and cried. I didn't want to sell my harp. But then I looked straight into my granddaughter's eyes—we both had tears in them—and I said: "I loved my harp. But do you know what? I love your mommy more than I loved my harp."

We sat there in silence for a few moments. I could tell she was processing the story—and then she ran off. A little while later she came back with a picture she had drawn to capture what she was seeing. There I was, with tears streaming down my cheeks, sitting out in a little boat, selling – sailing—my harp.

Even the little fishies have tears on their faces.

I love this sweet picture and I treasure it, not only for the memory of that moment we shared, but as a reminder of how often our words are misunderstood and how inadequate words can be to say what we want to say.

We use the same word—*awesome*—to describe the birth of a new baby, a sunset, and a quarter pound cheeseburger. Are they really all the same experience?

And the deeper our hearts feel something, the fewer words there are to express it. Remember the Nephites as they gathered around the resurrected Lord?: "…no tongue can speak neither can be written by any man… So great and marvelous things as we both saw and heard."

The deeps of the soul like the deeps of the ocean are silent—where words are concerned.

Yet, from the time a child can pick up a pencil, we lead him carefully into the world of words, eager to show him how to form letters and decode their sounds. And we begin to fill his head with facts and information.

Please don't misunderstand me. Words are wonderful and useful! But there are places in the heart too deep for words alone.

Let me offer a simple illustration.

Imagine you are walking down the street and you notice a man walking on the other side of the street. After a few moments, a second man comes up from behind and taps the first man on the shoulder. The first man turns around and after a brief interchange, he reaches into his pocket, pulls out his wallet and hands the second man a hundred-dollar bill. The two men then walk away in different directions.

What is the fact of what you just saw? You saw a hundred dollars transfer ownership from the first man to the second. It is an indisputable piece of information. Is that all you need to know?

Let's try again and this time I'm going to add the story so your heart can understand what you just saw. What if I told you the second man was a robber; when the first man turned around, he said, I've got a gun in pocket, hand over all your money, or else.

Or, let's try this. What if I said the two men were old friends. The second man was down on his luck and had previously phoned his friend and asked if he could borrow a hundred dollars and they had agreed to meet there.

Or what if it was the other way around? What if the first man had been the one to borrow the hundred dollars and he had asked his friend to meet him so that he could pay him back?

Let's go back to the first robber scenario. What if I told you the first man was a multimillionaire? No, let's say he had been unemployed for several months...no, let's say several years. He has just been to the bank and withdrawn his last hundred dollars. He has a little girl at home and she is sick. In fact, the doctor told him if he didn't get medicine for her right away, she was going to die. He was on his way to get that medicine and now his money is gone.

Isn't it interesting—that same hundred-dollar bill yielded greed, joy, sorrow, anguish, gratitude, love, despair and annoyance. The fact that it was a hundred-dollar bill really was the least important piece of information of all. It gave us a point of reference, but that was about it. And notice—if I were to ask you to tell me in words what greed or joy or anguish feels like, could you?

The heart understands things that cannot always be expressed in words or directly taught. But still, it knows. And as the fox in *The Little Prince* so rightly observed, "It is only with the heart that one can see rightly. What is essential is invisible to the eye." It is this realm of the heart that separates humans from machines and it's all these feelings that make life worth living.

The Apostle Paul teaches us to look not at the things which are seen, but at the things which are unseen; for the things which are seen are temporal—and temporary—; but the things which are not seen are eternal. (2 Corinthians 4:18)

On earth, the richest man is the one with the most money. In heaven, the richest man is the one with the greatest capacity for joy. Man is that he might have joy. God's greatest gift to us represented as the fruit on the tree in Lehi's vision is His love and in that love is a fulness of joy. Heaven's treasures are the unseen but very real gifts of the heart and they are everlasting.

> Thrust a man into prison and bind him with chains, and then let him be filled with the comfort and with the glory of eternity, and that prison is a palace to him. Again, let a man be seated upon a throne with power and dominion in this world, ruling his millions and millions and without that peace which flows from the Lord of Host—without that contentment and joy that comes from heaven, his palace is a prison. When a person is filled with the peace and power of God, all is right with him. (Brigham Young)

And outward circumstances fade in importance.

Heaven's ways are not man's ways. The last several months, I've had two images placed on my inward eye that I have been studying that has deepened my understanding of this idea of the seen and the unseen; of the differences between the world's ways and heaven's ways.

The first image is a tower—like the tower in Babylon. I notice the purpose of the tower is external. The tower is designed so that one can climb the path that circles round and round the outside of the tower with the intention that one will eventually be able to climb all the way to heaven by his own efforts. Although artists have depicted the tower with windows, when I look inside, it is dark and empty. It is not designed to go inside. The tower climber's progress is visible to everyone. Tower climbers can compare their progress with other climbers. Those higher up on the tower feel confident and self-assured; they are in control of their destiny, while those lower down often feel overwhelmed and discouraged. There are yet so many stairs to climb. And sadly, some of those highest on the tower look down upon those who are far behind. So focused are they on their own climb, they offer no helping hand to those farther down the tower.

Although the tower was never finished, I picture that had it been completed, it would have eventually come to a point at the very top where there is room for only one person to stand. I wonder how many other people the climber has to push out of the way to claim the spot. And although that tower climber will see how much higher the heavens are above him, he will be powerless to take one step further. He will have reached his limit; the peak of his performance.

The second image is a temple or a holy place. By contrast, I notice the temple is filled with Light because it is designed to go inside for in its innermost sanctuary is found a holy of holies where one can commune directly with God and be lifted by His power and glory. The work that goes on in the temple is not on display for public view or scrutiny. The temple dweller is compared with no one. The work that goes on within temple walls is private and personal.

Babylon is used to represent the ways of the world. And don't we see it all around us? The world is concerned with all the outward things— the size of our bank account; how many awards we have received, how many letters behind our name. We obsess over the size and shape of our body, how beautiful we are, what kind of clothes we wear. We are conditioned to climb to the top of the class, climb to the top of the corporate ladder. We must aim to be #1—to be the winning team, to be the fastest runner, the highest scorer. There is only one winner. The rest are all losers. It's an endless push to the top. Yet, for those who make it, they often look around and say, "Is that all there is?" And they look for another tower to climb. After all, it's lonely at the top.

We very much use a tower model in education. From the moment a child starts the climb, he is constantly compared with other climbers. We test and measure to see how high up the tower he has climbed. We talk about levels all the time. We congratulate ourselves when our children score on a higher level than the average child and panic when they fall below level. But we are only testing those outward things that can be tested and measured—which completely excludes the inward condition of the heart.

For most students in this system of learning, as they walk across the stage and pick up their diploma, rather than a commencement to a lifetime of learning, it's a conclusion. Studies show that the majority of graduates will never pick up another book, and if they do, it certainly won't be a book of history or poetry or great literature. They've reached their peak of learning.

Here is a visual of the difference I see between the world's way and heaven's way. The world works from the outside in. But heaven works from the inside out. Let me try and explain.

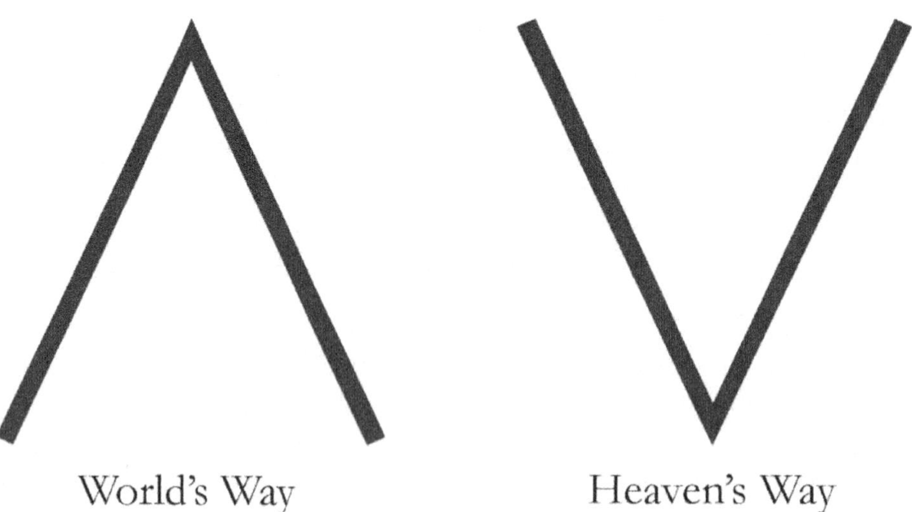

Everything the Lord teaches has layers of meaning. A single letter in the Hebrew alphabet is said to have 70 layers of meaning, with the number 70 also having a layer of meaning. When we stop at the literal or outward meaning, we are shortchanging ourselves. For example, from the days of Adam, man was taught to sacrifice animals unto the Lord. Yet, it wasn't the outward act that pleased God— through Isaiah, He said: I am sick of your sacrifices. Don't bring me any more of them. I don't want your fat rams; I don't want to see the blood from your offerings. He was trying to teach an inward meaning which they were so slow to grasp because they were so focused on the outward compliance.

In fact, at a Passover feast, while over a million diligent, obedient followers brought their unblemished lambs to be sacrificed, the true Lamb of God was being sacrificed on a cross just outside the city walls. And they knew it not.

It's significant that we are a temple building people. I love going to the temple where I am surrounded by peace and beauty and order. But I have to ask myself is there also an inward meaning?

Of course I believe there is. I believe one thing the Lord is teaching us is how to build an everlasting temple within our hearts—a place of beauty and peace where He can come and commune with us for He promises—"if a man love me, he will keep my words: and my Father will love him, and we will come unto him, and make our abode with him." Didn't Paul teach, "Ye are the temple of the living God and as God hath said, I will dwell in them, and walk in them." We go to the Temple to receive an endowment of power. An endowment is a gift and God's power is Love. Love—or Charity—is His greatest gift to us. "Without charity, ye are nothing." As my invited guest, He brings His gifts of love, joy and peace.

I cannot expect Him to dwell in my dirty bathroom. I must prepare a place where He can come—a place fit for a King.

No expense is spared in the building of our temples. The finest materials are gathered from around the world with great effort and attention is placed to the tiniest of details which are all designed to lift our thoughts heavenward. My inward temple requires nothing less. Every thought, every deed, every picture that hangs on the wall of my temple within must be pure and worthy of Him.

Marion G. Romney taught: "The only safety we have in the world for our children is what they build within themselves."

When the Lord is the center of our lives—the very core of our being—I see an upside-down tower. Everything which God does is about gathering, increasing, expanding, layering, multiplying, lifting–there is no end or limit. There is no peak. His joy is not that He made it to the top; His joy is that He is lifting myriads of His children to enjoy all He enjoys. They are made joint heirs to all He has. His glory and His influence will continue to expand infinitely. Eternal life means there is no end.

As you seek to educate your children, are you focused on climbing the tower or on building a temple where the Spirit of the Lord magnifies all we do? Are you more focused on that which is seen or on the unseen? Do you care more about test scores or the condition of their hearts?

Samuel lived in a world not unlike ours. A spiritual indifference had settled in. The Israelites were deserting God and drifting toward material gods they could see with their eyes and handle with their hands. And 'Everyone did what was right in his own eyes.'

Samuel's remedy to the conditions of his day was to establish a school for young men—a school of the prophets—as a barrier against the widespread corruption. These were not prophets as we might think of one—someone who has been called and ordained to a position of authority by one who is authorized to do so. These were prophets in a more general sense—A prophet was someone who saw the unseen things of life through spiritual eyes and who could recognize and comprehend the voice of the Lord, or as Elder Uchtdorf beautifully expressed it, they could "hear the music of the spirit." Because of their spiritual sensitivities, the Lord could write messages on their hearts that they would in turn deliver to the people. And as Amos taught, the Lord will do nothing, save He revealeth his secrets—his truths—unto his servants the prophets. Moses wished: "Would God that all the Lord's people were prophets, and that the Lord would put his spirit upon them!"

We see many, many prophets appearing among the people throughout the scriptures, who aren't necessarily called by one in authority, but they are delivering messages. John Widstoe taught: "In ancient and modern times there have been schools of prophets... These 'prophets' need not to be called to an office; they go out as teachers of truth." And yes—we are cautioned to beware of false prophets.

Samuel started this first school of prophets in his home at Ramah. I found this name interesting because it sounds just like the Greek word *rhema*, which means the spoken word of the Lord. It's divine illumination, a divinely inspired impression upon your soul, a flash of thought or a creative idea from God. It is the still, small voice deep within our hearts. The hard heart and literal mind cannot comprehend this voice. It is with this voice the Lord speaks within the temples of our hearts.

It appears Samuel's primary concern was helping these young men develop their spiritual sensitivities so they could hear the voice of the Lord. Other schools were started as well. The teacher was referred to as Father and the students were called sons of prophets, showing a warmth in relationship between student and teacher.

A couple of hundred years later the schools had fallen into decay and much of the work of Elijah and especially Elisha was to restore these schools and put them back in proper order. Which was vital to what came next—the scattering of the seed of Israel. Remember—the Lord promised that through the seed of Abraham, all nations would be blessed and this scattering of Israel was necessary to fulfill this promise. My reasoning tells me these schools prepared a remnant of prophet-servants who would carry and plant His messages throughout the world. We are given an account of where a couple of these seeds landed—Lehi, a prophet—carried the truth to the Americas and as I study the teachings and traditions of many of the Native American tribes, I see threads of truth that have been passed down for generations.

We know that Daniel landed in Babylon and was highly influential in the royal courts of both the mighty Babylonian and Persian Empires, which is primarily the land of today's Iraq and Iran.

And although we have no direct record of proof, I can't help but wonder if some wandering prophet met up with Socrates, who, not long after the scattering, started teaching of the inner light and the one true God or Confucius who, after his travels, returned home and started teaching to do unto others as ye would have them do unto you and the importance of family and honoring your ancestors among other truths designed to make one happy. Around that same general time, Buddha started teaching a people of an afterlife, of the importance of loving, kindness and compassion, to not lie or gossip or use rude speech, to not kill or cause injury, to not steal, to be morally pure, to not seek material gain but rather purity of thought and a focus—an eye single—to higher unseen things.

And although scholars don't agree as to when Zoroaster the Persian lived, many believe it was around 600 BC—which places him in the time of Daniel who was also in Persia. Could Daniel or his equally righteous friends, Shadrach, Meschach or Abed-nego have influenced Zoroaster who taught of the freedom of the individual to choose right or wrong. That by thinking good thoughts, saying good words, doing good deeds, we increase the divine force and come closer to being One with the Creator. The magi were the priests of Persia and hundreds of years later, they were watching the skies for the sign of the birth of a King.

In modern scripture, the Lord tells us He is gathering His elect from around the world. And who are His elect? He says: "...mine elect hear my voice and harden not their hearts." (D&C 29:7)

So wouldn't you like to know what curriculum was used in this ancient school of prophets that softened the hearts of these young men so they could hear the voice of the Lord? Although we have been given very few details of exactly what went on in these schools, we are given some scattered hints. We know they were taught the laws of God and were counseled to live lives of righteousness and purity. But here are a few other subjects that were taught.

Music

The sons of prophets learned sacred music.

Saul was told that maybe Samuel could help him find his father's lost donkeys. As he headed toward Samuel's home, a band of the sons of prophets met him coming down the hill playing various instruments of music.

Music has a powerful influence on our inner lives. Movie makers know that music makes the sad parts sadder, the happy parts happier and the scary parts scarier.

The greatest possession of The Daghda, the god of Irish mythology, was his harp. He could make anyone who heard it laugh for joy or weep for sorrow and by the playing of his harp, the seasons came in their correct order. When enemies came upon his fighting men, his playing would make his men forget their fear, and they would charge into the fight thinking of nothing but honor. At the end of the day, his song would take all the weariness out of the hearts of the survivors, and helped them forget their grief over their fallen comrades.

His enemies, knowing of the power of this marvelous harp, one day stole it. When the Daghda discovered it was missing, he immediately set out to search for it and found it guarded by a formidable guard of soldiers. He simply called to it and it flew to his hands, awakening the guards. His aid whispered, "I think you'd better play your harp."

The Daghda struck the strings with his hand, and called out the Music of Mirth. In spite of themselves, the enemies began to laugh. They laughed so hard that the weapons slipped out of their hands, and their feet began to dance. But when the music stopped, they snatched up their weapons again, and started to advance.

Again, the aid whispered: "I think you'd better play your harp!" And this time, when the Daghda struck the strings, he called forth the Music of Grief. All of the Formorians began to weep. The children wailed, and the men hid their faces in their cloaks so that no one would see the floods of tears they were in. But when the music faded, they took up their weapons again.

And then the Daghda struck the strings of his harp so softly that it seemed it would not make a sound. But he brought forth the Music of Sleep, and, though they struggled to keep their eyes open, every last guard fell down into slumber.

The Daghda and his men left them sleeping there, and stole away. And never again was the harp of the Daghda stolen.

Jehoshapat chose singers to lead his mighty army into battle, and they sang: "Thank the Lord, because His love continues forever." And the enemy was destroyed by unseen hands.

When Elisha's advice was sought in the fighting of a great battle, he first called for a harpist, and when the harpist played, "the hand of the Lord came upon him" and he saw clearly what to say.

When Captain von Trapp opened his mouth to sing in *The Sound of Music*, his hard heart was softened and joy came back into their home.

The voice is the great connector between mind and heart. It is said that it was the attention the Greeks placed on oral expression that caused them to be the most artistic of peoples. Greek children were raised on the recitation of poetry—evidently they didn't have a separate word for music—rather than on written language, like we do. Their writings were great because they were founded upon and developed by their speech—by their voice.

According to tradition, lessons in the schools of the prophets were primarily oral.

And if the voice is the grand connector of mind and heart, the hymn is the grand connector of heaven and earth. We receive divine communication through hymns that cannot be delivered in another way. There is a reason why we sing a hymn before the opening prayer is offered and before we take the Sacrament. It opens and prepares our hearts.

I serve as the organist in my ward and it falls on me to select the hymns we sing in Sacrament Meeting. A year ago, last January, I was choosing the hymns for January and February. I had just one hymn left—the intermediate hymn for the last Sunday in February. As I flipped through the hymn book, it opened to a hymn that we never sing and my first reaction was to keep looking because I know that my ward doesn't like to sing unfamiliar hymns. But as I went to turn the page, I had a strong impression: they may not like to sing unfamiliar hymns, nevertheless, someone is going to need that hymn that day. So I added it to the list I submitted and put it out of my mind.

The Friday before that last Sunday in February, I got a phone call from my daughter in Utah. I had been sick in bed for a week and was feeling miserable. Her baby was due in just a couple of weeks and I had my plane tickets in hand to go out and welcome this new little man-child into our family. In our family of girls, a boy is a rarity and we were all excited. After we chatted a bit, my daughter said, "You know, mom, the baby has been really quiet today." I said maybe it's time and he is resting up for the big event. But I told her she should probably check in with the doctor.

A couple of hours later, she called back. “Mom, there is no heart beat. I've lost the baby.” I've heard the question posed which hurts more—a broken bone or a broken heart. I know how I would answer that. She said they were going to induce labor that very night and I cried buckets of tears all night long as I thought of my daughter going through the pains of labor with no hope for a happy outcome.

She called about noon the next day. “Mom, he is so soft and warm. Practically perfect in every way.” There was no apparent reason why his little heart had stopped beating.

The first plane I could catch was Sunday afternoon so I went to church to play the organ Sunday morning. As we began to sing the intermediate hymn, that impression came back to me: Someone is going to need that hymn that day. And I realized that someone was me. There are only 3 hymns in the hymn book that are written as though the Lord is speaking directly to us. This is one of those hymns. These are the words:

> Lean on my ample arm, O thou depressed!
> And I will bid the storm cease in thy breast.
> Whate'er thy lot may be on life's complaining sea,
> If thou wilt come to me, Thou shalt have rest.
> Lift up thy tearful eyes, Sad heart, to me;
> I am the sacrifice offered for thee.
> In my thy pain shall cease, In me is thy release,
> In me thou shalt have peace eternally.

I shared the hymn with my daughter and her husband when I got there and it played through my heart that whole week. I watched its fulfillment as my daughter and her husband stood and bore testimony to a chapel full of friends and family of the love of God and that peace that surpasseth understanding.

Surely He speaks to the deepest parts of our hearts through the hymns and other inspired music.

In the midnight hour, in the dark, damp dungeon in which the naked, hungry and weary Paul and Silas were cast, they sang hymns and the prison walls crumbled around them and the prisoners were freed.

Is it a wonder that prior to entering the Garden of Gethsemane, Jesus prepared for the ordeal by singing a hymn? According to Jewish custom, the hymn that was sung following the Passover supper would have lasted nearly an hour, and included the words:

Thou art my God, and I will give thanks unto thee; For his loving kindness endureth forever.

President Nelson begins his day by playing the hymns and Johann Sebastian Bach on the organ. He says: "By the time I leave home in the morning, my mind is filled with good things—the scriptures and fine music. This gets my day off to a good start better than any other way I've found."

I'm afraid today's popular music is desensitizing our youth to this language of the heart. I listened to a young man from Sierra Leone tell his story of how he was kidnapped as a pre-teen and forced to kill as a child soldier. The way they numbed these young boys to commit such atrocious acts was to blast loud rock music 24 hours a day which kept them from feeling or thinking anything. Strong, repetitive beat shuts down feeling. And that is the nature of today's popular music.

I saw a video that showed all 40 of today's top hits are based on the same four repeating chords. The same two composers are writing nearly all the music for today's top performers and they are using familiar hooks to draw listeners in.

Leading them away from this kind of music is a challenge we face. One thing you can do is counter by using their tricks—make inspired music the familiar music to your children.

The great music masters approached their Maker in reverence as they sat down to compose. Their intent was to reveal the very glory of God to human hearts. What a priceless gift to us. Pay attention to the music that is surrounding your family in your home. And sing. I wish there was time to talk about the power of melody and harmony in the souls of our children. But that will have to wait for another day.

Let's turn to the second subject, which, for lack of a better word, I have labeled **Imagery**.

God spoke to His prophets through visions and dreams and through pictures He would place in their minds. Symbolism with its layers of meaning is used abundantly. And for good reasons. We say 'in one ear and out the other,' but we don't say 'in one eye and out the other.' Dr. Rich Melheim, wrote that "while the human ear can process 10,000 bits of information per second, the human eye can process up to 7 billion bits of information per second. Therefore, neurologically speaking, a picture is not worth a thousand words. It's worth 700,000 words." It's a very efficient means of communication.

Leonardo da Vinci said, "I hear it and it's gone. I see it and it is there again. And again. And again..."

When someone is explaining something to us, how often do we say, "I don't see what you are saying" and the response is "Let me illustrate it for you." Without the power of image-ination...imagination, the ability to create inner images, we cannot see God or heaven or eternity in this life. We cannot empathize with others because we cannot see what they are experiencing. We can only create that which we first 'see' in our mind's inner eye. Without vision, the people perish.

"Logic will get you from A to B. Imagination will take you everywhere."

So although we don't have specific evidence of what was used to increase in these sons of Prophets the power of Image-ination, it must have been part of their training.

And nurturing the Image-ination must be a vital work in the education of our children. One wonderful tool we have to work with are the visual arts. For many centuries, there was little written language. People relied upon paintings—pictures—to learn about the Bible. Consider this experience of one man:

"The first time I saw Raphael's *Disputa*, which decorates one of the walls in one of the rooms of the Vatican in Rome. I had set out with my guidebook, intending to study all the paintings by Raphael that decorate these rooms. I entered the first room, and I suppose looked around the other walls, seeing three other paintings, but all I recall during this visit was the *Disputa*. I sat down before it and remained seated! I do not know how long, but the morning slipped away. What I thought about as I looked at the picture I cannot tell you. My impression is that I did not think at all; I only felt. My spirit was lifted up and purified and strengthened with happiness. Returning to my hotel, I read about the picture in my guidebook. I noticed things that I had missed...[but]the whole subject as far as it could be put into words had escaped me. I had no knowledge what the painting was about; only I had felt its beauty."

Now contrast this experience with the learning objectives I pulled off the Virginia State Standards list, which begin in the First Grade:

"Demonstrate understanding of the elements of art: Color, form, line, shape, space, texture, value, balance, contrast, emphasis movement, pattern, proportion, rhythm unity, variety. Identify, analyze and apply criteria."

Again...starting in the First Grade.

Where is the part about opening children's inner eyes to see the beauty in all the world?

"The heart and soul of the masterpiece, the sheer beauty of it, are considered least of all, and students end up heartily hating something they might have enjoyed and loved... It is better to create a capacity to enjoy art than to have a technical knowledge of its pieces."

And now I have a sad story to tell you. By the mid-1800s, artists had discovered the greatest secrets of art—the rules—that made it possible to communicate profound messages to human hearts instantly.

When I came across this work of art, I was so captivated by it, I couldn't stop looking at it. It stirred feelings I can't put into words. It was painted by W. H. Gore and when it was first exhibited in a London gallery in 1885, one of the premier art critics of the day who was used to examining art through a critical eye, broke down and wept. Any sister, daughter, wife, mother,

Enlisted by William Henry Gore

friend who has sent a loved one off to war knows the meaning of this painting, which is entitled 'Enlisted' and the ribbon on his cap designates him as an enlisted soldier. But without even knowing that, I felt the sorrow of separation; of the resignation of doing a hard thing because it's the right thing to do, even when you don't want to.

This painting was created in an era of classical realism, which lasted from around 1848 to 1920.

About twenty years ago, a lover of art who had studied art history at a graduate level at Columbia University came across a work of art from that era that had stirred powerful emotions in him, like we've been talking about—and he couldn't figure out why he had never, in all of his studies, heard of the artist before. Upon investigation, he discovered the intellectuals of the early 1900s looked down on this kind of art as sentimental and unsophisticated. They despised storytelling in art. So they completely erased it from all the university textbooks and from all the courses of art history in our schools. Museums put many of the paintings into storage.

It has been his work through the Art Renewal Center to restore these beautiful works of art to public awareness and also to preserve the knowledge of those secrets the artists of this era had mastered and pass them along to a new generation of painters.

I went through all 80,000 art images that are archived in his site and guess who I bumped into all over the place? Mother! And although sometimes she is barefoot, she isn't repressed, miserable or trapped; she is content, joyful; she is beautiful.

And I found Father. In the last 50 years, we've gone from Father Knows Best to Father Knows Nothing to Who Needs a Father. But here he is! He is working hard to provide for his family. He is strong and protective. His children adore him and he adores his children.

I found sisters with their arms around each other. I found families happily engaged in work and play and learning—all over the world!

And I found dear, beautiful Mother Nature everywhere, nurturing her children!

Some years ago, the American Psychiatric Society estimated that the average American child will have seen some 200,000 violent acts and 14,000 murders by the time he is 18 years old. I suspect that number is much higher today. The visual impressions made on a child's tender heart last a lifetime. How many images of beauty and love will they have come in contact by the time they are 18? If you want to strengthen your families, let these be the last images they see hanging on their walls when they go to bed at night and the first they see when they rise in the morning.

"You must look at pictures studiously, earnestly, honestly. It will take years before you come to a full appreciation of art; but when at last you have it, you will be possessed of one of the purest, loftiest, and most ennobling pleasures that the civilized world can offer you." -- John Van Dyke

Now there is something else you can do to awaken that inward eye—sketch what you see.

When the camera was invented, John Ruskin traveled around teaching people to not stop sketching just because it was so much easier to capture a picture with a camera. He said the danger was that they would lose the ability to really see. And how prophetic he was. There is so much in the world we look at but never really see.

We would do so much to counter the damage we are doing to our children's hearts by encouraging them to draw before we teach them to form letters. Drawing produces an exactness of thought. Those who take a sketch book out into nature see infinitely more than those who do not.

Drawing is a way to capture feelings in a way words cannot.

Poetry

The Sons of Prophets were taught sacred poetry.

The prophets of the Old Testament were all poets—and to the literal mind, their teachings are difficult if not impossible to understand. A poet sees pictures in his mind. He doesn't say what he has to say in plain language, rather he gives one picture after another, giving us comparisons that make us think of his meaning. When you combine these images with the rhythm of music, the message is carried deeply into the heart.

History teaches us that when a people have lost their heroic spirit; when their hearts have grown cold, it's not the scholar or the scientist who fans the flame again. It's always the poet—a Pindar in Greece, a Thomas Moore in Ireland or a Lord Alfred Tennyson in England—who rises up and breathes new life and plants new hearts in nations. No wonder there were so many poet-prophets who appeared in Old Testament times. And it is exactly one of the prescriptive medicines we need today.

Do you remember that wonderful opening scene in the movie Dead Poets' Society where Robin Williams stands up in front of his class and tells his students to rip the dry introduction pages out of their poetry textbooks and then follows with these memorable words:

"We don't read and write poetry because it's cute. We read and write poetry because we are members of the human race. And the human race is filled with passion. And medicine, law, business, engineering, these are noble pursuits and necessary to sustain life. But poetry, beauty, romance, love, these are what we stay alive for."

I was at a library sale a couple of weeks ago and picked up a thick 1927 anthology of poetry. I was reading reviews of the book and smiled at this comment:

This book contains "all the classics you should know to get you through everything if you don't want to spend money on therapy."

> O poet, what power lies in thy magic wand! No sooner dost thou touch us, the dull gray day is aflame with color and sunshine.

A poet can capture in just a few lines what a scholar may attempt in 1000 pages and still fall short. In fact, poets have captured in these two short poems the message I will spend 90 minutes trying to convey.

King's daughter!—There is a volume of meaning right there!
Wouldst thou be all fair,
Without—within-Peerless and beautiful, A very Queen?
Know then;—
Not as men build unto the Silent One—
With clang and clamor, Traffic of rude voices,
Clink of steel on stone,
And din of hammer; —
Not so the temple of thy grace is reared.
But—in the inmost shrine
Must thou begin,
And build with care
A Holy Place,
A place unseen, Each stone a prayer.
Then, having built,
Thy shrine sweep bare
Of self and sin,
And all that might demean;
And, with endeavor,
Watching ever, praying ever,
Keep it fragrant—sweet, and clean:
So by God's grace, it be fit place—
His Christ shall enter and shall dwell therein
Not as in earthly fane—where chase
Of steel and stone may strive to win
Some outward grace—
Thy temple face is chiseled from within.

I love that last line—Thy temple face is chiseled from within.

Here is the second poem:

Two Temples

A builder builded a temple,
He wrought it with grace and skill;
Pillars and groins and arches
All fashioned to work his will.
Men said, as they saw its beauty,
"It shall never know decay;
Great is thy skill, O builder!
Thy fame shall endure for aye."

A mother builded a temple
With loving and infinite care,

Planning each arch with patience,
Laying each stone with prayer.
None praised her unceasing efforts,
None knew of her wondrous plan,
For the temple the mother builded
Was unseen by the eyes of man.

Gone is the builder's temple,
Crumpled into the dust;
Low lies each stately pillar,
Food for consuming rust.
But the temple the mother builded
Will last while the ages roll,
For that beautiful unseen temple
Was a child's immortal soul.

--Hattie vose Hall

Poetry seems to have fallen out of favor today. In our hectic ever-rushing noisy world, poetry requires us to slow down and feel; the meaning cannot be sensed by the literal mind; it requires a heart comfortable with imagery.

Story

A story is moving pictures attached to feelings. Sons of prophets were taught the stories and history of their people. They gathered all the legends and traditions of their heritage and it's largely due to the copywork of these stories in the Schools of the Prophets that they have been preserved for us.

Stories show us life in action and allow us to see life through a thousand different eyes rather than through the narrow view of our own experience.

Orison Swett Marden's sweet mother died at the age of 22 when he was only three years old. While he didn't get to keep any pictures, his entire life he could see with his inner eye her beautiful face and her auburn hair as she tucked him in his bed. His grief-stricken father—a tall, rugged 6-foot-2 man—took on the role of father and mother in their backwoods home in the hills of New Hampshire. He not only carried on his duties of farming, hunting and trapping, he took care of all the household tasks of cooking and cleaning and sewing and caring for the three little children left behind. Orison cherished the memory of the little Christmas outfit his father stayed up late to sew for him.

He loved his father. But one day, an accident with a bear trap ended his father's life. Orison now had no home. He was separated from his sisters, this little boy of seven, and was sent to homes who took him in as the 'hired boy' who was required to work hard to earn his keep. He would pass through five such homes before striking out on his own. He was cuffed and whipped, starved, worked to the limits of human endurance, abused and insulted. There was no one to give him comfort or love or answer his questions. Yet, it was out of the bitterness of his own experiences—his joyless childhood and the utter starvation of body and soul—that he was able to learn the glorious secrets of real happiness.

And he came to learn for himself to build a temple within his soul.

That journey began with a story. When he was in his early- to mid-teens, he happened upon a dilapidated copy of a book stored away in an attic. It was written by a Scottish man named Samuel Smiles—the book was called *Self Help*. It was written to give hope to the young people of Scotland who were living in such dire conditions. Orison wrote: "I felt like a poor man who had just by accident discovered a gold mine." It was a book of stories; stories of great men and women who had overcome hard challenges in their lives. It lit a fire of hope in his own heart, and by sheer perseverance and push, he went on to graduate from the Harvard School of Medicine and the Boston University School of Law within a year of each other as well as earning degrees in science and art. He put himself through school by working in hotels—which he later owned.

Then came the depression of the late 1800s and he experienced great financial loss, including the loss of his hotels. Yet, it wasn't growing a hotel empire that held his heart. For fifteen years, he had used every spare moment to gather stories of great men and women because he wanted to do for the youth of America what Samuel Smiles had done for the British youth—and for him. It was his way of paying it forward.

He was preparing the manuscript from his thousands of pages of notes he had gathered when a fire broke out in the hotel where he was staying. He escaped the fire with nothing but his nightshirt on. His labor of years went up in smoke.

But not one to be discouraged, he immediately walked down the street to buy some necessary clothes, and then he bought a twenty-five cent notebook, and while the ruins of the hotel were still smoldering, began to write from memory the manuscript of his dream book.

Of course he was overwhelmed and heartbroken. He had little money, but with what he had, he bought a train ticket to Massachusetts, rented a small, plain room and diligently continued his work of writing. After a short time, he made three manuscripts of the book, sent it to three local publishers, and all three of them offered to publish it.

Pushing to the Front became a runaway bestseller. Letters poured in from presidents like William McKinley, Theodore Roosevelt, the British Prime Minister William Gladstone, kings and rulers from around the world, telling him of how it had influenced their lives. A noted educator of the Italian Parliament strongly recommended the book be made obligatory reading in the schools of Italy, because he regarded it as a 'civilization builder.' The government schools of Japan and Peru and other countries adopted it into their studies. Thousands wrote and told how the book aroused their ambition, changed their ideals and aims, increased their confidence, and how it had spurred them to the successful undertaking of what they before had thought impossible.

He went on to write 50 more books. Yet, for all the fame and fortune, he understood the true secrets of happiness—the treasures of the heart—and that's what he taught and lived.

I have devoted most of my time for the last 15 years to the gathering of stories in my Libraries of Hope. It has not been an easy journey—in the beginning, most of what I did was met with apathy.

One day I was particularly discouraged and I knelt down in my basement and cried to the Lord. Could these stories really make a difference? And I immediately felt a strong impression, "Go upstairs and turn on the radio." which I did. Just then, the commentator on the radio said, "Stories can heal our nation."

I believe with all my heart that stories not only have the power to heal our nation, they can heal the world because they shape individual hearts. The destiny of the world does not lie in the outward battles—it lies within the hearts of individuals and the stories we come to love and believe in shape our hearts.

As we daily invite great and noble souls to dwell with us within our temples through their stories, they begin to serve as ministering angels to us and teach us the ways of happiness. Kings and queens, prophets, poets, sages, great musicians, artists, scientists and explorers can be the daily companions of our children through stories. If only we would be wise enough to quit using the study of history as a study of facts and information in youthful years and instead use it as a study of lives; if we would quit having our children analyze components of literature and instead let its life examples freely speak to their souls, we would see a seismic shift in our culture.

I keep a notebook of Great Souls. I create a page for each one who comes into my home and teaches me—adding pictures if I can find them, jotting down stories I want to remember and especially pieces of wisdom for happy living.

Sample "Great Souls" Notebook Page for Beatrix Potter

Oliver Goldsmith

1728-1774

Writer - The Vicar of Wakefield

IRELAND

Often he shared his pittance with some one more wretched than himself. One cold night he gave his blankets to a woman with five children, and crawled into the ticking of his own bed for warmth. p. 35

His clothes being too poor for him to be seen on the streets, he pledged the money to be received for four articles, bought a new suit, went up to the court of examiners . . .

. . . AND WAS REJECTED!

HAD ANY OF THESE POSITIONS BEEN OBTAINED, THE WORLD, DOUBTLESS, WOULD NEVER HAVE KNOWN THE GENIUS OF OLIVER GOLDSMITH.

His monument is in the Poets Corner at Westminster Abbey.

THE GREATEST HONOR ENGLAND COULD OFFER.

When he was buried, the stairs of the building were filled with the poor and the forsaken whom he had befriended. He conquered the world by hard work, kindness, and a gentleness as beautiful as his genius was great.

Still in debt, overworked, labouring sometimes far into the night and the morning hours, not leaving his desk for weeks together, even for exercise,

GOLDSMITH DIED AT 45.

broken with the struggle for life, but with undying fame.

LIVES OF POOR BOYS WHO BECAME FAMOUS

Sample "Great Souls" Notebook Page for Oliver Goldsmith

Here is my grandmother—who inspires me when I get discouraged. When a crop would fail…again…she would calmly say, "Next year will be better." And move on. I have a separate notebook for lessons I glean from great souls in literature. These are great treasures to me and have influenced me beyond anything I can describe.

Notebook page of my Grandmother, Esther Marie Lanzen Johnson

I'm not jotting down facts and information; I'm holding on to things that feed my soul.

When you consider the three brief years of Christ's earthly ministry, he didn't leave us volumes of brilliantly crafted written discourses to persuade us. He left us a handful of stories. The example of His life was the greatest story He ever told.

Music, Imagery, Poetry and Story—these are four languages of the heart. We call them the Arts. "Each art is a distinct language which expresses some aspect of the human soul and realizes some truth apprehended in no other way." Happy is the person who becomes fluent in all of them. These languages soften the heart and enable us to hear the delicate still, small voice of the spirit. Hard heartedness blocks it.

Childhood—especially the first eight years of life—is divinely reserved for awakening these languages of the heart through a process of immersion. What beautiful imagery we have in baptism by immersion as a symbol of being reborn into spiritual things—to be able to see the unseen kingdom around us through spiritual eyes. Blessed are the pure in heart, for they shall see God—they shall see God in the stars and the flowers and the trees, in works of fine art, music and literature, in the pages of history and in the chapters of their lives. To deprive a child of these languages is to cause them to remain dormant, or worse, to atrophy from disuse. Our focus on academic learning in childhood is hardening the hearts and blinding the spiritual eyes of our children.

Charles Darwin, the great scientist, experienced this atrophy:

> If I had to live my life again I would have made a rule to read some poetry and listen to

> some music at least once every week; for perhaps the parts of my brain now atrophied would thus have been kept active through use. The loss of these tastes is a loss of happiness, and may possibly be injurious to the intellectual and more probably to the moral character, by enfeebling the emotional part of our nature… Formerly I was led to the firm conviction of God and of the immortality of the soul… In my journal I wrote whilst standing in the midst of the grandeur of the Brazilian forest, 'It is not possible to give an adequate idea of the higher feelings of wonder, admiration and devotion which fill and elevate the mind.' ... But now the grandest scene would not cause any such conviction and feelings to rise in my mind… Disbelief crept over me at a very slow rate, but was at last complete. The rate was so slow that I felt no distress.

Pestalozzi, a heart educator of the 18th century, wrote: "When men are anxious to go too fast, and are not satisfied with nature's method of development, they imperil their inward strength, and destroy the peace and harmony of their souls… The schools hastily substitute an artificial method of words for the truer method of nature, which knows no hurry, and is content to wait."

Nature herself is a child's best first classroom, for it is filled with the languages of the heart—a perfect immersion experience.

Continuing with the story of Orison Swett Marden, he wrote:

> Everything in Nature seemed to speak to me to try to make up to me for my homelessness and loneliness. I loved every bit of it. Often in an ecstasy of emotion I would throw my arms around the trees and hug them—They filled me with a sense of the very presence of God, and I felt that I could read His thoughts in the flowers, in the grass, in the trees, in the birds—in all the beauty He created.
>
> Something spoke through all these things to me; gave me assurance and hope, and in a measure satisfied my hunger for love. When out in the sunshine, under the blue sky, I could not believe that I was left quite alone in this great universe… This love of Nature was a special refuge. I only knew that I was happy when out in the fields or in the woods, listening to the birds and watching the butterflies and the bees gathering honey from the wild flowers whose fragrance and beautiful color delight my heart…

And he offers a suggestion to you mothers: "When you are jaded and worn from the strenuous life of motherhood; when exhausted after a year's run, struggling with the daily problems that face you—it is to the 'everlasting hills' you must turn for help and renewal… 'I will lift mine eyes unto the hills, from whence cometh my help.' You must go into God's laboratory, the great outdoors, where Mother Nature will…lay her healing hand upon you…and in due time, send you back to your tasks, as new women."

I frequently hear moms say something like this: "I don't know what to do with my 6-year-old. He would play outside all day if I let him. He will not sit down so that I can do school with him." And what is it that she is so anxious to teach him? Periods, commas, semicolons and a smattering of facts and information.

There is a time for that. But please—childhood is for far more weighty things! Neuroscientists can see an intellectual shift in the brain of a child at around age 8. Prior to that age, their hearts are wide open to receive impressions that will lay a foundation for a lifetime. Yet, if your children are older, it is never too late. As C.S. Lewis wisely observed: "You cannot go back and change the beginning. But you can start where you are and change the end."

Jesus loved the sea, the mountains, the groves of trees, the gardens, the hills of Galilee.

Frederic Farrar in his *Life of Christ*, writes:

"The schools in which Jesus learnt were not the schools of the Scribes, but the school of holy obedience, of sweet contentment, of unalloyed simplicity, of stainless purity, of cheerful toil.

"Had Jesus received the slightest tincture of the technical training of the Scribes, he would have been less, not more..."

"In the depths of His inmost consciousness, did that voice of God...commune with Him. ... Written on His inmost spirit, written on His most trivial experiences, written in sunbeam, written in the light of stars, He read everywhere His Father's name. The calm, untroubled seclusion of the happy valley, with its green fields and glorious scenery, was eminently conducive to a life of spiritual communion...from which he drew food for moral illustration and spiritual thought."

It was in the hills around His home where He would have gathered the lessons of the sparrow, the mustard seed, the Good Shepherd.

Living among the poor in Nazareth, home was likely his school as a boy. His teachers were his earthly father, Joseph and his mother, Mary, who would have sung the beautiful hymns into his heart in infancy and would have planted the stories of the prophets into his imagination.

Mothers, like Mary, nurturing hearts of children is your divine gift. And I see evidence and events lining up that tell me that God intends to re-establish schools of prophets in our day of spiritual indifference—but this time, in homes with Mother and Father as teachers.

When Joseph Smith organized the Relief Society in 1842, he said, "I now turn the key in behalf of you" which Elder Packer interpreted as in behalf of all women and Emma said, "We are going to do something extraordinary."

History bears out that, from that time, something extraordinary started happening for women—for all women. Opportunities for education started opening up. She was given rights—no longer would she be chattel to her husband. In 1888, the women of the world gathered to organize a society for women. I am pretty sure the original organizers would be horrified to see what it has become. In the beginning, mothering was the central idea of the new movement. Ironically, the leaders of the movement—Frances Willard, Susan B. Anthony and others— were not married and had no children of their own. But they recognized the vital influence of the mother-heart and the importance of mother-love. In her inaugural speech, Frances said, "Mother-love works magic for humanity." "It is our task to make society more pure, more free from vice, than it has ever been before." Their call to 'home and humanity' was met with overwhelming enthusiasm.

The wonderful advances of modern technology have now freed women from many of the labor-intensive tasks she used to have to perform. Now we can push a button and a machine washes our dishes. Push another button and our clothes are washed. Drive to the store and pick up food. Instead of fighting off starvation, we are fighting eating too much!

What all this means is we have reached an age where women are free to take on holier and higher labors, if we will.

Marden wrote:

"The very foundation of our national life is laid in the home, and the wife and mother is the center, the mainspring of all true home life... Our wives and mothers have as yet hardly entered the outer chamber of the beautiful edifice of the ideal home of the future. It is the holy of holies...and in it lies the very secret of human progress. The highest civilizations have scarcely as yet glimpsed the possibilities of home."

And he added:

"The time will come when our children will be taught...to consider beauty as a most precious gift...and regarded as a divine instrument of education. Beauty is a quality of divinity, and to live much with the beautiful is to live close to the divine. Every beauty in any form...refines and elevates character."

Frances Willard echoed his thoughts:

"The time will come when we will be told as a relic of our primitive barbarism that children were taught the list of prepositions and the names of the rivers of Thibet, but were not taught the wonderful laws on which their own happiness is based, and the humanities by which they could live in peace and goodwill with those about them."

Frances and Orison said 'the time will come.' I believe that time is now and you are the first generation of mothers to arrive on the scene when all things have been prepared for you to accomplish something extraordinary and angels are standing by to assist you.

I say the first generation of mothers because look at the curriculum for the heart that has just been delivered to your homes—to your primary classrooms—for free. Mothers did not have access to this curriculum even ten years ago.

YouTube now makes it possible for you to listen to and watch the most inspired music ever composed, performed by the finest musicians around the world. Leonard Bernstein will bring his entire New York Philharmonic orchestra to your kitchen to play for you while you do your dishes. "Maestro—could I hear that one again?" "Certainly." You have front row seats to the Bolshoi Ballet or the Metropolitan Opera. Without leaving your living room.

A simple Google search will pull up hundreds of thousands of images of fine art that have previously been hidden away in private manors and estates, palaces and museums, accessed only by the very wealthiest. Our children, in a single afternoon, can take in more works of art than kings and queens of the past might have taken in during an entire lifetime.

Internet Archive has now digitized over 25 million books—and the number grows by hundreds every single day. They've made them available for us to read in our homes for free. While our public libraries are clearing their shelves of the classics and that which is ennobling and inspired, Internet Archive is providing enough of the best books at your disposal to last a lifetime. From your home, you can read ancient and modern poets; ancient and modern works of literature; endless works of history and stories of great lives. When you think of how few people in the history of the world ever learned to read let alone have access to books, our generation is blessed beyond measure.

We are living in the great day of the harvest. When those seeds of truth were scattered and planted in all nations, kindreds, tongues and people, they passed through the hearts of great and noble souls and were preserved in music, visual arts, poetry, and stories of folklore, history and great literature. If feelings, ideas, pictures, and deeds are the materials with which we can build our inner temples, this generation has just been gifted with the highest and noblest curriculum for the heart that has ever been created.

It is a day for the children to turn their hearts to the lessons learned by their fathers and then pass them along for the generations who follow. To ignore the work of the past is to make a waste of all the Lord has so carefully prepared in order to be able to raise up a generation capable of establishing His kingdom upon the earth.

As Luke reminds us: "A good man out of the good treasure of his heart bringeth forth that which is good."

It is time to gather the truths that have been scattered into one great whole. As I have been feasting on this great harvest of knowledge, I clearly see God's hand in the history of the world; that God loves all His children, for he has planted among all people everywhere seeds of truth that will lead them to live happy and joyful lives. The Hand of God is not revealed in the world of facts and information with which we commonly surround our children. It is revealed to the heart through the Arts.

Where much is given, much is expected. Sadly, we are surrounded by all stirring things, unmoved.

So what needs to happen next? We need mothers who are willing to re-learn the art of cultivating hearts through the arts because they must awaken a desire in their children to start reaping; we need moms who can sing songs into the hearts of their children.

Years ago, when I started my work of gathering stories, I was asked how I planned on marketing my books. I was told children don't like to read anymore, especially old books without pictures. The truth was, I had no marketing plans. In fact, I had no money to market them even if I had a plan. I was simply acting on an impression. And the thought that was planted deeply in my heart was that the Lord was preparing a network of mothers and when the time was right, He would begin to write messages on my heart that when these mothers heard them, they would resonate within them, and they would want to know more.

I believe you are the very mothers He has been preparing.

I am watching the fulfillment of that promise unfold and am humbled every single day when I get letters from mothers around the world, who frequently say they don't know how they found me, but when they heard the message, it resonated in their hearts and they want to know more. They are starting to gather together and form Mothers of Influence groups for the purpose of helping each other learn how to cultivate the arts—the languages of the heart—in themselves and in the hearts of their families. I've prepared a free Mother's University filled with resources to draw from. And moms tell me of the increased light and joy they are experiencing as they add more of the Arts into their lives. It's like a flood of living waters flowing on parched ground.

Which is exactly what Ezekiel saw in vison. He saw living waters flowing from the temple into the barren lands round about.

As temples dot the earth—not only the physical temples, but the temples within the souls of millions, the light of Christ that will fill them, His living waters, will flow outward and righteousness will flood the earth, as Isaiah saw.

And as desolating scourges and whirlwinds overtake the earth in the final scenes, those who have built temples within their souls will find a Holy Place to stand, wherever they are. And their shining example—like the shining stars against a black sky—will be an influence for good for everyone around them.

I think of the Apostle James. As he was being led to the place of execution where he was to be beheaded, because of his countenance and the conduct of his life; his perfect peace and joy within, his very accuser was converted to Christianity, and by the declaration of his new found faith, willingly went to the execution block himself that selfsame day.

I think of William Tyndale, who penned so much of the beautiful poetic language of the King James Version while in exile. The world, as it always does, thanked him by locking him up in a damp, dark prison cell for the last two years of his life before tying him to a stake and burning him. But because of his kindness, his humility, the conduct of his life, the jailer and all his family were converted.

And I think of Jesus Christ, mockingly clothed in purple robe and crown of thorns, standing in majestic silence before the most powerful worldly rulers of the day—when has a more influential sermon ever been preached? As Frederich Farrar wrote: "All things are done by Him in majestic silence."

Who we are always speaks far louder than the words we say. And for that person who has built a temple in his soul where the Spirit of the Lord feels at home, a power much greater than words always flows outward. While man organizes marches, slogans, studies and lavish PR campaigns to effect change in the world, Jesus' way is much simpler: Let your light shine.

Julia Ward Howe, who, under divine inspiration, gifted us The Battle Hymn of the Republic, wrote:

> One night I experienced a sudden awakening. I had a vision of a new era which is to dawn for mankind and in which men and women are battling unitedly for the uplifting of the race. There seemed to be a new, a wondrous permeating light, the glory of which I cannot attempt to put in human words—the light of new-born hope blazing. And then

> I saw victory. All of evil was gone from the earth. Misery was blotted out. Mankind was ready to march forward in a new era of human understanding—the era of perfect love, of peace, passing all understanding.

This is the dream of the ages, the hope of mankind from the beginning. It is your privilege to play a key role in its realization. "Awake! Awake! Put on thy strength, O Zion! Put on thy beautiful garment—and the Gentiles shall come to thy light, and the kings to the brightness of thy rising."

If you find yourself on that weary climb up the tower, I invite you to climb down and tend instead to gathering materials with which to build temples for you and the souls of your children.

When you leave this room, most of the more than 10,000 words I have thrown at you will have blown away. You may have captured a few words with your pen and pinned them onto your paper. But the rest are already gone. It is likely you have some images that have been stamped in your memory. Many of you will remember a story I told—at least enough to tell the essence of it to someone else—but already the details will feel hazy.

What will you hold on to? You will remember how you felt. And if I have done my job, a seed of desire has been planted in your heart to do something. And now if you tend and water that seed, it will begin to take root and will continue growing until one day it will bear fruit. If it is a good seed, you will multiply and replenish some measure of love, light, joy, peace and beauty in the world—for these are the heavenly and everlasting prized fruits the Lord of the vineyard is watching for.

In closing, This Is My Wish for You

> That the spirit of beauty may continually hover about you
> And fold you close within the tenderness of her wings.
> That each beautiful and gracious thing in life
> May be unto you as a symbol of good for your soul's delight.
> That sun-glories and star-glories
> Leaf-glories and bark-glories
> Flower-glories
> And the glories that lurk in the grasses of the field
> Glories of mountains and oceans
> And little streams of running waters
> Glories of song and poesy
> Of all the arts
> May be to you as sweet abiding influences
> That will illuminate your life and make you glad.
> That your soul may be as an alabaster cup filled to overflowing
> With the mystical wine of beauty and love.
> That happiness may put her arms around you and wisdom make your soul serene.
> This is my wish for you.

(Poem by Charles Livingston Snell, 1914)

"The whole world is full of unworked joy mines. Everywhere we go we find all sorts of happiness-producing material, if we only know how to extract it." (Orison Swett Marden)

May we diligently learn this art of joy extraction, using it to build our temples within, and then heed the invitation extended by hymnast Isaac Watt:

Come, we that love the Lord
And Let our Joys Be Known.

Come, We That Love the Lord: Using the Arts in the New *Come Follow Me* Curriculum

(Presentation delivered at LDSHE Homeschool Conference, Logan, Utah, May 2019)

I hope you had a chance to listen to the keynote yesterday because I laid a foundation for what I want to talk about today. Yesterday I gave the why and today I want to talk more about the how. But before I get started, you may be wondering where I am coming up with what I am telling you. So let me briefly tell you my story.

This is my family. You can see we specialize in girls. My husband, Brent and I have raised eight daughters and one son.

I have always been restless where education is concerned. So we public schooled, private schooled, charter schooled, homeschooled, unschooled, online schooled, and combinations of all of the above. By the current educational standards, you might say we were a success. All nine of our children have graduated from universities with several of them earning higher degrees. We are proud of their hard work.

But I always felt like something was missing.

Several years ago as our youngest was getting ready to leave home, I got involved in a project that made me seriously look at the question: What is the purpose of education? I had read a study where 365 people were asked what they thought the purpose of education was. And they received 365 unique answers. Isn't that interesting that we are trying to find a one-size fits all model of education when we can't even agree on the why. What I wanted to know was what is God's view? What is His purpose for education? And what are His methods?

I spent the next year or so in intense study, starting with 16 volumes of the *Teachings of the Prophets* as well as the four standard works. They became my measuring stick for truth as I then started studying various educational philosophies out there.

I took hundreds of pages of notes, and all those words distilled down to two simple essences:

I have come to believe that God's purpose for education is to prepare children to live lives of maximum joy. Does He not teach us "Man is that He might have joy?" Did we not shout for joy? Would His purpose for education be separated from the highest He hopes for us to achieve? A career may certainly be part of that path, but I don't see that as the ultimate objective.

And His method can be summed up in a simple phrase I found in Charlotte Mason's writings:

"True education is between a child's soul and God." He reserves, to Himself, the role of teacher.

When we read, "And all our children shall be taught of the Lord," I don't think it just means 'about the Lord.' I read that the day will come when "all our children shall be taught by the Lord."

So, in my mind, it shifts our role as the disseminator of knowledge—something even a machine can do—to that of an artist, preparing the hearts of our children to be taught by Him, which I talked about yesterday.

But how do we do that?

As part of my search, I was led to a wonderful circle of educators who I call the heart educators. They have become some of my dearest friends. I happen to spend a lot of time with dead people. Through their writings, which have only recently surfaced again, I feel surrounded by them and they teach me something new every single day.

I have been gathering and sorting and sharing their writings through my website, Libraries of Hope where you will find, among many things, a Mother's University. Mothers are joining with other mothers in Mothers of Influence groups to learn how to use the arts to cultivate hearts. It's all free and you can learn more at welleducatedheart.com.

As I continued to learn, a simple pattern for learning emerged.

Today's schools are very much focused on training the minds of our children. You know you are in the realm of the mind when what you are teaching can be measured and tested. What is 9x9? Who was the first president of the United State? The mind is fed with facts and information. We associate the mind with the realm of science, which is all about discovering the laws, rules and principles upon which everything in the universe functions. So we teach our children the rules of spelling, the rules of grammar, the laws of thermodynamics. Rules and laws create order. They are good and desirable.

Learning for the mind is systematic and sequential. You need to know arithmetic before you can study algebra. But the big challenge of this kind of learning is it's very hard to hold on to by itself. We test kids on Friday and on Monday, a lot of what they learned is gone.

We call this kind of learning academic learning. Have you ever looked up the word 'academic'? I did. Some of you know this. The dictionary says: having no practical importance, not involving or relating to anything real or practical, having no practical or useful significance.

And we don't just want academic learning. We want rigorous academics. *Rigorous* and *rigor mortis* have the same root word—*rigor*—which means stiff even voluntary submission to pain.

Over 2000 years ago, Aristotle understood something we seem to have forgotten—Educating the mind without educating the heart is no education at all.

Learning in the heart cannot be measured or tested. Lessons are delivered through feelings and impressions and through the imagination. Love is the foundation of all lasting and meaningful learning. This kind of teaching requires the use of the arts that reach deeply into the heart where words alone cannot travel. Yesterday I talked about these languages of the heart which stir our souls and awaken desire. This stage of learning can be spontaneous and random because it goes into long term storage. So we have the luxury of time to connect and make use of it. By the way, we can prolong the lifespan of facts and information by attaching them to a language of the heart. For example, we are able to hold on to 26 letters of an alphabet in a certain order because we attached them to a song. What does that tell you that you can do to help doctrines and principles stick?

And now, the third and most important and most neglected part of the pattern for learning—the role of the Spirit, which comes to us through Light or a sort of Spiritual Sunshine. The source of this Light is Jesus Christ.

I believe Parley Pratt sums up the role of the spirit very nicely:

This Light "...quickens all the intellectual faculties, increases, enlarges, expands, and purifies all the natural passions and affections, and adapts them, by the gift of wisdom, to their lawful use. It inspires, develops, cultivates, and matures all the fine-toned sympathies, joys, tastes, kindred feelings, and affections of our nature; inspires virtue, kindness, goodness, tenderness, gentleness, and charity. It develops beauty of person, form, and features. It tends to health, vigor, animation, and social feeling. It invigorates all the faculties of the physical and intellectual man. It strengthens and gives tone to the nerves. In short, it is, as it were, marrow to the bone, joy to the heart, light to the eyes, music to the ears, and life to the whole being."

No wonder the Lord is so anxious that we receive the Spirit into our lives!

The Spirit operates in the realm of faith because we cannot tangibly see or touch it. We can only sense its presence.

The Spirit is all about Creation—fitting a right-use—or rightuseness—righteousness—to all our learning for the purpose of increasing love, beauty, joy, goodness and truth in the world—all the riches of eternity. Our learning needs an expressive outlet; an application. The difference between the beautiful sea of Galilee and the Dead Sea is the Dead Sea has no outlet. When we start piling up learning for which there is no use, the learning starts stagnating inside of us and deadens us. Like Mr. Rogers taught: "It's not what you possess, but what you do with what you possess, that really matters."

The world was not created from nothing. The Lord went to where there was matter unorganized, and organized it. The biggest obstacle to the work of the Spirit in our lives is we give it so little to work with. What are our questions—our interests—what are we bringing from our own studies?

As we fill our hearts with all that is good and true and beautiful and then align ourselves with correct principles and laws, the Spirit can do much with our lives and put our learning to good use.

Michelangelo filled his heart and labored hard to master important skills, but he acknowledged that 'his Unassisted heart was barren clay.' He recognized the necessity of divine influence on his work.

Heaven is anxious to help us as we learn and can fill in gaps and make sense of our learning. For example, I was at a large book sale and out of all the hundreds of books laid out on a table, I felt drawn to a book about Greece. In it, I learned about the poet Pindar—who I had never heard of before—and how scholars credit his influence with ushering in the Golden age of

Greece, which was of special interest to me because I was learning all about the importance of the arts on civilizations.

But I wondered in my heart who had influenced him and stirred his heart. I happened to be standing in front of one of the bookshelves in my basement and felt drawn to a particular volume of children's stories I had never looked at before. I pulled it off the shelf, and it opened to a page about Pindar and there I learned there were two women, Clyrtis and Myrna—two renowned singers—who sang songs into his heart as a boy. I was astonished! I never would have found that on my own. I wanted to share this story of Pindar and I wanted to have an illustration of these two women and a Google search had come up empty. As I went to bed, I heard something fall off of my nightstand. So I got down on my hands and knees to see what it was. While I was down there, under my bed, I found an old children's book—among other things—that I forgot I even owned. I picked it up and the first picture it fell open to was this picture of Pindar as a boy with the two women, Clyrtis and Myrna. You may call it a coincidence, but coincidences like this happen all the time in my learning. Many of you have experienced the same thing.

The Spirit is very purposeful in its teaching. Each one of us has come into the world with a divine purpose—a special contribution each of us is to make. Only the spirit can help us navigate the tsunami wave of information we are surrounded by and lead us to the things which we need to know to accomplish our purpose. There are hidden treasures of knowledge buried all over the world and the spirit is waiting for the chance to lead someone who cares enough and is open enough to be led.

But look what we are doing. For the first 15 or 20 years of a child's life, every single day we tell him what he will learn, what book he will read, what we expect him to get out of it. We ask all the questions and let the child know when we are satisfied that he has learned what we have determined is important for him to know. It's an outside-in model of teaching. What room do we leave for the Spirit to teach? What opportunities do we give our children to be guided in the way I have described? I believe we have got to quit interfering with the spirit's role as teacher in the lives of our children. Our job is to prepare their hearts, teach them the importance of correct principles and then get out of the way.

All learning under the influence of the Spirit is infinite and eternal.

Take away the spirit and the heart in education, and all that's left is purely academic.

I now find this pattern for learning all over the place. Just as a few examples—

In our time, we were first given the Book of Mormon—primarily a book of stories, starting with a family. Then came the Doctrine and Covenants—a book of laws and principles—and then the Temple where spirit-to-spirit learning takes place.

I find it in individual scriptures everywhere—even our Sacrament prayer—where we are taught to always remember Him, the realm of the imagination, keep His commandments that we might always have His spirit to be with us.

There was a John the Baptist to stir and prepare the hearts of a people to receive Jesus and His law of the gospel which was to prepare them to receive the gift of the Holy Ghost who would teach them all things that they must do.

I find it in history—the Greeks are remembered for their love of Art and Beauty. The Romans, for law and justice and then came Jesus, teaching of a spiritual kingdom.

It's in nature. A seed will lie dormant until the ground warms up. Without a strong root system—the part that is unseen, just like our hearts—the plant will never bear fruit or flower. And it's within the fruit or flower that the seeds are contained by which to multiply and replenish the earth.

You may notice that yesterday I tried to plant a seed of desire in your heart so that you want to know more. Today, I'm teaching principles and giving you more information. But the most important part will happen after you leave when the Spirit gives you understanding and helps you apply what you have learned into your life.

I could go on all day giving you examples, but I hope you catch the idea. The takeaway here is always tend to the heart before you tend to the mind.

This pattern very much applies to the teaching of the new Come Follow Me curriculum. I've noticed how much it is designed around these very principles. Let me recap a few of the things Elder Holland taught.

"What the Lord is really hoping to change is you and me... He wants to change our hearts."

I am not alone in noticing that we have a heart surgeon leading our church today. The heart is the center of our desires and moves our actions. Change the heart, and you change the world.

"This kind of learning is...too big to fit in a classroom to be wrapped up in a 45-minute lesson... The everyday curriculum of life itself provides opportunities for us to learn about God for surely 'all things bear record of Him.' He is willing to teach us...anywhere and anytime.

"Home is classroom and lab, where learning and living the gospel are so seamlessly combined that they are almost indistinguishable."

I love all these things he said. There is no separation between temporal and spiritual learning in the Lord's eyes. One thing that means is that your study of History, Math, Nature, and Literature can be a continuation and provide examples of the principles you are learning in Come Follow Me...if you are looking.

I noticed there are fewer words in the new manuals as compared with older manuals. Mr. Rogers taught that all true learning happens in the white spaces between the lines and we have been given a lot of white space. It is purposely designed to allow for adaptation, personalization and inspiration as to how to best teach your family.

And there are many suggestions for incorporating the arts because the arts reach places in our hearts that words alone cannot. I was in Ireland a few weeks ago and we visited the Book of Kells exhibit at Trinity College. I noticed they named the exhibit: Turning darkness into Light. And it struck me—how did they do it? They used colorful art to illuminate the words of the scriptures. The more you apply the arts in your teaching, the more light you will bring. And the way that they made the illumination pop off page was by the use of layering. We learn line upon line, precept upon precept, here a little and there a little. That's layering and one day it's like the light goes on.

So let me offer some resources and ideas, starting with Music.

A song is a wonderful kind of thing, so lift up your voice and sing.

Just start a glad song, let it float, let it ring, and lift up your voice and sing. We shall make music to brighten our day. Music will help us to lighten the way.

Lift up your voice, lift up your voice, lift up your voice and sing.

I hear so many moms say they are sad because they can't afford music lessons for their children. But guess what—children come equipped with their first and most important instrument—their voices. We have made singing a performing art and if we can't sing like a performer, we say we can't sing. But it's simply not true. I just demonstrated that you don't even have to sing on key to receive all the benefits.

Music is a language all children—even the very youngest—can understand. We are all deeply and profoundly musical. If you don't believe me, when you leave this class, try walking to your next class out of rhythm. Or try talking out of rhythm. It is nearly impossible.

I was thrilled when I saw that sharing time in the new Primary program is to be all singing. What other activity can every child participate in at the same time? Voice is the great connector of heart and mind and the doctrine that our Primary songs and hymns will plant in our children's hearts will last a lifetime. Singing these songs, according to the First Presidency preface found in the front of all our hymnbooks, will invite the Spirit of the Lord, bring families a spirit of beauty and peace, inspire love and unity among family members, lift our spirits, give us courage, and move us to righteous action. Those are wonderful promises, aren't they?

Like I said yesterday, movie makers understand the power of music. Musical soundtracks make the sad parts sadder, the happy parts happier, the scary parts scarier. Hymns and Primary songs can provide the soundtrack to gospel doctrine. Especially in childhood, I would rely more on singing than on speaking words.

There is a goldmine of Primary songs and hymns that go unsung. If you are unfamiliar with them, there is help. If you go on the church website, you'll find accompaniment versions and versions with voices singing. In the Primary Come Follow Me manual, you will find Primary song suggestions to go along with the message being taught. I suggest that you don't bog down the process by trying to teach the songs—just sing them and your children will easily learn by repetition.

And then sing them as you work, as you play, as you travel together or as lullabies, as is recommended in the Preface of the hymn book.

And if you want to tie it into any nations you might be studying, you will find versions in many languages in the church website. You will notice in the corner search field, you can select a language. Now you can print the music out with words of the language of your choice.

Maybe see if there are returned missionaries in your ward who can help with the pronunciation. Or there are lots of online tools. You'll find many of the Spanish, French and Portuguese versions have audio recordings that you can listen to. Isn't this part of the spirit of gathering when you realize that children all over the whole world are singing the same songs?

Don't overlook all the wonderful songs in the music library. There are sing-along-songs. There is simplified piano music for young musicians to play. Songs with American Sign Language. You can find music from the *Friend*. The downside to these songs is that you can't listen to most of them and if you don't play the piano or read music, it's hard to figure out how they are supposed to sound. But I bet you know someone who can help you out.

The other thing I mentioned yesterday is that the great composers like Handel and Brahms and Bach have gifted us music that was intended to purify us and lift us closer to heaven. But for many of our youth, this language of music is too rich for their tastes. The strong repetitive beat of popular music is deadening their sensitivities.

My heart-educator friends addressed this issue. What did they recommend? Basically, it was follow the Pattern for Learning by first focusing on the melody which is like the heart of a song. Let them hum along or draw a Pitch melody in the air with their hands. Let them try and find the melody in the piano keys. Then let them feel the rhythm—the rhythm of music maintains order and then, quite naturally, they will start to feel the beautiful harmonies layered around it.

There are some wonderful music books in the Mother's University that will fully guide you through this process. The other recommendation was that if you want children to appreciate fine music, you need to make the unfamiliar become familiar. The more you play fine music in your home, the more friendly it will feel.

How do you kill a love of music? Start with notation and technical drills—the realm of the mind—which has convinced more people that they are not musical than just about anything else. Every single person is deeply musical and as Martin Luther said, "Music is the art of the prophets, and the only art that can calm the agitations of the soul...it is one of the most magnificent and delightful presents God has given us."

So lift up your voice and sing!

Let's turn to the second language: Imagery

A young father in our ward was telling me that they keep their Come Follow Me manual in a cubby in their couch and every night when he says, "Who wants to do Come Follow Me" his little kids come running in: "What picture are we on tonight daddy?" Children love pictures because it's a language that is familiar to them. And the images will remain on their hearts—maybe even forever.

I love all the Fine art that is now included in the Primary manuals and the home manual.

This dad said that when the kids open up the manual, he uses the pictures to tell a story or has his kids tell the story of what they are seeing. A lesson can be as simple as that.

There are great truths and principles buried in much of the Fine Art of the world, and you certainly don't need to limit their exposure to just religious paintings. Let's take a look at an example.

In Gedanken by Friedrich Prolls

This is a painting by the German artist, Friedrich Prölls.

Go ahead. Look really, really hard at this painting. Are you looking? Is that helpful?

Let me offer three tools that I learned from John Muir Laws who teaches workshops on nature journaling to open eyes to what we see in nature. When I started applying the three tools to Fine Art, I started discovering all kinds of details in the paintings I had previously missed. The three tools are simple; I notice, I wonder and That reminds me of.

Let's apply them to this painting:

I notice there's a kind of a light that seems to be shining from the book into the faces of the children who are looking at it. I wonder if it's a Bible—it looks like one and the light reminds me that the word is a lamp unto my feet—a light in my life. I notice how the brother has his arm around his sister; how comfortable they seem around each other. How much they must love each other. I notice the brother is so engaged in what they are reading, he has put his piece of bread down on the floor. It reminds me that the word of the Lord is often referred to as the bread of life. And he who eats of this bread will never hunger again.

I notice that they don't appear to be rich, at least materially. Their home is simply furnished.

The children are sitting on the floor. But I notice the look of contentment on the mother's face. I notice she has an appreciation for beauty—she has taken the time to grow a rose on her windowsill and I wonder if she is the one who has painted the roses on her cabinet? I also notice the letter on the windowsill with the rose by it. I notice whoever gave it to her must know of her love for roses. It's the perfect gift. I wonder if the letter is from her husband. I wonder if he is away from home. Is he a soldier? Does he travel for work? Or is he just thoughtful and has given her a love letter that has made her smile with contentment?

Of course I notice the books overhead. And I notice the open window—I can almost feel the fresh breezes blowing through and I notice in the center of the window and really the central part of the painting, a chapel. It reminds me of how faith is the center of my soul and my life.

I notice the spinning wheel in front of the mother. There is work to be done. There is always work to be done. But it reminds me of those rare moments when I pause, and just feel contentment in the moment for life and reflect on my blessings and the goodness of home and family and everything that really matters. I notice the heart in the chair where she sits—I believe love is the foundation of that home.

Now, I have no idea if the artist intended these things. But these are the things I noticed and connected to and it makes me love this painting. And as I take the time to notice and wonder, it's as though each detail of the painting is etched on the wall of the gallery in my own heart and I can close my eyes and see the painting and feel all the feelings associated with it. And it makes me happy.

Did you notice how many gospel principles this painting is teaching?

As you do this picture talk with your children, it will help to bring paintings to life for them and in time, they'll start discovering principles to apply in their lives—for themselves. Just be careful to not kill it by making it a chore or an assignment. And please—no assigned essays on what the painting means to you. But you wouldn't do that, would you?

If you are looking for pictures like the ones I showed you in yesterday's presentation, I've been collecting them. These are wonderful to begin with because to awaken a love of fine art, you have to first connect your children to a subject that is familiar to them. So I look for paintings of children and animals and flowers and families and home. There is a time to talk about the elements of art, but childhood is not that time, in my opinion. Let them just enjoy it.

To go to my collection, the most direct way is to visit welleducatedheart.com and in the search field at the bottom of any page, enter 'Art home and family.' Or visit simplejoyart.com.

If you hang around my website, I'll connect you with what I'm finding as well as a lot of other art resources to help your children appreciate fine art.

Another suggested activity you will frequently find in the new Come Follow Me manual is drawing. Drawing produces an exactness of thought. It doesn't matter if the drawings are perfectly sketched. In the attempt to recreate what you are seeing, it helps the heart to process the lesson. Little children who don't have our adult inhibitions are very creative in expressing themselves through illustrating what they are learning. Give them a chance. And by the way, everyone can learn to draw. It's a skill that has been sorely neglected and consequently, we see much less than we could.

Nature journaling is a perfect way to acquire the skill and God has hidden so many teachings there that are revealed as we sketch. If you go to johnmuirlaws.com, you will find much to inspire and teach you about nature journaling. And it's all free. I hosted Jack at a couple of workshops last year and he is a living testament of the power of sketching as a means of learning. He's profoundly dyslexic—he grew up thinking he was stupid. But a high school teacher opened a door for him and he uses pictures to learn. He earned graduate degrees by listening rather than reading. And the thing I noticed about him that is so remarkable is his power of memory. He can't rely on the written word so he has to remember things. But it's hardly a handicap. If anything, I think he sees things much more deeply than those of us who rely so heavily on written words.

Poetry.

A poet can capture a profound truth in just a few words. And the poems we take the time to memorize will teach us throughout our lives. Poetry can be like jewels in our life. They can sweeten the most painful of experiences. Is anything more painful than the separation of death? I was recently reading a brief biography of one of my heart-educator friends—Jane Taylor. She held a little school in her home and was beloved for her storytelling. When she became very ill and the doctor said she had just hours left, she had arranged that this poem be read to family and friends who had gathered to say goodbye.

Prepare the house, kind friends, drape it and deck it
With leaves and blossoms fair;
Throw open doors and windows, and call hither
The sunshine and soft air.
Let all the house, from floor to ceiling, look
Its noblest and its best;
For it may chance that soon may come to me
A most imperial guest.
A prouder visitor than ever yet
Has crossed my threshold o'er.
One wearing a royal sceptre and a crown
Shall enter at my door.
Shall deign, perchance, sit at my board an hour,
And break with me my bread;
Suffer, perchance, this night my honored roof
Shelter his kingly head.
And if, ere comes the sun again, he bid me
Arise without delay,
And follow him a journey to his kingdom
Unknown and far away;
And in the gray light of the dawning morn
We pass out from my door,
My guest and I, silent, without farewell,
And to return no more—
Weep not, kind friends, I pray; not with vain tears
Let your glad eyes grow dim;
Remember that my house was all prepared,
And that I welcomed him.

Isn't that beautiful?

I can tell you how to kill a love of poetry in your children. Make sure you assign them a poem that you have decided is important they learn. Have them look up all the vocabulary words they don't know—and bonus points if you make them create sentences, demonstrating they can use the word correctly. Have them analyze the poem, identifying its meter and rhyme—request they place appropriate accent marks. And then assign them to write an essay on the meaning of the poem.

I hope your school experience was different than mine. It took me decades to make friends with poetry again. But now I love it. It was my heart-educator friends who helped me. This is their simple method for helping children love poetry.

First step—Fall in love with poetry yourself.

Step two–Read it aloud. Poetry is not meant to be read silently to yourself. Your voice brings the music so fill their ears with Mother Goose rhymes when they are babies and toddlers. If you want your children to love Homer when they are older, give them Mother Goose when they are babies. Nursery rhymes have a tremendous ordering effect on young brains. Recognize that your little children are not listening for meaning—they are listening to the music and children have a natural love for it. So don't be afraid to read to them that which is way over their heads.

Then, third, start gathering the poetry that makes your heart sing into a personal anthology. I picked up a blank journal at the craft store and every time I come across a poem that stirs my heart, I copy it in my poetry book. Let your children see you doing this and share your favorites with them. When they are ready, buy them a blank journal for them to start gathering their own favorites. If they are not yet writing, you can copy the poems of their choice for them and let them illustrate them, if they would like to. This first book of poetry can become their first reading book. You can have them practice handwriting by copying sentences that don't mean anything to them, or you can let them practice by copying poems they love into their very own book of favorite poetry.

Four—Collect worthy and beautiful books of poetry that you keep on a shelf that is easily accessible. Many families are regularly having poetry tea times where they come together and share the poems they have found that they love or are memorizing. And don't forget the cookies and hot chocolate.

So do use poetry to enhance and deepen the lessons in the Come Follow Me manual. Here are a few of my favorite poetry collections.

Best Loved Poems of the LDS People is out of print, but I regularly find copies at DI or you can look for used copies online. These are not necessarily written by LDS people, but the majority are poems that were quoted in General Conference. By the way, President David O. McKay was said to have memorized 1000 poems. I like this book because the poems are sorted by topics that can make them easy to find something that will tie in with the lesson.

For a general poetry collection that is still in print, check out *Favorite Poems Old and New*, originally published in 1957 by Helen Ferris. Or another favorite is *The Golden Treasury of*

Poetry selected by Louis Untermeyer, illustrated by Joan Walsh Anglund. It is no longer in print, but there are quite a few used copies running around out there.

Another book that is out of print but which there are usually quite a few used copies online is *Christ and the Fine Arts*. It not only contains poetry, but also fine art, hymns and stories. It was compiled for young people because the compiler realized that it is through the arts that young people will best come to know and love their Savior. She also has a book for the Old Testament. I love this book so much and it will work so nicely with Come Follow Me.

Back in the early 60s when I was a little girl, one of the Relief Society lessons was called Cultural Refinement and they used as their text a series of five books called *Out of the Best Books*. If you would like to deepen your appreciation for poetry—and all the arts—this is a great self-instructive collection. I have learned so much and it is sorted by topics like:

Faith in God and Man
The Place of Suffering in Man
Refinement Creates Beauty
Humility Yields Strength
Virtue Nourishes the Soul

So you can see you can easily find selections that can tie into your Come Follow Me topics.

I don't see many used copies online, but I see them at DI all the time. Or ask your mothers or grandmothers or older women in your ward if they would be willing to part with their copies.

One more poetry resource: If you go to welleducatedheart.com and select Categories in the search bar, go to the Other section and you will find a link to a lot of older poetry books. Just click on the little heart and it will open up a free digital copy of the book.

Story.

I remember one Christmas several years ago. We have a large family so Christmas was always stressful, but this particular day, I was in charge of some ward event or something and feeling crunched for time. I pulled into a gas station and when I put my credit card in, it said I had to go into the store, which really irritated me. I was very indignant and made sure the clerk knew it. "What kind of a gas station is this that the pumps won't read the cards?" I paid and went back out, pumped the gas and drove off.

And then came that still small voice. "Marlene, you know, that clerk didn't deserve that. That is hardly the Christmas spirit. " And I felt really badly. So I turned the car around, went to the grocery store and bought a big bag of Christmas candy, went back to the gas station and found the clerk. I looked him in the eyes and said, "You didn't deserve to be treated like that and I am so sorry. Please forgive me. I hope you have a Merry Christmas." And I handed him the bag of candy.

I have no idea what he thought, but I know how I felt.

You can explain the steps of repentance, or you can show it in action, which a story does. It's the story that makes the heart desire it.

Your personal stories of answered prayers and rewarded faith will carry much more deeply than explanations. Phrases like 'applying the Atonement' and 'walking the Covenant path' are hard for the heart to wrap around without a story to illustrate.

Many years ago, when my children were small, I served as the Stake Primary President in a stake that had lots of young families. There were 12 wards in our stake and it was common for nurseries to have 75 or more children. Elder Neal Maxwell came to visit one time and a few days later, he was performing a sealing in the temple. He didn't know a member of our stake was in the group when he said, "I visited a Stake a couple of days ago that was so loud and noisy, you could have fired a cannon and no one would have heard it."

It was no surprise that the Stake President came to me and asked if I would organize a Primary lesson for the kids the next Stake Conference, which was a bit of a logistical challenge. But we did it. We had the kids rotate rooms and in one of the rooms I had them show a video. It was Easter Sunday, so I thought it would be appropriate to show the Easter story from the church's children's scripture stories.

Soon, one of my counselors came running to find me. "Sister Peterson, we can't show that video to those little children! It's too sad."

It is sad. And that's exactly why we do show it to our little children. I don't remember a lot about being three years old, but I remember hearing the story of Jesus on the cross. That single story bound my heart to His in a way that has lasted my entire life. In fact, that is the point of the story—to draw all men unto Him. It stirs our deepest sympathies and makes us love Him.

The first commandment is not to obey; the first commandment is to love, which is the first step in the Pattern. If we teach our children to obey the commandments, but they never feel that personal love and connection to the Savior, they are as the Pharisees and scribes who prided themselves on perfect adherence to the law, but there was no love for the Lord—or really anyone else—in their hearts. They didn't need a Savior—they were perfecting themselves. On the other hand, if we teach them to love, but not to obey, they are as the hypocrites to whom Jesus said, "Why call me Lord, Lord and do not what I say." In either case, the Spirit will not be manifested in their lives.

Here is the pattern again: If ye love me, keep my commandments, and I will pray the Father send you another Comforter—the Spirit of Truth. First, we love. And to teach our children to love, we need to share lots of stories and pictures to bring Jesus to life in their hearts. They need to feel a personal connection.

My patriarchal blessing tells me how varied my children would be in dispositions, abilities, objectives, purposes and callings. The only requirement placed on me was to teach them to know and to love the Lord. Everything grows out of that love. I wish I had known the things I am teaching you while my children were growing up.

Attach their hearts to His, and they will grow up wanting to be near Him and to be like Him. So many things we stress about teaching them somehow resolve themselves.

Did you see President Nelson's counsel to the Samoans? "There are difficult days ahead. Please protect your families. Please protect your children. Help them to know the Lord and love Him and keep His commandments."

The lesson about the Crucifixion is coming up in a few weeks. I challenge you to put the book down, and tell the story from your heart. In fact, try to tell all the stories of Jesus 'by heart' and experience for yourselves the difference it makes.

Here is the story filtered through my own heart. Yours will be different.

It was about 9:00 in the morning when the Roman soldiers drove large nails through the hands and feet of Jesus, fastening his body to wooden beams. Jesus had not slept all night. He had been dragged from ruler to ruler, his hands bound behind his back. He had been mocked, and insulted, spat upon, even cruelly whipped. His accusers had to work quickly in the dark of the night. They had seen how all those adoring crowds of followers had welcomed Jesus a few days earlier as their king. What they were to do must be done while those who loved Jesus slept, or they might interfere with their plans.

And now in these early morning hours, when few knew what was happening, his cross was lifted between two thieves, just outside the city gates. And there he was to hang until he died.

And yet, even in his agony, his thoughts were turned to others. He could hear the Roman soldiers passing the time laughing, joking, gambling for his robe. To them, he offered forgiveness. "Father, forgive them for they know not what they do. "

To the thieves, he offered hope. "Today you shall be with me in paradise." To his grieving and heartbroken mother, Mary, who was close enough that he could speak to her, he gave comfort. "John—please—take my mother to your home and care for her."

Forgiveness, hope and comfort—the same gifts he offers to us still.

By noon, thick black clouds blocked the sun, casting an eerie darkness over the scene. Rumbles of thunder, flashes of lightning—the winds began to blow.

Pilate insisted a sign be nailed to the top of the cross—it read King of the Jews in three languages. A crown of thorns remained pressed into his head. Passersby scornfully wagged their finger at him. "If you are who you say you are, come down from the cross and then we'll believe you." And then, laughing, moved on.

Jesus made no reply.

His disciples, when word came to them, rushed to the site in confusion, bewilderment, disbelief, profound sorrow. How could this be happening? The kingdom has not been established. We are still under Roman rule. Surely some miracle will deliver him. He can't leave us now.

A ladder was brought nearby along with linens to wrap his body. All things must be ready. It would go against their strict Jewish laws to lay him in the tomb after the sun had set and the sabbath had begun.

1:00. 2:00. Still he suffers in silence. As excruciating as the physical pain has been, Jesus now feels a much deeper pain. "My God, my God, why has thou forsaken me?" He has now hung on the cross for nearly 6 hours when, for the first time, he asks something for himself.

"I thirst. " Twice before he has been offered wine, but he has refused it. The first time, it was to be mixed with a drug to lessen his pain. But now, he accepts the wine-soaked sponge that is lifted to his parched lips and dry throat. And then, with a loud voice, cries out: "It is finished.

Christ on the Cross, by Carl Heinrich Bloch

Father, into thy hands, I commend my spirit."

> It shouldn't be hard to sit very still and think about Jesus, His cross on the hill
> And all that He suffered and did for me; it shouldn't be hard to sit quietly
> It shouldn't be hard, even though I am small, to think always of Jesus, not hard at all.

Then, let silence be the teacher. Don't be too quick to start interpreting. If there are questions or comments, let them rise up out of your children's hearts and go from there.

By the way, this is the Carl Bloch painting included in the lesson manual. You'll notice I wove elements of the painting into the story I told. I probably wouldn't show the picture during the story because I want the listener to paint the images on his own heart first. The painting is just a reinforcer.

Do take your classroom out under the stars or under the trees as often as you can. Especially when you are telling stories. Elder Eyring's son said one of his favorite classrooms was on the sandy beach of Baja California, where, with the rhythmic rolling of the waves in the background and the sky and the song of birds overhead, his mother read pages of great literature to her family.

Keep in mind, most of the words you speak will likely be forgotten. But what your children will remember is how they felt when they were near you; what home felt like. In the *Teaching in the Savior's Way Manual*, it says: "The Savior's power to teach and lift others came from…the kind of person he was."

You are the most important lesson. Your children are watching you.

One of my favorite great soul friends is Jon G. Paton, a Scottish Presbyterian missionary who felt the call to share the love of Jesus Christ with the cannibals of the New Hebrides islands. He wasn't deterred by the stories of missionaries who were killed and all the dangers he would be facing. He had a deep and abiding faith and what he accomplished with God's help is miraculous. Where did that kind of faith come from?

He leaves us a little glimpse in his description of his home-centered gospel learning. Let's join him on a tour of his home:

> The "closet" was a very small apartment. This was the Sanctuary of that cottage home. Thither daily, and oftentimes a day, generally after each meal, we saw our father retire, and "shut to the door"; and we children got to understand by a sort of spiritual instinct (for the thing was too sacred to be talked about) that prayers were being poured out there for us, as of old by the High Priest within the veil in the Most Holy Place. We occasionally heard the pathetic echoes of a trembling voice pleading as if for life, and we learned to slip out and in past that door on tiptoe, not to disturb the holy colloquy. The outside world might not know, but we knew, whence came that happy light as of a new-born smile that always was dawning on my father's face: it was a reflection from the Divine Presence, in the consciousness of which he lived. Never, in temple or cathedral, on mountain or in glen, can I hope to feel that the Lord God is more near, more visibly walking and talking with men, than under that humble cottage roof of thatch and oaken wattles. Though everything else in religion were by some unthinkable catastrophe to be swept out of memory, or blotted from my understanding, my soul would wander back to those early scenes, and shut itself up once again in that Sanctuary Closet, and hearing still the echoes of those cries to God, would hurl back all doubt with the victorious appeal, "He walked with God."

Continuing:

> Each of us, from very early days, considered it no penalty, but a great joy, to walk with our father to the church; the four miles were a treat to our young spirits, the company by the way was a fresh incitement...
>
> Oh I can remember those happy Sabbath evenings; a holy, happy, entirely human day, for a Christian father, mother and children to spend. There were eleven of us brought up in a home like that; and never one of the eleven, boy or girl, man or woman, has been heard, or ever will be heard, saying that Sabbath was dull and wearisome for us… But God help the homes where these things are done by force and not by love!

I hope I've given you some useful ideas. As I have spent much more time in all the arts, carefully watching for principles of truth in them and applying them, I have felt such an increase of light and joy in my life. And I receive letters almost every day from moms telling me how applying this pattern for learning is changing the lives of their families and the spirit of their homes.

Celebrating Libraries of Hope's Tenth Birthday

When mothers get together, we love to share our labor and delivery stories, don't we? Well, it was exactly ten years ago this month that Libraries of Hope was officially born. Or at least announced to the world. Some of you were there at the very beginning—and your kids are already grown! Maybe some of them have children of their own. So much can happen in just ten years. So I hope you'll indulge me in a little trip down memory lane as I share a few labor and delivery stories—and consider lessons learned along the way that apply to all of us because you are part of the story, as well.

The idea of Libraries of Hope had been conceived several years before and it had been forming close to my heart. But there came a day when I wanted to make a formal announcement and introduce Libraries of Hope to the public. So I rented a hotel room for June 12, 2009, and sent out 300 invitations to friends.

About twenty-five people came. I told them my vision and dream and talked about the power of stories in our lives. By that point, I had gathered most of the stories for the first series—the Freedom Series which was American History stories. But all I could show them were sample covers. At that time, there was no print-on-demand technology. To get the price down to any reasonable amount required that we print at least a thousand copies. And we had no money.

The idea came to me to offer them on a subscription basis and release one title a month. I felt to set a $15 a book price and I left with 25 subscriptions in hand, but no idea how I was going to print them.

Within a few days, my husband and I set off for Virginia. A series of events had left us destitute and without a home. A few years earlier, it had taken us 6 26-foot trucks crammed full to move our stuff from Colorado to Utah. Now, after selling everything we could, what we needed fit into a small trailer we towed across country behind our car. In a short amount of time, I had gone from living in a beautiful 6000 square foot home in a neighborhood of million-dollar homes to now setting our bed on a concrete floor in my daughter's unfinished basement in Virginia. I woke up to insulation hanging from the ceiling and cinder block walls, surrounded by storage boxes. But we had nowhere else to go.

We had intended to only stay for a few months. My daughter's husband had joined the army and would be away at boot camp when their third baby was due to arrive. So we were happy to go be there with her. When he deployed for another year, we stayed. They have long ago moved away. But we're still here. Only I don't live in the basement any more. And I have most certainly fallen in love with Virginia. We live out in the beautiful countryside where I can sit on the porch and listen to the birds and watch the fireflies.

I wasn't sad. Really. I loved being with my little grandchildren and my daughter. The feeling that came to me was: "Good. Now that we have all that stuff out of your life, let's get to work." And both my husband and I put our hearts and souls into growing Libraries of Hope. Every other path for us had been hedged up.

My first problem was I had 25 subscription orders and just needed 975 more to be able to fill them. Then one day I was searching for something and an ad or an article caught my eye and led me to a printing company that specialized in short runs. They were just south of us. We drove down and talked to them. I explained I wanted to offer hard cover dust jacketed books. They said they could do it for just less than $15 each—and the minimum order was 25.

That's exactly what I had and we were on our way and were able to finish the Freedom Series.

At this time, Glenn Beck was soaring in popularity. Everyone kept telling me I needed to get hold of him and show him my books. I started watching his show and he pled with parents to teach their children American History stories—especially from books written before 1923. He said we need to teach them the principles of liberty and was pushing the 5000 Year Leap, which presented 28 principles, all of which were woven into the stories in my books. We had exactly what he was talking about!

One day when I was so discouraged, I knelt down in the basement and prayed. What were we doing! Were all these sacrifices worth it? Would these stories really make any difference? And the impression came to go upstairs and turn on the radio. Glenn Beck's program happened to be on and at that very moment, he said: "Stories will heal our nation."

It made complete sense to get in touch with him. So I tried in every way I could possibly think of. But with no success. I had saved a set of books just for him and I had them boxed up ready to go, but had no idea how to get them to him. Then the words came into my mind, "Marlene, I created the universe. Do you not believe that I can get these books into Glenn Beck's hands?" And I laughed at my lack of faith. Of course! I looked up his general address and put them in the mail, trusting they would find their way.

Some weeks went by and nothing happened. And then one night I had a strong impression:

"Marlene,"—these impressions always addressed me by name—"Would you be willing to call into Glenn Beck's radio program tomorrow?" Nothing could have stricken more terror in my heart. I am pretty sure I made it through my entire school career—from kindergarten to college graduation without once raising my hand to ask or answer a question or make a comment in class. I lived in dread terror of saying something stupid. And the thought of going on a live national radio program with millions of listeners and making a fool of myself was the worst possible thing that could be asked of me. I just knew I was going to be the talk around the water cooler at work the next day.

No. I'll do anything but that. But I had promised I would do anything He asked of me. A promise is a promise. I took some comfort in the fact that I had known a few people who had tried to call into his show without success. Some days he didn't even take callers. So the next morning I tried to think of something to say, and with trembling fingers dialed the number. My call was answered immediately. The screener said Glenn would be very interested in talking to me and to hold the line.

I've listened to enough of his shows to know that he usually only takes a few calls a day, if that.

But this particular day, he took calls for all three hours. I was watching the program on my computer screen with my headset on, literally in a death grip of fear. The screener occasionally came back to check that I was still there—and told me that Glenn would still take my call.

The hours were agonizing. I can't even tell you. Finally it was close to the end of the three hours and if you have ever watched the program, sometimes Glenn will go into this low, soothing voice, which he did at this time and these were the words spoken into my ears: God has not forgotten you.

And the program was over.

My husband asked if I was going to try again the next day and I said, "Are you crazy?" I kept my promise. It wasn't for the lack of trying. And I didn't particularly feel like I needed to try again.

A few weeks later I got a phone call. :This is Natasha. I am Glenn Beck's producer. He has become aware of your work and he loves what you are doing and he was wondering if you would send him two sets of your Freedom Series."

I can't help but wonder if I came to his attention during that radio program—I'll never know—but I learned later that he had warehouses packed with products that people were sending him with the hopes he would endorse them on his show. And here he was calling me and asking me to send him my product?

I was awestruck—and so quick to give credit to where credit was due. "Lord, thank you." I had to box up my own set and piece together another set from my daughters. That's all I had. I was given special instructions how to send it so it would get to him.

I kept watching his show. Nothing happened.

And then about a week later, a strange course of events had brought me to a large beach house in Florida where I was in a room with about 12 to 15 women. On my right was Lori Parker. She had called into Glenn's program and overnight had gathered over 80,000 moms and As A Mom was born. I had previously tried to get hold of her without success—and here she was, sitting next to me. On the other side of the couch was Yvonne Donnelly who was heading up Glenn's 912 project that had over a million participants. Right after I shared my books with the group, Yvonne's phone rang. "Oh, hi Glenn. You know those books you just got from Marlene Peterson—the Freedom Series? Yeah, yeah. She's sitting right here on the couch next to me." I couldn't hear what he was saying but she cupped the phone and said, "He loves them!" and she left the room to finish her call.

My mind was reeling. This was impossible. This was a miracle. So surreal. Glenn Beck loved my books. I was sure she would say something. I kept watching the program. Nothing happened.

A couple of weeks later Yvonne texted me a picture. She was in Glenn's New York apartment and there were my books, in a place of honor on a table with book ends.

I kept hearing him say you need to get stories like these into your children—I knew he had the books and loved them—why wasn't he telling people about them!

Finally, I said, "Lord, I don't understand." And I could almost feel the smile behind it—"That was your idea, not mine."

And I laughed aloud again. It was my idea! He had kept His promise—He got the books into Glenn's hands which evidently is a miracle right up there with parting the Red Sea. But that was not His idea. That was mine.

And with my perspective today, I am a million times grateful that Glenn didn't promote those books at that time. Had he done that, most of what followed which is infinitely more important in my estimation would likely never have happened.

I came away from that experience with greater trust in the Lord. But more importantly, a firmer commitment to quit trying to figure everything out. Instead, I have tried to live by daily asking, "Today, What wouldst thou have me do? Where wouldst thou have me go? What wouldst thou have me say?"

And I continue to watch His Hands perform wonders.

After the Freedom Series, I had several more series in mind. I loved the stories I was gathering and was so anxious to find a way to share them with families. But I couldn't continue doing it the way we were doing. I had gathered stories for at least five dozen more books and I still only had a handful of subscribers.

Then I was given an invitation to speak at a homeschool conference in Fredericksburg and felt to go. At the last minute, they asked if I would do a vendor class. I wasn't even sure what that was. Only two or three ladies came to it and I talked about the books, but they seemed disinterested. Afterwards, one of the women pulled me aside and said that she had no idea why she came to my little presentation. She came from a family of storytellers and didn't feel a shortage of stories in her life, but she felt she should sit in on the class. And as she sat there, she had the strongest impression to connect me with a man she knew who was a high-power business consultant. I contacted him and he was very cordial and nice, but way out of my league. I couldn't figure out what we needed to talk about. And then he casually mentioned a book he had just finished and somewhere in the course of conversation, he told me about a fairly new company called CreateSpace that printed books on demand.

I immediately checked them out—this was a turning point for us. They could print a single book at less than the cost we had been quoted for printing a thousand books. And they would print one title at a time. The downside was I had to give up my beautiful hardcover dust-jacketed books and could only offer softcover, but the gate was opened to move forward and I was so grateful.

We could now offer books as fast as we could get them formatted.

Now more ideas kept coming and we would work long 18-hour days to try and keep up. And opportunities to begin to spread a message started dropping in my lap. I noticed the Utah Governor's First Lady was sponsoring a giant family conference at the Salt Palace when I was going to be in town and felt the nudge to offer to speak, which I really didn't expect to be accepted. I was a nobody and there were a lot of very recognizable speakers. But the invitation was extended and I spoke again of the power of stories in our lives. Out of 185 presenters, it was my picture that was posted on the front page of the Deseret News and my presentation was the featured talk. From that, I was invited to meet with an executive at the KSL studios who were interested in filming me in some segments about storytelling that would reach families around the world in a program they were developing. It didn't work out for different reasons, but I was stunned at the attention.

Another time, two weeks before the World Congress of Family was to be held for the first time in the United States, I got a call. A presenter was unable to make it—would I fill in for him. He was someone I had followed for years and was a well-respected man. I couldn't fill his shoes. I was told it needed to be a well-crafted, 18-minute speech that would be videotaped and given a worldwide distribution. I would be presenting to the entire group—over 4000 delegates from all over the world. With all my heart I wanted to say, "Are you kidding me??" But that gentle voice inside said, "Go. I'll be with you."

The message I was to deliver was written on my heart, but I was quaking in my shoes. The night before I was to speak, I went to dinner with my family. My daughter has a Jeep and my 94-year-old mother at the time was with us, so she needed the front seat. Which meant I had to climb into the back. Somehow in the climb I twisted my body the wrong way and pinched my sciatic nerve. At least I think that's what it was. All I know is I was in agony and couldn't move without excruciating pain. I kept thinking the pain would go away, but it got worse. I didn't know what to do. There were many prayers.

I tossed and turned all night in pain and tried to figure out how I was going to manage this. The setup was that I was to be part of a five-man panel. They had big soft chairs on this huge stage that, as we were presented one at a time, we would walk out on the stage and sit in one of these chairs and wait our turn. I couldn't imagine how I was going to sit down without help and far worse, how I could possibly pull myself out of the chair. I thought should we get a wheelchair? Should I just tell them I'll stand off stage until it's my turn to speak?

I will say the pain crowded out the fear. And the feeling that came to me in the night was, "Trust me." So I got up and got ready, very, very slowly, all the time not knowing what I was going to do. I was speaking in the first session of the morning. And then, the second I stepped outside my room, the pain went away. Completely. I was rushed backstage and got there just as they were about to announce us.

Our panel leader was a distinguished man from Poland who had previously hosted the conference in his country. There was an orthodox priest, a man who had held a high position in the government of the Philippines, and a man who had a high position in the CIA. And me. The Sesame Street song kept running through my head—"One of these things is not like the other." It didn't boost my confidence when, the day before, the man who had invited me to speak told me that the chairman of the event had reached out to him and said, "What does the power of stories have to do with this Congress? You need to find a new speaker." I was on board with that. He assured her all would be well.

So I stood and delivered the message that was written on my heart. And, oh my goodness, I watched its message resonate in hearts. Everywhere I went for the next three days, people would surround me and tell me how deeply the message had moved them.

I know where that credit goes.

Saturday morning, when I was finally done with the final session that I took part in, the pain returned and I suffered for a couple of more weeks. Maybe just in case I doubted the miracle. Which, believe me, I never did.

I think back to the time when Libraries of Hope was in its infancy; when I was asked what my business plan was; how I planned on marketing this. And my reply was always the same. I have no plan. But the feeling planted in my heart, as I have frequently shared, is that the Lord was preparing a network of mothers who, when they heard the messages, would resonate in their hearts and they would be drawn to the work.

If I had millions of dollars and could have hired New York's finest marketing agency, they could never have gathered the wonderful families that have been quietly gathering from all over the world to a message of the influence of a mother and the need to cultivate our hearts through the arts.

One time I expressed frustration to the Lord—this work would be so much easier if I had money. And the thought immediately came to my mind, "If you had money, you would do it your way. I need you to do it My way."

And He continues to teach me His way is always better. And He has provided for our needs.

Libraries of Hope has never been about selling books. It has always been about building reservoirs of stories that are broad and deep in the hearts of our children. I don't know all that lies ahead in the future of Libraries of Hope. But I do know there are likely wonderful surprises. There is a great orchestrator and we are all part of His grand orchestra. Some of you will be the trumpet section. Others will play sweet melodies on your violins. I always hope I get to pluck a few harp strings. He will perform miracles in your lives and help you to do exactly what you need to do.

Sometimes I get little glimpses. I have a sense of a safety net lying over the land, unknown to the world, but made up of homes like yours where goodness and beauty are being safeguarded in the hearts of the coming generations. Sometimes I worry there are so few of us. And I am reminded that a little yeast raises the whole loaf of bread. But I am also reminded how quickly an idea can spread. If you plant the seed of an idea in just two friends who live in another town or another state or even another country, and those two friends share it with two friends, and so forth it's amazing how quickly a safety net can grow.

I think the world is headed for a necessary winter. But today's harvest will see us through until spring when new green shoots will appear— and beauty will rise from the ashes. That is not a gloomy thought. I am filled with a brightness of hope.

Enough of memories. Time to get back to work. Happy 10th Birthday, Libraries of Hope! I can hardly wait to see what's in store for you. I can hardly wait to see what's in store for all of us!

Inspirational Quotes

Ah! Vous dirai-je, Maman.
Ce qui cause mon tourment?
Papa veut que je raisonne,
Comme une grande personne;
Moi, je dis que les bonbons
Valent mieux que la raison.

Ah! Let me tell you, mother,
What's the cause of my torment?
Papa wants me to reason
Like a grown-up.
Me, I say that candy has
Greater value than reason.

Art credit: *Mother and Child* by Leon Perrault

"The motive power of the moral life is Will. The motive power of the intellectual world is Imagination. In virtue of his power to imagine or re-create through mental images, man sees the past, forecasts the future, and has made whatever advances has been ever made into the fields of the Unknown.

"We cannot give Imagination to another, but we may arrest its development; and where it is ignored or suppressed, all intellectual life must quickly decline and perish. Now, as of old, wherever for one reason there is no vision the people perish."

Fairy tales are a prime tool and so vital in nurturing thc Imagination! Don't underestimate their power and usefulness.

Art credit: *Take the Face of a Fair Woman* by Sophie Gengembre Anderson

"The time will come when it will be told as a relic of our primitive barbarism that children were taught the list of prepositions and the names of the rivers of Thibet, but were not taught the wonderful laws on which their own...happiness is based, and the humanities by which they could live in peace and goodwill with those about them."

--Frances Willard

Art credit: *At the Shrine* by John William Waterhouse

Is it possible to read too much? I think so. Too much food and too much reading can give us indigestion. Like President Gilman of John Hopkins said: "...let us read less and think more."

Notebooking can help digest ideas.

Art credit: *The Elder Sister*, by James Tissot

"You can live more on less when you have more to live for."

--Sterling Sill

Art credit: *Le Jeu de Krouta* by Nasreddine Dinet

"Wouldst thou write a living book thou must first live."

--From the Mother's University book on Language Arts.

Art credit: *The Farmer and His Son at Harvesting* by Thomas Pollock Anschutz

The Teacher

Lord, who am I to teach the way
To little children day by day,
So prone myself to go astray?

I teach them knowledge, but I know
How faint the flicker and how low
The candles of my knowledge glow.

I teach them power to will and do,
But only now to learn anew
My own great weakness through and through.

I teach them love for all mankind.
And all God's creatures, But I find
My love comes lagging far behind.

Lord, if their guide I still must be,
Oh, let the little children see
The teacher leaning hard on Thee.
--Leslie Pinckney Hill

Art credit: *Falling Apple Blossoms* by Hamilton Hamilton

"A good man out of the good treasure of his heart bringeth forth that which is good." (Luke 6:45)

What 'treasure' is filling the hearts of your children? What are the 'fruits' of your learning?

Art credit: *The Apple Picker* by Leon Bazile Perrault

"[D]on't ever sell yourself short as a woman or as a mother... Do not let the world define, denigrate, or limit your feelings of lifelong learning and the values of motherhood... Lifelong learning is essential to the vitality of the human mind, body, and soul. It enhances self-worth and self-actuation. Lifelong learning is invigorating mentally and is a great defense against aging, depression and self-doubt." --Robert D. Hales

Art credit: *A Young Girl Reading* by Jean-Honore Fragonard

In an article about nature shared by one our group members, there is a phrase that I loved: "cultivating wonder."

I would say that sums up our task as mothers in educating the hearts of our children. WEH is not just letting your kids do anything they want. You role is 'to cultivate wonder' and the principles shared in the mother's university is all about how to do that.

Art credit: *A Garden Scene with Children* by Charles Edouard Boutibonne

"I never let anyone walk through my mind with their dirty feet."

Art credit: *In the Spring Meadow* by Ludwig Knaus

Today I am transferring and adding additional resources on the Oceans page and I stopped to read the introduction to one of the books, which are so frequently loaded with good thoughts about educating children.

It talked about how important books are for "making a child a participant in the results of experiences of all mankind." BUT "the book knowledge, containing as it does the precious lessons of human experience, may be so taught as to bring with it only dead rules of conduct, only dead scraps of information, and no stimulation to original thinking…

"Its contents may be memorized without being understood…resulting in loading the mind with materials which he cannot use to advantage…

"Some minds are so full of lumber that there is no space left to set up a workshop."

Are you leaving space for a workshop?

Art credit: *On the Sands* by Harold Harvey

"When things fall apart…make art."

Art credit: *The Little Dressmaker* by Pierre Edouard Frere

I just had a 1921 book show up randomly in my search for a book about John Smith. The title intrigued me: *Why We Should Read Books* by S.PB. Mais. So I opened it and this caught my eye:

"The object of any man who enjoys life is to share his enjoyment with others."

I would paraphrase a bit—"The object of any mother who enjoys life is to share her enjoyment with her children."

Are you enjoying life?

Art credit: *A Mother's Love* by Gaetano Chierici

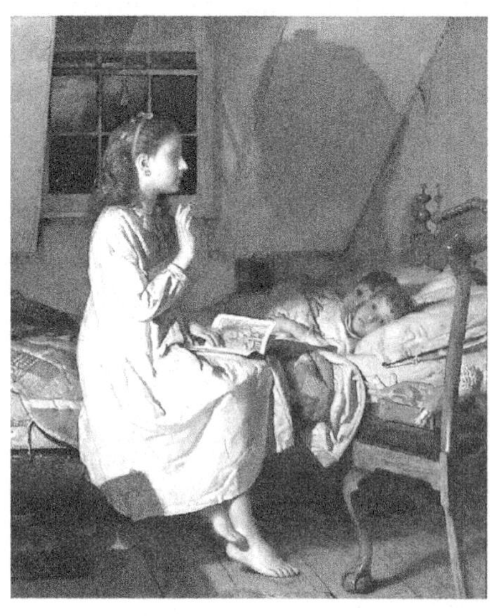

"A good children's book strikes a vibration in the soul that lasts a lifetime. And when a reader or collector achieves maturity and a special sense of values, he may recognize that the best books are really those that children have loved for generations of lifetimes."

--William Targ

From an 1844 literary critic: A children's books should be a "union of the highest art with the simplest form."

Art credit: *The Story of Golden Locks* by Seymour Joseph Guy

"Nothing touches the soul but leaves its impress, and thus, little by little, we are fashioned into the image of all we have seen and heard, known and meditated; and if we learn to live with all that is fairest and purest and best, the love it all will, in the end become our life."

--Bishop Spaulding

Art credit: *Gather Ye Rosebuds While Ye May* by John William Waterhouse

"Logic will get you from A to B. Imagination will take you everywhere."

--Albert Einstein

Art credit: *Children Playing* by Charles Bertrand d'Entraygues

"If we were all determined to play the first violin, we should never have a complete orchestra. Therefore respect every musician in his proper place."

--Robert Schumann

Children deserve that respect as well. Are you overlooking a child's unique gifts and talents because you are focused on that first violin position?

Art credit: *The Music Lesson* by Eduard Charlemont

In educating children, the pattern is:

"From within…outward. A rosebud blooms from the pressure outward of inner fulness."

--Dr. S.S. Curry (1885)

Art credit: *Flower Garden* by Abbott Fuller Graves

"Woman has always recognized as her chief business the task of making the world a better place to live in…men strive for the means of living, and women make the living worth striving for."

--Delphian Handbook

Art credit: *The Homecoming* by Jennie Augusta Brownscombe

The Pattern for Learning in this morning's scripture study, John 14:15:

Art credit: *Christ with Mary and Martha* by Henryk Siemiradzi

If ye love me (Heart, Desire)
Keep my commandments (Mind, Law)
And I…shall give you another Comforter…even the Spirit of Truth (Spirit)
Whom the world cannot see—(Only the heart can see rightly; blessed are the pure in heart for they shall see God)
But he know him, for he dwelleth in you. (You feel something the eye cannot see—Faith)

The act of decoding words does not make a child a reader. The act of constructing sentences does not make a child a writer. Only the imagination can do that.
Imagination = The thinking of the heart.
The thinking of the heart can only be cultivated through the Arts.
WEH is about cultivating the heart through the arts—Music, Pictures, Poetry, and Story.

Art credit: *Die Lesestunde* by Simon Glucklich

I just pulled this out of another old book I found with more children's plays. The writer affirmed it's through the voice that we develop a love of reading and literature. And why do we teach reading?

"Does not the teaching of reading really mean teaching our children to understand all the mighty thoughts of the world, whether they be expressed in music, or poetry, or art, or in the characters of the heroes of literature?"

Art credit: *Knowledge is Power* by Seymour Joseph Guy

The study of Great lives is the study of History.

Art credit: *Cincinnatus* by Alexander Cabanel

I just posted a new book in the library—actually, of course, it's an old one—*Modeling My Life* written by American sculptor, Janet Scudder.

Here is learning by heart:

"I had been out in the garden playing with the flowers. The colors evidently stirred something latent in me for I can remember, as distinctly as though it had happened yesterday, the feeling of intense excitement that swept over me and carried me into the house and up to my grandmother…

"How did they ever get these beautiful colors?" I demanded breathlessly, holding a small bunch of flowers out towards her.

"She put her hand and touched me and then the flowers—for she had been blind for many years—and very solemnly and impressively explained that colors were given flowers by God.

"He painted them!" I gasped.

She nodded, still very solemn.

"How?"

At this she laid down her knitting and her voice came a bit uneasily. "Why do you ask me that, my child?"

"Because I want to paint some just like them. I've got to! I must!"

I am sure the creative instinct was born at that moment. I knew that I had to make something beautiful. I just had to express in some tangible way the strong emotion I was experiencing over the beauty of the flowers…

Poets and writers have grown into the habit of calling this desire to create something beautiful the divine fire. Divine fire! Perhaps it is that. Surely it is divine in the joy it gives. I have always thought that incident with flowers—even though I was only six—must have been a tiny little flame from a great fire.

Art credit: *Girl in a Field* by Ludwig Knaus

I came across a painting I loved of Hans Christian Andersen reading his story of "The Angel" to the children of the painter. I posted it on the Enrichment page for Scandinavia along with a link to the story of The Angel…which some scholars think was inspired by Jenny Lind.

Art credit: *H.C. Andersen Reads "The Angel"* by Elisabeth Jerichau-Baumann

I have especially loved learning many of the Swedish folk songs with their love of nature and of God, and I thought this one was appropriate for this group. Here's the song, translated, called *Blomman*:

When our Lord creates a flower,
He makes the stem soft and beautiful.
Then he places small leaves upon it;
then His strong hand takes
the color of the earth and the dark dusk
and then blows His spirit into it.
Then the flower stands here,
glowing with clear, loving colors
that came out of God's own hand
to give us joy.
Flower! Flower! Be the joy of my heart!

When our Lord makes a girl,
He does it the same way:
first a beautiful little body, so soft and lean
Then His strong hand takes
all the light color of the earth
and mixes them and creates her soul.
Then the girl stands there glowing
among the Lord's other beautiful flowers
that come from God's own hand.
To comfort us—Girl! Flower!
Be the comfort of my heart!

Art credit: *Springtime, the First Anemones* by H.A. Brendekilde

It has been interesting to watch the different reactions to the call to make our homes the center of our learning. I'm hearing a little panic in some mothers—"How am I going to make my kids sit down and listen to my lesson?"

For many of you, I have a feeling it will be a seamless transition. You already know of your influence as a mother and that learning and teaching happen as you go about the normal affairs of life; that the most powerful lessons are wrapped in stories, art, music, and poetry. And the most wonderful classroom is Nature.

Art credit: *In Thought* by Friedrich Prolls

"One knows thoroughly only what one learns oneself; and I advise you earnestly, as far as possible, to have recourse to no aid other than relection."

--Jean Henri Fabre

Art credit: *Afternooon Along* the River by Emile Claus

"We need more music in the world, because we need more culture, more beauty, more sweetness, and music makes for all of these."

--Harriet Seymour

Art credit: *Two Young Girls* at the Piano by Renoir

I was just thinking of something. Although my kids are all grown with homes of their own, I'm still a mom. Lately, several of them have had really hard challenges come their way, most of it through no fault of their own. Of course, we want everything to be OK. I hurt for them and try to offer words of encouragement and help as I can.

But here's the deal. Life is messy. It's designed to be that way because that's how humans grow. We have to learn to sort and prioritize and adapt and endure and overcome. To learn joy in the journey. It's a never-ending process.

And I thought of comments so many of you have made where you feel so out of control—that you dream of that moment when everything aligns and runs smoothly. But life keeps happening and interferes with your carefully made plans.

I remember a card I got from a friend once that said on the cover, "Let's get together when life gets back to normal." And inside it said, "But what if this is normal?"

And that's the point of this post—if you are constantly working to achieve that home where everything is perfectly in place and every day goes just as scheduled, is that real life?

My experience says absolutely not.

So learning to go with the flow and the challenges and the disruptions and the changes of plans may be the very best preparation for life you can give your children! Much more so than the perfectly ordered and clockwork home you may feel so guilty that you are unable to achieve.

Just my two cents.

Art credit: *The See-Saw* by Giovanni Battista Torriglia

I avoid politics in this group, but I do have a plan for a course correction:

"Educate the women and the men will be educated. Let the ladies understand the great doctrine of seeking the greatest good, of loving their neighbors as themselves, let them indoctrinate their children in this fundamental truth, and we shall have wise legislators:

--Mary Lyon

Art credit: *The Reading Lesson* by Pierre Jean Edmond Castan

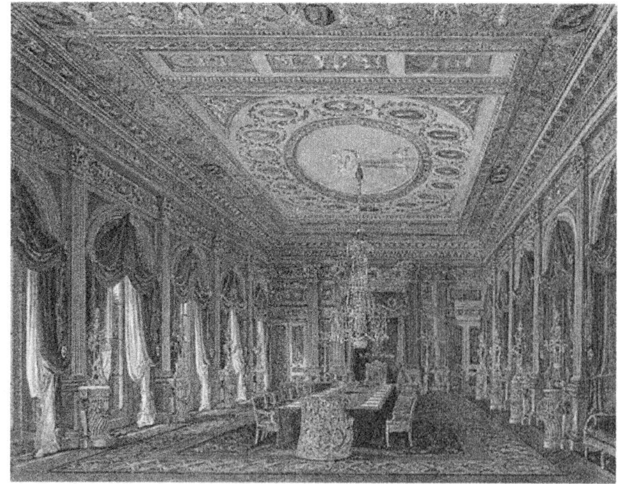

"If anybody would make me the greatest king that ever lived on condition that I would not read books, I would not be a king. I would rather by a poor man in a garret with plenty of books than a king who did not love reading."

--Macaulay

Art credit: *Carlton House, Throne Room* by Charles Wild

I am frequently asked in the stories in my books are 'true,' meaning are they 'accurate.' And I always say there is a difference between 'true' and 'truth.' 'True' where a study of people is concerned is a really hard thing to come by. You can get a few facts right, like date and place of birth, but much of the rest is interpretive.

Our efforts toward 'true'—i.e., documentation, citations, evidence, original source—do not belong in childhood in my opinion, and I believe it has weakened us as a people in some ways. We have lost our vision of greatness and as Alfred North Whitehead wrote: "Moral education is impossible apart from the habitual vision of greatness."

The author of 'In Search of Heroes' wrote: "...irreverence, skepticism and mockery permeate the culture to such a degree that it is difficult for young people to have heroes and presenting reality in the classroom is an empty, education goal if it produces disillusioned, dispirited students."

...which I see happening.

So are all the stories in my books 'true?' I can't verify that. I do know the authors of these books were scholars. They did their homework. Even they acknowledge that much had to be filled in from their 'imagination,' but they were clear in their intentions—to build noble and virtuous human beings.

As Ralph Waldo Emerson wrote, "Go with mean people and you think life is mean...with the great, our thoughts and manners easily become great."

I'm trying to give your children some really 'great' souls to hang out with. The 'facts' of their lives can come later when they are mature enough to measure it all in proper balance.

Art credit: *Homecoming Marine* by Norman Rockwell

"Whosoever acknowledges himself to be a zealous follower of truth, of happiness, of wisdom, of science, or even of the faith, must of necessity make himself a Lover of Books."

--Richard deBary

Art credit: *The Reading Lesson* by Knut Ekvall

"Art comes from within, not from without. Do not force; do not fuss; be quiet; wait for the child to hear the still, small voice from within."

--Richard Wyche, *Some Great Stories and How to Tell Them*

Art credit: *Ragazza Che Legge* by Johann Georg Meyer von Bremen

"Mothers, let your minds be sanctified before the Lord, for this is the commencement, the true foundation of a proper education in your children...

"The mothers are the moving instruments in the hands of Providence to guide the destinies of nations."

--Brigham Young

Art credit: *Leibevolle Mutter* by Hans Bachmann

"The normal [child] demands a story. The Bible does not open with a scientific disquisition upon the evolutionary hypothesis of anthropological origins—it begins with the story of Adam and Eve. Even the Great Teacher did not speak without a parable.

"This is the law of life. It is more; it is as vital as breathing."

--Everett Tomlinson

Art credit: *Jungle Story* by James Jebusa Shannon

I learned something new as I read about Marie Curie. The word used for high school was Gymnasium and the reasoning was that it was used as a place to 'exercise' the mind in preparation for the rigorous studies ahead at the University level.

That's how I feel about our focus—it's not about mastering content at this level. It's about exercising and stretching a child's learning faculties in preparation for a lifetime of learning. When students graduate from formal schooling, they attend a Commencement ceremony—a commencement of learning. Not a conclusion to it.

Art credit: *Preparing for the Next Day*, by Seymour Joseph Guy

"Art comes from within, not from without. Do not force; do not fuss; be quiet; wait for the child to hear the still, small voice from within."

--Richard Wyche, *Some Great Stories and How to Tell Them*

Art credit: *Hide and Seek* by James Jacques Joseph Tissot

"I have no patience with the stupidity of the average teacher of grammar who wastes precious years in hammering rules into children's heads. For it is not by learning rules that we acquire the power of speaking a language, but by daily intercourse with those accustomed to express themselves with exactness and refinement, and by the copious reading of the best authors."

--Erasmus

I have seen this principle at work in the lives of some of our greatest authors!

But it doesn't apply just to the grammar. We acquire the 'power' of living life 'by daily intercourse with those accustomed to [living life] with exactness and refinement, and by the copious reading of the best [lives]'...not by pounding rules and doctrines of right living into our heads.

Art credit: *Grandfather's Tale* by Edward Thompson Davis

"Educating the mind without educating the heart is no education at all." –Aristotle

But remember educating the heart without educating the mind is also no education.

Heart AND Mind

Faith AND Reason

Art AND Science

Warmth AND Light—Consider the sun can shine on a seed all winter long, but until the ground warms up, that life force within remains dormant.

Your children are no different. Heart—Warmth—first to start the growing process. The ARTs for the heART.

And don't forget Roots AND Stems—the roots are unseen, but without a strong root system, the plant will never flower.

I find it interesting we even call the Mind subjects the STEM subjects.

Lesson over.

Art credit: *Hummingbird and Passionflowers* by Martin Johnson Heade

We've had quite a few new members join our group recently and we welcome you! I hope you feel that you are among friends. If you are brand new to the Well-Educated Heart, I recommend going through the free Catch the Vision intro court at welleducatedheart.com.

You will notice two unique things about my approach—I focus on tending to mother's hearts because I believe it is out of the abundance of a mother's heart that our children are blessed. "Only the warm heart can kindle warmth in another." And secondly, while traditional schooling and curriculum focuses on those things that are seen, my priority is with those things that are unseen—love, joy, kindness, all the riches of the heart.

If you are looking to fill your own heart in order to bless those around you and you understand the value of those things which are 'unseen,' you have come to the right place.

Art credit: *The Writing Lesson* by Eugenio Zampighi

John Wanamaker was once asked to finance an expedition to recover treasures which had lain for years in sunken frigates off the coast of the Bahamas. "Young man," he replied, "I know of a much better expedition than that right here. At your own feet lie treasures untold, and you can have them all by faithful study."

When learning is a chore, there is something wrong. We are surrounded by so many treasures of knowledge waiting to be mined! Who can possibly be bored in a world like ours??

Art credit: *Bookworm* by Carl Spitzweg

"Reading furnishes us only with the materials of knowledge," said John Locke; "it is thinking that makes what we read ours."

"In order to get the most out of books, the reader must be a thinker. The mere acquisition of facts is not the acquisition of power. To fill the mind with knowledge that cannot be made available is like filling our houses with furniture and bric-a-brac until we have no room to move about.

"If you wish to become intellectually strong, after reading with the closest attention, form this habit: frequently close your book and sit and think, or stand and walk and think--but think, contemplate, reflect. Turn what you have read over and over in your mind.

"Many people have an idea that if they keep reading everlastingly, if they always have a book in their hands at every leisure moment, they will, of necessity, become full-rounded and well-educated.

"But they might just as well expect to become athletes by eating at every opportunity. It is even more necessary to think than to read. Thinking, contemplating, what we have read, is what digestion and assimilation are to food.

"Some of the biggest fools I know are always cramming themselves with knowledge. But they never think. When they get a few minutes' leisure they grab a book and go to reading. In other words, they are always eating intellectually, but never digesting their knowledge or assimilating it."

By every reader Let Milton's words be borne in mind:

"Who reads
Incessantly, and to his reading brings not
A spirit and judgment equal or superior...
Uncertain and unsettled still remains,
Deep versed in books and shallow in himself..."

Elizabeth Barrett Browning says: "We err by reading too much, and out of proportion to what we think. I should be wise, I am persuaded, if I had not read half as much..."

"It is a grand thing to read a good book--it is a grander thing to live a good life."

(From *Pushing to the Front* by Orison Swett Marden)

So for all of you who think that I am suggesting you read books all day long, not at all! A big par of educating the heart well is to find that balance--daily feeding your heart, but allowing plenty of time for digestion. Your children need that 'digestion' time, as well. And on the outside, it may appear as play or even doing 'nothing' or having a conversation. Notebooking is part of that digestion process, as well.

Art credit: *Summertime* by Joseph Farquharson

"Of this thing be certain: wouldst thou plant for Eternity, then plant into the deep infinite faculties of man, His Fantasy and Heart. Wouldst thou plant for Year and Day, then plant into his shallow superficial faculties, his self-love and arithmetical understanding…"

--Thomas Carlyle

Art credit: *Children in the Garden* by Wladyslaw Podkowinski

"In the best books, great men talk to us, and give us their most precious thoughts… They give to all who will faithfully use them the society and the presence of the best and greatest of our race."

--Channing

Art credit: *A Walk by the River* by Alfred Augustus Glendening, Jr.

"It instead of a gem or even a flower, we could cast the gift of a lovely thought into the heart of a friend, that would be giving as angels give."

--George MacDonald

Art credit: *Gossips* by Daniel Ridgway Knight

This month's Mother's University topic is imagination. Here's a crash course from an 1896 text, Imagination and Dramatic Instinct by S.S. Curry, PhD.

Why should the imagination be trained?

1. Its perversion is one of the leading causes of the degradation of character.

2. It is the chief creative faculty.

3. It gives man taste and refinement.

4. It raises him out of a narrow prison into communion with the universe.

5. It lifts him into relation with all things and all men.

6. It develops the comprehension of universal principles.

7. All true appreciation of art and literature is dependent on its exercise.

8. It enables man to appreciate not only the art of his own age and his own country, but that of all other lands and times. By its power he can become a Greek, and see as the Greeks saw, and feel as the Greeks felt.

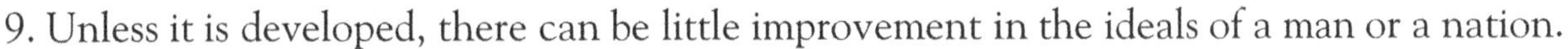

9. Unless it is developed, there can be little improvement in the ideals of a man or a nation.

10. It enables us to enter into sympathy with our fellow-man. By its power alone can we appreciate the point of view of those different from ourselves.

11. It gives us the power to penetrate to the heart of Nature.

12. It is the faculty which sees beauty and loveliness.

13. It discovers grace in the motion of the storm.

14. It is the faculty which enables man to realize eternity and God.

15. Work without imagination is drudgery, but with it the humblest employment is lifted into the realm of beauty and art.

16. The imagination is the source of all inspiration and interest in life; its activity creates beauty in the commonest objects of handicraft, and gives charm to the humbles home.

Yet, the development of the imagination has been given little or no place in the courses of study in our schools.

How much time are you allowing for the development of the imagination in your busy days?

Art credit: *Dressing Up* by Fritz Zuber-Buhler

"I do not like to read lies to my child," is the verdict of many a mother. "I give him only histories, biographies, and useful books."

She does not know, this really earnest mother, than she is shutting the door of her child's imagination, and that she may be hampering his power to do great things in after life, by thus closing to him the storehouse of imaginative literature. For later he will not be able to draw full sustenance from classic writings unless he has been fed in youth on the best of folk-literature.

The action of the picture-making power of the mind—the imagination—is a part of almost every mental process.

--Frances Jenkins Olcott

Or, as Albert Einstein puts it: "If you want your child to be intelligent, read him fairy tales. If you want him to be more intelligent, read him more fairy tales."

Art credit: *Sleeping Beauty* by John Collier

May I reach
That purest heaven, be to other souls
The cup of strength in some great agony,
Enkindle generous ardor, feed pure love,
Be the sweet presence of a good diffused
And in diffusion ever more intense!

So shall I join the choir invisible
Whose music is the gladness of the world.

--George Eliot

Art credit: *Windswept* by John William Waterhouse

I know we are all horrified by the massacre of Muslim worshipers in New Zealand.

One of this month's topics is the study of Islam. What impressions will you place on your children's hearts? Will they fear people of other faiths or will they seek to understand them? Remember the danger of the single story.

Like the song says in South Pacific:

You've got to be taught to hate and fear
You've got to be taught from year to year
It's got to be drummed in your dear little ear
You've got to be carefully taught

[Verse 2]

You've got to be taught to be afraid
Of people whose eyes are oddly made
And people whose skin is a diff'rent shade
You've got to be carefully taught

[Verse 3]

You've got to be taught before it's too late
Before you are six or seven or eight
To hate all the people your relatives hate
You've got to be carefully taught

Tomorrow's world will be shaped by what you teach your children today.

Art credit: *Evening Prayer* by Jean Leon Gerome

"The vision that you hold in your mind, the ideal that is enthroned in your heart—this you will build your life by; this you will become."

--Orison Swett Marden

(Why imagination matters…)

Art credit: *Verkleidete Kinder* by Richard Borrmeister

"Childhood is happiness. Every child is happy if no brutal hand is interposed between it and happiness. Air, light, liberty, a little sand and mud—in childhood we need nothing more for being happy. And God gives us these things."

--Armando Palacio Valdes

Art credit: *At Scarborough* by Frederick Morgan

"Every great is a special language of the human spirit, and he who desires to awaken his artistic nature will learn to read all these languages…

"What form of art should be studied? Every form as far as possible; for each art is a distinct language, which expresses some aspect of the human soul and realizes some truth apprehended in NO OTHER WAY."

--S.S. Curry (*Imagination and Dramatic Instinct*)

Art credit: *Apollo and the Muses* by Claud Lorrain

"Beauty is a quality of divinity, and to live much with the beautiful is to live close to the divine. Every beauty in any form…refines and elevates character…

"The time will come when our children will be taught…to consider beauty as a most precious gift…and regarded as a divine instrument of education."

--Orison Swett Marden

Art credit: *Apple Time* by Frederick Morgan

"The world is a colossal university, and no matter how far removed you may be from great institutions of learning, if you are alert and eager to learn you can always absorb something from your environment. We are all God's great kindergarten, where everything is trying to teach us its lesson."

--Orison Swett Marden

Art credit: *The Garland* by Frederick Morgan

"The very foundation of our national life is laid in the home, and the wife and mother is the center, the mainspring of all true home life…

"Our wives and mothers have as yet hardly entered the outer chamber of the beautiful edifice of the ideal home of the future. It is the holy of holies of evolution, and in it lies the very secret of human progress…

"The highest civilizations have scarcely as yet glimpsed the possibilities of home."

--Orison Swett Marden

Art credit: *Heimkehr* by Paul Barthel

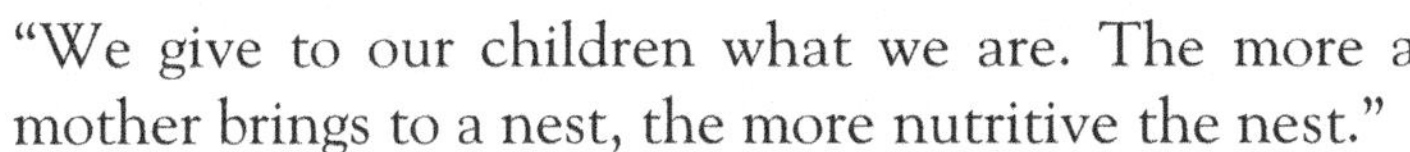

"We give to our children what we are. The more a mother brings to a nest, the more nutritive the nest."

--Neal A. Maxwell

Art credit: *Maternal Admiration* by William-Adolphe Bouguereau

I was just cleaning off my desk and my old friend Orison stopped by to remind me to tell you something he wanted you to know…

"There are a thousand evidences in us that we were intended for temples of beauty, of sweetness, of loveliness, of beautiful ideas…

"There is nothing which will pay so well as to train the finest and truest, the most beautiful qualities in us in order that we may see beauty everywhere and be able to extract sweetness from everything.

"The cultured ear will find harmony in forest and field, melody in babbling brooks, and untold pleasure in all Nature's song.

"The great majority of us are living in the basement of our beings.

"If we would all cultivate a love of the beautiful and scatter beauty seeds as we go through life, what a paradise this earth would become!"

My friend William Wordsworth was listening and said, "I bet I can say that in much fewer words:

"'…with an eye made quiet by the power
Of harmony, and the deep power of joy,
We see into the life of things…'"

I just love it when they hang out with me. But I told them I really have to go grocery shopping now.

Art credit: *Departure for the Field* by Jules Breton

"Mothers who love your children. Do not set them too soon to the study of history; let them dream while they are young."

--Edouard Laboulaye

Art credit: *Boys in Pasture* by Winslow Homer

Written by a poet who never had children of her own...

Two Temples

A builder builded a temple,
He wrought it with grace and skill;
Pillars and groins and arches
All fashioned to work his will.
Men said, as they saw its beauty,
"It shall never know decay;
Great is they skill, O builder!
Thy fame shall endure for aye."

A mother builded a temple
With loving and infinite care,
Planning each arch with patience,
Laying each stone with prayer.
None praised her unceasing efforts,
None knew of her wondrous plan,
For the temple the mother builded
Was unseen by the eyes of man.

Gone is the builder's temple,
Crumpled into the dust;
Low lies each stately pillar,
Food for consuming rust.
But the temple the mother builded
Will last while the ages roll,
For the beautiful unseen temple
Was a child's immortal soul.

--Hattie Vose Hall

Art credit: *The Lily* by Frank William Warwick Topham

I frequently hear moms tell me, after they discover this 'new' way of learning, "I only wish I had known this when my children were younger."

C.S. Lewis offers some insight on that:

"You can't go back and change the beginning, but you can start where you are and change the ending."

Good advice.

Art credit: *On the Heights* by Charles Courtney Curran

A mom in our group alerted me to a beautiful book about mothers as teachers written in 1838—Letters to Mothers by Lydia Sigourney. I'm going to go back and spend more time, but this quote struck me:

"...no universal agent of civilization exists, but through mothers. Nature has placed in their hands, our infancy and youth. I have been among the first to declare the necessity of making them, by improved education, capable of fulfilling their natural mission.

"The love of God and man, is the basis of this system. In proportion as it prevails, national enmities will disappear, prejudices become extinguished, civilization spreads itself far and wide—one great people cover the earth, and the reign of God be established. This is to be hastened, by the watchful care of mothers over their offspring, from the cradle upwards."

Art credit: *Moederzorg* by Evert Pieters

"If you are giving a child a piece of cake, it adds nothing to his enjoyment to tell him that it contains ingredients and was made by certain rules or that it will contribute to his nourishment.

"If it is good, he eats it and wants more."

--Estelle Hurll

That is what you are striving for in a childhood learning—a desire for more.

Art credit: *Birthday Cake* by Auguste Ludwig

"That country is the richest which nourishes the greatest number of noble and happy human beings."

--John Ruskin

Art credit: *The Storybook* of Heinrich Hirt

I frequently quote a line from a poem Michelangelo wrote: "My unassisted heart is barren clay..."

I thought you may enjoy more of the poem, which demonstrates the third step in the Pattern of Learning, which he evidently understood.

My unassisted heart is barren clay,
That of its native self can nothing feel.
Of good and pious works Thou are the seed,
That quickens only where Thou sayest it may,
No man can find it. Father! Thou must lead!
Do Thou then breathe those thoughts into my mind,
By which such virtue may in me be bred,
That in Thy holy footsteps I may tred.

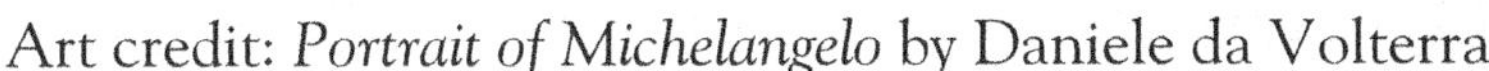

Art credit: *Portrait of Michelangelo* by Daniele da Volterra

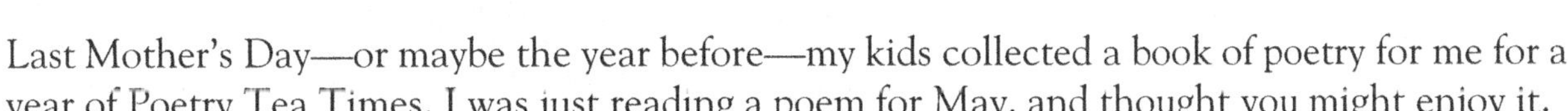

Last Mother's Day—or maybe the year before—my kids collected a book of poetry for me for a year of Poetry Tea Times. I was just reading a poem for May, and thought you might enjoy it.

Red Geraniums by Martha Haskell Clark

Life did not bring me silken gowns,
Nor jewels for my hair,
Nor signs of gabled foreign towns
In distant countries fair,
But I can glimpse, beyond my pane,
a green and friendly hill
And geraniums aflame upon my window sill.
The brambled cares of everyday,
The tiny humdrum things,
May bind my feet when they would stray,
But still my heart has wings
While Red Geraniums are bloomed
against my window glass,
And low above my green-sweet hill
the Gypsy wind-clouds pass.
And if my dreamings ne'er come true,
The brightest and the best,
But leave me lone my journey through,
I'll set my heart at rest,
And thank God for home—sweet things, a green and friendly hill,
And red geraniums aflame upon my window sill.

Art credit: *Geraniums* by Johann Baptist Reiter

"That country is the richest which nourishes the greatest number of noble and happy human beings."

--John Ruskin

Art credit: *The Children's Storybook* by Sophie Anderson

"We are taught nearly everything except the very thing we ought to know—the art of living."

--Orison Swett Marden

Art credit: *Madchen mit dem Rotkehlchen* by Richard Borrmeister

A little food for thought:

Oscar Wilde: "Nothing that is worth knowing can be taught."

David Bednar: "The most important learnings of life are caught—not taught." "An answer given by another person usually is not remembered for very long, if remembered at all."

Art credit: *Resting in the Wood* by Anton Dieffenbach

Kate Douglas Wiggin was one of the heart-based education pioneers who founded the kindergarten movement in the US, starting in California. You may recognize her as the author of *Rebecca of Sunnybrook Farm*.

I just found this Foreword she wrote to a children's reader and thought it was worth passing along:

"Christ it was who disdained not the use of objects and symbols, remembering that it was the childhood of the race. He it was who spake in parable and stories, laying bare soul of man and heart of nature, and revealing each by divine analogy. He it was who took the little ones in His arms and blessed them; who set the child in the midst, saying, 'Except ye become as one of these.'

"May the afterglow that inspired teaching ever shine upon the path we are treading. May we bathe our tired spirits in its warmth and glory, and kindle our torches at the splendor of its light."

Art credit: *Making a Flower String* by Evert Pieters

A little Monday morning inspiration:

If You Can Smile

If you can smile when things go wrong
And say, "It doesn't matter,"
If you can laugh off care and woe
And trouble makes you fatter;
If you can keep a happy face
When all around are blue—
Then have your head examined, Bud,
There's something wrong with you!
For one thing I've arrived at:
There are no "ands" and "buts";
The guy that's grinning all the time
Must be completely nuts.

--Author Unknown

Art credit: *The Night Alarm the Advance* by Charles West Cope

"Beauty is everywhere—in white clouds against the blue, in the gray bole of the beech, the play of a kitten, the lovely flight and beautiful colouring of birds, in the hills and the valleys and the streams, in the wind-flower and the blossom of the broom. What we call Nature is all Beauty and delight, and the person who watches Nature closely and knows her well, like the poet Wordsworth, for example, has his Beauty Sense always active, always bringing him joy."

--Charlotte Mason

Art credit: *Junge Gansemagd auf Einer Wiese* by Paul Wilhelm Keller-Reutlingen

I am in Utah with a new grandbaby, but my husband can't come until later. I got a text from him on Sunday:

"I don't understand it! The more sugar I put in the potatoes the saltier it gets. Yikes!"

But the time I got the text, the damage was done and he had to throw out the potatoes that were supposed to go with the roast beef.

What he didn't know was that just before I left, I had filled an empty canister on the counter with a box of salt I had just bought. He assumed because of the size of the container, it was sugar. Sometimes if the potatoes had gotten too salty, adding a little sugar helped. So he kept adding 'sugar' and it kept getting worse!

I thought how that applies to learning. Sometimes we accept false assumptions about how children learn and we think if we just keep doing more of what we are doing, things will improve.

But really, the problem is we are operating under a false assumption.

That is why it is so important to keep an open heart and to keep learning about how children learn. When you find the right way for your child, the experience should be sweet—just like the potatoes were supposed to be.

Art credit: *Girl Peeling Potatoes* by Albert Anker

"A man with an experience is never at the mercy of a man with an opinion."

A person can study WEH principles for a long, long time and still waver. But once you actually experience the power of a story or music or art or poetry in your own lives, or experience the freedom of learning outside a curriculum, what other people say about what you are doing matters less and less, don't you think?

Art credit: *The Difficult Lesson* by William-Adolphe Bouguereau

As you gear up for the new school year, remember:

"For God hath not given us the spirit of fear; but of power, and love, and of a sound mind." (2 Timothy 1)

You can do this!

Art credit: *Maternal Joy* by Adolf von Becker

"It's man's life, the mere living! How fit to employ

All the heart and soul and the senses forever in joy."

--Robert Browning

Art credit: *Summer and Playing Children* by Nikolai Astrup

"We are able to feel and learn very quickly through music, through art, through poetry some spiritual things that we would otherwise learn very slowly."

--Boyd K. Packer

Art credit: A *Summer's Day* by Charles Baugniet

From today's reading in Farrar's *Life of Christ*—consider this in light of the education of your children:

"If they would see the star which should at once direct their feet and influence their destiny, they must look for it not in the changing skies of outward circumstances, but each in the depth of his own heart."

Art credit: *The Golden Hour* by Thomas Moran

"Study without thought is vain;
Thought without study is dangerous."

--Confucius

Art credit: *Small Abbate with Books Under his Arms* by Axel Helsted

I started reading the new history of The Church of Jesus Christ of Latter-day Saints and couldn't help noting the first paragraph of the Preface:

"True stories well told can inspire, caution, entertain, and instruct. Brigham Young understood the power of a good story when he counseled Church historians to do more than simply record the dry facts of the past. 'Write in a narrative style,' he advised them, and 'write only about one tenth part as much.'"

It reminds me of Rudyard Kipling:

"If history were told in the form of stories, it would never be forgotten."

Stories are the most valuable tool in your teaching tool box! And notice the attention of these children in the painting. Nothing will hold their attention like a story told 'by heart.'

Art credit: *Grandmother's Tales* by Rudolf Gessler

It seems like every day when I read from Farrar's *Life of Christ*, I read something that pertains to this group. Here is today's offering:

"It is not the influence of external forces, but it is the germinal principle of life within, which makes the good seed to grow; nor can the hard heart by converted by portents and prodigies (think threats and fears or even visions of grandeur), but by the inward humility, and the grace of God stealing downward like the dew of heaven, in silence and unseen."

Art credit: *Still Life with Blossom* by Margaretha Roosenboom

"...when the soul is as full of beautiful things as an overflowing river, some of them are sure to get out where people will see."

Art credit: A *Nibble* by Edmund Blair Leighton

"Grapes must be crushed to make wine.
Diamond form under pressure.
Olives are pressed to release oil.
Seeds grow in darkness.
Whenever you feel crushed, pressed, or in darkness, you're in a powerful place of transformation.
Trust the process.

Trust God."

Art credit: *The Grape Harvest* by Leon-Augustin L'hermitte

"Joy is the serious business of heaven."

--C.S. Lewis

Art credit: *Mädchengespräche auf der Gänsewiese* by Luigi Chialiva

From Delphian Book 10, p. 115:

"The man should be the master, not the slave of his learning… It is better to be the master of a little knowledge, with the capacity to use it creatively, than to be the unproductive carrier of all the learning in the libraries."

A creative use for our learning is the final step in the Pattern for Learning. Without an outlet, even pure waters become stale and stagnate.

Art credit: *Mother and Child Reading a Story* by Carlton Alfred Smith

In a book about education written a hundred years ago, I found:

"Formerly, the question was, What does a man need to know? Now the question is being asked, What does he need to be?"

The same question is on the table today.

A heart-based education is focused on 'being'—being curious, kind, honest, diligent, loyal, faithful, etc.

A mind-based education is focused on 'knowing'—the year of the American revolution, the order of the planets, the capital of Arkansas.

What is more important to you? The 'knowing' or the 'being'?

You have to decide that for yourself. And then pay attention to what you are spending the most time doing. Does it align?

Art credit: *The Fairy Tale* by James Sant

Be a light, not a hammer.

Art credit: *Mother and Children in Front of a House* by Hermann Sondermann

I've been talking about Imagination resources in the Take 5s the last couple of weeks. Someone pulled up an old post and I think this is worth posting again. It was in response to a mom who said she is a literal thinker. She likes her days mapped out.

You are describing the mind-culture we are as a people—very much in control. It's the system almost all of us have been raised in. Yes—you are a literal thinker. And so is just about everyone else. It's the lack of 'imaginative' power-the thinking of the heart-that is causing problems in the world in my opinion. Imagination is the seat of empathy, motivation, hope, vision, dreams. And we shut down its development by focusing on that which we can test and measure in childhood. The act of decoding words does not make a child a reader. The act of constructing a sentence does not make a child a writer. ONLY the imagination can do that. And the imagination can ONLY be developed in the atmosphere of freedom and a generous supply of the arts--story, music, poetry and picture. Mechanized learning interferes.

So what does leaving the shore look like? The risk is you lose control. You let your child bloom according to the seeds planted within individual hearts. You allow for failure.

The plus side--an awakening to beauty, love, joy--all expressions of the heart. The heart cannot be accessed through the mind. But the mind, that is accessed through the heart, will be whole. Scientists who studied Einsteins brain said the connections between the two sides were massive. He used his whole brain--that is the secret of his genius and the secret to ours.

Art credit: *The Fairy Tale* by Walther Firle

I love the solution that someone just offered in another post for when you are overwhelmed and don't know where to go next.

Just. Start. Reading.

I couldn't agree more.

Art credit: *Alice in Wonderland* by George Dunlop Leslie

"Imagination is the key by which we unlock the doors of beauty."

--Estelle Hurll

Art credit: *Blick Aus Dem Entree* by Henrik Nordenberg

"My son, I tell the soothfastly
No gift is like to liberty."

--William Wallace

Art credit: *The Trial of William Wallace* by Daniel Maclise

John Wanamaker was once asked to invest in an expedition to recover from the Spanish Main doubloons which for half a century had lain at the bottom of the sea in sunken frigates.

"Young men," he replied, "I know of a better expedition than this, right here. Near your own feet lie treasures untold; you can have them all by faithful study.

"Let us know be content to mine the most coal, to make the largest locomotives, to weave the largest quantities of carpets; but, amid the sounds of the pick, the blows of the hammer, the rattle of the looms, and the roar of the machinery, take care that the immortal mechanism of God's own hand—the mind—is still full-trained for the highest and noblest service."

(From Orison Swett Marden's *Pushing to the Front*)

Art credit: *Astronomer by Candlelight* by Gerrit Dou

"Everyone dies, but not everyone lives."

--William Wallace

Art credit: *Wein, Weib und Gesang* by Josef Danhauser

An ounce of morning is worth a pound of afternoon!

Art credit: *Early Morning* by Moritz von Schwind

My daughter texted me—at midnight—that I should go read Delphian Volume 4 pp. 40-43. It talks about Early Christianity in the days of Rome. This idea struck me:

Jesus left no writings. Nothing was written down until some time after his death. Yet, "we know much of his wonderful personality, which the greatest students of Christianity admit to be the essence of the faith. It was the striking personality which gave such a pulse of life to his teachings... Their religion was something to be felt rather than expressed in words."

We spend so much time worrying about teaching skills to our children, but what we are trying to accomplish here at WEH is to develop their personalities.

There is a section in the Restoring the Art of Storytelling book where the storytellers talk about warming your own heart first:

"The parent...should first enrich his own personality through an understanding of the essential values of literature and of life. The person whose life is colorless, whose emotions are pallid, whose experience is narrow, whose appreciation of beauty is undeveloped, whose knowledge of literature is limited, should face squarely the fact that he is not the one to guide the development of a child. He should kindle the flame in his own life before he attempts to pass on the torch." (Esenwein)

(P.S. Don't let that statement discourage you! You only have to be one step ahead of your kids.)

How to obtain a rich personality: "By loving the beautiful, by reading the worth-while, by filling the mind with those things that are worth passing on, by cultivation of a cheery disposition, by striving towards high ideals." (Eggleston)

"Love paints the pictures, writes the poems, sings the songs, bears the burdens and does all the great and abiding deeds." (Wyches)

"A deep and abiding soul life is more important than the mouthing of many words. The measure of our influence is not what we say but what we are..." (Wyches)

"The story which lacks an inner spiritual quality is...devoid of power to stir a soul." (Edward St. John)

Why do I not focus on academics? Because there is something deeper within all of us!

Art credit: *Jesus at the Home of Mary and Martha* by Harold Copping

I copied this passage this morning from Farrar's *Life of Christ*. It is Jesus' last journey to Bethany.

"Jesus did not love cities, and scarcely ever slept within their precincts…and though the necessities of His work compelled Him to visit Jerusalem… He seems to have retired on every possible occasion beyond its gates—partly because He loved that sweet home of Bethany—and partly, too, because He felt the peaceful joy of treading the grass that groweth on the mountains rather than the city stones, and could hold gladder communion with His Father in heaven under the shadow of the olive trees, where, far from disturbing sights and sounds, He could watch the splendor of the sunset and the falling of the dew…

"The exquisite beauty of the Syrian evening, the tender colors of the spring grass and flower…the distant hills bathed in the primrose light of sunset, the coolness and balm of the breeze after the burning glare—

"[W]hat must these have been to Him to whose eye the world of Nature was an open book, on every page of which He read His Father's name!"

Art credit: *Christ and Child* by Carl Bloch

I'm now to the chapter on the trial in Farrar's *Life of Christ*. He talked about how sceptics (his spelling) use the discrepancies between the four gospels to raise doubt and I thought his response applies to our study of history.

He talks of "histories honest and faithful up to the full knowledge of the writers, but each, if taken alone, confessedly fragmentary and obviously incomplete.

"After repeated study, I declare, quite fearlessly, that though the slight variations are numerous—though the lesser particulars cannot in every instance be rigidly and minutely accurate—though no one of the narratives taken singly would give us an adequate impression—…it is perfectly possible to discover how one Evangelist supplements the details furnished by another, and perfectly possible to understand the true sequence of the incidents by combining into one whole the separate indications which they furnish."

My conclusion: Read widely and do not allow yourself ever to let one book of history be the final word. Truth will eventually emerge even though 'facts' seem contradictory. There is a danger in the single story.

This principle of learning is even woven into the Bible in the most important story ever told.

Art credit: *Christ Before Caiaphas* by Mattias Stom

I have been pondering this passage from one of Orison Swett Marden's writings:

"Fortunate is the person who has been educated to the perception of beauty; he possesses a heritage of which no reverses can rob him. Yet it is a heritage possible to all 'who will take the trouble to begin early in life to cultivate the finer qualities of the soul, the eye and the heart.

"'I am a lover of untainted and immortal beauty,' exclaims Emerson. 'Oh, world, what pictures and what harmony are thine!'

"A great scientists tells us that there is no natural object in the universe, which, if seen as the Master sees it, coupled with all its infinite meaning, its utility and purpose, is not beautiful. Just as the most disgusting object, if put under a magnifying glass of sufficient power, would reveal beauties undreamed of, so even the most unlovely environment, the most cruel conditions, will, when viewed through the glass of a trained and disciplines mind, show something of the beautiful and the hopeful.

"A life that has been rightly trained will extract sweetness from everything; it will see beauty everywhere."

The cultivation of the finer qualities of the soul, the eye and the heart is the work of WEH.

Art credit: *Evening* by Corot

A little inspiration from Wordsworth:

"Nature never did betray
The heart that loved her; 'tis her privilege
Through all the years of this, our life, to leap
From joy to joy; for she can so inform
The mind that is within us, so impress
With quietness and beauty, and so feed
With lofty thoughts, that neither evil tongues,
Rash judgments, nor the sneers of selfish men,
Nor greetings where no kindness is, nor all
The dreary intercourse of daily life,
Shall e'er prevail against us, or disturb
Our cheerful faith, that all which we behold
Is full of blessings."

Art credit: *La Guirlande de Fleurs des Champs* by Virginie Demont-Breton

"It isn't how much we have, but how much we enjoy that gives us happiness."

--Charles Spurgeon

Art credit: *Grosvaters Tranzun-terricht* by Franz von Defregger

"All of humanity's problems stem from man's inability to sit quietly in a room alone."

--Blaise Pascal

Art credit: *Der Brief* by Johann Joseph Geisser

"Real happiness is not dependent on external things. The pond is fed from within. The kind of happiness that stays with you is the happiness that springs from inward thoughts and emotions. You must think of this now, while you are young. You must cultivate your mind if you wish to achieve enduring happiness. You must furnish your mind with interesting thoughts and ideas. For an empty mind grows bored and cannot endure itself. An empty mind seeks pleasure as a substitute for happiness." – William L. Phelps

Inside Out.

"The happiest person is the person who thinks the most interesting thoughts." –Timothy Dwight

Art credit: A *Chestnut Tree by a Pond* in Autumn, by Peder Mork Monsted

"Doing better does not always mean doing more."

--Sharon Eubank

Art credit: *Blackberry Picking* by James Clarke Hook

"The grand essentials to happiness in this life are something to do, something to love, something to hope for."

--Joseph Addison

Art credit: *The Lanterns* by Charles Courtney Curran

Longfellow understood this business of tending to the 'temple' within:

Let us then labor for an inward stillness,
An inward stillness and an inward healing,
That perfect silence where the lips and heart
Are still, and we no longer entertain
Our own imperfect thought and vain options,
But God alone speaks in us, and we wait
In singleness of heart, that we may know
His will, and in the silence of our spirits,
That we may do His will, and do that only!

Art credit: *Thoughtful Reader* by Frantisek Dvorak

"The cure for everything is salt water—sweat, teas or the sea."

--Karen Blixen

Art credit: *Women by the Sea* by Sergey Vinogradov

"If we could have but one generation of properly born, trained, educated and healthy children, a thousand other problems of government would vanish."

--Herbert Hoover

Art credit: *Singende Kinder* by Ferdinand Georg Waldmuller

"It is better to put the yeast into the bread before the bread is put into the boy.

"The normal [child] demands a story. This is the law of life. It is more; it is as vital as breathing.

"The Bible does not open with a scientific disquisition upon the evolutionary hypothesis of anthropological origins—it begins with the story of Adam and Eve. Even the Great Teacher did not speak without a parable."

--On the *Historical Story* by Everett Tomlinson

Art credit: *The Boyhood of Raleigh* by John Everett Millais

"The Lord recognized…it would take man thousands of years to make the earth habitable for self-governing individuals."

--David O. McKay

Are we helping our children take advantage of the wisdom learned through the ages? Or do we ignore it and, in essence, cause a new generation to start at square one? Let them 'stand on the shoulders of giants' so that they can be the generation for which all the souls of the past have labored.

We are living in the great day of the harvest. Thrust in your sickles and reap!

Art credit: *Kleiner Gartner Schnuppert an Blumen* by Jean-Paul Haag

"One of the most tragic things I know about human nature is that all of us tend to put off living. We are all dreaming of some magical rose garden over the horizon—instead of enjoying the roses that are blooming outside our windows today."

--Dale Carnegie

Art credit: *The Soul of the Rose* by Waterhouse

"True genius is impossible without heart; no amount of intellect alone or of imagination, no, nor of both together, can make genius. Love is the soul of genius."

--Gottfried von Jacquin

Art credit: *Zither-Playing Girl* by Franz von Defregger

I was reminiscing with my family this morning about living in the 'olden days' when there were no skinless, boneless chicken breasts to cook with. I remember a RS homemaking night that taught us how to remove bones from chicken, but it was too hard. I rarely cooked chicken recipes.

The my 98-year-old mother posted this in our family group: "My mother had to clean the insides out of the chicken (after my dad killed it and hung it up to bleed). Then she defeathered it, cut it in pieces and cooked it. The defeathering was before the gutting. I never learned to cook at home. Wonder why?"

If there is nothing else in your life today that you are grateful for, take a moment to be grateful for boneless, skinless chicken breasts!

(Unless you are a vegetarian, of course. If I lived in my mother's day, I think that's exactly what I would have been. Or starved.)

Art credit: *Plucking the Fowl* by William Henry Hunt

"If instead of a gem or even a flower, we could cast the gift of a lovely thought into the heart of a friend, that would be giving as angels give."

--George MacDonald

Art credit: *Strazny Andel* by Frantisek Dvorak

"It is better to light a candle than to curse the darkness."
Art credit: *Junge Mutter* by Albert Anker

"Anything will give up its secrets, if you love it long enough."

--George Washington Carver

Art credit: *De Vlinders* by August Allebe

"Love paints the pictures, writes the poems, sings the songs, bears the burdens, and does all the great and abiding deeds."

--Richard Wyches

Art credit: June Sunlight by Joseph decamp

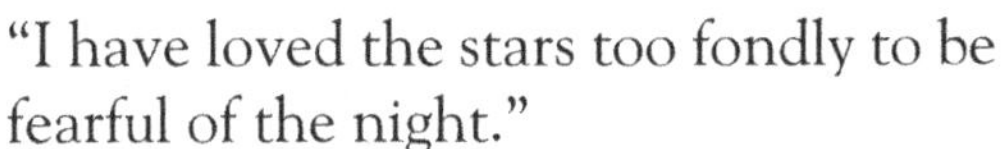

"I have loved the stars too fondly to be fearful of the night."

--An old astronomer to his pupil

Art credit: *Kyrkrodd, Dalarna* by Bengt Nordenberg

I loved this quote shared by Lisa Underwood:

"Let us learn of the handiwork of God by the study of nature, search out her flowers, her moods, her laws;

"Let us study to improve our thoughts, reaching up toward our Heavenly Father, praying for the inspiration of the Holy Ghost;

"Let us improve the language in our homes and among our children, that our words be not idle, complaining, nor vain, but, as nothing can be lost, cheerful, hopeful, intelligent, reflecting a charitable spirit.

"Let us open the books of life and salvation and study also the great authors, poets, and painters, that our minds may be clothed with intelligence and our hearts about with human feeling.."

--Bathsheba W. Smith

If you are looking for a curriculum guide, this sounds like a good one!

Art credit: The Golden Rays by Herbert James Draper

"If sunrise could be witnessed but once a year, who would be abed on the morning of that more than imperial pageant; yet is the splendor less, because almost every day it streams across the sky?...

"The fault of spiritual poverty is in ourselves, not in our surroundings…the eye must be clarified to see the vision, the ear opened to hear the beatific tidings."

--W.H. Milburn

Art credit: *Pythagoreans Celebrate Sunrise* by Fyodor Bronnikov

"Things that matter most must never be at the mercy of things that matter least."

--Goethe

Art credit: *Young Lord Hamlet* by Philip Calderon

"He who neglects his finer spiritual sentiment shall find that the inner light hath failed."

--Newell Dwight Hills

Art credit: *Otroci v Travi* by Ivana Kobilca

"The highest civilizations have scarcely as yet glimpsed the possibilities of home."

--Orison Swett Marden

Art credit: *Idyllic Family* by Eugenio Zampighi

"Better to limp on the right road than to speed on the wrong one."

Art credit: *Children on a Country Road* by H.A. Brendekilde

A global pandemic, economic collapse and now an earthquake certainly has a way of bringing what really matters in focus, doesn't it?

How concerned are you about math scores today?

Art credit: *Good Morning* by Friedrich Eduard Meyerheim

"Grapes must be crashed to make wine.
Diamonds form under pressure.
Olives are pressed to release oil.
Seeds grow in darkness.
Whenever you feel crushed, pressed, or in darkness, you're in a powerful place of transformation.
Trust the process. Trust God."

--Lalah Delia

Art credit: *Coin de Vigne* by Edouard Debat-Pondsan

Art credit: *A Helping Hand* by Eugene de Blaas

The Kitchen Prayer

"Lord of all pots and pans and things,
Since I've not time to be
A saint by doing lovely things or watching late with Thee,
Or dreaming in the dawn of light or storming
Heaven's gates
Make me a saint by getting meals and washing up the plates.
Although I must have Martha's hands,
I have a Mary mind
And when I black the boots and shoes—,
Thy sandals, Lord, I find.
I think of how they trod the earth,
What time I scrub the floor
Accept this meditation Lord, I haven't time for more.
Warm all the kitchen with Thy love; and light it with Thy peace
Forgive me all my worrying and make my grumbling cease.
Thou who didst love to give men food, in room or by the sea
Accept this service that I do,
I do it unto Thee."

One important lesson we are learning through WEH is how to keep hearts from failing in difficult times. Don't underestimate the power of small and simple means: a story, a poem, a song, a picture, a simple walk outside.

All free, by the way.

Art credit: *Familienidylle vor der Feuerstelle* by Johann Georg Meyer

"Reading gives us someplace to go when we have to stay where we are."

--Mason Cooley

Art credit: *Boy with Apple* by Karl Witkowski

"Those who would see wonderful things must often be ready to travel alone."

--Henry van Dyke (The Other Wise Man)

Art credit: *Femme au Jardin* by Claude Monet

While the kingdom 'without' has been put on hold, this is your opportunity to do some serious building of the kingdom 'within.'

Art credit: *Grossmutter mit drei Enkelkindern* by Ferdinand Georg Waldmuller

I was reminded this morning of something I said when I addressed the World Congress of Families a few years ago. I don't believe we are in full blown winter yet, but nature and history cycles teach us it will come.

Keep harvesting.

"This is the day of harvest. It is a day to thrust in your sickle and reap with diligence because you know what follows Fall's harvest. Already you may be seeing signs of approaching winter. The leaves are changing color and starting to drop off the trees. There's a bit of a chill in the air. But you don't have to be afraid. Within the harvest are lessons on how to survive harsh winters. And if you've been wise, you will have stored enough to sustain yourself through cold winter months when nothing grows. Winter can be a time to rest from heavy labors, to wrap up in a warm blanket, sit in front of a fire and reflect on things that really matter. Even on the coldest day of winter is found great beauty. Some of the greatest masterpieces of literature, art and music have come from history's winters. And if the winter's day seems especially long and dark and dreary, you can hold on to the hope and promise of spring, because spring always follows winter. Always. It will be a time of new beginnings; of clearing away rotting leaves and digging new furrows in the earth to plant the seeds saved from the fruits of fall's harvest. And there will be fresh scented breezes."

Art credit: *La Seconde Recolte* by Julien Dupre

"Earth's crammed with heaven. And every common bush afire with God. But only he who sees takes off his shoes. The rest sit round and pluck blackberries."

--Elizabeth Barrett Browning

Art credit: *Three Little Girls Picking Blackberries* by H.A. Brendekidle

A little WEH instruction from Dieter Uchtdorf:

"Would you honestly want everything spelled out in every detail? Would you honestly want every question answered? Every destination mapped out?

"...most of us would tire out pretty quickly from this kind of heavenly micromanagement.

"We learn the important lessons of life through experience; we learn through our mistakes."

Art credit: *Recado Dificil* by Jose Ferraz de Almedia, Jr.

"The word heart...often denotes the inner feelings of an individual. Our hearts—the sum total of our desires, affections, intentions, motives, and attitudes—define who we are determine what we will become."

--David A. Bednar

That's why so much focus on a well-educated heart here!

Art credit: *Maternite* by Elizabeth Jane Gardner

Happy hearts and happy faces
Happy play in grassy places—
That was how, in ancient ages
Children grew to kings and sages.

--Robert Louis Stevenson

Art credit: *An Archipelago with Children* by Lotten Ronquist

I have been gathering folk songs for awhile now as I have slowly come to understand why learning folk songs of other nations should matter to us.

I just read the foreword of an old folk song book I picked up and I think this sums it up:

"If we, in America, are going to be good neighbors with the rest of the world, it is important that we come to know how people in other lands think and feel. The songs of a people reveal more truly than do anything else the spirit and mood of their daily lives... Some of them are very old and all of them have for generations been used to express the spirit of the people from whence they came.

"Because we are such a young nation we, in America, have not yet developed very much fine music of our own. If, however, all of the boys and girls are given an opportunity for training in music, in the course of time we too shall have a great American musical art."

The Arts are the great preservers of Truth through the generations. What will we be leaving behind from which generations to come will learn about our hearts?

Art credit: *Sunday Evening in a Farmhouse* by Amalia Lindegren

"Fortunate is the person who has been educated to the perception of beauty; he possesses a heritage of which no reverses can rob him...

"A great scientist tells us that there is no natural object in the universe which, if seen as the Master sees it, coupled with all its infinite meaning, its utility and purpose, is not beautiful."

"Beauty is God's handwriting. Just as the most disgusting object, if put under a magnifying glass of sufficient power, would reveal beauties undreamed of, so even the most unlovely environment, the most cruel conditions, will, when viewed through the glass of a trained and disciplined mind, show something of the beautiful and hopeful.

"A life that has been rightly trained will extract sweetness from everything; it will see beauty everywhere." --Orison Swett Marden

Art credit: *Sommarang* by Fanny Brate

"Never mistake knowledge for wisdom. One helps you make a living; the other helps you make a life."

--S. Carey

Art credit: *Jeune Fille d'Orphelinat* by Nicolaas van der Waay

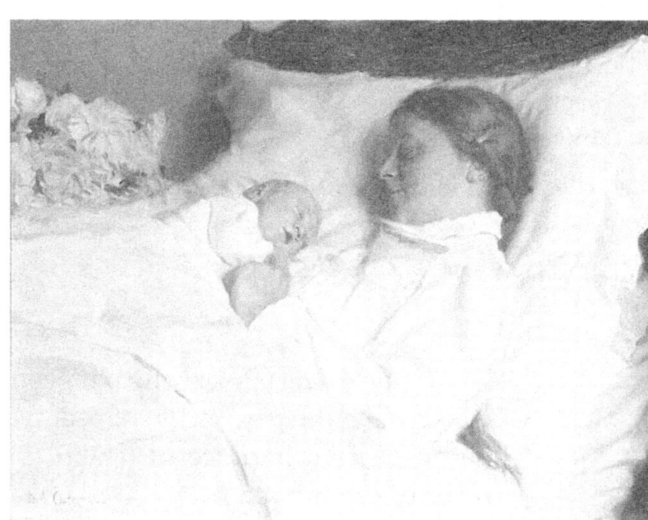

"What happens in society all begins with a baby."

--Mrs. Anwar Sadat

Art credit: *Mother and Child* by Emil Osterman

"Give me good mothers and I will change the world."

--Pius IX

Art credit: *Mutter beim Ankleiden des Kindes* by Rudolf Epp

"Mother love works magic for humanity."

--Frances Willard

Art: *An Algerian Mother* and Child by Guillaume-Charles Brun

"The world has enough women who are tough; we need women who are tender. There are enough women who are coarse. We need women who are kind. There are enough women who are rude; we need women who are refined."

--Margaret Nadauld

Art credit: *Pardon Mama* by Emile Munier

"All true trophies of the ages
Are from mother-love impearled;
For the hand that rocks the cradle
is the hand that rules the world."

--William Ross Wallace

Art credit: *The Cradle* by Berthe Morisot

"Let us keep our children for our own, during their earlier years. The world will have them long enough afterward."

--From *Letters to a Mother* by Lydia Sigourney

Art credit: *Mother and Child* by Mary Cassatt

"When the real history of mankind is fully disclosed, will what happened in cradles prove to be more controlling than what happened in congresses?"

--Neal Maxwell

Mother's matter!

Art credit: *Lulled to Sleep* by Adolph Artz

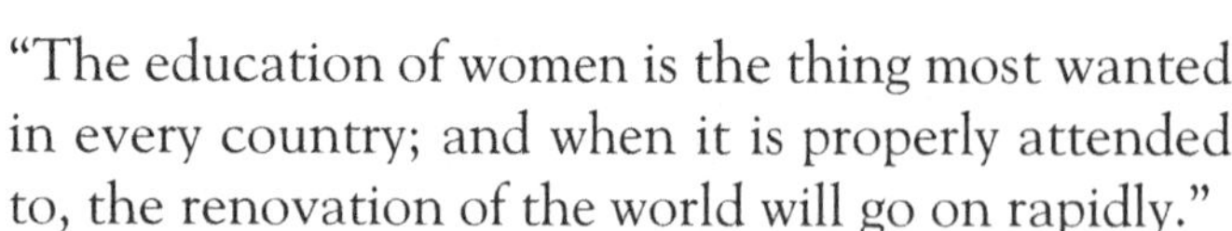

"The education of women is the thing most wanted in every country; and when it is properly attended to, the renovation of the world will go on rapidly."

--James Thomson

Art credit: *The Evening Hour* by George Hardy

Renowned educator, Marva Collins, taught: "If you can't make a mistake, you can't make anything."

And this connecting thought just popped up in my feed: "Never make the same mistake twice. There are so many new ones—try a different one each day!"

I can definitely do that!

Art credit: *Getting Ready* by Carlton Alfred Smith

Happy is free.

Art credit: *Kinderreigen* by Mieczyslaw Reyzner

"By words, one transmits thoughts to another; by means of art, one transmits feeling."

--Leo Tolstoy

Art credit: *Idealismo y Realidad* by Juan Comba Garcia

In Flander's Fields originated in remembrance of lives sacrificed in World War I, a Month 10 topic. In three days, on June 6, we'll remember the lives sacrificed on Normandy Beach in WWII. This poem reminds us of the sacrifices of all who have given their lives for others—and what we owe them.

In Flanders Fields

In Flanders fields the poppies blow
Between the crosses, row on row,
That mark our place; and in the sky
The larks, still bravely singing, fly
Scarce heard amid the guns below.
We are the Dead. Short days go
We lived, felt dawn, saw sunset glow,
Loved and were loved, and now we lie,
In Flanders fields.

Take up our quarrel with the foe:
To you from failing hands we throw
The torch; be yours to hold up high.
If he break faith with us who die
We shall not sleep, though poppies grow
In Flanders fields.

--John McCrae

Art credit: *Coquelicots* by Robert Vonnoh

Books are keys to wisdom's treasures;
Books are gates to lands of pleasure;
Books are paths that upward lead;
Books are friends. Come, let us read!

--Emilie Poulsson

Art credit: *The Half Holiday* by Elizabeth Adela Forbes

"No longer talk at all about the kind of man that a good man ought to be, but be such."

--Marcus Aurelius

Art credit: *The Two Brothers* by Firmin Baes

"Outward circumstances do not determine the course of our lives as much as the thoughts that habitually occupy our minds."

--Howard W. Hunter

Art credit: *Summer* by Jules Breton

"It is good to love many things, for therein lies the true strength, and whosoever loves much performs much, and can accomplish much, and what is done in love is done well."

--Vincent Van Gogh

Art credit: *12 Sunflowers* by Vincent Van Gogh

"When the multitudes cease to flow into the sanctuary to bathe themselves in God's divine ether, to wash the grime from the soul's garments, to sharpen the dulled instrument of the spirit, that moment the bloom and beauty will begin will to pass from our arts, our literature, our music, our laws, and the very springs of civilization will dry up."

--President Hopkins of Williams College

Art credit: A *Prayer* by Frederick Daniel Hardy

"Rivers do not drink their own water; trees do not eat their own fruit; the sun does not shine on itself and flowers do not spread their fragrance for themselves.

"Living for others is a rule of nature. We are all born to help each other.

"No matter how difficult life is…

"Life is good when you are happy; but much better when others are happy because of you." –Pope Frances

Art credit: Beerensammler by Fritz Ebel

"What you make a child love and desire is more important than what you make him learn."

--Alice O'Grady

Art credit: *At the Garden Bank* by H.A. Brendekilde

"The education of even a small child…does not aim at preparing him for school, but for life."

--Maria Montessori

Art credit: *In the Nursery*, by Albert Edelfelt

"I am not afraid of storms, for I am learning how to sail my ship."

--Louisa May Alcott

Art credit: *Stormy Sea at Night* by Ivan Aivozovsky

"Our liberties are safe until the memories and experiences of the past are blotted out and the Mayflower with its band of pilgrims forgotten, until our public school system has fallen into decay and the nation into ignorance."

--Woodrow Wilson

Art credit: *The First Thanksgiving* at Plymouth by Jennie A. Brownscombe

"The world's history is a divine poem…to the humble listener—there has been a divine melody running through the song which speaks of hope and peaceful days to come."

--James Garfield

Art credit: *Moulin du Boulonnais au Soleil Couchans* by Henri Duhm

"A difference of opinion in one question must not prevent us from working unitedly in those on which we can agree."

--Elizabeth Cady Stanton

Art credit: The First Grief by Daniel Ridgway Knight

"There is no such thing on Earth as an uninteresting subject; the only thing that can exist is an uninterested person."

--G.K. Chesterton

Art credit: *Summerlust* by Hermann Seeger

Harriet Beecher Stowe's reflections on the mother as teacher:

"The most fearful thing about this education matter is that it is example more than word. Talk as you will, the child follows what he sees, not what he hears. The prevailing tone of the parent's character will make the temper of the household; the spirit of the parent will form the spirit of the child."

Art credit: *Mutter und Kind Rasten under einem Baum* by Imre Gergely